T5-BSI-736

STRAND PRICE
5.00

EU Accession – Financial Sector
Opportunities and Challenges for Southeast Europe

Ingrid Matthäus-Maier
J. D. von Pischke
Editors

EU Accession – Financial Sector Opportunities and Challenges for Southeast Europe

With 9 Figures
and 41 Tables

Ingrid Matthäus-Maier
KfW
Palmengartenstraße 5–9
60325 Frankfurt
Germany
ingrid.matthaeus-maier@kfw.de

Dr. J. D. von Pischke
2529 Trophy Lane
Reston
VA 20191-2126
USA
vonpischke@frontierfinance.com

Cataloging-in-Publication Data applied for
Library of Congress Control Number: 2004113829

ISBN 3-540-23426-8 Springer Berlin Heidelberg New York

This work is subject to copyright. All rights are reserved, whether the whole or part of the material is concerned, specifically the rights of translation, reprinting, reuse of illustrations, recitation, broadcasting, reproduction on microfilm or in any other way, and storage in data banks. Duplication of this publication or parts thereof is permitted only under the provisions of the German Copyright Law of September 9, 1965, in its current version, and permission for use must always be obtained from Springer-Verlag. Violations are liable for prosecution under the German Copyright Law.

Springer. Part of Springer Science+Business Media

springer.com

© Springer Berlin · Heidelberg 2005
Printed in Germany

The use of general descriptive names, registered names, trademarks, etc. in this publication does not imply, even in the absence of a specific statement, that such names are exempt from the relevant protective laws and regulations and therefore free for general use.

Cover photograph: Jasmin Fazgalic
Hardcover Design: Erich Kirchner, Heidelberg

SPIN 11333623   43/3130/DK-5 4 3 2 1 0 – Printed on acid-free paper

FOREWORD:

Policy Input and Dialogue for Accelerated Financial Sector Development in Southeast Europe

Ingrid Matthäus-Maier[1] and J.D. von Pischke[2]

[1] Member of the Board of Managing Directors, KfW Bankengruppe
[2] President of Frontier Finance International, Inc., Washington DC, USA

KfW Entwicklungsbank has made special efforts to focus on Southeast Europe (SEE). Its strategic importance for the region is based on the imperative of ensuring peace throughout Europe, on hastening the revival of employment and enterprise in SEE, on reconstruction and development of physical infrastructure and the housing stock, and on the economic, social and cultural benefits that will be secured throughout Europe by the accession of more states to the European Union (EU).

KfW Entwicklungsbank, part of the KfW Group owned by the German government and the German Länder, provides economic cooperation on a broad scale, offering finance, investment and policy advice to help achieve these objectives. It targets its assistance to institutions that serve the private sector, especially micro, small and medium scale firms because of their central role in creating employment and furthering development.

An important part of KfW's contribution to promoting development on behalf of the German Ministry for Economic Cooperation and Development consists of taking stock and exchanging views among interested parties on progress or the lack thereof. At the operational level, testing the responsiveness of project design and monitoring project implementation provide a basis for evaluation of results. At the policy level, KfW has led policy discussion and review, moving beyond the technical parameters of economic cooperation.

The Inaugural Berlin Symposium: Financial Sector Development

KfW accords a high priority to financial sector development: finance touches all markets and thus plays a pivotal role in growth, employment, enterprise, reconstruction and stabilisation. Included in this thrust is a series of symposia launched in November 2002. The first of these was titled "Innovative Approaches to Financial Sector Development in a Volatile Environment: Experiences, Lessons, Challenges – The Case of Southeast Europe."

That first meeting in Berlin was attended by representatives of key stakeholders in the financial development of Southeast Europe. The presentations and discussion had a relatively broad scope and made several themes clear:

- Progress in transition varies greatly throughout the region.

- Unemployment rates throughout the region are unacceptable and in certain countries remain persistently high.

- Micro, small and medium scale enterprises are numerous throughout the region and account for a relatively high portion of new jobs and economic activity.

- At the retail level the financial sector in the region has been more like a piggy bank – a convenient place to keep money – than an intermediary transforming savings into working capital and investment loans.

- Strategic financial sector interventions by donors can have very positive impacts, especially when these actions are initiated quickly after peace is restored or crises abate. The KfW Group, IFC and EBRD have successfully applied a financial systems approach, focusing on institutions while searching for reliable partners.

- Dynamic, for-profit target-group oriented microenterprise banks have made a very good start in supporting businesses and offering financial services to households on a sustainable basis. These activities attract investment from a variety of sources: IFIs,[1] bilateral investment institutions, foundations and private banks such as Commerzbank AG.

- European commercial banks, primarily Austrian, serve large firms, but are also building a consumer clientele and beginning to serve small and medium enterprises. In addition, some local commercial banks have downscaled to serve the target group of micro and small enterprises.

- Impact analysis properly undertaken offers insights into the role of finance as a development tool at the household level and at the level of financial institutions. Information produced by impact analysis can be useful for donors and for retail lenders. Improvements in impact analysis have reinforced the traditional links between research universities and public policy.

---

[1] International financial institutions such as EBRD, IFC and others.

- KfW, EBRD, IFC, the EU, FMO, and other investment and development assistance institutions based in Austria, Germany, the Netherlands, Switzerland and elsewhere have played a major role in rebuilding the housing sector, providing funding for enterprise development, sharing risks with local financial institutions, protecting consumers, and fostering macroeconomic stability through financial regulation and, in some countries, deposit insurance.

- Official investors in banks and enterprises require an exit when their development mandate has been accomplished or is no longer achievable. This challenge is likely to attract more attention in policy circles.

- Finally, experience from Bolivia and other countries outside Europe suggests that microfinance loan portfolios tend to be stronger and more resilient in crises than the portfolios of commercial banks.

The 2002 Symposium was essentially a measured examination of successful development assistance to financial sectors of SEE. Given the difficulties in building institutions in developing and transition economies generally, the 2002 event was in fact a celebration as well as a stock-taking. It highlighted Germany's role as a leader and as a partner with other governments and private sector consultants and contractors in the reconstruction and development of the region based on initiatives in the financial sector. These results, presented at the symposium, are documented in *The Development of the Financial Sector in Southeast Europe: Innovative Approaches in Volatile Environments*, published in 2004 by Springer Verlag on behalf of KfW.

The Second Berlin Symposium: EU Accession and Its Implications for the Financial Sector in Southeast Europe

The success of the 2002 meeting encouraged KfW to make a broader examination of financial markets in SEE in a second Berlin symposium in November 2003. Five themes related to EU accession guided this meeting. Each is treated in this book, which is organised into five sections. The first is economic policy and government performance, which provides an overview of the economic and political framework conditions in Southeast Europe. It highlights the successes achieved and points out the significant challenges in moving towards EU accession. The second is financial regulation and its implications posed by prospects for EU accession and by Basel II. The subsequent two sections review bankers and clients' perspectives on financial market performance and developments in providing financial services to microenterprise and SME clients. The final theme is public-private partnerships and their potential contributions to financial market development, featuring an example supported by KfW that focuses on developing micro and small business finance institutions.

Each theme paper is complemented by response papers, primarily by practitioners who provided further information, different points of view, and discussion of situations in the countries in which they work. The book concludes with an editorial summary that identifies lessons that have emerged in promoting financial sector development in Southeast Europe and the main steps required to prepare the financial sectors in Southeast Europe for EU accession.

Looking Ahead

The context for continued symposia contains several dynamic features. One is the development of SEE economies in transition and their financial markets. Another is EU accession and the incentives this possibility creates. A third is the insights provided by new economic approaches and their applications to development, primarily through building robust institutions that move economies and policies towards efficient modes of conduct. These issues and developments are palpable and timely: by mid-2004 it was clear that the success celebrated in 2002 has continued. Conditions in Southeast Europe have improved in most respects, but not uniformly so across the region.

Acknowledgements

Finally, the efforts of those who have contributed to this book deserve acknowledgement. We include the authors and the many others who have provided time and effort to gather and present data, to share experience and to offer advice and criticism. Their efforts and commitment have made it possible to identify the main forces driving continued financial sector development in Southeast Europe.

The 2003 Symposium was financed by two sources. The first is the FEFAD Foundation, an entity established by the Albanian government and KfW almost a decade ago to support microenterprise and SME development in Albania and elsewhere in Southeast Europe. The second is KfW.

The editors are grateful to Wolfgang Kroh, Hanns-Peter Neuhoff, Norbert Kloppenburg, Doris Köhn and Klaus Glaubitt of KfW for their consistent support in promoting the commercial approach to microfinance, microenterprise and SME development. We also offer our profound thanks to Lauren Day and Haje Schütte, who conceptualized the Symposium, coordinated thematic inputs and devoted hours of professional energy to advising the editors of this book. Tina Butterbach's outstanding organisational and management skills were invaluable in processing and developing the manuscript.

PREFACE:

Opportunities and Challenges Facing Financial Sectors Moving Towards EU Accession

Ingrid Matthäus-Maier

Member of the Board of Managing Directors, KfW Bankengruppe

Ten countries joined the European Union in 2004. In 1988, almost all of these countries lay behind the Iron Curtain.

The fall of the Iron Curtain and the end of Communism was relatively peaceful and bloodless for Eastern Europe. But the transition from Communism to democracy and the market economy has not, by any measure, been easy.

Rebuilding and Restructuring: From Transition to Accession

It is fair to say that no country has more in-depth or unique experience with these transition challenges than Germany. Strategies that we developed when rebuilding West Germany after World War II have been applied by KfW in the former East Germany, most importantly in the financing of investments via the banking sector. Furthermore, the support and promotion of financial sector development beyond our borders is one of KfW's core *raisons d'être*.

Relations with our European neighbours to the east are for us of paramount importance.

For almost fifteen years, KfW has promoted small and medium-sized enterprises (SMEs) in the EU candidate countries in Central and Eastern Europe. We have supported the establishment of promotional institutions and their loan and credit programmes for SMEs, and for housing and infrastructure development. Furthermore, we have assisted small and medium-sized German companies that invest abroad and have provided global loans to partner banks in the region which fund individual loans to SMEs. Since 2000, we have administered the SME Finance Facility for the EU accession countries on behalf of the European Union. For ten years, our advisory Transform Programme has been helping our public and private sector partners in Eastern Europe – including the current EU accession countries – with their transition to market-driven economies.

On May 1, 2004, these ten countries merged, politically, economically, and culturally into the European Union. This is a triumph: a mark of financial and political stability, of identity, and of community. The process of enlargement holds great promise of unparalleled partnership, prosperity and peace.

Now, we are looking ahead to the next wave of EU accession and beyond, to the future candidates waiting in the wings of the world stage. The experience of transition gained by the countries that gained EU membership in 2004 can serve as an analytical, historical, and political reference for the nations of Southeast Europe.

Exploring the Challenges of Financial Sector Development

In November 2002, KfW's first Financial Sector Development Symposium made its debut. It was an expression of KfW's desire to create a unique international forum at which leaders in the field could meet, share knowledge, and exchange experiences about the challenges of financial sector development in volatile environments, particularly in Southeast Europe (SEE). With EU accession as a backdrop, the 2003 KfW Symposium employed a political focus to examine the latest challenges facing financial sector development in Southeast Europe. Two major forces animated our efforts:

- the current issues raised by the EU accession process and Basel II;
- the expanding role of the private sector in developing Southeast Europe's financial landscape.

The 2003 symposium began with a comprehensive review of the political setting and then proceeded to outline the perspectives of central and commercial bankers, donors and clients. Finally, it identified areas of cooperation and partnership.

The symposium was a dialogue in which ideas, experiences, and knowledge were presented and shared. To achieve its objective, KfW invited highly experienced decision-makers who had been central in shaping the financial sector in Southeast Europe and who would engage in open and lively discussion, drawing on their wide-ranging professional know-how and expertise. In additional, there were opportunities for informal discussion and networking. Participants included central bankers, commercial bankers, policymakers, entrepreneurs, academic advisors, and representatives of microfinance institutions, international financial institutions (IFIs) and donor organisations. These leaders shape the financial sector environment and have intimate knowledge of the region in which they are engaged. Their ultimate purpose was to shift the focus towards shaping the financial future of the countries of Southeast Europe.

Implications for the Banking Sector

We must reflect on the significance of the progress made towards EU accession. In spite of recent reports highlighting the obstacles that still stand in the way of accession and the importance of further reform, the results to date have generally been positive. This is particularly true in the banking sector, which continues to make good progress in implementing reforms and promoting development. Furthermore, private actors have taken a leading role in shaping the region's financial sectors.

These encouraging indicators offer a perspective on the ongoing challenges that we face and on their changing nature. For example, political instability continues to burden risk assessments in SEE, retarding reforms and their implementation to the detriment of investment. The real economy continues to be sluggish. In a number of countries, economic growth is not yet sustainable and still heavily reliant on external transfers.

Specific challenges facing the banking sector's supply side include risk aversion, the lack of trained and experienced staff, and mismatched term structures that inhibit term lending. On the demand side, credit histories are just one of the challenges being faced. Information on credit histories is either not available or inadequate as a tool for lending.

Looking Forward

How can we capitalise on the progress being made and improve the effectiveness of our efforts to meet these challenges?

The nineteenth century German poet, Heinrich Heine, observed that "Experience is a good school, but the fees are high." The paths that we are following are also illuminated by experience, and this can also be very costly. By pooling experience and thus making a wealth of knowledge accessible, our symposium is designed to help reduce the "school fees" for the lessons learned the hard way.

The exchange of experience and know-how has always inspired KfW's approach to financial sector development, which is guided by commitment to sustainability, a focus on pro-poor growth, the promotion of SMEs as the backbone of the economy, and dedication to technically sound and efficient business practice. In particular, KfW stresses the promotion of private sector involvement through risk-sharing, market development, and catalytic investments.

KfW's activities in SEE have three vehicles:

- funding and advice: as the political and financial landscape evolves, KfW will continue to support microfinance banks, commercial banks, and microfinance NGOs with refinancing and advice in order to assist private sector involvement;

- innovation: we will encourage our partner institutions to develop and implement new products and services;

- facilitation of broader financial sector development: we will promote financial sector development beyond the banking sector into such areas as capital markets and insurance.

These three thrusts can be achieved only through close cooperation with others in the region.

I am confident that the vision of the KfW 2003 Symposium will be realised.

Table of Contents

Foreword:

Policy Input and Dialogue for Accelerated Financial Sector Development in Southeast Europe V

Ingrid Matthäus-Maier and J.D. von Pischke

Preface:

Opportunities and Challenges Facing Financial Sectors Moving Towards EU Accession IX

Ingrid Matthäus-Maier

Part I: Stimulating the Economy of Southeast Europe 1

Chapter 1:

Setting the Stage for Stability and Progress in Southeast Europe 7

Paul Hare

Chapter 2:

The Scenario for EU Accession by Southeast European Countries 39

Marc Franco

Chapter 3:

Infrastructure Finance, Accession, and Related Policy Issues in Southeast Europe 43

Ewald Nowotny

Chapter 4:

Making It Easier to Do Business in Southeast Europe 47

Khaled F. Sherif

Part II: Financial Regulation for Stability and Protection in Southeast Europe 55

Chapter 5:

Financial Sector Development in Southeast Europe – The Roles of EU Accession and Basel II 61

Evan Kraft

Chapter 6:

Implementing European Standards of Banking Regulation in Georgia 93

Merab Kakulia

Chapter 7:

Issues Concerning Foreign Banks' Operations in Bosnia and Herzegovina 99

Peter Nicholl

Chapter 8:

The Role of Foreign Banks in SEE 103

Mihai Bogza

Chapter 9:

The Impact of Basel II on Banking in Albania and Southeast Europe 107

Eris Sharxhi

Chapter 10:

Financial Stability in Southeast Europe – Basel II and the Challenges Ahead 113

Christian Fehlker, Arnaud Mehl, and Adalbert Winkler

**Part III: Bankers' Perspectives – Dynamic Banking in the
Changing Market of Southeast Europe** 125

Chapter 11:

Bankers' Perspectives – Dynamic Banking in a Changing Market 131
Sylvia Wisniwski

Chapter 12:

**Evolution of the Banking Sector in Southeast Europe – The Role
and Business Strategies of Domestic Banks** 163
Per Fischer

Chapter 13:

Financing Small and Medium-Sized Companies 169
Mita Katic

Chapter 14:

**The Business Strategies of Domestic Banks in the Long Run –
SME Lending as an Attractive Market Segment** 173
Evgeny Gospodinov

Chapter 15:

**Building a Market Niche Also Builds a Market – Opportunity
Bank in Montenegro** 179
Keith Flintham

**Part IV: Clients' Perspectives on Access to Financial
Services for Micro and Small Enterprise in
Southeast Europe** 183

Chapter 16:

**Clients' Perspectives – Providing More Effective Financial
Services for Micro and Small Enterprises** 189
Sarah Forster

Chapter 17:

Access to Finance: Issues and Opportunities in Southeast Europe 213

Albrecht Mulfinger

Chapter 18:

Nonfinancial Obstacles to SME Financing in Serbia 219

Igor Brkanovic

Chapter 19:

**Constraints to Business Development in Bulgaria and the Case
for Action 227**

Stefan Kossev

Chapter 20:

**Degrees of Competition in Serving Target Groups –
They May Be Closer than You Think 233**

Christoph Freytag

Chapter 21:

**A New Approach to Business Development Services in
Southeast Europe 239**

Hayder Al-Bagdadi, Dirk Steinwand, and Frank Wältring

**Part V: Looking Ahead – Public-Private Partnerships in
the Financial Sector in Southeast Europe 243**

Chapter 22:

**Public-Private Partnerships for Financial Development in
Southeast Europe 251**

Reinhard H. Schmidt and Nina Moisa

Chapter 23:

**Replicable and Transparent PPP Models for Financial Sector
Development 277**

Klaus-Eckhard Hartmann

Chapter 24:
Using PPPs to Facilitate Transactions in Financial Markets............283
Ira W. Lieberman

Chapter 25:
Sustainable Microfinance Banks – IMI as a Public-Private Partnership in Practice............289
Helen Alexander

Chapter 26:
Opportunities for Public-Private Partnerships in Financial Sector Development............297
Syed Aftab Ahmed

Chapter 27:
Public-Private Partnership – Results in the Banking Sector in Southeast Europe............303
Klaus Glaubitt and Haje Schütte

Chapter 28:
Microfinance Investment Funds – An Innovative Form of PPP to Foster the Commercialisation of Microfinance............323
Doris Köhn and Michael Jainzik

Part VI: Summary and Conclusions............337

Chapter 29:
An Overview of Banking, Financial Regulation, and Access to Financial Services in Southeast Europe in the Context of EU Enlargement............339
Ingrid Matthäus-Maier and J.D. von Pischke

Index of Names............353

Index of Countries............355

Index of Banks and Organisations............359

Index of Terms............363

List of Abbreviations

ALL	Albanian Lek
ATM	Automatic teller machine
AR	Annual report
BEEP	Business Environment and Enterprise Performance Survey
BCR	Banca Comerciala Romana
BGL	National currency of the Republic of Bulgaria prior to redenomination
BGN	National currency of the Republic of Bulgaria after redenomination
BNB	Bulgarian National Bank
BOO	Build-operate-and-own agreements
BOT	Build-operate-and-transfer agreements
CBBiH	Central Bank of Bosnia and Herzegovina
CEB	Central Europe and the Baltics
CFP	Certified Financial Planner
CIS	Commonwealth of Independent States
CZK	Czech
DM	Deutsche Mark
EBRD	European Bank for Reconstruction and Development
EU	European Union
EUR	Euro – Currency of the European Monetary Union
FbiH	Federation of Bosnia and Herzegovina
FDI	Foreign Direct Investment
FTA	Free trade agreement
GDP	Gross domestic product
GNI	Gross National Income
HIPC	Highly indebted poor countries
HRK	Croatian Kuna
HUF	Hungarian
HVB	Hypo Vereinsbank

IAS	International Accounting Standards
IDP	Internally Displaced Persons
IFC	International Financial Corporation
IFI	International finance institution
IRB	Internal rating base
IS	Infrastructure
IT	Information technology
IMF	International Monetary Fund
IMI	International Micro Investments
KM	Convertible Mark
MEB	Micro enterprise bank
MFB	Micro finance bank
MFN	Most Favoured Nation
n/a	Not available
NGO	Nongovernmental organization
NPK	National payment card system
NPO	Not-for-profit organization
PCA	Partnership and Cooperation Agreements
PLN	Polish
POS	Point of sale
Q	Quarter
ROL	Romanian Leu
RS	Republika Srpska
SBC	Soft budget constraint
SDIF	Savings and Deposit Insurance Fund
SME	Small and medium enterprise
USAID	US Agency for International Development
USD	US Dollar
WTO	World Trade Organisation
YUM	Yugoslav Dinar

PART I:

Stimulating the Economy of Southeast Europe

Introduction to Part I

Does support for the development of Southeast Europe do the job it is designed to do? To provide an adequate answer, the question must be approached from two angles. First, is support from public and private sources well-designed in the sense that its objectives are realistic and workable within the environment in which it has to operate? Poorly designed subsidies, loans and investment are unlikely to have a significant positive impact, and may even be counter-productive as they raise transaction costs and divert resources from more productive uses. Second, does the support fall on fertile ground? If local institutions are not receptive, subsidies, loans and investment are likely to be wasted or diverted to uses unintended by the providers. However, if local institutions are receptive, support can leverage local aspirations, on the one hand, and promote the establishment of entirely new institutions, on the other, thus helping create sustainable momentum for development.

The Theme Paper's Focus: Labour Markets, Investment and Trade

Professor Paul Hare explores these issues in his theme paper: "Setting the Stage for Stability and Progress in Southeast Europe." The paper examines three critical areas of the economy in Southeast Europe (SEE): the labour market, investment and trade.

- First, labour markets create the jobs that will lift households out of poverty. Employment generation depends on achieving rapid rates of enterprise formation, and here micro, small and medium-sized industrial development is essential, along with foreign direct investment (FDI). Other labour market elements that have a bearing on jobs and poverty include job displacement in the restructuring of agriculture and large-scale industry, and poverty alleviation effects resulting from voluntary migration and the creation of social safety nets.

- The second critical area is investment in physical infrastructure and other productive activity. High rates of investment, both foreign and domestic, are required to stimulate growth. This is best achieved through market institutions that effectively support property rights and the resolution of disputes, at the same time ensuring transparency, reducing transaction costs and facilitating risk management. Efficient banks that function as risk-taking intermediaries are also a critical ingredient.

- Third, trade is essential in the small, open economies of SEE. Post-conflict aid is declining, underscoring the importance of attracting FDI.

Trade can be facilitated through supportive domestic policies that reduce transaction costs and uncertainty between buyers and sellers.

Several constraints are slowing the pace of reform and acting as a brake on investment: ethnic and religious divisions that threaten stability and weaken the spirit of trust, political fears about the impact of reforms, lack of familiarity with the market economy, and barriers to efficient trade within and also beyond the region.

Response Papers

Three response papers are presented in Part I. Marc Franco of the European Commission deals with EU accession. Bulgaria and Romania are on track to be the first SEE countries to accede to the EU; they are expected to join in 2007. The basic requirements for admission are known as the Copenhagen Criteria: respect for democratic principles and the rule of law, a functioning and competitive market economy, and the capacity to implement and enforce EU legislation. The Stabilisation and Association Agreements, flanked by corresponding implementation assistance, provide the framework for accession.

Compared to the degree of change demanded by the transition process in other sectors in the accession countries, the financial sector faces the most profound reform. In the past, this sector was largely a passive instrument that executed the government's economic plans. Now, it is accorded a central role as a facilitator and risk-taker in the three segments of financial markets: credit, equity finance, and guarantees and insurance products. In each of these three market segments, risk management is essential. Financial deepening is also critical: the financial sector must grow faster than the real or nonfinancial sector if finance is to promote growth effectively. FDI plays an important role in this process.

Professor Ewald Nowotny, formerly vice president of the European Investment Bank, emphasises the interaction between infrastructure and financial development. Private sector investment in infrastructure plays an important role in applying market criteria to investment in this sector and thus in enhancing its efficiency. Given that many SEE states are relatively small, regional participation in infrastructure development takes on particular importance.

The European Investment Bank (EIB) has pioneered local currency bond issues as a way of opening up and developing capital markets. Efforts in the Czech Republic, Hungary and Poland helped to extend yield curves, making long-term investment more attractive. This, in turn, creates more channels for domestic savings and hence investment in projects in which revenues more than cover costs.

The widely diverging income and investment levels in the region will present serious challenges in the accession process. Professor Nowotny hopes that these do not delay accession unnecessarily, assuming that flexibility and pragmatism will be applied, especially regarding the poorer countries, when the costs of meeting EU standards are massive in local terms.

Khaled F. Sherif of the World Bank concentrates on the costs of doing business in transition economies and the changes required to bring SEE economies up to the performance levels of the countries that joined the EU in 2004. The challenges he cites include the currently rudimentary financial sectors in these countries, inconsistent tax and regulatory systems that distort incentives, uncertainty and delays in policymaking and implementation, poor judicial structures, and corruption. The legal framework touches on all of these problems and therefore deserves special attention.

Recognising that these shortcomings raise the transaction costs of doing business, discourage enterprise and make it difficult to establish a broad tax base, the SEE countries are now taking a proactive line. The problems themselves can be seen *inter alia* in the lengthy delays involved in starting up legitimate businesses and the time required to enforce contracts and to close businesses. This has been documented in research carried out by the World Bank, which also cited the numbers of procedures and the time typically required to work through the bureaucratic maze. One result of these impediments is the burgeoning underground economy, whose participants attempt to circumvent the government-imposed administrative, regulatory and fiscal obstacles to formalised economic development.

These problems can be addressed by developing a clear vision and translating this into strategic plans, by establishing a stable macroeconomic framework, expanding the fiscal base but with lower tax rates, imposing prudential financial regulation, supporting open trade and investment, strengthening the legal framework as a secure base for contracts and transactions, upgrading staff in the auditing and accounting profession, and by adopting other pro-growth strategies.

Toward these ends, the World Bank has devoted much effort and funding worldwide in order to professionalise public services in ways that stimulate private sector growth. This synergy can be especially important in managing the trade-off between using local business as a tax base and also as a source of growth and jobs.

CHAPTER 1:

Setting the Stage for Stability and Progress in Southeast Europe

Paul Hare

Director of Research and Professor of Economics, Heriot-Watt University, School of Management and Languages, Edinburgh[1]

Five Propositions

Five propositions – P1 through P5 – about the region are derived from the political developments, economic reforms and the requirements for longer term economic success in Southeast Europe (SEE) that are reviewed in this chapter:

P1. Recent weak economic performance is partly the result of political conflict and the subsequent fragmentation of the region into small states with poor inter-regional links, and partly a consequence of subsequent slow or badly designed economic reforms.

P2. Sustained growth in the region requires substantial increases in domestic investment and in foreign direct investment (FDI), considerable job creation including massive small and medium enterprise (SME) formation, as well as highly open trade.

P3. For such growth to occur, wide-ranging institutional reforms will be needed. These include very important reforms in banking systems and the financial sectors of each country. A badly designed or poorly functioning banking sector can seriously impede growth, while a well designed one can make a valuable contribution in some cases.

P4. Small, poor countries that are not on track to join the EU for a number of years cannot be advised to adopt the *acquis communautaire* wholesale. The *acquis* is a complex and costly economic mechanism, better suited to more prosperous states such as most transition economies that acceded to

---

[1] I am grateful to the participants at KfW's 2003 Berlin Symposium for helpful comments and suggestions that have enabled me to clarify and develop parts of the paper. Remaining errors and omissions are wholly my own responsibility.

the EU in 2004. Hence the SEE countries should be encouraged to adopt only those parts of the *acquis* that are likely to prove helpful at their present stage of development.

P5. An important condition for economic success across the SEE region will be the willingness of its national governments to undertake cooperative and coordinated economic policies in many key areas. Such willingness has been disappointingly limited, despite the establishment of many groups seeking to promote such cooperation.

Introduction

Southeast Europe means different things to different organisations and in various contexts,[2] so a definition is necessary. In this paper Southeast Europe refers to the following states: Albania, Bulgaria, Romania; from the former Yugoslavia: Bosnia and Herzegovina (BiH), Croatia, the former Yugoslav Republic of Macedonia (often referred to as FYR Macedonia, or FYROM), and the federation of Serbia and Montenegro; and from the CIS: Moldova. These states have experienced extremely diverse histories since the fall of communism, including the most severe ethnic conflict in Europe since the Second World War, various degrees of economic collapse and recovery, and rather mixed fortunes in building stable and effective states. The international community, together with these eight countries, has responded by establishing a Stability Pact to foster a long-term conflict prevention strategy.[3]

The political background conditions in the region are briefly summarised in Table 1. Table 2 summarises recent macroeconomic statistics for each country.

SEE is currently growing rather faster than the CEB countries (Central Europe and the Baltics) that joined the EU in 2004. However, political strife in SEE and economic policy failures of the 1990s are clearly visible in the column of Table 2 showing real GDP in 2003 as a percentage of that in 1989. To a significant extent, current high growth might simply reflect recovery from the initial post-communist

---

[2] For the EU, Southeast Europe (SEE) consists of Albania, Bosnia and Herzegovina, Croatia, FYR Macedonia, Serbia and Montenegro. Bulgaria and Romania are not included as they are regarded as accession states, even though their entry to the EU is not expected before 2007. For the EBRD, SEE commonly excludes Croatia but includes Bulgaria and Romania. However, in the context of discussions relating to the 1999 Stability Pact (and subsequent developments), SEE is defined as the eight Stability Pact countries: Albania, Bulgaria, Romania, Bosnia and Herzegovina, Croatia, FYR Macedonia, Serbia and Montenegro, and Moldova. This is the definition adopted in this paper. Hereafter, the countries will no longer be grouped geographically; instead, they will simply be listed alphabetically.

[3] For fuller information about the Stability Pact and its activities, see the Pact website at www.stabilitypact.org.

Table 1. Political conditions in southeast Europe: brief overview

Country	Year(s)	Comments
Albania	Mid-1990s	Serious economic crisis due to large-scale financial pyramid collapse.
		Albania appears not to be a candidate for EU accession in the near future (i.e. not before 2010).
Bosnia and Herzegovina (BiH)	Mid-1990s	Civil war and ethnic cleansing, fostered by involvement of the then Yugoslavia under its leader, Milosevic (now on trial at The Hague). Some military involvement by Croatia in Western Bosnia (e.g. around Mostar).
	Dec. 1995	Dayton Peace Accords under which BiH became a two-state federation. The Serbian part, capital Banja Luka, is called Republika Srpska. The rest (mostly Croat plus Bosnian Muslim) is the Federation, capital Sarajevo.
		Extensive use of the euro in the Federation.
Bulgaria		Candidate for EU accession in second wave, entry expected around 2007.
		Slow reforms in early-1990s, financial crisis led to introduction of currency board system.
Croatia	1991–93	Yugoslavia breaks up, Croatia gains independence after heavy fighting with what is now Serbia and Montenegro.
	1992–95	Involvement in Bosnian wars; strong EU and US pressure to pursue more liberal, democratic policies.
	2003–10	Could join the EU by 2010 (hence a probable exception to P4).
FYR Macedonia		Strains between the Slav and Albanian populations leading to political instability.
	2001–03	Open ethnic conflict between Slavs and Albanians led to a NATO mission to disarm Albanian insurgents and promote stabilisation. From April 1st 2003, this mission came under EU control.
Moldova	1991–93	Moldova gains independence from Soviet Union, civil war as Russian enclave of Transnistria in the east of the country opposes the new state. Ceasefire supervised by OSCE (Organisation for Security and Cooperation in Europe), but Transnistria still refuses to accept the Moldovan government.
		Limited autonomy for southern region, the Gagauz Republic.
		Good start to reforms, which then slowed down badly.
Romania		Candidate for EU accession in second wave, entry expected around 2007.
		Slow and inconsistent reforms until later 1990s.
Serbia and Montenegro	Late-1990s	Attempts by Serbia to terrorise the Albanian majority in Kosovo, large scale ethnic cleansing eventually prompting NATO bombing. Kosovo is now under UN administration.
		Some pressure for Montenegrin independence, but the status quo is a high degree of autonomy within the Federation.
		Milosevic voted out of power, faltering moves towards democracy and more coherent economic reforms.
	2001	Montenegro uses the euro rather than the dinar.

Source: Various, including EBRD Transition Report, various years.

Table 2. Southeast Europe: basic economic statistics

Country/Region	Population 2003 (millions)	Growth in real GDP (%)			Real GDP in 2003 (% of 1989)	GDP per capita (2003, US$)	Inflation based on consumer price index (%)		General government balance[f] (2003, % of GDP)	Current account balance (2003, % of GDP)	Cumulative FDI inflows per capita, 1989-2003 (US$)
		2001	2002	2003 (preliminary)			2002	2003 (preliminary)			
Albania	3.4	6.5	4.7	6.0	136	1765	5.4	3.3	-5.6	-8.4	329
Bosnia and Herzegovina	3.8	4.5	3.8	3.5	59	1857	0.7[a] / 2.4[b]	-0.3[a] / 0.2[b]	0.3	-17.8	282
Bulgaria	8.0	4.0	4.5	4.5	88	2505	5.9	2.3	0.0	-8.3	775
Croatia	4.4	3.8	5.2	4.5	94	6409	2.4	3.2	-4.6	-6.8	1923
FYR Macedonia	2.0	-4.1	0.0	2.8	80	2357	2.4	1.1	-1.6	-6.3	478
Moldova	4.3	6.1	7.2	6.3	43	451	5.3	11.8	0.2	-8.0	210
Romania	21.7	5.3	4.9	4.9	96	2520	22.5	15.4	-2.4	-6.1	486
Serbia and Montenegro	8.3[d] / 1.7-1.9[e]	5.5	4.0	2.0	53	2507	21.4	11.2	-2.5	-11.6	350
SEE[g]	57.7	4.5	4.6	4.2	89	2564	11.0[c]	6.7[c]	-2.0	-9.2	568
CEB[g]	73.1	2.5	2.5	3.7	123	6421	3.0	2.8	-3.5	-5.6	1715

Source: *Transition Report 2003* and *Transition Report Update*, April 2004, London: EBRD; *Fact Sheet Kosovo*, UNMIK, May 2003.

Notes: (a) Federation; (b) Republika Srpska; (c) excluding Bosnia and Herzegovina; (d) without Kosovo; (e) Kosovo. (f) The general government balance is the consolidated sum of the national-level government balance (commonly called the government surplus or deficit), all lower-level government balances (e.g. from regional and local governments), and so called off-budget public sector balances (e.g. social security funds are off budget in many countries). (g) SEE is defined as for this paper; CEB (Central Europe and the Baltics) is the EBRD definition without economic collapse and subsequent crises. It is debatable whether high growth can be sustained unless accompanied by large increases in new investment. There is clearly much catching up to be done, with the exception of Albania which bounced back very rapidly from its mid-1990s economic and political crisis. Other economic indicators shown in Table 2, excluding the general government balance, suggest that the SEE countries are generally in a far less favourable position than the CEB countries. It is important to bear these very significant differences in performance in mind in the subsequent discussion.

Macroeconomic stabilisation is fundamental to any attempt to achieve sustainable growth. This means, above all, getting inflation down to manageable and fairly stable levels; keeping the external accounts in good shape, using an appropriate exchange rate policy, and keeping firm control over the government's own spending and revenue. The 1990s witnessed some very bad mistakes in these policy areas in some countries, with painful lessons. But for the most part, the SEE countries have now established the conditions for macroeconomic stabilisation. They have done so much more slowly than the CEB countries. This was partly due to the pressures brought about by armed conflict, and partly due to the power of economic and political ideologies that prevented political leaders from understanding fully the links between their decisions and the macroeconomic disasters that followed.

Likewise, the selected transition indicators in Table 3 show that there is a qualitative difference between the reform progress achieved by the eight accession States (CEB) compared to that of the SEE countries. In some respects, including its progress with banking reforms, Croatia is closer to the CEB countries, and Bulgaria has made notable progress with large-scale privatisation. In most other respects, though, the SEE region has a lot of ground to recover. These differences in the pace of reform, according to a great deal of empirical evidence assembled since the 1990s (Hare, 2001), translate into marked differences in economic performance. Generally, liberal trade and well protected property rights are systematically linked with stronger economic growth. For the SEE region, institutional reforms to strengthen the business environment will encourage business start-ups in the official economy (rather than in the informal or black economy) and create the conditions necessary to encourage far more FDI. More favourable international trading conditions would support both these aspects of development.

The remainder of this chapter is structured as follows. A section on labour markets starts from the position that economic development is fundamentally about raising living standards, and that this most often occurs through job creation, accompanied by social policy measures to alleviate the most extreme poverty. SEE progress in these respects, as compared to the CEB countries, is summarised. A section on investment discusses how investment – in basic infrastructure and in directly productive assets (buildings, equipment and the like) – is vital for sustained growth in the longer term. The same section also sketches the region's nascent banking systems and financial markets, in part as an introduction to later chapters, in part due to their potential role in facilitating efficient investment and trade.

Table 3. Southeast Europe: progress with market reforms

Country / Region	Private sector share of GDP, mid-2002 (%)	EBRD Transition Indicators[b]				
		Large scale privatisation	Competition policy	Banking reforms	Nonbanking financial markets/services	Infrastructure
Albania	75	2+	2-	2+	2-	2
Bosnia and Herzegovina (BiH)	50	2+	1	2+	2-	2+
Bulgaria	75	4-	2+	3+	2+	3-
Croatia	60	3+	2+	4-	3-	3-
FYR Macedonia	60	3	2	3	2-	2
Moldova	50	3	2	2+	2	2
Romania	65	3+	2+	3-	2	3
Serbia and Montenegro	45	2+	1	2+	2	2
SEE[a]	60	3-	2-	3-	2-	2+
CEB[a]	75	4-	3-	4-	3	3+

Source: *Transition Report 2002* and *Transition Report Update*, May 2003, London: EBRD.
Notes: (a) Last two rows - author's calculation by simple averaging.
(b) For the EBRD Transition Indicators, a score of 1 denotes that virtually no reform has occurred, while a score of 4 indicates that reform has been sufficiently far reaching to create conditions equivalent to those of a well functioning market economy. Scores of 2 and 3 represent various stages of partial reform, with plus and minus signs denoting finer judgements (e.g. 2+ means a little better than 2).

Attention then turns to trade. All countries belonging to the SEE region have to be considered small, open economies. Their future prosperity will be found through integration with the wider world economy, including especially their immediate neighbours and the EU. Hence the trading environment in which the SEE countries operate is a critical feature of their economic progress, with both political and economic dimensions. The factors likely to influence other international flows such as aid and FDI are also listed.

Why have reforms in the SEE region not proceeded faster, and what constraints does the reform process face? These are very difficult questions, but the penultimate section attempts to pinpoint the most important constraints and to outline possible ways forward. The final section highlights a few issues of a more general nature that currently impede the region's economic progress.

Labour Markets and Poverty Alleviation

In most countries, including the SEE region, creating jobs is the most effective way of reducing poverty and improving general living standards. But the dislocation and disruption of the old economic structures that relied on regional markets, together with further shifts in economic structures during the 1990s, have resulted in very high rates of unemployment (Table 4). The more successful of the CEB countries already have unemployment rates below 10% of the labour force. These rates are generally falling, but Poland, with a large share of employment in agriculture (which is undergoing restructuring), has rates closer to 20%, as does Slovakia. The SEE countries that stand out with high levels of unemployment are BiH, FYR Macedonia, and Serbia and Montenegro. The relatively low rates for Albania and Moldova mask a great deal of underemployment and poverty in still largely unreformed agricultural sectors.

Most of the CEB countries have economic structures with higher shares of industry than the average across the SEE region, and lower shares of agriculture. This would be expected for economies significantly more developed than the SEE countries (again, Croatia does not quite fit the SEE pattern).

This structural difference means that getting SEE unemployment rates substantially down will be even more challenging than it has proved to be in the CEB countries. Jobs will be needed to engage the currently unemployed, those displaced from existing medium and large scale industry as it is finally privatised and restructured, and those likely to move out of agriculture as it restructures. In several SEE countries, existing farming patterns cannot realistically support higher incomes without restructuring.

Migration to seek work elsewhere in the region and beyond has proved attractive to many workers in some SEE countries. Many people have also moved out of conflict zones and areas where inter-ethnic conflict remains an everyday experience. The counterpart to such migration has been massive flows of remittances to a few SEE countries, notably Albania and to some extent the successor states of the former Yugoslavia; more modest flows have benefited Bulgaria, Romania and Moldova.

Table 4. Southeast Europe: unemployment and economic structure

Country / Region	Unemployment rate in 2002 (%)	Share of industry in GDP (%)^a	Share of agriculture in GDP (%)^a
Albania	15.8	11.4	48.1
Bosnia and Herzegovina (BiH)	40.6	22.5	16.0
Bulgaria	18.2	24.5	11.0
Croatia	14.8	19.8	6.9
FYR Macedonia	31.9	17.5	9.8
Moldova	7.4	20.5	26.0
Romania	8.2	28.2	13.2
Serbia and Montenegro	28.9	25.5	25.1

Source: *Transition Report Update*, April 2004, London: EBRD.
Note: (a) Mostly for 2002; most recent earlier year when data for 2002 not available.

Most remittances appear to contribute to household consumption – maintaining or improving current living standards – rather than investment.

While migration provides a useful alternative route to employment and raises incomes back home through remittances, there is a downside. Except under the most extreme political conditions, when entire populations are forcibly shifted from one area to another, migration is essentially voluntary. But it is widely perceived as a high-risk and probably costly option for those who move. This helps to explain its selective character: most migrants are relatively young, predominantly male, and often better educated than those who stay behind. In some cases, losing so many of those with energy, initiative and drive makes economic development in the home country even more difficult. Given this situation, it would make sense for the countries of the SEE region to create domestic economic conditions that would slow the outflow and start to bring back some of their more entrepreneurial migrants.

Aside from voluntary migration, the ethnic conflicts afflicting the region since 1991 have left Southeast Europe with about 1.7 million internally displaced persons (IDPs, or refugees; see World Bank, 2000). Their situation remains a potential source of conflict. Steps are being taken to make it safe for people to return to their former homes. Many thousands have done so, but many cannot and are faced with building new lives in new places, usually with little or no compensation to help. In such circumstances it is only to be expected that feelings still run high, and that cooperation across the new, "harder" ethnic boundaries should prove so difficult.

Employment generation depends on achieving rapid rates of new firm formation that will more than offset the shedding of jobs in agriculture and redundancies from relatively large industrial firms that are not yet privatised or just starting the process. This can take place in two ways:

- SME development: starting up new small and medium businesses, mostly using domestic capital or lines of credit set up by development banks and the like. (Serious constraints to this process range from the inexperience of the banks in evaluating borrowers to problems of finding acceptable collateral.)

- forming new large and medium businesses financed by FDI, which is the subject of later sections.

All SEE countries claim to have a favourable business environment supportive to SMEs. Evidence from the Business Environment and Enterprise Performance Surveys (BEEPS) carried out jointly by the World Bank and EBRD in 1999 and 2002 shows solid improvement in the business climate across the SEE countries, which are catching up on the CEB countries which improved at a slower rate. This is very encouraging news because the BEEPS surveys look at the business environment in a broad, multi-dimensional way covering macroeconomic management, taxation, business regulation, corruption, crime, the judiciary, finance and infrastructure (Fries et al., 2003). The critical issue is how quickly such improvements will translate into faster rates of business formation, and how quickly the SEE area will continue to improve conditions for doing business. Interestingly, the IMF (2003d, pp. 5–6) indicates that at least in FYR Macedonia, business turnover in recent years has been healthily high: while about 60% of the firms that existed in 1994 had ceased trading by 2000, two-thirds of the firms operating in 2000 did not exist in 1994, indicating a dynamic market and relatively free entry.

However, actual numbers of SMEs operating in most of the SEE countries are still not sufficiently high, as compared to some of the CEB countries that embarked on reforms much sooner. Table 5 sums up the situation as it was in 2000. Aside from Bulgaria, the other SEE countries have numbers of SMEs per 1000 inhabitants that are at or below the lower end of the Visegrad countries.[4] Hence the notable improvements in the business environment that were noted above need to be transformed into a stock of businesses at least double the stock that existed in 2000. Progress is being achieved, but it is very doubtful whether the countries concerned are even close to such a goal. When they are, unemployment rates will be far lower than those reported above.

Regardless of job creation efforts, it is important in the meantime to have social policies in place to alleviate poverty. Some form of income support is needed for those not economically active: the retired, those unable to work (e.g. due to disability), adults undertaking training and education, and so on. Especially in relatively

---

[4] The Czech Republic, Hungary, Poland and the Slovak Republic.

Table 5. Number of enterprises in southeast Europe (2000)

Country / Region	All SMEs (incl. micro)	Micro only	Large	SMEs per 1000 inhabitants
SEE				
Albania	56,442	55,143	76	16.5
Bosnia and Herzegovina (BiH)	n.a.	n.a.	n.a.	n.a.
Bulgaria	224,211	207,643	741	27.6
Croatia	59,907	47,368	529	13.7
FYR Macedonia	27,938	25,985	194	14.0
Moldova	18,898	15,138	2,525	5.2
Romania	306,073	270,843	1,991	13.6
Serbia and Montenegro	68,207	n.a.	1,032	8.0
CEB-Visegrad				
Czech Republic	876,990	830,601	1,671	85.1
Hungary	275,671	249,388	1,030	27.4
Poland	1,762,982	n.a.	3,071	45.6
Slovak Republic	60,310	48,662	610	11.2

Source: EBRD survey of national authorities; table taken from Falcetti et al. (2003).
Note: According to the old European Union (EU) definition, an SME is defined as an enterprise with less than 250 employees, and a micro-enterprise is one with 1–9 employees. These definitions have recently been revised by the EU to incorporate annual turnover limits specified in Euros, but these are not used here. "Large" enterprises in Moldova are those with more than 50 employees, and most are therefore medium-sized according to the EU definition.

poor countries, there is a delicate trade off between the benefits paid and the tax rates that must be levied on business activity to finance them. The higher the benefits, the higher the resulting tax rates, which in turn translate into slower rates of new business formation (Blanchard 1998). The resulting dilemma can be managed using a combination of three approaches. The first is to target benefits very strictly to those in direst need, which can be administratively quite tricky. The second is to pay benefits at extremely low rates. The third is to slow down restructuring, so that fewer new entrants join the labour market. The last of these options is often tempting politically but also costly, requiring some mix of protection and/or subsidies to keep ailing firms alive and preserving the very damaging "soft budget constraints."[5] It also limits competition, contributing to an already poor business environment by discouraging the entry of new firms.[6]

Investment and the Financial Markets

To sustain growth, investment rates in most of the SEE area need to be higher. While FDI can make an important contribution (discussed in the next section) it has not yet done so due to the poor investment environment and unstable political conditions that investors would face, together with the small and fragmented markets that characterise the region. Much of the capital investment that takes place is funded either by aid donors or from the usual domestic sources – retained earnings by firms and savings by households. It is commonly claimed that people are "too poor to save," and that therefore most investment must be funded from outside. But this is simply wrong except for very short periods. As the economic situation stabilises and improves, enabling people to see clear benefits from the real returns they can achieve by saving, they will start to save more. Part of the process of making savings more effective is the development of financial institutions to mobilise savings and to ensure that they are allocated where they can be used most productively.

Table 6 starts this discussion by reviewing savings and investment in the SEE countries, and comparing these with CEB countries. The comparison makes clear that in the CEB countries, except Poland and Lithuania, investment ratios are high (generally over 25% of GDP), while domestic savings ratios are also high, mostly above 20% of GDP, again with the same two exceptions. This means that relatively small fractions of the savings used for investment typically come from abroad, suggesting that the observed growth is likely to prove sustainable.

The situation is not yet so satisfactory among the SEE countries, except Croatia. Investment rates are mostly below those in the CEB countries, domestic savings rates are a lot lower: these countries rely heavily on foreign savings, mostly from remittances and foreign aid rather than FDI. Much aid in recent years has been directed towards the post-conflict restoration of physical infrastructure. When this inflow declines, aggregate investment could fall considerably in some SEE

---

[5] The soft budget constraint (SBC) notion was first introduced by Kornai; see, for instance, Kornai (1980), Kornai (1992), and for a more recent theoretical exploration of various interpretations of the SBC, Kornai et al. (2002). It is exemplified by firms in financial distress that might be able to set artificially high prices, defer tax and social security payments (or not make them at all), defer payments to suppliers, fail to meet credit obligations, and take similar steps to remain in business. In an environment of hard budget constraints, firms can engage in these practices only within quite strict limits before being forced to merge or to go bankrupt.

[6] The key issues associated with the design of social policies in relation to problems of industrial restructuring are analysed in Hare (2003).

Table 6. Savings and investment: SEE and CEB comparisons

Country / Region	Domestic savings (% of GDP)	Foreign savings (% of GDP)	Investment (% of GDP)
	(Data for the year 2001 wherever possible)		
SEE Countries [a]	9.9	10.3	20.2
Albania	16.4	6.2	22.5
Bosnia and Herzegovina (BiH)	3.9	15.5	19.4
Bulgaria	13.0	7.7	20.7
Croatia	19.8	3.8	23.6
FYR Macedonia	5.2	13.1	18.3
Moldova	13.3	7.7	21.0
Romania	14.9	7.7	22.6
Serbia and Montenegro	-7.2	20.8	13.6
CEB Countries [b]	21.4	5.2	26.6
Czech Republic	25.3	4.6	30.0
Estonia	20.2	6.5	26.7
Hungary	23.9	3.4	27.3
Latvia	21.0	9.6	30.6
Lithuania	17.0	4.8	21.8
Poland*	15.6	3.6	19.2
Slovakia	22.9	9.0	31.9
Slovenia	25.6	-0.2	25.4

Source: IMF (2003a-m), IMF (2002a-c)
Note: (a) and (b) Entries in these rows are simple averages of the entries for the corresponding country groups.
* denotes 2002 data.

countries. To improve longer term growth prospects, and the sustainability of their respective development paths, domestic savings ratios therefore need to rise and the resulting investment must be allocated efficiently.

Banks and financial markets are normally expected to play a significant part in achieving such goals. There is a good deal of evidence from around the world, as noted by Mehl and Winkler (2004), of a long-term causal link running from financial development to economic growth. But the most appropriate financial architecture for a given country depends on the structure of its business community. Tadesse (2002) presents evidence from a wide range of countries showing that those dominated by small firms can be expected to perform better in a predominantly bank-based financial environment, while countries dominated by larger firms do better with a more market-based financial structure. For SEE, small firms predominate and therefore banks will be the providers of financial services. However, until very recently the SEE countries had weak and fragile banks operating in poor institutional environments, with virtually no other formal financial markets in existence. There was then more reason to expect the banks to impede growth rather than to assist it. Policies to help change this situation are suggested later.

Strengthened financial sectors in this region will not necessarily accelerate economic growth. In the more successful transition economies that joined the EU in 2004, there is no noticeable correlation between their observed performance and the diverse paths of financial sector development they each chose. Berglof and Bolton (2002) point out that the financial sector has contributed rather little to the industrial restructuring that has occurred even in the more successful countries. They argue that the key to economic success is "the ability of governments of transition countries to enforce contracts and to achieve fiscal and monetary responsibility, together with a commitment to refrain from excessively bailing out failing banks or loss-making enterprises...." (p. 78). This important observation is taken up later in this chapter.

What is the basic shape of the existing financial structures across the SEE region? The traditional mono-bank system that prevailed under socialism has everywhere been replaced by two-tier banking with a central bank overseeing various sorts of commercial banks. Several countries have stock markets: across the region there are eight separate markets. This has to be highly inefficient, since all markets are tiny with few listed securities and very thin trading consisting largely of equity shares resulting from privatisation. Recent suggestions that the exchanges are starting to discuss cooperation can only be welcomed. Most countries have few or at best very weak nonbank financial institutions such as insurance companies and pension funds. Government paper, mostly very short-term, is the principal type of marketable financial asset. There are a few corporate bonds.

Financial systems are therefore predominantly bank-based, the more successful ones being those with a significant foreign ownership stake. In the countries that have not reached this point, significant further restructuring of the banking systems is needed to improve liquidity, deal with accumulated nonperforming debt, and so on. Most bank lending is to governments and to a smaller extent to households, rather than to firms, which fund most of their investment through retained profits and FDI inflows. However, Cottarelli et al. (2003) does suggest that bank credit to the private sector is now rising, is likely to expand more rapidly than GDP, and may even create macroeconomic instability from excessive credit growth.

Outstanding issues for the financial sector include the progress in banking reforms and the state of the other financial markets and institutions (Table 3) and the following:

- How independent should the central bank be, or what degree of independence would be politically acceptable and credible?
- Who should have responsibility for banking sector regulation – the central bank or a separate agency?
- What model of regulation should be used, e.g. a model based on EU and BIS (Bank for International Settlements) rules, or something different?
- How rapidly should the banking sector be privatised and on what model – in particular, what role might be expected for foreign participation?
- What degree of depositor protection should be offered?
- What arrangements should be in place to deal with bad debt, including the underlying bankruptcy laws?

A final issue concerns the exchange rate policy and regime that a given country should pursue, which is often a joint responsibility of the central bank and the ministry of finance. These are difficult and often controversial issues, especially for small countries with little experience of modern commercial banking. None of the items in the list refers to other parts of the financial sector, including the stock market, because these other markets are unlikely to assume great importance for most SEE countries in the near future.

Trade, FDI and Aid

Romania is the only SEE country having a population that exceeds ten million. Most of the others have fewer than 5 million inhabitants (Table 2). Small, low-income countries cannot hope to achieve high living standards unless they adopt strongly export oriented economic policies and take the fullest possible advantage of the opportunities offered by the international division of labour. This is easier said than done, because the region faces awkward constraints, some of which it could overcome through actions taken within the region, some of which require the cooperation of other countries.

Restraints to Trade

There is a complex network of mostly bilateral free trade agreements across the region, encouraged by the Stability Pact. But in practice firms wishing to export to a neighbouring country face numerous separate conditions and restrictions, as well as the standards and customs procedures of each country, which are not yet harmonised. It is very important to extend the network of bilateral agreements into a single multilateral free trade agreement across the region, with as few exceptions to free trade as possible. Unfortunately, the SEE countries have resisted such a multilateral initiative.

The EU has Partnership and Cooperation Agreements (PCAs) or Stabilisation and Association Agreements with most of the SEE countries. These provide very welcome trade liberalisation but also incorporate quotas and other restrictions on so called sensitive sectors, which are somewhat different for different regional partners. Moreover, the local content rules (rules of origin) in these agreements are often unnecessarily restrictive, as they were until the late-1990s for the first wave of Accession States. As Michalopoulos (2003) points out, these agreements can create a hub and spokes structure that tends to direct most of the benefits to the hub (i.e. the EU).

The CIS countries notionally form a free trade area that includes Moldova, but this is not an operational reality. Moldova faces great difficulties in exporting through Ukraine and on to Russia where it formerly had large markets (e.g. for its wine). The other seven SEE countries do not receive special access to CIS markets, though those that join the EU later in the decade might well expect to benefit from the PCAs already in place with Russia and Ukraine.

Six of the eight SEE countries already belong to the World Trade Organisation (WTO), though four (Albania, Croatia, FYR Macedonia, and Moldova) are very recent arrivals. BiH and Serbia and Montenegro have applied to join the WTO. Their applications are still at an early stage. Hence the region does not yet enjoy the full benefits and protections of universal WTO membership, such as automatic most favoured nation (MFN) treatment by other WTO members, and access to the WTO's dispute resolution procedures.

The physical infrastructure to support trade in the SEE region is patchy at best, with roads, rail links, telecommunications, and the electric grid needing substantial investment. Much of the aid effort in the region is being directed towards this area. The European Investment Bank (EIB), for instance, has concentrated its contribution to the region in physical infrastructure.[7]

The institutional infrastructure for government services and private sector provision is also poor. Border controls and customs formalities are frequently corrupt and inefficient to an extent that causes delays in transit of goods and significant increases in transaction costs. The design of tariffs and other regulations governing trade are often needlessly complex and therefore virtually impossible to administer effectively without resorting to corrupt practices. Private sector deficiencies include a lack of banking services to support trade, such as export credits, and efficient means for effecting international financial transfers plus insurance and freight services. Joint public-private services would include export promotion activities like trade fairs, as well as export credit guarantee schemes. These services are weak or nonexistent in several SEE countries.

---

[7] In doing so, it has had to face considerable political pressure from the region's governments, each advancing particular projects that might or might not prove economically viable or desirable for the region as a whole. Hence the EIB has had to apply careful investment appraisal to all proposed projects to weed out those based on political opportunism.

Trade Flows and Tariffs

Basic statistics on the major trade flows and average tariff rates (not trade weighted) indicate the scale of the trade problem in SEE countries (Table 7). It is evident that for such small, potentially highly open economies, trade volumes in relation to GDP are quite low. They are well below the ratios of the smaller CEB countries, and especially low as far as exports are concerned, which are sustainable only with continuing inflows of external financing. Indeed, a recent paper by Babetskii et al. (2003) used a gravity model to project potential trade flows for transition economies. It found that the SEE countries have a massive "trade gap," indicating that under the right conditions trade within the region and between SEE countries and other partners ought to be able to expand enormously. Thus for several SEE countries, policymakers and advisers should devise ways to boost exports not merely by a few percent here and there, but by factors of at least three or four. This presents a serious challenge, but it is vital both for job creation and poverty reduction within the countries and for regional economic integration.

Average tariff rates are not terribly high for most countries in the region, and the number of rates is not too bad except for Croatia. However, a regional SEE free trade zone would certainly contribute to greater and more efficient trade. In addition, numerous non-tariff barriers also need to be lifted – but more on that tricky issue later.

Foreign Direct Investment

The SEE countries have not attracted very much FDI and some have serious debt problems. Table 8 summarises the situation across the region. Cumulative FDI inflows have been low everywhere except Croatia. All the other countries had per capita FDI inflows well under half the levels typical for CEB countries, and in most instances much smaller than that. A somewhat better picture emerges in 2003; as a percentage of GDP the flows are, for the first time, somewhat above the current rates in the Accession States. Nevertheless, the sums involved remain low. The low levels of FDI partly reflect the slow pace and sometimes the unsatisfactory forms of privatisation in the SEE countries, and partly reflect continuing deficiencies in the business environment. Moreover, the small size of most of the countries means that foreign investors will usually expect to engage in trade in addition to supplying domestic markets. Foreign investors would therefore be especially influenced by the regional trading environment, which remains far from open and flexible.

Development Assistance

Aid flows to the SEE countries are set out in Table 9, which shows net official development assistance (ODA) receipts from 1999 to 2002 expressed as a percentage of Gross National Income (GNI). Aid flows to the SEE countries fall into

Table 7. Trade flows and tariffs of the SEE region

Country	Exports of goods and services (% of GDP)	Imports of goods and services (% of GDP)	$(X+M)/Y^a$ (%)	Average tariff (%)	Tariff bands (%)^b
SEE Countries	(Data for the year 2000 wherever possible)				
Albania	6.9**	28.8**	35.7	8.1	2,10,15
Bosnia and Herzegovina	8.8**	31.4**	40.2	6.8	0,5,10,15*
Bulgaria	55.7	63.2	118.9	n.a.	n.a.
Croatia	49.1	54.7	103.8	7	100+ rates
FYR Macedonia	48.3	62.4	110.7	n.a.	n.a.
Moldova	50.1	74.4	124.5	n.a.	n.a.
Romania	33.5	41.6	75.1	n.a.	n.a.
Serbia and Montenegro	18.4	44.4	62.8	9.5	1,5,10,15, 20,30
Kosovo	n.a.	n.a.	n.a.	10	Uniform
Montenegro	n.a.	n.a.	n.a.	3	1,3,5,10,15

Source: World Bank (2003); UNECE Country Statistics; EBRD *Transition Report Update*, May 2003.
Note: * plus about 250 specific tariff duties for agricultural products; ** goods only.
(a) This column shows each country's total trade (exports plus imports, $X + M$) as a fraction of total GDP (Y).
(b) Countries vary enormously in their choice of tariff rates. Some, such as Kosovo, apply a uniform tariff to all imports; other set numerous rates, often running into the thousands. Hence the presence in this column of countries setting only three or four rates is very encouraging; simple tariff structures are easier to administer and are less vulnerable to corruption than more complex structures. To explain the numbers, consider Albania: the tariff bands of 2, 10 and 15% mean that some goods pay an import duty of 2% of the declared border value of the import, some pay a 10% duty, others 15%. The published customs schedule for a given country lists which goods attract each rate of duty.

two distinct groups. Bulgaria, Romania and Croatia are either currently on track for EU entry later this decade or hope soon to join that group.[8] Aid flows as a percentage of their GNI are low, in all cases below 3%. For the remaining five countries, aid flows as a percentage of GNI, typically exceed 6%, and in BiH they exceeded 12% for three of the four years reported in the table. Germany was

---

[8] In fact, Commission (2004b) formally recommended that negotiations be opened with Croatia regarding its accession to the Union, and more recently it has been announced that negotiations can start in 2005.

Table 8. Foreign direct investment and external debt in southeastern Europe

Country	Cumulative FDI (1989–2003)	Cumulative FDI/capita (1989–2003)	FDI Inflows in 2003	Debt Stock in 2003	Debt Service in 2003
	US $ million	US$	% of GDP	US $ billion	% of exports
CEB Countries	116867	1715	2.6	223.6	9.4
SEE Countries	32191	568	4.0	76.2	14.6
Albania	1128	329	3.2	1.4	5.1
Bosnia and Herzegovina	1073	282	4.5	2.5	9.3
Bulgaria	6178	775	6.7	11.4	9.0
Croatia	8499	1923	6.0	23.7	16.6
FYR Macedonia	956	478	0.9	1.7	12.6
Moldova	893	210	2.5	1.7	13.9
Romania	10547	486	2.8	19.5	17.4
Serbia and Montenegro	2917	350	5.7	14.3	13.4

Source: EBRD *Transition Report Update*, April 2004.

Table 9. Aid flows to the SEE countries, 1999–2002 (% of GNI)

Country	1999	2000	2001	2002
Albania	13.0	8.3	6.3	6.6
Bosnia and Herzegovina	21.6	15.3	12.7	10.7
Bulgaria	2.2	2.5	2.6	2.5
Croatia	0.2	0.4	0.6	0.8
FYR Macedonia	7.6	7.1	7.3	7.5
Moldova	8.9	9.1	7.7	8.0
Romania	1.1	1.2	1.6	1.6
Serbia and Montenegro	6.9	13.2	11.3	12.5

Source: Development Assistance Committee of the OECD, Paris, various years.

among the top ten donors for every country and was in the top five for all except Moldova and Bosnia and Herzegovina.

Most of the larger aid flows were for post-conflict reconstruction and recovery, and can therefore be expected to decline; this tendency is especially evident for BiH. Some of the aid literature draws attention to absorptive capacity and aid dependence when flows remain large for long. These concerns might also lead to an expectation of declines in aid flows to the region fairly soon. Consequently, governments in the region, especially those with large flows relative to GNI, should develop two strategies: (a) how to make best use of the aid flows that are in place; and (b) how to adapt their economies to manage with less aid. These are both difficult challenges.[9]

Constraints on Reforms: Internal and External Conditions

To sum up key points: To achieve sustainable economic growth at rates of at least 4% per annum, and ideally 5–7% per annum, the countries of Southeast Europe need: (a) more investment, especially financed from domestic sources; (b) a much improved business environment to encourage new business formation and FDI; (c) a more liberal trading environment including substantial measures towards cooperation within the region and with major partners such as the EU; (d) further reforms in and consolidation of financial systems, notably the banks; and (e) commitment to the whole range of institutional reforms associated with the transition process, most importantly the effective implementation of new laws and practices consistent with a liberal society.

It is easy to put forward such a list of reforms. It is more useful to identify the constraints to their immediate adoption throughout the region, since that is a crucial precondition for understanding why progress has not been more rapid and for formulating new policies to promote faster development. It is also important to clarify how conditions facing the SEE countries differ from those of the more developed CEB countries.

The more severe internal and external constraints facing the SEE region are listed below as I1 through I3 and E1 through E5:

Internal Constraints

I1. Continuing ethnic and religious divisions, suspicion and mistrust, and associated political instability retard progress.

I2. Political fears slowed down many reforms, especially those that might have generated high unemployment through the closure of large, loss-making state-owned enterprises. Privatisation was delayed, as was a great deal of enterprise restructuring, including in the banking sector.

I3. Lack of understanding among political and business elites of the requirements for a well functioning market economy have often precluded dynamic reform. These requirements include the strict separation be-

---

[9] Interesting analysis and discussion of the political economy of aid, and practical experience with aid programmes, can be found in Easterly (2002) and Martens et al. (2002).

tween state and economy, the importance of macroeconomic stabilisation, the need to promote competition, the application of economic "rules of the game" uniformly rather than being subject to negotiation, lobbying, bargaining, corrupt deals and the like.

External Conditions Requiring Better Management

E1. Links with neighbours in the SEE region – regional cooperation.

E2. Links with the EU – trade and investment, and the impact of EU enlargement.

E3. Links with other trading partners, such as countries belonging to the CIS.

E4. Links with the EU – whether and how far to adopt the *acquis*.

E5. The role of the international community.

Civil Order

Condition I1 remains overwhelmingly the most important for several SEE countries: Moldova, Serbia and Montenegro, FYR Macedonia, and BiH have experienced international conflict, civil war, or at least serious internal disputes between ethnic groups. These led to international intervention by NATO, the EU, the OSCE or the UN. All are still under international supervision with Kosovo effectively a UN protectorate, and Bosnia and Herzegovina overseen by a High Representative appointed following the Dayton Peace Accords signed in 1995. In contrast, no such international intervention has occurred in the Accession States, all of which are politically stable and increasingly committed to democratic practices, including – albeit sometimes as a result of EU pressure – respect for minority groups.

While the international community can sometimes intervene to stop bloody conflict, it cannot compel the erstwhile warring parties to like each other or to cooperate seriously over matters of economic policy and reforms. To this extent, therefore, the role of the international community is necessarily rather limited (condition E5). Ultimately, the groups involved must want to cooperate before anything more than token progress can be achieved. While they decline to cooperate, sustained growth and high rates of investment are unlikely to occur.

Incentives to Accelerate Reforms

Could some form of "incentive" be offered to such states to induce cooperation that would benefit the entire region? A natural way forward in this regard might be through demonstration effects. The visible economic success of countries such as Croatia might finally encourage elites and governments in less successful states to support reforms. A similar sort of demonstration effect could arise if one part of a state, such as Montenegro within Serbia and Montenegro, started to grow rapidly and attract lots of investment; a success that might be emulated by the rest of that state. While an appealing idea, evidence from around the world suggests that if this approach works at all, it is extremely slow, often because the brightest and best people choose to move out rather than wait endlessly for political stability. Northern Ireland is such an example: it has been by far the poorest UK region for generations, racked by religious divisions.

Another type of incentive is provided by EU membership or the offer of such membership. Croatia, Bulgaria and Romania are clearly on track for such membership. To achieve it, they have to meet the Copenhagen criteria, as well as implement the detailed conditions of virtually all chapters of the *acquis communautaire*. These are demanding conditions but they are attractive for countries that want to lock in their reforms and belong to a club of highly developed market economies, especially as the EU is already their major trading partner. For the three countries mentioned, the prospect of EU membership by 2010 provides a very strong incentive to push reforms across the board, and hence create good conditions for growth.

The other five SEE countries are significantly poorer than the first three and much less advanced in market oriented reforms. The prospect of EU membership is included in most of the formal agreements between the EU and these states, but there is no realistic likelihood of entry for at least a decade, and quite possibly for a lot longer. Hence EU entry cannot provide much of an incentive to political elites. Given that, it is quite surprising to find that PCAs and other agreements linking these states with the EU envisage an increasing harmonisation of regulatory conditions through adopting more and more elements of the *acquis*. But it is very hard to see the attraction to the *acquis* (Condition E4), especially as the adoption of large chunks of the *acquis* would be unavoidably complex and costly. For poor, small states, it is also beyond their likely implementation capacity. Even worse, misguided attempts to implement parts of the mechanism, such as complex tax rules to do with VAT, might open up new opportunities for corruption in states already quite fragile and administratively weak. However, foscusing on a "core" of the *acquis* such as the single market, competition policy and state aid, and on prudential rules that protect savers, investors and the like, might well offer a more appealing way forward for these states.

Trade and Protectionism

SEE countries have displayed some willingness to conclude bilateral free trade agreements (Conditions E1, E2, E3). But the diversity of limitations and restrictions in these separate agreements itself constitutes a trade barrier, and an adequate multilateral agreement is not yet in place. A regional free trade area with zero tariffs on most intra-regional trade, and ideally on most trade with major partners like the EU, but not necessarily a common external tariff, would have tremendous advantages compared to the plethora of nontariff barriers that are currently the main impediment.

Nontariff barriers include efforts by governments to protect "their" firms from competition, through disputes over technical standards, restrictions on freight operators and inefficient border controls. They also include shortcomings in the financial institutions and instruments needed to support trade. All of these problems raise the transaction costs of trade: many institutional reforms may be regarded as means of reducing these costs. At this level many of the concrete problems might be regarded as largely technical in nature, and hence suitable for amelioration through various well foscused aid programmes. However, in most instances a good deal of political will is still needed to overcome these problems.

Comparison with the CEB countries that entered the EU in 2004 demonstrates the effectiveness of an early commitment to reforms that promote industrial restructuring, stimulate trade, and sooner or later, attract foreign direct investment. FDI is also contingent on credible agreements regarding the treatment of accumulated external debt, including debt forgiveness and rescheduling where appropriate. Poland's satisfactory resolution of its external debt problems helps to explain the very low levels of FDI flowing in before the mid-1990s, and its subsequent rapid rise. Moreover, far from generating intolerable unemployment, most of the CEB countries found that quick and sometimes tough reforms often fostered new business formation and faster growth that quite soon reduced regional unemployment rates, despite the initial, wholly understandable fears of many political leaders.

Regional Implications of an Expanded EU

The impact of EU enlargement (part of Condition E2) will be significant for those parts of Southeast Europe that now have common borders with the EU following enlargement in 2004: Croatia, Serbia and Montenegro, and Romania. Albania, FYR Macedonia and Bulgaria already border Greece, of course. Daily cross border movements of people seeking work could become more difficult in places, and some trade flows might be subject to controls which, though more rules-based and less corrupt than is sometimes the case at present, could restrict business. It is hoped that EU enlargement will not disadvantage the small countries around its southeast frontiers.

The Quality of Reforms

A few examples are probably useful to illustrate the distinction between relatively bold reforms and misguided or weak reforms. Examples of bold policies include:

- Estonia, early-1990s: abolished virtually all tariffs and introduced a currency board system, tying their currency to the DM, then to the Euro.

- Hungary, 1992–93: introduced a tough bankruptcy law and enforced it. Many outsiders criticised the country for being too tough, and to some extent it was, but Hungarian firms no longer expect state rescue. Many perform very well internationally.
- Czech and Slovak Republics (or CSFR until end-1992), early-1990s: introduced imaginative model of voucher-based privatisation and, to the surprise of many observers, implemented it successfully.

The contrast with some of the SEE countries is highly instructive, as illustrated by the following examples of more hesitant or poorly founded approaches to reforms:

- Romania, 1990s: quick to establish the institutions to promote privatisation, but based on a very unsatisfactory model and in any case poorly implemented, in part due to politicians' fears of creating unemployment.
- Albania, early- to mid-1990s: pyramid financing that attracted most citizens' savings, resulting in a serious financial crisis. The IMF had advised that the scheme was fraudulent and would end in tears, but the government at the time did not take their advice.
- Bulgaria, mid- to late-1990s: failed to manage the government budget well and ran into a severe foreign exchange crisis. Eventually set up a currency board system to help stabilise the country's finances, with good results.
- Serbia and Montenegro, mid- to late-1990s: unrealistic conceptions of privatisation, including the claim that so called socially-owned firms could be regarded as private, helped to slow down reforms in general.
- Moldova, late-1990s: still maintained low electricity prices and then failed to enforce them, with non-payers rarely cut off and many payments taking the form of barter.

Numerous other examples could be cited: all fall under the headings of Constraints I2 or I3. To overcome them, political elites have to be persuaded to be bolder in their reform efforts. There is also an evident requirement for wider education about the nature of a market economy and its critical institutional underpinnings.

Conclusion: Critical Issues and Next Steps

This concluding section of this chapter focuses on four issues that are most important for economic recovery and success in the SEE region and that touch financial sector development.

Before proceeding to specific points, it is worth noting that a great deal of valuable material has recently been published that summarises the first 10–12 years of transition experience, seeking to draw out practical lessons. Mitra and Stern (2003) review taxation structures in the transition economies,[10] Estrin (2002) reports on corporate governance, Djankov and Murrell (2002) examine enterprise restructuring, Campos and Coricelli (2002) review what we know, or still do not know, about growth in transition, and Hare (2001) analysed institutional reforms. These papers provide a backdrop to what follows. Concrete recommendations emphasise simple, practical steps that yield tangible benefits relatively rapidly.

Investment and Growth

Investment has already been emphasised at several points. It is an area where the performance of the SEE countries (except Croatia) lags well behind that of the Accession States, the CEB region. High levels of domestic investment and a positive business environment strengthen business confidence at home while also encouraging much needed FDI.

To encourage investment, financial market reforms will help, as will positive measures to improve the business climate (e.g. Paddy Ashdown's "Bulldozer Initiative" in BiH, 2002–03), such as simplified tax rules, simpler registration requirements, elimination of most licensing obligations, limitations on business inspections such as for alleged health and safety reasons, and numerous others.

There is also a virtuous circle to promoting investment: people are usually more willing to save when they perceive that their community is developing and living standards are visibly improving. This point explains why communities and countries sometimes find themselves locked into a low-level equilibrium, with low savings and investment, slow growth, and generally negative attitudes. Yet once growth starts and people become more confident that it is sustainable, so it proves to be. The same community, with more positive, optimistic attitudes about the future, can then achieve a high-level equilibrium. The challenge for much of the SEE region is to bring about the shift from a low-level to a high-level equilibrium development path.

Trade

The easy part of trade policy is securing agreement on such structures as free trade areas and the like, where much but still not enough progress has already been achieved. Much the harder part of making trade policy work well lies in the most micro-level regulation. Here are a few ways of improving trade in the SEE region:

---

[10] Although beyond the scope of this paper, Mitra and Stern argue that transition countries should aim for tax revenue to GDP ratios in the range of 22–31% (depending on their level of development), comprising VAT (6–7%), excises (2–3%), income tax (6–9%), social security/payroll taxes (6–10%), other taxes, e.g. on trade and property (2%). All percentages here are percentages of GDP, not proposed tax rates.

- Look at *border crossings* by road and rail, as well as the major international waterways such as the Danube River. Carry out surveys to find out how long a typical shipment is held up at border points, other check points, customs offices, etc., and also calculate the various costs resulting from these delays, including the legal tariffs, additional bribes paid to reduce delays, etc. While doing this, it would be useful for comparative purposes to find out about similar data for Hungary, Estonia, or elsewhere in the CEB countries. Once the right data are available, even roughly, set targets at border crossings to limit the time delays and cut the costs associated with normal trade. To be really effective, such measures require a fairly high degree of international cooperation. For instance, if Serbian exit controls are quick and cheap, the impact on trade is still bad if the corresponding Bosnian entry controls are slow and expensive.

- Strengthen the *financing of trade* by offering export credit guarantees and trade-related finance on a more routine basis. Apart from requiring improvements in the region's financial institutions within each country, there is an evident need for international cooperation among banks to ensure that international credits are quickly and reliably honoured so that exporters *from within the region* get paid on time. It is clearly not good enough if the banks deal only with internationally known firms.

- *Stop protecting local firms* that supply poor quality products, often at relatively high cost. Politicians may think they are protecting local jobs, but in practice workers often vote with their feet. Once they perceive a firm to be in poor shape they seek jobs elsewhere. Many poorly performing firms in the region have very high rates of voluntary quits. What is often quite astonishing is that despite performing badly they also take on lots of new workers as a result of the political pressures that enable them to remain in business. This is seriously bad economics and also bad politics except from a very short-term standpoint. It limits competition in the domestic market, discouraging the entry of new firms that might be able to perform better. It also discourages intra-regional trade.

Micro-level Institutional Reforms

The main problem is nearly always effective implementation of reforms, since many of the SEE countries have much of the right legislation in place. Some countries have chosen very complex regulatory models, and then prove unable to carry it through. The basic approach may be better, but it can still fail as a result of sectoral or regional political pressures for special treatment. The smallness of the countries is a serious problem when thinking of micro-level policies in this region. In many local markets there will be few agents on either side, most whom know each other. Hence the usual assumptions of competitive analysis – that markets are essentially impersonal institutions with no agents receiving special treatment or possessing special information – frequently fail. This makes the design of well functioning market institutions unusually difficult.

Three examples illustrate this problem:

- *Electricity pricing.* Electricity prices must be high enough to cover production and distribution costs, including an allowance for capital costs when the system operates close to capacity. Charges to different users must reflect differential supply costs. In most developed countries per unit charges to households are much higher than those to firms, while the opposite has tended to be the case in many transition countries. Even worse, transition countries have frequently proved unwilling or unable to disconnect customers who fail to pay, and have tolerated nonmonetary payments. Significant improvements are occurring, but there is a long way to go. Moreover, poor pricing of electricity can distort the pricing of downstream products that use it as a major input, such as aluminium production. Poor pricing can in turn distort privatisation decisions.

- *Bankruptcy provisions.* When firms fail they should exit to make way for new ones. This is a fundamental part of the market economy, and one of the principal mechanisms through which productivity improves and incomes rise. Efforts to impede the process are mostly self-defeating in the long run, both for small and large firms. For banks to function properly, they must have the right to call in loans that do not perform, even if this forces a firm to close. One can argue about exactly how a bankruptcy law should be written, how creditors should be ranked and what conditions must be fulfilled for a firm to cease operation: there is much academic literature on this topic. For present purposes it is sufficient to insist that suitable legislation be in place, and enforced as far as possible, through procedures which are simple, quick and cheap.

    Excluding firms that are worthless except as industrial museums, bankruptcy normally means the demise of a particular firm (an organisation), not the loss of its physical assets. Rather, bankruptcy is often accompanied by the sale of assets either as a whole – to be run by another already existing business, and hopefully better managed – or in pieces, to be incorporated productively into the production processes of other firms. Either way, the assets of a bankrupt business remain in productive use, making the social costs of bankruptcy much lower than is commonly assumed.

- *Property and collateral.* Similar points apply to the use of immovable property and other assets as collateral, e.g. when a firm or an individual seeks a bank loan to develop a new business venture. Such provisions are ineffective if the bank is prevented from realising the assets offered as collateral in the event of default. For instance, if people cannot be turned out of their houses by the courts, such property cannot be offered as collateral and this can prevent many potentially sound businesses from starting up. Also, if there is no market in agricultural land, such land cannot be offered as collateral. To be effective, collateral thus requires the associated development of other property markets, such as those for housing, agricultural land, and so on. In several SEE countries these markets barely function, creating scope for substantial assistance programmes to help develop these vital "missing" markets.

Financial Market Development

A few points on the most urgent priorities: since the region mostly comprises small, low-income countries, it can be expected that financial markets will mostly be thin, fragile and unstable, with few assets to trade and few significant traders. That reality will likely remain for some time. Experience from the CEB countries strongly suggests that government securities will remain the main traded assets, provided governments manage their finances very prudently. There will be a few corporate bonds, but initially not much else. Consequently, even where stock markets exist, they cannot possibly assume much importance unless some form of regional confederation or association of markets can be established. For political reasons as well as for a variety of local, technical reasons, such an association does not appear very probable, though early discussions have started as noted above.

The financial sector will remain largely bank-based, and its effectiveness will therefore depend above all on how well the banks operate, how well they are regulated. Experience in the CEB countries argues in favour of foreign ownership stakes in the banks, since that improves service standards and enhances competition. It also helps to cut or weaken some of the damaging links between banks and large, failing firms that have contributed to poor bank performance in some transition economies. It then becomes more realistic to imagine that the new and inexperienced central banks in the region might be able to cope with the demands of banking regulation. Banking and real sector development should move in step: if the real sector moves ahead, it could be held back by deficiencies in the banking sphere; if the banks develop too fast, they could find that they have deposits but far too few sound borrowers. This balance is hard to get right.

The banks will mostly lend to government. Credit for the household sector and companies will develop more slowly, depending on the parallel development of other markets, together with enforcement of legal provisions to protect lenders. It is especially important that SME finance be developed. The international community has already made useful contributions in this field, with a number of the region's banks offering special credit lines targeted at SMEs (see, for instance, several chapters in Matthäus-Maier and von Pischke, 2004).

Vigorous development of mortgage markets is unlikely without strong legal title to property, adequate systems of surveying and valuing property for mortgage purposes, and legal provisions that allow lenders to repossess property in case of default. Otherwise lenders will perceive the market as too risky. Similar remarks hold for pension funds. These will become more important, but at present few firms in the region require pension contributions in addition to existing state-determined payroll taxes, and there are not yet many reasonably secure long-term assets for funds to hold.

In summary, a useful start for financial sector development is a network of well run banks, preferably with significant foreign ownership, able to finance the governments of the region as well as the region's trade and SMEs.

Outlook

The SEE countries evidently have a long way to go before they complete their market reforms and achieve political stability. Nevertheless, their improved economic performance of the past few years provides grounds for cautious optimism, as does the improving business climate. Commission (2004a) highlights some of the challenges ahead, but also notes (p. 26), "The Commission is particularly encouraged by the increase in regional co-operation, notably in the areas of infrastructure, trade, transport and energy." If it can build on these foundations and avoid further serious conflict, the SEE region can look forward to a prosperous future.

References

Babetskii, Ian, Babetskaia-Kukharchuk, Oxana and Raiser, Martin (2003): "How Deep is your Trade? Transition and international integration in eastern Europe and the former Soviet Union," *EBRD Working Paper 83*, London: EBRD, November.

Berglof, Erik and Bolton, Patrick (2002): "The Great Divide and Beyond: Financial Architecture in Transition," *Journal of Economic Perspectives*, vol.16(1), pp. 77–100.

Blanchard, Olivier (1998): *The Economics of Post-Communist Transition*, Clarendon Lectures, Oxford: Oxford University Press.

Campos, Nauro F. and Coricelli, Fabrizio (2002): "Growth in Transition: What We Know, What We Don't and What We Should," *Journal of Economic Literature*, vol. XL(3), pp. 793–836.

Commission (2004a): *The Stabilisation and Association Process for South East Europe: Third Annual Report*, Com(2004)202/2 final, Brussels: Commission of the European Communities, March 30th.

Commission (2004b): *Opinion on Croatia's Application for Membership of the European Union*, Com(2004)257 final, Brussels: Commission of the European Communities, April 20th.

Cottarelli, Carlo, Dell'Arricia, Giovanni and Vladkova-Hollar, Ivanna (2003): "Early Birds, Late Risers and Sleeping Beauties: Bank Credit Growth to the Private Sector in Central and Eastern Europe and the Balkans," *IMF Working Paper WP/03/213*, Washington, DC: IMF, November.

Djankov, Simeon and Murrell, Peter (2002): "Enterprise Restructuring in Transition: A Quantitative Survey," *Journal of Economic Literature*, vol. XL(3), pp. 739–792.

Easterly, William (2002): *The Elusive Quest for Growth*, Cambridge MA: MIT Press.

EBRD (various years): *Transition Report* and *Transition Report Update*, London: EBRD.

Falcetti, Elisabetta, Sanfey, Peter and Taci, Anita (2003): "Bridging the gaps? Private sector development, capital flows and the investment climate in southeastern Europe," *EBRD Discussion Paper 80*, London: EBRD.

Fries, Stephen, Lysenko, Tatiana and Polenac, Saso (2003): "The 2002 Business Environment and Enterprise Performance Survey: Results from a survey of 6,100 firms," *EBRD Discussion Paper 84*, London: EBRD, November.

Hare, Paul G. (2001): "Institutional Change and Economic Performance in the Transition Economies," chapter 3 (pp. 77–99) in *Economic Survey of Europe*, 2001(2), Geneva: UN Economic Commission for Europe.

Hare, Paul G. (2003): "Social Aspects of Industrial Restructuring and their Financing," background paper for UNECE Regional Forum on Social Aspects and Financing of Industrial Restructuring, held in Moscow November 2003 (available on author's website: www.sml.hw.ac.uk/ecopgh).

IMF (2003a): *Albania: Second Review under the Three-Year Arrangement under the Poverty Reduction and Growth Facility – Staff Report*, IMF Country Report 03/218, Washington DC: IMF, July.

IMF (2003b): *Bosnia and Herzegovina: Second and Third Reviews under the Stand-By Arrangement – Staff Report*, IMF Country Report 03/204, Washington DC: IMF, July.

IMF (2003c): *Croatia: Request for Stand-By Arrangement – Staff Report*, IMF Country Report 03/27, Washington DC: IMF, February.

IMF (2003d): *Former Yugoslav Republic of Macedonia: Selected Issues and Statistical Appendix*, IMF Country Report 03/136, Washington, DC: IMF, May.

IMF (2003e): *Bulgaria: Third Review under the Stand-By Arrangement and Request for Waiver of Performance Criteria – Staff Report*, IMF Country Report 03/206, Washington DC: IMF, July.

IMF (2003f): *Romania: Third Review under the Stand-By Arrangement and Request for Waiver of Performance Criteria – Staff Report*, IMF Country Report 03/123, Washington DC: IMF, May.

IMF (2003g): *Serbia and Montenegro: First Review under the Arrangement – Staff Report*, IMF Country Report 03/151, Washington DC: IMF, June.

IMF (2003h): *Republic of Slovenia: 2003 Article IV Consultation – Staff Report*, IMF Country Report 03/108, Washington DC: IMF, April.

IMF (2003i): *Slovak Republic: 2003 Article IV Consultation – Staff Report*, IMF Country Report 03/234, Washington DC: IMF, August.

IMF (2003j): *Republic of Poland: 2003 Article IV Consultation – Staff Report*, IMF Country Reports 03/187, Washington DC: IMF, June.

IMF (2003k): *Hungary: 2003 Article IV Consultation – Staff Report*, IMF Country Report 03/124, Washington DC: May.

IMF (2003l): *Republic of Lithuania: Third Review under the Stand-By Arrangement – Staff Report*, IMF Country Report 03/55, Washington DC: IMF, March.

IMF (2003m): *Republic of Latvia: 2003 Article IV Consultation – Staff Report*, IMF Country Report 03/113, Washington DC: IMF, April.

IMF (2002a): *Republic of Moldova: 2002 Article IV Consultation, First Review Under the Three-Year Arrangement Under the Poverty Reduction and Growth Facility and Request for Waiver of Performance Criteria – Staff Report*, IMF Country Report 02/190, Washington, DC: IMF, August.

IMF (2002b): *Republic of Estonia: 2002 Article IV Consultation – Staff Report*, IMF Country Report 02/134, Washington DC: IMF, July.

IMF (2002c): *Czech Republic: 2002 Article IV Consultation – Staff Report*, IMF Country Report 02/167, Washington DC: IMF, August.

Kornai, János (1980): *The Economics of Shortage*, 2 vols, Amsterdam: North Holland.

Kornai, János (1992): *The Socialist System: The Political Economy of Communism*, Princeton NJ: Princeton University Press.

Kornai, János, Maskin, Eric and Roland, Gérard (2002): "Understanding the Soft Budget Constraint," Harvard University Working Paper.

Martens, Bertin, Mummett Uwe, Murrell Peter and Seabright, Paul (2002): *The Institutional Economics of Foreign Aid*, Cambridge: Cambridge University Press.

Matthäus-Maier, Ingrid and von Pischke, J.D. (eds) (2004): *The Development of the Financial Sector in Southeast Europe: Innovative Approaches in Volatile Environments*, Berlin: Springer-Verlag.

Mehl, Arnaud and Winkler, Adalbert: "The Financial Sector and Economic Development: Evidence from Southeast Europe," chapter 2 (pp. 11–41) of Matthäus-Maier and von Pischke (2004), q.v.

Michalopoulos, Constantine (2003): *The Western Balkans in World Trade*, ch. 3 of World Bank (2003), q.v.

Mitra, Pradeep and Stern, Nicholas (2003): "Tax Systems in Transition," *World Bank Policy Research Paper* 2947, Washington DC: The World Bank, January.

Tadesse, Solomon (2002): "Financial Architecture and Economic Performance: International Evidence," *Journal of Financial Intermediation*, vol. 11, pp. 429–454.

World Bank (2000): *The Road to Stability and Prosperity in South Eastern Europe: A Regional Strategy Paper*, Washington DC: The World Bank, March.

World Bank (2003): *Trade Policies and Institutions in the Countries of South Eastern Europe in the EU Stabilization and Association Process*, Report No. 24460, Europe and Central Asia Region, Washington DC: The World Bank.

CHAPTER 2:

The Scenario for EU Accession by Southeast European Countries

Marc Franco

Deputy Director General, European Commission

In 2007, Bulgaria and Romania are expected to become EU Member States. Other Balkan countries will follow. The scenario for accession depends to a large extent on the countries in Southeast Europe themselves. The EU has set the framework and defined the benchmarks and the criteria for accession.

The Copenhagen Criteria and Other Enabling Instruments

The Copenhagen Criteria, agreed in 1993, specify the basic requirements for accession. The conditions that apply to the potential SEE candidates are the same as those applied to the ten new Member States admitted in 2004. They can be summed up as follows:

- respect for democratic principles and the rule of law;
- a functioning and competitive market economy;
- capacity to implement and enforce EU legislation.

In mid-2000, the European Commission (EC) launched the Stabilisation and Association Process (SAP), constituting the framework for the accession of the countries of the Western Balkans. At the Zagreb Summit in November 2000, these countries expressed their agreement to the objectives and conditions of the process in return for the EU's offer of a prospect for membership.

The Stabilisation and Association Agreements (SAA) to be entered into with the Balkan countries are the equivalent of the Europe Agreements concluded with the Central European countries and constitute the framework for completing the transition to accession. Agreements have been concluded with Croatia and the Former Yugoslav Republic of Macedonia, to be superseded by a ratification of the SAA Interim Agreement which relates to trade and trade-related matters. The negotiations on the SAA with Albania have started. A feasibility study is underway regarding the decision to start negotiations with Bosnia and Herzegovina. In Serbia and Montenegro, progress has been made through the adoption of the Constitutional Charter and of the Internal Market and Trade Action Plan. This will provide a basis for collaboration with the European Commission, creating the conditions for launching the feasibility study for these two entities' entries.

Croatia's application for EU membership is under examination and it is expected that negotiations may begin in 2006. The Thessaloniki Council noted the need for reform in some sectors, in particular the judiciary, and stressed the importance of refugee return and full cooperation with the International Criminal Tribunal on matters relating to the former Yugoslavia.

Moreover, the June 2003 Summit endorsed the "Thessaloniki Agenda for the Western Balkans: Moving towards European Integration." The measures proposed give new impetus to preparation for EU membership and include initiatives that were highly successful in preparing the accession of the new Member States in Central Europe. These are also applicable to the Western Balkans:

- European Partnerships will be drawn up for each SAP country, identifying priorities for action in the "approximation process" towards legal and regulatory consistency;

- the "twinning" programmes – in which officials from Member States provide technical assistance to support the processes of legal approximation and institution building – will be extended;

- monitoring mechanisms for the implementation of the commitments by SAP countries will be strengthened and streamlined;

- community programmes will be open to SAP countries, allowing them to start cooperation with Member States on education, research, energy, environment, etc.

The EU has reiterated its support for preparation for accession. The main instrument for this support is the CARDS programme (Community Assistance for Reconstruction, Development and Stabilisation). To assist in meeting the requirements for EU rapprochement, funds totalling €200 million are being provided to reinforce the programme's activities from 2004 through 2006.

In short: the SAP framework was clearly laid down in Zagreb. The steps leading to accession have been defined, support is available and the monitoring mechanisms are being established. The process is largely identical to that which led to the accession of the Central European countries. As was the case for the new Member States, it is impossible to fix a date far in advance: the countries of the Western Balkan will become members when they are ready. This depends first and foremost on the results of their efforts to fulfil the Copenhagen Criteria.

EU Accession and the Financial Sector: Benefits and Challenges

The preparation for accession will stimulate the reform and approximation process in the countries of the Western Balkans, offering the financial sector a modern, market oriented environment in which to operate.

Accession also means participating in the free flow of goods, services and capital in the internal market. This implies increased competition with international financial groups in the financial services market. Whether the financial sector in the Western Balkans will benefit from accession or suffer from the increased competition within the broader European market depends on its competitiveness. The sector's future rests on its capacity to take up the challenge of reform and transition, and its ability to offer modern financial services that businesses want to use.

The Western Balkan countries are still in the process of transition towards a modern market economy, and the financial sector plays a crucial role in this process. However, the financial sector itself has to pass through the most profound transformation of all economic sectors. Indeed, banking in a planned economy and in a market economy are totally different activities. In the planned economy, banking has a largely passive function, designed to assist the implementation of the state's economic planning. In the market economy, the banking sector plays a central role as facilitator, a provider of credit and as a major player in the allocation of resources.

To ensure the success of the economic transition process and the preparation for accession, it is therefore essential that the necessary and far-reaching banking sector reforms are tackled first. Specifically, this means:

- Completing the reform process: ensuring central bank independence, placing commercial banks on a sound footing, moving ahead with privatisation in this sector, cleaning up the banks' balance sheets, setting up a modern nonbanking financial sector.

- Further developing financial intermediation in general and banking services in particular: at present, the relative importance of the banking sector in the economy (measured as deposits/GDP or credits/GDP) is far below the norm in developed market economies. To stimulate economic growth, it is crucially important to develop banking and other financial services for the local enterprise sector. Special attention must be given to small and medium-sized enterprise (SME) and to the transformation of the informal sector.

- Promoting the approximation of legislation, i.e. setting up a harmonised regulatory framework to enable the financial sector to function within the internal market. In this context, conformity with EU directives is only the first step. Effective institutions that are able to monitor and enforce the legislation are a sine qua non for accession. This is of particular importance for the application of all prudential rules, such as those pertaining to licensing and the supervision of financial institutions.

Some of these reforms can be undertaken by each individual state. However, in order for them to be fully effective, international cooperation is of paramount importance. The EU CARDS programme offers technical support for the transformation of the financial sector and the approximation of legislation. Other institutions, such as the EBRD (European Bank for Reconstruction and Development), have made important contributions to financial sector reform.

Moreover, foreign direct investment (FDI) is necessary to stimulate the emergence of a modern banking sector. The EBRD has played an important role in this effort, and international investors are developing an interest in participating in the sector. This is a manifestation of increased confidence in the economic prospects of the Western Balkan countries – the result of increased political stability and the countries' efforts to transform their economies and to create a legal environment geared to the modern market system.

CHAPTER 3:

Infrastructure Finance, Accession, and Related Policy Issues in Southeast Europe

Ewald Nowotny

Vienna University of Economics and Business Administration, formerly Vice-President of EIB for operations in Southeast Europe and Turkey

The European Investment Bank (EIB) is an important provider of long-term financing in Southeast Europe. In this capacity, it enjoys excellent cooperation with KfW and EBRD. Long-term financing is used predominately for infrastructure projects, and this has important implications for both financial sector and real sector development.

Planning, Constructing and Financing Infrastructure in SEE

Building and, even more importantly, repairing and adequately maintaining infrastructure (IS) is an essential condition for further stimulating private investments and thus economic development. Nevertheless, it is still necessary to subject each IS project to a rigorous cost-benefit analysis. In SEE – as in other regions – a great number of projects are driven by a combination of political ambition (and perhaps other motivating factors) and suppliers' interests. There is an attendant risk of building "white elephants," the maintenance and capital costs of which have to be borne by future generations and future governments.

In some cases, a smaller version of a project is economically more efficient than one of spectacular dimensions. But it is also essential to insist on regional coordination and cooperation for many projects. This has been achieved in electricity production for example, where plans to expand national generating capacity also have to include the efficiency-enhancing effects of building or reconstructing interregional transmission lines that create regional energy markets. In fact, in all such IS projects, regional coordination is a condition for financing by international financial institutions (IFIs) – a condition with obvious political implications.

Physical Infrastructure Investment and Capital Market Development

The role of capital markets is to a large extent related to national economic development, to political and economic stability, and to the range of investment and financing alternatives that are or will become available. In the light of these factors, there will be a limited but growing role for capital markets in SEE.

Local currency bond issues by top-rated IFIs can promote longer time horizons in capital markets in transition economies. EIB has played a pioneering role in this respect in practically all recent and future EU accession states. The Bank's long-term efforts to open up and develop capital markets came to fruition in 2002 and are beginning to pay off. The issuance of € 535 million in bonds denominated in Czech, Polish and Hungarian currencies was innovative. These issues included the first 15-year domestic zero-coupon Polish (PLN) bond, extending the PLN yield curve and offering more opportunities for long-term investors, such as insurance companies; the first Czech (CZK) international bond with a maturity of 20 years; a maiden Hungarian (HUF) issue that was designed to be merged with a "standard" EIB benchmark issue following Hungary's membership in the European currency union.

This activity has made the EIB the leading nonsovereign borrower in the future accession states, in keeping with its position as the largest lender in these countries. EIB is also prepared to implement this policy in SEE. For the IFIs involved, the design, coordination and marketing of these innovative instruments is quite labour-intensive. However, this effort is outweighed by the obvious advantages of offering top-quality investment opportunities that make long-term saving in the relevant countries more attractive. This, in turn, reduces capital flight and eliminates exchange rate risks for local investors in infrastructure and in other sectors. In contrast, the extremely damaging effects of uncovered exchange-rate risks have been demonstrated in a dramatic way in Turkey.

IS investments can be vehicles for access to European capital markets – providing infrastructure financing opportunities to foreign investors who are able to refinance themselves on Western capital markets. The attractiveness of this approach depends, of course, on the profit perspectives for these investors. The telecoms and energy sectors present obvious opportunities for foreign direct investment.

This opportunity does not generally occur in environmental investments in water, wastewater and transportation (for example, toll roads) because of the very low income levels in most SEE countries. Although this also implies lower investment costs, it is usually extremely difficult to generate cost-covering fees and tolls, given the low income base. Foreign investors may provide important know-how transfer through public-private partnerships, but usually a substantial direct or indirect grant element will be necessary to achieve socially compatible prices.

EU Policy in SEE

The theme paper's unconventional, but well-taken, points concerning EU policy in SEE call for careful consideration.

Even for those countries that are likely to attain EU membership, per capita GDP adjusted for purchasing power parity remains well below the EU average. In 2002, real per-capita GDP at purchasing power parity in Romania was 26% of the average for the 15 EU Member States; in Bulgaria the figure was 34%.[1] The most advanced country in the region is Slovenia (which does not want to be considered as part of the region). It had an income level equivalent to 73% of the EU average in 2002, and its per-capita GDP has surpassed that of Greece. Slovenia is followed by Croatia at 53%.

On a less positive note, Serbia (21%), Macedonia (24%), Albania (21%) and Moldova (5%) are – according to some economic criteria – still (or once more) in the range of the developing countries. They are much further from Western Europe economically than geographically, and this is part of the political problem. These huge differences within SEE and the development gaps exhibited by some of the countries tend to be somewhat neglected in diplomatic discussions on the prospects for eventual EU membership.

The theme paper rightly considers it essential to have a realistic view of the timetable and possibilities for EU membership. Given the time required to overcome their substantial economic and institutional problems, the prospect for full EU membership for Romania and Bulgaria by 2010 is realistic. The same should hold true for Croatia. It is extremely counterproductive to delay membership negotiations on the grounds of the ever new demands arising at the International Criminal Court in The Hague. *Fiat justitia, pereat mundus* – justice at all cost – may be of great value in principle, but the complicated geopolitical situation that emerged following the horrible wars in the Balkan countries may make the economic and political costs of delaying membership negotiations also very high. The Hague Court actions, if stretched out over a long period and not fully transparent, could create a permanent source of political instability, which is especially harmful for those wanting to move their countries closer to EU standards.

For countries other than Romania, Bulgaria and Croatia, there is and should be a prospect of joining the EU – even if this will happen only in the very long term. Given the length of time involved, it is problematic to ask these countries now to adopt the *acquis communautaire* wholesale. A number of aspects of the *acquis* are based on the perspectives of much more prosperous states; in countries with much lower incomes, the socio-economic conditions and cost-benefit calculations may look quite different.

Let us consider just one example: environmental regulations. EIB and other IFIs have to ensure that all EU environmental regulations are observed in all pro-

---

[1] Statistics are based on calculations of WIIW (Wiener Institut für Internationale Wirtschaftsvergleiche – Vienna Institute for International Economic Studies).

jects. This, despite the fact that social preferences and conditions in low-income countries may be quite different from those in high income countries. And we should not forget that environmental standards were different in high income countries when their incomes were lower.

The EU, IFIs and international organisations must follow strict international procurement and tendering rules for all projects they finance. This can be a valuable safeguard against the ever-present dangers of corruption. However, there is no provision for the preferential treatment of local suppliers, except in procurement contracts financed by the World Bank. The long-term development impact of a project is much greater if it creates a substantial degree of supply integration with the local and regional economy. Closer integration, appropriately managed, would increase the overall economic efficiency of international investment and development programmes.

All these issues are very sensitive, but the theme paper provides a way through: given the very complex nature of the changing economic and political developments, a rigid legalistic and therefore also bureaucratic approach should be avoided, in favour of more pragmatic economic policies and, in some cases, even common-sense approaches. This message is certainly of special importance for SEE, but it may also be relevant to other parts of Europe.

CHAPTER 4:

Making It Easier to Do Business in Southeast Europe

Khaled F. Sherif

Sector Manager, World Bank

Recognising the significant diversity among the SEE countries and variable levels of progress and development, the SEE region faces several broad obstacles in its effort to close the income and competitiveness gap with the EU and first-tier accession candidates. These obstacles burdening SEE broadly include:

- financing: weak, under-capitalised, risk-averse banks; poorly functioning securities markets (if at all); the absence of institutional investors (insurance, pension funds); weak specialised nonbank financial institutions (leasing, mortgage finance);

- tax and regulation: distorted incentives, inconsistent treatment, unpredictability;

- policy instability: uncertainty undermines investment prospects;

- judiciary: poor institutional framework and enforcement reduces willingness to take risk;

- corruption: costly in terms of money and time, reduces public sector effectiveness, adds to uncertainty and the risk premium.

Building Legal Systems That Reduce Business Transaction

The legal framework touches all of these obstacles. The integrity of this framework is fundamentally affected by the degree to which these obstacles constrain growth, development *and* perceptions of fairness and equity. Together, these obstacles add to the cost of transactions in the region, and all of them present challenges to SEE countries.

Positive Beginnings

But not all is negative. There has been significant progress in recent years, as reflected in greater stability, real GDP growth, and long-term optimism that the region is destined to integrate more closely with the European Union and, in the case of Bulgaria and Romania, will continue to negotiate for an eventual formal invitation to accede. In the banking sector, most countries now have two-tier systems, and few state banks remain. Fiscal reforms have led to the introduction of VAT, improved tax and customs administration, and efforts to improve budget management. Business registration systems have slowly improved, reducing the number of procedures and the time and cost involved in business start-up.

Governments have come to recognise the importance of investment, and in some cases are trying to sustain consistent policies to reduce business uncertainty. The judiciary remains slow and inefficient, yet several countries are in the process of reforming their judicial systems in order to achieve greater responsiveness and efficiency. Corruption remains problematic, but is now on the radar screen for reform. Thus, while lagging the 2004 accession countries, SEE is making progress in areas that exhibited varying degrees of weakness a decade ago.

Strengthening Property Rights

On the other hand, the SEE countries must be realistic about the persistence of these obstacles and the impact they have on overall economic growth. Inadequate or inefficient collateral or pledge registries, weak secured transactions frameworks, insufficient creditor protection or foreclosure procedures, and weak protection or abuses of minority shareholder rights all promote risk aversion by financial institutions, severely reducing credit and investment for growth. Such risk aversion is reinforced by the absence of financial discipline in many enterprises, reflecting inadequate governance, weak management, poor business planning, and/or a closed and nontransparent mode of operation that makes it difficult for banks and other financial institutions to play their proper role in the evaluation and management of credit risk. When loans or investments are made, such characteristics add to borrowers' costs and risk premium, all of which slows growth in the real sector and adds to enterprise costs.

These obstacles are intensified by the persistence of corruption, inefficiency and malfeasance of public sector institutions. Bribes and kickbacks are common in the processes required to obtain permits, licences, and other types of registration. These are informal taxes that grease the wheels of individual transactions, yet perpetuate a system of inefficiency and corruption that serves as a disincentive for civil servants to provide services to the public and markets in accordance with their job descriptions and mandates. Such malversation disillusions most people and reduces their incentive to pay taxes. The circularity of this lack of integrity and confidence makes it difficult for those civil servants who are professional and dedicated to public service to behave accordingly, owing to the weakness of revenue flows. In the end, such behaviour adds to macroeconomic pressures in the form of

Table 1. SEE business environment indicators

Country	Informal sector as % of economy	Business start-up	Contract enforcement	Business closure
Albania	33	11 procedures; 47 days; 65% of per capita income;* minimum capital 52% of per capita income	37 procedures; 220 days; 73% of per capita income	n.a.
Bosnia and Herzegovina (BiH)	34	12 procedures; 59 days; 52% of per capita income; minimum capital 379% of per capita income	31 procedures; 630 days; 21% of per capita income	1.9 years; cost = 8% of estate
Bulgaria	37	10 procedures; 30 days; 8% of per capita income; minimum capital 134% of per capita income	26 procedures; 410 days; 6% of per capita income	3.8 years; cost = 18% of estate
Croatia	33	13 procedures; 50 days; 18% of per capita income; minimum capital 51% of per capita income	20 procedures; 330 days; 7% of per capita income	3.1 years; cost = 18% of estate
FYR Macedonia	n.a.	13 procedures; 48 days; 13% of per capita income; minimum capital 138% of per capita income	27 procedures; 509 days; 43% of per capita income	3.6 years; cost = 38% of estate
Moldova	45	11 procedures; 42 days; 26% of per capita income; minimum capital 86% of per capita income	36 procedures; 210 days; 14% of per capita income	2.8 years; cost = 8% of estate
Romania	34	6 procedures; 27 days; 12% of per capita income; minimum capital 3% of per capita income	28 procedures; 225 days; 13% of per capita income	3.2 years; cost = 8% of estate
Serbia and Montenegro	29	10 procedures; 44 days; 13% of per capita income; minimum capital 357% of per capita income	40 procedures; 1,028 days; 20% of per capita income	7.3 years; cost = 38% of estate

Source: summarised from "Doing Business," World Bank - http://rru.worldbank.org/DoingBusiness/
* *Note:* Cost of procedures and capital relative to per capita gross domestic product.

monetary and fiscal costs; it intensifies distortions, weakens the overall environment for free and fair competition, and makes it difficult for firms and the economy to achieve high standards of performance.

Table 1 summarises some crucial business environment weaknesses exhibited in SEE countries.

Formalisation for Efficiency

Compared to the EU and other "high" OECD countries, in which the informal sector generally produces less than 20% of economic activity, most SEE countries:

- have an informal sector that constitutes about one-third of their economy;
- require more procedures to enforce contracts effectively, and the process takes twice as long – even longer in the successor states of the former Yugoslavia;
- take longer to effect business closure and at higher cost;
- are slower to formalise the registration of new businesses, partly due to an excessive number of procedures;
- often have outmoded and excessive minimum capital requirements for real sector enterprises, reducing their incentive to register and become part of the formal tax system.

These weaknesses show that there are administrative, regulatory and fiscal obstacles to formalised economic development. Generally, these impediments add to the cost of transactions for business in the SEE countries. Even in Romania, where the indicators are generally the closest to EU and other "high" OECD countries, the informal sector accounts for 34% of gross national income. Add to these factors such problems as organised crime, basic street crime and theft, and inadequate infrastructure, and the transaction costs mount.

Ultimately, the effects are broadly felt. For instance, small scale enterprises need freedom in order to operate, incentives for growth, and a minimum of interference from bureaucracy and administration. For these enterprises, simplicity is essential. They are vital for long-term fiscal sustainability and ongoing job creation. Thus, impediments and/or excessive taxation drive them underground, as shown in the high estimates of informal GDP above. Medium-sized firms are in many cases young and dynamic: usually small enough to be agile, yet large enough to muster resources. These firms need consistency, a minimum burden of taxes and procedures, and inducements to grow. As with small firms, too many constraints encourage informal activity to the detriment of the economy. Meanwhile, large scale firms must be subject to regulatory oversight in order to ensure compliance. As they play an anchor role in their respective business sectors, they should be encouraged to build clusters, to increase research and development, etc.

Harassment encourages these firms to move offshore, or at least to transfer funds out of the country.

How Can These Barriers Be Reduced? Is Progress Likely?

Several measures can be taken to reduce these impediments to growth and competitiveness. They include:

- establishing a strategic plan and vision, such as accession to the European Union combined with medium-term competitive performance targets for the economy relative to regional and global peers;
- providing a stable macroeconomic framework based on low inflation, low fiscal deficits, and relatively stable exchange rates;
- expanding the fiscal base and lowering rates, possibly with the adoption of a flat tax for individuals and companies across the board;
- adopting and enforcing sound regulation to improve financial stability and to boost depositor and investor confidence; establishing reasonable consumer protection regulations would encourage contractual savings;
- having a competitive, adequately regulated and supervised market-based framework in the real sector that is based on open trade and investment,;
- modernising the legal framework for secured transactions, contract enforcement, and creditor/investor rights; reinforcing the legal framework through effective use of implementing regulations; introducing standardised contracts, specialised courts, and out-of-court mechanisms for dispute resolution;
- professionalising the civil service, making it more focused, technology based, specialised, and offering more attractive remuneration;
- streamlining business registration and exit procedures and making them more automatic;
- using electronic means of information dissemination, for example for status reports on investment, permit and licensing requests and applications;
- strengthening the role of specialised business associations to generate essential market information;
- strengthening the role of self-regulatory organisations (SROs) to assist with regulatory compliance;

- strengthening and professionalising the accounting and auditing profession in order to raise standards of governance; producing reliable financial data for better financial management.

The SEE countries are addressing their business environment weaknesses in varying ways. However, the reforms cannot be designed and implemented overnight, because they frequently imply reversal of practices that have been in effect for decades. Rather, the approach requires vision, with the short-, medium- and long-term goals and objectives clearly mapped out. But for many of these reforms, changes in the incentive structure, cultural architecture, and institutional landscape alone with not be sufficient. They require time, training and experience. This applies particularly in areas such as judicial reform, where a new body of laws and considerations need to be taken into perspective when adjudicating on such issues as bankruptcy, foreclosure, repossession, and liquidation.

Local Businesses: A Tax Base or a Source of Growth and Jobs?

Local businesses are important for development. They can be taxed, thus providing a source of revenue for public sector activities. However, taxes reduce their productivity and diminish their contribution to growth and job creation. Key policy guidelines for managing this conflict include:

- Adherence to a policy of macroeconomic stability in order to maintain confidence, to aid long-term business and household planning and to facilitate general risk management. Relatively recent experiences with hyperinflationary chaos and deep fiscal deficits triggered an erosion of purchasing power, living standards, and the provision of social services and infrastructure.

- Recognition that good governance is indispensable for both public and private sector effectiveness. This depends on the rule of law, absence of corruption, a functioning and well supervised financial sector, and professional oversight of banks, other financial institutions and companies based on modern management information systems and "fit and proper" standards.

- Focus on human capital and the knowledge economy. Human capital is central in an increasingly knowledge-based world. It is necessary to make a long-term commitment to education at all levels, to promote intensive cooperation between research and development centres, universities, schools and think tanks and others in order to increase opportunities while avoiding duplication of effort.

- Establishment of sound infrastructure as a precondition for speed, efficiency, and competitiveness.

With respect to taxation, basic principles and guidelines include:

- Broadening the base: The larger the number of taxpayers, the lower the rates and the smaller the burden of any specific type of tax. The more exemptions that exist, the smaller the base, which translates into higher rates, accusations of politicisation and unwarranted targeting, and the increased attractiveness of operating in the informal sector.

- Lowering rates: The lower the tax rates, the less the perceived burden, and the greater the willingness to comply.

- Simplifying the tax code: The easier it is for households and companies to understand, the easier it is to comply and collect.

- Introducing sound incentives: Positive incentives should be in place for registration and licensing, such as access to formal financial services. Meanwhile, negative incentives should also be in place for illegal informal sector activity, i.e. tough penalties.

- Benchmarking performance: Countries should benchmark their performance (relative to others) and set a timeframe for achieving goals, such as reducing informal sector shares of GDP to below 15%.

- Demonstrating good governance: Households and companies will resent paying taxes if funds are misallocated. Thus, efforts to promote a balanced fiscal policy in which revenues are commensurate with expenditure without imposing an unreasonable burden must be backed up by a professionally managed civil service.

Pro-growth Professional Standards

The World Bank has observed that public sector professionalisation is very closely linked to progress in the private sector. Private sector development has encouraged the public sector to rationalise, raise standards of governance, and improve service delivery. While the Bank has focused significantly on private and financial sector development, it has also provided more than $ 1 billion in assistance to help modernise the civil service and public administration of transition countries. It has provided this assistance because good governance in all quarters is an essential requirement for private sector growth and sustainable economic development. Today's public sector is much better equipped to provide fundamental government services than in the early-1990s, and is increasingly focused on improving the targeting of social assistance.

Public sector capacity-enhancement measures have included increasing the regulatory capacity in critical areas in order to make investment more attractive, ensuring sound delivery and fair pricing, and to provide consumer protection under market conditions. Adequate services, fairly priced tariffs for critical infrastructure, social support for the most vulnerable in society, and the fair enforcement of consumer rights are important building blocks. These factors, plus upholding creditors' rights based on contractual agreements, are all part of creating a soundly functioning institutional framework. When such a framework is in place, households and companies appear more willing to pay taxes, particularly if an effort has been made to reduce the financial burden and the time involved.

The housing finance market is also an important building block and a target of further development. This market has begun to take off in many countries, including most of SEE. One of the benefits is that it provides households and companies with asset-based security that can be collateralised, while also providing a fiscal foundation for local government. This, of course, is predicated on a number of other preconditions. These include the willingness of central government to provide reasonable levels of local autonomy, a clear mandate that is not excessively complex or duplicative of other governmental functions, professionally managed and effective budget and planning departments, adequate information systems for the accurate archiving and updating of data, and a commitment to establishing transparent procedures to facilitate public access to and use of information.

Property taxes are an essential source of funding for local government and for the development of municipal bond markets. Modern appraisal and accounting standards, including mark-to-market valuations, are needed for the assignment of asset values. Based on these two factors – tax-based funding and appraisal standards – it is possible construct cash flow projections for budgetary management and planning purposes based on any given property tax formula. Once these and other sources of data are available and systems are operating, it becomes possible for local governments to obtain credit ratings, which is a prerequisite for issuing municipal bonds. This additional tool will enhance the public sector's capacity to render services for communities, including local businesses.

PART II:

Financial Regulation for Stability and Protection in Southeast Europe

PART III

Introduction to Part II

To what extent can financial regulation improve the investment climate and confidence in financial systems in Southeast Europe (SEE)? This question is important because banking crises and inflation created an aversion to banks and mistrust in institutions during the early stages of transition. Restoring citizens' confidence and attracting local and foreign direct investment (FDI) is crucial in stimulating finance to play its part in creating robust growth and development in the region. A matter of increasing interest is the influence or adoption of EU regulations and the Second Basel Accord (Basel II) that sets international banking and regulatory standards. How will SEE governments respond?

Banking Regulation and Stable Growth

The theme paper by Evan Kraft, "Financial Sector Development in Southeast Europe: The Roles of EU Accession and Basel II," discusses two major issues. The first is the role of financial regulation in realising the opportunities opened by the EU accession process. These opportunities include improved access to FDI, capital markets, and official loans and subsidies. The second major issue is the challenge facing financial regulators in adapting supervisory practices to local circumstances, which include political interference, the institutional capacity to administer regulations, and relatively low levels of financial development.

The improved protection of creditors' rights is a prequisite for financial sector development. Achieving this legal objective depends on administrative will and political commitment. The best place to begin is the banking sector, because banks dominate SEE formal financial markets. Banking supervision can help to provide sectoral and macroeconomic stability, to limit risks and to provide discipline and respect for law. This is most easily achieved when supervisors enjoy political independence, which is usually maximised when they are part of the central bank, and when they are protected personally against liability for corrective and cautionary actions justly undertaken and properly implemented.

A number of questions surrounds the large and generally positive presence of foreign banks in SEE: Will they take responsibility for risks incurred by their subsidiaries and affiliates? Will they dominate retail markets while ignoring small and medium enterprise (SME)? Will they use their vast resources in ways that destabilise small economies? Are they more skilled than their SEE regulators? Will they fuel debt-driven bubbles? Will their home-country and host-country regulators be sufficiently well coordinated to avoid embarrassments?

The integration of SEE financial sectors into larger regional systems need not be rushed. In general, no major changes are required to comply with EU banking directives. Basel II practices that govern banking in rich, diversified economies should not be adopted until sufficient databases have been compiled to meet rating criteria and when regulators' skills are more fully developed. Affordability suggests that deposit insurance coverage should be lower than the EU level. The market for SEE sovereign debt is more bullish than Basel ratings would suggest and therefore this debt should not be rated. It is recommended that local bank capital requirements that exceed Basel minima should be retained. Collaboration among local regulators and those of the home countries of foreign banks active in SEE will be a useful part of this process.

Response Papers

Five response papers address regulatory and related issues in specific SEE countries as well as at a more general level. Merab Kakulia of the National Bank of Georgia provides an example of standards that are tighter than those of the EU. Key differences between the Georgian banking legislation and EU Directives include: a) Georgian capital adequacy requirements are tighter; b) no single owner except banking institutions may hold more than 25% of a bank's stock, and there are therefore no bank holding companies in Georgia, and c) minimum initial capital requirements for banks are being progressively raised to reach the EU standard by the end of 2008.

However, supervisors face information constraints in licensing banks because they are required to complete due diligence searches within specified, short time periods, and because court actions, rather than regulatory findings, are required to disqualify parties that are not "fit and proper." In addition, EU deposit insurance coverage limits should not be adopted in Georgia because they are far too high and hence costly.

Peter Nicholl, governor of the Central Bank of Bosnia and Herzegovina (BiH), addresses the role of foreign banks in improving banking practices and standards in SEE. Foreign banks from Austria, Croatia, Italy, Serbia, Slovenia and Turkey currently operate in BiH. Their quality varies considerably, based on their age, size and home country practices, which makes generalisations dangerous. The better foreign banks have the confidence of depositors and have introduced new products and systems, spurring the better domestic banks to innovate and adapt in order to compete. The deposit base continues to rise rapidly, but remains primarily short-term. Foreign banks, especially the older and larger ones, have tremendous reputational capital at risk: their failure in any country would have a significant impact on their standing in the international financial community and among depositors.

Lending to households, including home reconstruction and home improvement loans, is a very important segment of retail business for banks in BiH. Housing loans are very attractive to the banks because they can be reasonably well collateralised by real property, in contrast to other types of property, and guarantors are also used. The courts work slowly and cannot be depended upon to protect creditors' rights. Efforts are underway to improve collateral law, to establish special courts for financial claims, and to stimulate longer credit terms for small and medium scale firms, using donor-funded credit lines.

Mihai Bogza of the National Bank of Romania explores the contrasts between foreign banks (owned by foreign capital) and local banks (with a majority of domestic shareholders). His account is especially interesting because of the performance, verging on comic opera, of a foreign bank that failed spectacularly in Romania. Romanian authorities have found that foreign banks have widely different approaches to doing business, and that these can be roughly categorised by the structure of foreign ownership and by the banking traditions and standards of the home countries in which the foreign parties are based. Due to the priority attached to building the banking sector during the early transition period, when it was very difficult to attract foreign banks, entry requirements were kept low. Subsequently, they have been upgraded as foreign banks showed more interest and as failures occurred. The authorities learned the hard way that "supervisors should never relax."

Another concern is rapid growth in bank credit expansion. This has occurred at the consumer level in Romania, and also at the aggregate level. As a transition country without an historical basis for creating benchmarks, debate has raged in Romania about the implications of rapid growth in the credit supply.

Eris Sharxhi of the Bank of Albania focuses on risk management and its implications, especially in the context of the Basel II package of regulatory improvements. The implications are quite broad, extending from the board room and executive suite to the economy and to society in general. Improvements in risk management have occurred in banks and in regulatory practices. However, attempts to manage risks through regulation may have negative consequences when rules are not aligned with the risks they are intended to manage. Hence, using a range of tools can produce more accurate risk assessments.

One such tool is credit rating. However, the majority of small firms in transition countries are not rated because of costs and lack of a data base. The use of risk weightings in such cases may be problematic because of their uneven application. Unrated firms are automatically placed in the highest risk category according to Basel standards, requiring bankers to provide the highest level of capital to support such loans. However, loans to some unrated firms would no doubt be less risky than implied by their categorisation. These firms would probably be rationed more severely and their costs of borrowing, the amount of credit obtained and loan tenors would tend to be more restrictive than if they were rated.

More public disclosure of the conditions of banks according to Basel recommendations is problematic because of the public's general lack of ability to place numbers in context, and because good news is discounted while bad news is compounded.

Flexibility in content and timing is required to permit SEE regulators to adapt to Basel II and EU standards. In addition to rating issues, the location of supervisory authority over foreign shareholders and institutions is important. Dynamic provisioning in response to business cycles or other circumstances is useful because it builds reserves in good times and draws against them in bad. Failure to adopt dynamic provisioning would tend to cause banks to lend less in downturns than they would otherwise do, accelerating economic recession. In short, pragmatism is key to the reform and enhancement of supervision.

The paper by Christian Fehlker, Arnaud Mehl and Adalbert Winkler (European Central Bank) looks at the challenges of financial regulation in SEE. They note that the immediate task is bringing SEE practices up to international standards, a challenge which is compounded by the relatively rapid evolution of international best practice. They address three issues. The first concerns the preconditions for effective supervision. Their starting point is that supervisors are not the only guarantors of financial stability, that the economic environment needs to be conducive to financial stability and that financial sector developments affect and may endanger the effectiveness of the supervisory framework.

The second issue concerns the conduct of supervision, where two periods are distinguished. In the first, improvement in SEE supervisory practice requires a focus on achieving compliance with international standards. Upon compliance with these standards, a second period unfolds whereby supervisory challenges in SEE and the EU converge in an effort to preserve financial stability and protect consumers. Thorny issues that will remain include the definition of the proper supervisory focus, the allocation of supervisory responsibilities among competent authorities, the definition of the role of central banks in supervision and establishing workable crisis management procedures. In the EU, these challenges are being addressed against the background of the advancement of the single market and the introduction of the euro, which add to the complexity of the task.

The third issue concerns the supervisory framework, which comprises a wide range of instruments. Minimum capital requirements, an important component of the framework, are currently being reviewed in an internationally harmonised framework (the so-called Basel II reform). The authors elaborate on the potential consequences of this reform for European business, noting that further analysis is in order. They conclude by providing an outlook on the currently accepted reform agenda in Southeast Europe, emphasising that its smooth implementation is a key challenge. They conclude that, in all likelihood, catching up with international standards means chasing a moving target.

CHAPTER 5:

Financial Sector Development in Southeast Europe – The Roles of EU Accession and Basel II

Evan Kraft

Research Department Director, Croatian National Bank

Introduction

Recent research has stressed the importance and strength of the link between financial sector development and economic growth in most countries (Levine et al. 2000; Wachtel 2001; Berger, Hasan and Klapper 2003). However, the connection seems empirically weak in transition countries (Berglof and Bolton 2002) and Southeast Europe (SEE).[1] Indicators of banking system development, such as credit to the private sector as a percentage of GDP, have deteriorated as economic growth has improved (Mehl and Winkler 2002).

This paradox is probably more apparent than real. Transition countries necessarily had to "clean up" portfolios of bad assets accumulated under communism and the first years of transition in order to stabilise their financial systems and their economies. Thus, it is reasonable to presume that, as in most countries, further economic development in SEE requires further financial development. Even if financial sector development may not have a big impact on growth, due to various other factors impeding business expansion, sensible financial sector policies and further progress in financial development should minimise the likelihood of financial sector instability that could damage growth.

Two external factors influence policy issues relating to financial development: the EU accession process and the Basel II Accord. The approach taken by the SEE countries to these policy issues is discussed here in the broader context of how these countries can achieve the desired goals of financial development and economic growth in general. Of course, the SEE countries are economically and politically heterogeneous: there certainly is no one-size-fits-all approach to the issues raised here.

The basic themes of this paper are two-fold. First, progress towards EU accession should bring greater political stability to SEE countries and raise investor

---

[1] Southeast Europe is defined here as Albania, Bosnia and Herzegovina, Bulgaria, Croatia, Kosovo, Macedonia, Romania, and Serbia and Montenegro. In some cases other countries are also included or only a partial set is discussed.

confidence. In turn, this is expected to improve access to resources, including increased foreign direct investment (FDI), strengthen links to international capital markets and lead to higher levels of official development assistance. These flows can make great contributions to stabilising and deepening SEE financial systems.

However, these opportunities are bound up with important challenges. The growing presence of foreign banks, which has increased financial sector stability and encouraged financial sector development, poses new questions. For example, how will the owners of foreign banks react if their subsidiaries in transition countries fail? Will the foreign banks be interested in small and medium enterprise (SME) lending? Also, heightened capital inflows created by foreign bank entry may produce credit booms, raising concerns about prudential lending and exacerbating current account problems and exchange rate volatility.

Second, SEE banking supervisors will face major challenges. The decision whether, when, and how to adopt Basel II is one of these. More fundamentally, supervisors are faced with the challenge of adapting supervisory practices to local circumstances, including the level of financial development, administrative capacity, and relations between supervisors and political authorities. SEE countries should strive for organisational structures appropriate for banking supervision and provide adequate incentives to supervisors. Neither task is simple.

The remainder of this paper is organised as follows. The second section provides an overview of the current situation of the financial sector in SEE. The third section discusses key policy issues facing financial sector regulation, with special attention paid to the organisational structure of banking supervision and to supervisory incentives. The fourth section examines the EU accession process and priorities in SEE financial sector development. This includes the adoption of the EU's financial regulation framework along with issues raised by the increased presence of foreign banks and the policy dilemmas caused by lending booms. The fifth section focuses on issues for SEE raised by Basel II, suggesting a cautious approach to adopting the new standards. The sixth offers a conclusion.

The Current State of SEE Financial Sectors

Financial systems in the Southeast European (SEE) countries are relatively undeveloped and highly bank-centred. Table 1 lists five of the basic indicators of financial sector development found to be significant in growth regressions. The SEE countries are compared with those in Central and Eastern Europe (CEE).

Beginning with total bank assets to GDP, SEE countries clearly lag far behind the eurozone. As of 2001, they also lagged quite far behind CEE, especially when Croatia is excluded. The sharp fall in this indicator in SEE from 1996 to 2001 is due primarily to financial developments in Bulgaria, which suffered hyperinflation and a banking crisis in 1996 and 1997. But part of the decline reflects the recognition that many of the assets on SEE banks' books in 1996 were actually worthless, especially in Romania and Albania. To the extent that decreases in bank assets simply reflect past losses, they are not worrisome economic phenomena but rather attempts to come to grips with the actual state of affairs.

Table 1. Indicators of financial sector development

Country	Total bank assets/GDP (%)		Credit to private sector/GDP (%)		Commercial bank deposits/GDP (%)		m2/GDP (%)		Stock market capitalisation as % of GDP	
	1996	2001	1996	2001	1996	2001	1996	2001	1996	2001
SEE										
Albania	73.0	55.0	3.9	4.0	38.0	46.5	38.4	62.1	n.a.	n.a.
Bosnia*	81.3	54.5	n.a.	7.0	16.0	28.6	18.8	47.0	n.a.	n.a.
Bulgaria	158.2	38.5	35.3	14.6	63.6	27.1	71.0	40.9	0.2	3.7
Croatia**	62.6	87.5	21.4	34.2	29.8	59.7	34.0	65.1	15.3	16.8
Macedonia	36.2	42.4	26.5	12.5	7.7	21.3	10.5	29.3	2.3	0.4
Moldova	19.4	25.3	6.8	14.8	7.9	14.7	14.6	16.8	2.3	2.4
Romania	39.0	26.1	11.5	8.0	23.5	21.0	27.9	24.0	0.2	6.0
AVERAGE	67.1	47.0	17.6	13.6	26.6	31.3	30.7	40.7	4.1	5.9
Average without Croatia	66.8	37.4	16.0	11.4	23.7	22.5	28.6	31.6	1.0	2.5
CEE										
Czech Republic	100.4	96.7	47.2	24.5	62.6	66.1	71.5	76.9	31.4	15.4
Hungary	56.5	59.5	21.9	30.6	40.7	44.4	48.1	45.6	5.8	16.7
Poland	47.4	52.9	15.9	18.4	31.1	40.3	36.7	44.3	6.6	14.0
Slovakia	81.4	93.0	30.4	27.6	60.4	61.3	68.7	68.4	11.5	3.3
Slovenia	64.1	87.1	26.4	40.4	36.6	54.1	44.4	60.3	3.6	15.3
AVERAGE	70.0	77.8	28.4	28.3	46.3	53.2	53.9	59.1	11.8	12.9
Eurozone		243.2		108.4		81.1		84.8		72***

Source: International Financial Statistics, IMF; and EBRD.
*total bank assets/GDP and commercial bank deposits/GDP for 1997 rather than 1996.
m4/GDP instead of m2/GDP. * average for Euro area countries (Thimann, 2002).

The figures on credit to the private sector relative to GDP reinforce these observations. The decrease in Bulgaria is the most striking. By 2001, all of the SEE countries except Croatia had ratios below 15%, while Croatia at 34% was actually above the CEE average of 28%.

The low levels of deposits relative to GDP indicate the limitations facing the banking sectors in SEE. In 2001, all SEE countries except Albania and Croatia had deposit/GDP ratios below 30%. The gap between SEE and the CEE average of 53% is enormous and is shaped by varying aggregate savings ratios and by differences in depositor confidence in the banking system. The degree of payment systems sophistication and the size of the unofficial economy are also important determinants of deposits. M2/GDP ratios basically tell the same story.

Finally, the stock market capitalisation/GDP ratios remain in low single-digit figures in SEE, again with the exception of Croatia. In the CEE countries, only Slovakia has such a low level of stock market development. With few high-quality companies, limited disclosure and transparency, inconsistent rule of law and inexperienced regulatory agencies, the short-run prospects for stock market development in SEE are limited.

The data in Table 1 presented a picture of the "quantity" of financial development in SEE. Table 2 addresses quality criteria.

Interestingly, the market share of foreign banks in SEE and CEE based on their capitalisation is similar, especially if Slovenia, which has been rather closed to foreign investment in banking, is excluded. SEE may be attractive to foreign entrants due to the lack of strong local competition and weaker government bargaining positions. The CEE environment is more stable and predictable, and it seems that both groups of countries are quite attractive to foreign banks.

There is little difference in bad loan ratios in the two country groups, although there are important differences among individual countries. Furthermore, comparison of the numbers may be misleading: Hungary's 3.1% bad loan ratio should be viewed in the context of relatively stable economic growth and firm banking supervision, while Romania's 3.4% was achieved under conditions of unsteady economic growth and less well-developed banking supervision. These similar bad loan ratios do not imply that the banks in both countries are equally good at managing risk, or that bank supervisors apply equally strict loan classification criteria with equal consistency.

The EBRD ratings provided in the next three columns of Table 2 indicate that overall banking sector progress is, on average, one rating point better (on a four-point scale) in CEE than SEE. This means that the CEE countries are substantially closer to meeting the EU standards of a functioning market economy than are the SEE countries. This is a big gap; transition countries have usually taken several years to advance by a full point. For example, Hungary, considered a leader in banking reform, remained a "3" from 1993 to 1996, despite major bank recapitalisations and privatisations, moving to "4" in 1997. Slovenia remained at "3" from 1993 to 1998, despite the rehabilitation of three of its largest banks and significant regulatory improvements. In 1999, Slovenia received a "3+".

The gap between SEE and CEE regulatory effectiveness is less in terms of extensiveness (0.6) than in effectiveness (1.0).[2] This is characteristic of SEE's prob-

---

[2] Extensiveness is the degree to which laws concerning banking and securities regulation generally conform to international standards. Effectiveness refers to the comprehensive enforcement of laws, that is, whether laws are supported by appropriate regulations and whether they are enforced by bodies having adequate powers and independence. (See EBRD *Transition Report 2002*, p. 41.)

Table 2. Foreign bank presence, bad loans and EBRD ratings (*2001 data*)

Country / Region	Foreign bank share as % of total bank capital	Bad loans as % of total portfolio	EBRD banking reform index	EBRD Financial regulations index		Transparency International Corruption perceptions index 2002
				Extensiveness	Effectiveness	
SEE						
Albania	86.1	6.9	2.3	2.0	1.7	2.5
Bosnia	63.1	7.0	2.3	1.3	1.0	n.a.
Bulgaria	66.7	7.9	3.0	3.0	3.0	4.0
Croatia	74.8	15.0	3.3	3.0	3.0	3.8
Macedonia	43.5	24.7	3.0	3.3	2.0	n.a.
Moldova	60.9	9.9	2.3	4.0	3.0	2.1
Romania	60.6	3.4	2.7	4.0	3.0	2.6
Serbia and Montenegro		24.4	1.0	3.3	2.0	n.a.
AVERAGE	65.1	12.4	2.5	3.0	2.3	3.0
CEE						
Czech Republic	70.0	13.7	3.7	3.3	3.0	3.7
Hungary	62.2	3.1	4.0	3.7	3.7	4.9
Poland	61.3	20.1	3.3	4.0	3.0	4.0
Slovakia	60.6	24.3	3.3	3.0	3.0	3.7
Slovenia	16.0	8.2	3.3	4.0	3.7	6.0
AVERAGE	54.0	13.9	3.5	3.6	3.3	4.5
without Slovenia	63.5					

Source: Foreign bank share of total capital, Banking Supervisors of Central and Eastern Europe Review 2002. Transparency International data from www.transparency.org. All other data from EBRD Transition Report 2002. Scores on the Corruption Perceptions Index range from 10 (no corruption at all) to 1 (maximum corruption).The EBRD indexes range from 1 (no change from rigid central planning) to 4 (reform consistent with a functioning market economy).

lems: laws and regulations may be in place, but they are not well enforced. To be fair, we should note that effectiveness ratings are lower than extensiveness ratings in CEE as well. But the larger gap between CEE and SEE in effectiveness underlines SEE's weaknesses in that area.

Finally, the last column provides the Transparency International Corruption Perception Index for 2002. While there is a big difference between the SEE and CEE average, it is interesting to note that Bulgaria and Croatia actually did slightly better than the Czech Republic and Slovakia. Less encouraging, however, are the scores for Moldova and Albania and, importantly, EU candidate Romania.

Key Regulatory Issues in Financial Sector Development in SEE

Summarising the previous section: SEE financial systems are shallow, with low levels of intermediation and deposit mobilisation. The regulatory systems are improving, but enforcement lags behind improvements in the laws.

What can be done to improve this situation? The following section looks at five major issues facing policymakers in SEE. The subsequent two sections focus on two issues that have recently generated substantial controversy: the organisation of supervision and supervisory incentives.

1. *The primary strategic issue in financial sector development is improved protection of creditor rights.*

At present, the courts often cannot be relied upon to enforce claims, and political influence often makes debt collection slow or impossible. Laws on foreclosure and bankruptcy may be re-examined, but often the problem is not the letter of the law, but enforcement. The issues involved are therefore administrative and political.

Recent research has begun to document the impact of these problems. Laeven and Majnoni (2003) find that better creditor protection lowers the cost of credit; and La Porta et al. (1997), Demirgüç-Kunt and Maksimovic (1998) and Galindo (2001) find that better protection of creditor rights improves access to external finance.

The demand for creditor protection exists in SEE, although this may not be strongly articulated in the political arena. Nevertheless, providing creditor protection is the key issue. SEE countries need to realise that a strong system of creditor protection and rule of law is actually economically and socially superior to a system of arbitrariness and political influence. The next section returns to this issue in the context of European integration.

2. *Never lose sight of the macroeconomic prerequisites for financial development.*

These prerequisites include low inflation, moderate fiscal deficits, reasonable real interest rates, and manageable balance of payments and foreign debt positions. As Berglof and Bolton (2002) point out, macroeconomic stability complements creditor protection. Governments that cannot enforce bankruptcy and that continue to subsidise loss-makers have great difficulty maintaining macroeconomic stability.

3. *Given weak creditor protection and weak financial infrastructure, financial systems in SEE are likely to remain bank dominated, and reform efforts should focus primarily on banking.*

In particular, it would be unrealistic to expect too much from the stock markets.[3] Mechanisms to transfer equity stakes are important to facilitate exit and create a market for ownership, but formal stock markets require high levels of transparency and strongly enforced rules and procedures. Furthermore, some of the best SEE companies have already listed on western stock exchanges,[4] and some have delisted when bought by foreign strategic investors.

Insurance has great potential. Reforms that create mandatory individual pension funds can also stimulate development by spreading the experience gained in financial investment and by creating demand for securities. But experience in Croatia, for example, shows that pension funds are likely to invest mainly in government paper. This is not only due to legal requirements, but also to the lack of alternative low-risk securities. Thus pension reform, while having a positive effect on financial market development, cannot now be expected to produce major steps forward.

Other capital market players, such as investment funds and venture capital, will not develop rapidly. Investment funds created via privatisation have not had a major impact in the region, and venture capital has mainly been foreign and small scale.

4. *Banking supervision can play an important role by limiting risk taking, facilitating the exit of unsound institutions, and establishing discipline and respect for the law.*

Banking supervision exists for two broad reasons: to ensure the stability of the system and to protect the interests of depositors. Bank failures do not necessarily indicate supervisory failures. In fact, prompt recognition and resolution of failed institutions helps minimise costs, and is crucial to maintaining discipline and ensuring stability.

Bank supervisors in transition countries in general have faced difficult challenges in establishing credibility. An important initial hurdle was to show that failed institutions could and would be closed. Furthermore, supervisors have to show that they will not tolerate late and inaccurate reporting. Finally, supervisors must demonstrate their ability to identify excessive risk-taking and to implement measures to ensure that banks meet compliance criteria and, if this fails, to shut them down.

---

[3] Berglof and Bolton (2002) argue that "bank-led finance may be inevitable at certain stages of development, and efforts to develop stock exchanges in some countries may have been premature." p. 93.

[4] In some cases, however, these listings are mainly for prestige purposes, and the main trading in the company's shares continues on the home exchange. I owe this point to Arnaud Mehl.

5. *Vigilance is required to prohibit pyramid schemes and other nonbank financial institutions from creating havoc.*

Regulatory frameworks must have clear authority to deal with *all* financial institutions, including conventional nonbank financial institutions and the more exotic institutional or informal manifestations of pyramid schemes. The selection of the regulatory institution with authority over pyramid schemes is less of an issue than ensuring that someone is in charge.

Two specific issues are crucial to the development of financial sector regulation in SEE. The first is to organise banking supervision in a manner that will minimise political interference and maximise effectiveness in the current political and economic context. The second is to provide adequate incentives to banking supervisors. The next two sections consider each point in turn.

The Organisational Structure of Banking Supervision

Banking supervision must be organised such that political interference is kept to a minimum. Decisions on whether bank owners and managers are "fit and proper," on whether banks are solvent, or on the most appropriate remedial measures or resolution procedures in particular cases should be left to the judgement of experts and should not be the subject of political lobbying. Political involvement is appropriate in establishing broad policies, for example when setting criteria for licensing or determining the manner of resolution when public funds are involved. However, political involvement in individual cases is certainly not desirable. In any case, supervisory authorities can and should be held accountable for their work.

Achieving the proper balance between the unhindered functioning of supervisory expertise in particular cases and political accountability over broad policies and cases of supervisory misconduct or error is a major challenge in all countries. The challenge is all the greater in transition countries, where political involvement was pervasive during the communist period and often remains considerable.

Options for Supervisory Locus

A glance at the organisation of banking supervision around the world reveals that these matters are resolved in different ways in different countries. In some cases, central banks are responsible for bank supervision; in others, separate government agencies are responsible; and in a third group, responsibility lies with ministries of finance. Generally speaking, supervision by the finance ministries is the most politicised and least effective option, while there is little systematic evidence to distinguish between the effectiveness of supervision undertaken by either a central bank or a separate agency (Barth, Caprio and Levine 2001).

In the SEE countries studied here, central banks are responsible for bank supervision, except in Bosnia and Herzegovina (BiH) where the political circumstances surrounding the Dayton Agreement led to the establishment of separate banking supervision authorities in the individual entities. The only way to devolve supervision to the entities of BiH was to keep it outside the central bank. However, the Governor of the Central Bank of Bosnia and Herzegovina has advocated that the central bank take over supervision in the near future.

Supervision by the central bank was probably a logical solution for SEE countries at the beginning of transition. Central banks have a relatively high degree of independence from political interference and are usually responsible for managing the payments system – a key to systemic stability. Further, central banks usually have substantial income from their management of the country's foreign exchange reserves. While there may be pressure to turn profits over to the government budget, the central bank generally does not have to go to the treasury for funds. Quite the opposite: the treasury often has to squeeze the central bank in order to extract its profits.

In addition, the strong reputation of the Deutsche Bundesbank and the growing consensus in the 1990s that central bank independence tends to result in low inflation led to the adoption of laws that, at least on paper, granted high degrees of independence to SEE central banks (Cukierman, Miller and Neyapti 2000). While *de facto* independence is often less than *de jure*, it seems reasonable to believe that central banks are more independent of political influence than separate government agencies would have been.

Unified Supervisory Agencies as Watchdogs over Integrated Markets

What has changed in the meantime? Starting with the establishment of the Kredittilsynet (a unified financial services regulator) in Norway in 1986, there has been a growing trend to unite the various agencies supervising financial institutions into a single, all-encompassing financial regulator. Single regulators exist in 13 countries: Austria, Denmark, Germany, Estonia, Hungary, Iceland, Ireland, Japan, Korea, Latvia, Norway, Sweden and the UK (Briault 2002). At least two other countries, Australia and the Netherlands, have reorganised their regulatory agencies into two bodies, one for prudential supervision to ensure the safety and soundness of the operations of financial institutions and one for conduct of business supervision focusing on fraud, misleading advertising and insider trading (Jonk, Kremers and Schoenmaker 2001). Finland has a Financial Services Authority linked to its central bank and a separate agency to supervise mandatory pension funds (Taylor and Fleming 1999).

The main driving force behind these organisational changes is the increasing integration of financial markets. Demarcations between banking and insurance, and between banking institutions and capital market institutions are breaking down as financial conglomerates become more important in OECD countries. These developments led regulators to reappraise their organisations and practices, eliminating overlapping mandates and filling gaps where firms or products were not regulated.

The benefits of regulatory unification include comprehensive supervision that plugs gaps or eliminates overlaps; economies of scale in data gathering and support services; the greater influence of the single regulator; and more consistent approaches across financial instruments. Drawbacks include the costs of merging separate agencies into one entity, culture clashes between prudential regulators and business compliance regulators, and possible diseconomies of scale due to the excessive size of the new agency.

It is not entirely self-evident whether unification, even if desirable, should result in the formation of one or of two agencies. The Dutch and Australian authorities argued that prudential supervisors could be grouped together profitably to oversee the stability of the financial system. Business compliance supervision should be separate, as these supervisors have little to do with the assessments of balance sheets and risks that prudential supervisors focus on.[5]

Considerations for SEE

What are the implications of these debates for SEE countries? Several accession countries with strong foreign bank presence (Estonia, Hungary and Latvia) have unified their financial services supervisory authorities. The home countries of these foreign banks – mainly Germany, Austria and Scandinavia – have single financial supervisors. Thus it may be easier for these transition country supervisory agencies to communicate and cooperate with their EU counterparts if they are organised in the same way, as single agencies. In addition, the foreign banks have started to function as financial conglomerates.

The argument for this model is weaker in SEE because financial conglomerates do not yet exist and capital markets are small, posing little threat to systemic stability. Goodhart (2000) argues against separating central banking from banking supervision in developing and transition countries for three reasons:

- The financial structure tends to be less complex in developing and transition economies, where financial conglomerates are also less complex and have less clout.

- Developing and transition economies have been more prone to systemic instability. Effective reaction to systemic instability requires that the central bank maintain the best possible information about banks by keeping supervision in-house.

- The status and quality of central bank personnel in developing and transition countries tends to be substantially higher than in other local regulatory institutions. This is due to the relatively high degree of

---

[5] The Dutch model keeps the central bank involved in prudential supervision, while the Australian model rests on an independent prudential agency. In addition, the Dutch model has two closely cooperating but distinct prudential supervisors, the central bank and the Pension Supervision Agency, while Australia has a single prudential supervisor, the Australian Prudential Regulation Agency.

independence of central banks, and the high status enjoyed by those central banks that have succeeded in keeping inflation low and maintaining macroeconomic stability. Central banks not directly funded from the national budget pay better salaries and offer better chances of education, training and career advancement (but remain vulnerable to competition from commercial banks for the best cadre).

Goodhart's three arguments apply to SEE countries and thus support the view that central banks should be responsible for banking supervision. This does not preclude movement towards the Finnish or Dutch solution by bringing other supervisory functions that deal with prudential issues into an enlarged agency tied to the central bank. Insurance and pension fund supervision are probably prime candidates for such a merger, which would increase the status and clout of the nonbank regulators and enhance the central bank's ability to monitor and defend the stability of the financial system.

This consolidation is not urgent. It will take time for SEE regulatory agencies to master the skills necessary to supervise stock markets, insurance funds, pension funds and investment funds. And radical organisational change may prove disruptive and destroy the fragile progress already made. Even EU membership does not require a change in the structure of financial supervision. For example, the Banca d'Italia supervises banks, even though Italy is a member of the EU and the Eurozone. Although a European banking supervisory authority has been proposed (Vives 2001), it is far from clear whether it will happen or whether such an authority would be a banking supervisory authority only or a financial services authority. In the absence of a clear model, SEE countries have no reason to make major changes at this point.

The Problem of Supervisors' Incentives

Bank supervisors are often expected to behave with perfect impartiality, using their expertise to make the most accurate judgement possible about the soundness of regulated institutions. However, as Boot and Thakor (1993) pointed out in their aptly titled article "Self-Interested Bank Regulation," it is naive to expect that supervisors would not have their own interests. "Self-interested" regulation can lead to two kinds of problem: those created by political influence and corruption, and those created by the career interests of the supervisors.

If corruption is a general problem, it cannot be expected that bank supervisors will be immune. It would be helpful to pay supervisors well, but supervisors will generally be paid less than private sector bank employees. This creates personnel retention problems for the supervisory agency and leaves the door open to bribery. The National Bank of Romania, for example, has recently increased banking supervisors' salaries for these reasons.

In a related vein, supervisory incentives can be distorted if supervisors fear political or legal reprisal for undertaking corrective actions against banks. The Core

Principles on Banking Supervision state that supervisors should have "protection (normally in law) from personal and institutional liability for supervisory actions taken in good faith in the course of performing supervisory duties" (Basel Committee on Banking Supervision 1997, p. 14).

Tison (2003) disputes this, arguing that European case law "allows to duly take into account the complexity of prudential supervision and the discretion left to supervisory authorities in performing their functions." But it is hard to be enthusiastic about reliance on courts to arbitrate banking supervision cases. Arguably, even in the EU, such an approach could have a chilling effect on supervisors, and could lead to large numbers of very complex and expensive lawsuits. In SEE, where courts are far more subject to political and interest group influence, the case for leaving these matters to the courts seems even weaker. Where the independence and professionalism of public servants has hardly been adequately established, it seems extremely unwise to make supervisors individually legally responsible.

Even the idea of making supervisory institutions legally responsible in SEE countries should be dealt with very carefully. Financial institutions, as all constituent parts of society, must have the democratic right to appeal against government decisions. However, given the strong pressures likely to be exerted by wealthy and powerful interested parties and political stakeholders, complainants should be required to show that the regulator has not acted in good faith and/or is guilty of gross negligence. In other words, there must be very good reasons for overturning regulatory decisions.

The second aspect of the supervisory incentives problem is that supervisors may allow considerations about their own reputations and careers to distort their prudential action. Supervisors may practice forbearance and refrain from taking harsh measures against a bank, in the hope that the situation will improve of its own accord and that the supervisor will not be blamed for allowing the bank to fail. However, experience shows that problems almost invariably get worse, not better, and that the eventual cost of resolution rises if action is delayed.

Forbearance became a major theme in the debate surrounding the US savings and loan debacle in the 1980s. Forbearance was seen not only in the practice of individual supervisors, but in legislative rulings that lowered capital adequacy standards in the face of widespread insolvencies in the savings and loan (S&L) industry in the early-1980s (United States GAO 1985; Lindgren, Garcia and Saul 1996).

The main remedy in this situation was to introduce the Federal Deposit Insurance Corporation Improvement Act (FDICIA) in 1991, which calls for prompt corrective action. FDICIA requires supervisors to take specified action against capital-impaired banks, including withdrawing the bank's licence if the capital ratio falls below 2%. The key point is that supervisory discretion is limited by mandatory steps required by law.

FDICIA also introduced the principle of least cost resolution to protect the interests of taxpayers. It requires resolution of problem institutions according to specified criteria and prevents supervisors from attempting to cater to particular interests by compensating depositors or investors beyond the minimum required by law.

FDICIA-style limitations on supervisory discretion tend to be opposed by supervisors and banks alike. Supervisors argue that discretion is useful and allows them to handle problems with appropriate flexibility, avoiding closure of viable but troubled banks. Bank owners similarly argue that closing down a solvent but poorly capitalised bank infringes shareholder property rights. They similarly oppose legislation allowing supervisory authorities to limit bank actions or to remove managers and owners at undercapitalised banks.

Information available to the author indicates that no SEE country has effective legislation along the lines of the FDICIA. In Croatia, for example, prompt corrective action powers were substantially strengthened by the Banking Law of 2002, but supervisory discretion remains relatively wide. The principle of least cost resolution is not clearly stated in law. Thus the question of adapting legislation to provide appropriate incentives to supervisors has yet to be fully addressed.

EU Accession and Financial Sector Development

Broadly speaking, the main potential benefit of the EU accession process is increased political stability and stronger democratic institutions. To the extent that these are achieved, economic development in general, and financial development in particular, will doubtless be strengthened (Kaminski and de la Rocha 2003).

Benefits of EU Accession and Challenges Posed by Foreign Banks

Moves towards EU accession send favourable signals to potential investors, strengthening the prospect of greatly improved access to resources on the international capital markets and to the special facilities of the EU and its member states. In addition, growing political stability and the strengthening of the legal framework, due in part to the accession process, should attract foreign direct investment (FDI).

Easier access to resources and increased FDI are favourable to SEE countries. FDI through the entry of banks from EU countries has already played a major role in stabilising the financial systems of the current accession countries and several of the SEE countries (notably Bosnia and Herzegovina [BiH], Bulgaria, and Croatia). Foreign banks often have superior capital strength, risk management and marketing skills, diversified portfolios and banking experience. Their entry into SEE markets should be welcomed.[6]

While the overall picture is positive, SEE policymakers face dilemmas and challenges regarding foreign banks:

---

[6] Of course, not all foreign banks are good banks. The simple fact that a bank is headquartered in a developed country does not guarantee the bank's quality.

- *Can foreign banks be expected to stand by their progeny in SEE when they get into trouble?*

If the answer is no, or no in some cases, SEE regulators cannot be complacent about the failure of foreign banks. Indeed, the case of Rijecka Banka in Croatia, in which a rogue trader incurred losses exhausting almost all the capital of the bank, should be a warning. The majority owner, Bayerische Landesbank (BLB), walked away from the bank, returning its stake to the Croatian government for one dollar. BLB had failed to detect the fraud during due diligence, and for two years thereafter when it was the majority owner of the bank. It is not coincidental that the largest cases of operational risk have occurred at foreign subsidiaries of large banks, such as Barings and Allied Irish.

The point is simply this: regulators must continually strengthen their procedures for resolving bank failures, whether or not foreign banks are present or even predominant. They must maintain the banking system's attractiveness for potential entrants so that, in case of failure, investors can easily be found.

- *Are foreign banks especially biased towards retail lending in SEE?*

Foreign banks have a major advantage in the retail area due to their superior marketing knowledge and their standardised products. In several countries in the region (including BiH, Croatia and Romania), retail lending has grown rapidly since the entry of foreign banks. Domestic banks have attempted to keep up, seeking to capitalise on the advantages offered by a large client base: high demand, relatively low default rates and risk dispersion.

During 2003, the Croatian National Bank imposed a reserve requirement on loan growth above 4% per quarter, without any distinction between types of loans. This led to a decrease in lending to enterprises, a result that is not considered desirable but is accepted as an unfortunate by-product of measures to reduce the risk associated with credit growth. The policy issue here is quite important and far from settled.

- *Will foreign banks serve SMEs?*

There is a considerable body of literature in the USA on the interest, or lack of interest, on the part of large banks in SME lending (Peek and Rosengren 1998, Berger et al. 1998, Strahan and Weston 1998). In Latin America, many large banks were sold to foreign buyers, making the behaviour of the foreign banks an issue. The argument is that large banks and foreign banks have competitive advantages in dealing with standardised loans to consumers or to larger firms with relatively transparent accounting. The soft, localised knowledge crucial for SME loans is likely to be unavailable or too expensive to acquire relative to other opportunities for large and foreign banks (Berger, Klapper and Udell 2001, Berger and Udell 2002).

At the same time, research by Clarke et al. (2001) suggests that foreign bank entry raises competition and increases the supply of funds, lowering interest rates and improving lending conditions, which indirectly stimulates the supply of SME loans. For this reason, even if the first argument is correct, the global effect of foreign bank entry on SME loans may still be positive.

In SEE, there may be room for cautious optimism. First, there are very few large local firms with transparent balance sheets. Competition to lend to such firms is extremely strong, forcing many banks to look for other clients. Second, some of the foreign banks arriving in SEE have strong SME orientations in their home countries. And third, at least in Croatia, foreign banks have tended to employ local managers who have the personal relationships and soft knowledge that make such lending feasible.

- *Foreign bank entry may make it more difficult for the authorities to control and stabilise capital inflows, complicating exchange rate management and increasing the foreign debt.*

Foreign banks often have much higher credit ratings than domestic ones, and in any case can usually borrow from their parent banks. In addition, a decision by a large foreign bank to allocate an extra 1% of its global portfolio to one of the smaller SEE countries may be overwhelming, due to the sheer size of foreign banks. The larger foreign banks active in SEE have total assets well above € 200 billion, while the total assets of banking systems in most SEE countries are less than € 20 billion.

The situation is further complicated for countries with Stabilisation and Association Agreements with the EU, committing these countries to full liberalisation of capital flows over a four-year transition period.

The importance of these issues will be clear in the next section, which discusses the connection between capital inflows and lending booms.

The Lending-Boom Dilemma

Strong capital inflows have been a leading cause of lending booms worldwide. And experience in many countries suggests that rapid lending growth is often connected to asset quality deterioration and balance of payments problems (Caprio and Klingebiel 1996, Gavin and Hausman 1996, Eichengreen and Arteta 2000). Asset quality deterioration may result from lower underwriting standards as banks expand their client base to include new, less creditworthy borrowers (Gavin and Hausman 1996). Or it may occur because the banks' internal processes are strained by greater numbers of loan applications. Finally, deterioration may occur because the share of new borrowers increases, decreasing the average length of relationships and the bank's experience with the quality of its clients (Niinimaka 2001).

The connection between rapid lending growth and macroeconomic problems is even clearer. Rapid lending growth may be caused by capital inflows, which in turn may attract even larger capital inflows. Income and price effects combine to create current account problems and, in extreme cases, currency crises.

Gourinchas et al. (2001) examine whether lending booms are indeed always troublesome. They show that the frequency of banking or currency problems following lending booms has been much higher in Latin America than elsewhere. They also point out that lending booms necessarily have the positive effect of promoting financial deepening, which is believed to cause higher rates of GDP growth. Thus, a serious policy dilemma exists between the desire to avoid lending booms that turn into banking or currency crisis, and the desire to encourage financial deepening. Several approaches are possible. One is to prevent lending booms by imposing "speed limits" that discourage banks from growing too rapidly. The alternative is to adopt a wait-and-see attitude, acting only when problems emerge. One of the problems with the preventive approach is that banking problems are very hard to assess in real time: asset quality indicators are subject to a time lag and do not reflect the up-to-the-minute portfolio status. Furthermore, it is doubtful whether developing or transition countries possess the data necessary for accurate credit risk modelling. This is the result of the extensive structural changes which have taken place and the very short data series available, especially in transition countries (Kraft and Jankov 2004).

To address these factors, it seems logical to look for policy measures that either moderate the boom or increase bank safety during the boom. An innovative tool called dynamic provisioning is now in force in Spain. It requires banks to smooth their provisioning over the cycle, holding general dynamic provisions based on historic provisioning averages (Fernandez de Lis 1999, Mann and Michael 2002).

The dynamic provision, a new instrument, is not directly related to any specific provisions for losses realised by the bank. The dynamic provision is created in good years when provisions against specific losses are lower than normal because portfolio quality is above average. The dynamic provision is tapped during bad years in which provisions for specific losses are higher because portfolio quality declines. This countervailing structure has the effect of reducing bank profits in good years, putting a brake on new lending, while in bad years provisions are released, increasing bank profits and providing a basis for new loans. In this way, dynamic provisioning, a microeconomic tool, is used to assist macroeconomic stabilisation in a way that reduces cyclicality in the economy and in bank income and lending.

Dynamic provisioning is relatively untested, and it relies on the availability of sound estimates of historical provisioning averages. An alternative would simply be to require banks to hold higher capital levels if their growth exceeds certain thresholds; such a system was implemented in Croatia in 2003.

Table 3. Percentage point difference between the real credit growth rate and twice the real GDP growth rate

Year	Excess of real credit growth over 2 x real GDP growth (Caprio criterion)					
	Albania	Bosnia	Bulgaria	Croatia	Macedonia	Romania
2000	1.2	-7.2	-5.7	-4.8	-12.4	-24.4
2001	3.5	-1.6	17.8	14.1	21.3	14.5
2002	19.3	19.7	29.1	18.5	4.0	32.5
2003	23.7	14.8	32.4	4.4	14.0	57.1

Source: national central banks and author's calculations; 2003 GDP is based on the estimates in World Economic Outlook, IMF, September 2003, Statistical Appendix Table 7, p. 183.

How relevant is all this for SEE? Caprio and Klingebiel (1997), based on a large multi-country study, find that the probability of banking problems occurring grows significantly if real credit growth exceeds two times real GDP growth for three consecutive years. Although further research has not always supported this finding, it can be used as a rule of thumb to explore the question of rapid loan growth in SEE.

Table 3 shows the simple application of the Caprio and Klingebiel rule of thumb using recent SEE data. Where the result is positive, lending has grown "too fast" in most of the countries in at least two of the last three years.

What explains such rapid credit growth? Relatively strong economic growth certainly contributes to loan demand. Substantial capital inflows have strengthened loan supply. Foreign banks now hold majority shares in most SEE banking systems, greatly improving the supply of funds. And low interest rates in developed countries, along with low levels of profitability in home markets such as Italy, Germany and Austria, have also contributed to this. Strong capital inflows are thus both a sign of successful reform and a potential source of new problems.

How should the central banks and governments in SEE react? Clearly, loan growth must be examined in the context of banking system soundness and the overall macroeconomic picture. Given the weaknesses of banking systems in SEE countries, generally poor current account performance and, in some cases, problematic external debt ratios, there seems to be cause for concern. Certainly, when credit/GDP indicators are low, policymakers want credit to grow more rapidly than GDP. But the substantial overshoots in the rule-of-thumb values shown in Table 3 should raise warning flags.

But, a mitigating factor may be at work. In some countries, the recent lending boom has targeted households rather than enterprises. Insofar as households tend to have better repayment records, this would decrease the probability of asset quality problems. However, household lending is often for purchases of imports such as cars and appliances, which can exacerbate current account problems.

Table 4. Ratio of household loans to total loans (*percentage*)

Year	Albania	Bosnia	Bulgaria	Croatia	Macedonia	Romania
1997	n.a.	5.2	10.3	28.9	6.5	4.4
1998	5.1	8.8	20.1	32.5	7.3	4.9
1999	48.1	9.8	18.2	37.9	9.9	4.5
2000	36.2	12.9	17.6	42.3	7.6	4.7
2001	14.3	20.6	19.4	43.8	7.4	5.6
2002	18.3	34.5	19.4	47.5	10.7	8.5
2003	23.1	38.2	22.6	52.7	20.7	17.2

Source: national central banks.

Table 4 shows that the share of lending to households has increased substantially in BiH, Croatia, Romania and Macedonia. The share in Bulgaria has been relatively stable following a big jump in 1998, although a somewhat larger increase was seen in 2003. Albania experienced a consumer lending boom in 1999 that ended in major loan write-offs. It appears that consumer lending in Albania started to recover again in 2001, but it still has not regained the large share it held in total loans in 1999. The overall picture is clearly one of increased consumer lending in SEE.

It is difficult to predict whether the lending booms in SEE will create in prudential problems. The high proportion of new loans to households somewhat mitigates such concerns, but it would seem worthwhile considering some form of increased capital requirements as insurance against future problems. Albania, BiH, Bulgaria, Croatia and Moldova already require minimum capital ratios of 10 to 12%, above the 8% Basel standards. Other SEE countries could consider this, along with measures to raise capital requirements for fast-growing banks.

Even if SEE central bankers feel that prudential concerns are not acute at the moment, they are keenly aware of their current account deficits. Lending booms may well require fiscal and monetary policy reactions, as they already have in Croatia. Controlling lending could prove a significant challenge; lending is not nearly so easy to control as interest rates or exchange rates.

EU Accession and Financial Sector Regulation

Most EU directives on banking actually codify the recommendations of the Basel Committee on Banking Supervision. (For a list of the main directives, see Appendix 1.) For example, the Second Banking Directive (89/646/EEC) required member states to follow the 1988 Capital Accord. Since SEE countries generally attempt to harmonise bank regulations with Basel Committee on Banking Supervision (BCBS) standards, these aspects of European regulation do not represent an additional burden.

Furthermore, as discussed in detail later, these directives do not have legal force until SEE countries become EU members. And it may be possible to negotiate delays and exemptions where implementation seems inappropriate at the time of accession. While specific changes, such as consolidated supervision, will be required, EU accession will not generally entail major regulatory changes beyond the continuing efforts to improve supervision and implement the core principles.

As accession approaches, it will be necessary to amend or rewrite banking laws to allow information sharing with the EU and its organs, and to grant the automatic right of establishment to EU banks. These changes can be safely postponed by those countries that do not expect to accede in the near future.

Some other EU directives set particular parameters that will affect SEE countries if and when they become members. Most notably, the deposit insurance directive (94/19/EC) sets the minimum level of deposit insurance that EU member states must provide. The current €20,000 level, well above those currently provided by SEE countries, is certainly too high. Comparative studies by the IMF suggest that deposit coverage averages about three times GDP per capita throughout the world (Garcia 1999).

Research that is still somewhat tentative suggests that the introduction of deposit insurance when the institutional framework is extremely weak can actually increase financial sector instability (Demirgüç-Kunt and Detragiache 2000). It seems clear that deposit insurance that is inadequately funded and untested will not have the same stabilising effect on depositors as well funded and well established systems. For these reasons SEE countries that do not yet have deposit insurance schemes should not feel obliged to comply with EU directives immediately.

For SEE countries entering the EU in the near future, the €20,000 minimum will come into effect upon accession. All EU members should have the same coverage level because banks located in states with lower coverage would be at a strong competitive disadvantage. Under the EU's single market rules, nothing would prevent savers in countries with lower levels of deposit insurance coverage from moving their deposits to EU countries with higher levels.

The entry of CEE and SEE countries into the EU and the concomitant increase in deposit insurance coverage to €20,000 would result in an extraordinarily high level of coverage in these countries, as would the immediate adoption of EU norms in SEE countries prior to accession. Very few uninsured depositors would remain, decreasing the potential market discipline that a large depositor group could exert, not to mention the potential fiscal liabilities involved. Nenovsky and Dimitrova (2003) argue that this situation could increase banking risk and financial instability in the Eurozone as a whole, and that it would penalise accession country banks, in particular, through higher per capita deposit insurance premia. Despite the competitive disadvantage argument above, Nenovsky and Dimitrova advocate modifying the coverage level in accordance with member states' GDP per capita. This argument should be given serious consideration. It may well be the case that the competitive disadvantage of lower deposit insurance coverage is in fact outweighed by the competitive disadvantage of higher deposit insurance premia per capita and the resulting increase in moral hazard.

Finally, EU banking directives also require the division of authority between host and home country supervisors. For example, Directive 2001/24/EC stipulates that the authorities of the home state of a bank with branches in one or more host member states have the legal right to initiate the reorganisation or winding up of the institution as a whole. The home member authorities are obliged only to inform the host member authorities; they are not obliged to consult them.

Deciding who is lender of last resort for a branch or a bank subsidiary in a host country is just one important issue in this context. While the answer in principle is clear, the practicalities are not, mainly because no such cases have yet arisen. However, these issues refer to the situation obtaining after EU membership. Although important, they will probably remain low on SEE states' agendas.

Basel II in SEE

The Basel Capital Accord of 1988 represented a major step towards the goal of creating a level playing field for international competition among banks. In addition, it created awareness of the importance of bank capital as a buffer against losses. The Accord was intended to increase the stability of financial systems. However, some economists have pointed out that regulations forcing banks to hold more than their desired level of capital may actually lead these banks to increase the riskiness of their portfolio. This happens because the capital regulations restrict the risk-return frontier, and the banks may choose to obtain this lower, constrained level of utility by increasing risk or by decreasing return (Koehn and Santomero 1980, Kim and Santomero 1988 and Rochet 1992). In addition, there has been widespread concern that rigid minimum capital requirements could lead to "credit crunches" during recessions. (e.g. Bernanke and Lown 1991).

The empirical evaluation of these claims is complex. Jackson et al. (1999) find indications that the Accords did induce weakly capitalised banks to rebuild their capital ratios more rapidly than they would otherwise have done. The same authors regard evidence on the Accord's effects on banks' overall portfolio risk as inconclusive. Despite this, Berger, Herring and Szego (1995) conclude that the empirical evidence rather strongly suggests that overall bank risk is lower with higher equity. For example, Avery and Berger (1991), using US bank data from 1983 to 1989, find that the risk weights implemented under the Basel I Accord lead to capital requirements that are better predictors of write-offs and bank failure than unweighted assets.

Regulatory Incentive Issues

Thus, there is some evidence that the Capital Accord had an impact on bank capital ratios and that it provided a better approximation of bank risk. At least three issues remain, however:

- The first is whether the first Accord tended to produce credit crunches. Peek and Rosengren (1997 and 2000) and Hancock and Wilcox (1997 and 1998) find evidence of effects on particular sectors, such as real estate or small business, due to pressure on capital at banks in the United States during the early-1990s. But they do not find any major effects at national level, nor for other countries.

- The second issue is whether the exact risk weights prescribed by the first Accord accurately reflect asset risk. The answer is clearly no. Jones and King (1995), for example, show that the correlation between risk-weighted assets and the probability of failure can be substantially improved if the risk weights are increased on assets that are classified as substandard, doubtful or loss by bank examiners.

- The third issue is whether the first Accord creates substantial incentives for regulatory arbitrage. The answer must be yes. For example, since all noncollateralised loans to firms are assigned a 100% risk weight, loans to low-risk firms are actually charged a capital requirement above the true economic level, while loans to high-risk firms may actually be charged a capital requirement below the true economic level. Since banks are required to allocate the same amount of capital for each euro of loan to the high-risk firm and to the low-risk firm, it is actually cheaper to favour high-risk, high-yield loans within the capital requirement category.

Recognising these problems, the Basel Committee on Banking Supervision sought to amend the first Accord to adapt regulatory capital requirements as closely as possible to the "true" economic level. In addition, developments in risk modelling made it possible to use much more sophisticated techniques to measure risk and therefore economic capital. The Basel II Accord allows banks to use these techniques not only for their own internal risk management purposes but also to determine regulatory capital.

The Basel II Accord incorporates three "pillars": capital requirements, supervisory review, and market discipline. They are intended to be mutually reinforcing. Capital requirements, although determined in a greater variety of ways, continue the basic thrust of the first Accord. The supervisory review is strengthened and made more explicit, in part because of the greater responsibility devolved to banks. In particular, supervisory review is crucial in testing and certifying banks' credit-risk models. Finally, market discipline is explicitly introduced, relying heavily on public disclosure to inform market participants and to enable them to exert pressure on the banks' behaviour. This whole approach leads to several very tricky issues.

- First, banks are required to calculate their own regulatory capital requirements, which creates severe incentive problems. The Basel II process attempts to build in safeguards to avoid abuses. But, if banks are to be given incentives to devote substantial resources to constructing sophisticated risk models, they must perceive some benefit to doing so. And the logical benefit is decreased regulatory capital requirements.

- The second tricky issue involves the development of risk models, which are still relatively new. Their robustness to structural changes in the economy and the financial markets has yet to be fully tested. Historical data can be used to backtest the models and to simulate their performance in hypothetical scenarios, but more experience will be needed to make the models perform well when used widely.

- A third tricky issue is the possible procyclicality of the Basel II capital requirements. The Basel I capital requirements were based on broad classifications of the types of assets held in a bank's portfolio. Capital *per se* was not directly affected by cyclical forces, but provisioning of course was. Basel II requires that when a bank downgrades its assessment of a borrower's creditworthiness during a recession, it would have to increase its provisions accordingly, and it would also have to increase its capital to reflect its increased expected losses.

Since raising capital would be especially difficult in such times, banks could be forced to reduce their holdings of risky assets, exacerbating the credit crunch. Catarineu-Rabell, Jackson and Tsomocos (2003) point out that the degree of procyclicality depends crucially on the banks' modelling procedures. If banks use models that consider over-the-cycle creditworthiness, as some rating agencies now do, the problem would be minimal. But if banks use models that revise creditworthiness estimates frequently to incorporate the most recent information, procyclicality could be quite significant.[7]

Considerations for SEE

These issues are of major importance for the functioning of Basel II in general. But what are the most important issues for SEE? These can be identified by providing an overview of the changes in capital requirements contained in the Accord and the options most likely to be used by SEE countries. It is very important to note that the Basel II Accords provide a menu of options to supervisors, including limiting banks' choices by declaring some of the more complex menu options unacceptable.

Arguably, the most important menu choices in the whole Accord are among a) the Standard System, b) the Foundation Internal Ratings Based System and c) the Advanced Internal Ratings Based System for determining capital. The Standard

---

[7] However, Carpenter, Whitesell and Zakrajšek (2001) use historical rating agency data to simulate the cyclical effects of the Standard approach (treated in the text below) in situations in which most firms have ratings. They find no significant evidence of procyclicality.

approach closely resembles the Basel I system. Assets are classified into a somewhat larger number of risk categories, each of which has its own capital weighting. The internal rating base (IRB) approaches use the banks' own risk models: the Foundation IRB variant uses many parameters set by supervisors, while the Advanced IRB Approach uses relatively few parameters set by supervisors.

The Standard approach deserves the greatest attention. The requirements of the IRB approaches are unattainable for SEE banks and supervisors because they require at least 5 years of historical data, and ideally should be based on data for an entire business cycle. IRB is to be phased in from 2006 to 2009. Theoretically, SEE banks could start collecting data now and have sufficient data by 2009, but this is extremely unrealistic because the full testing of such models requires much more data.

In addition, IRB models assume reasonably stable macroeconomic conditions. The major changes currently underway in SEE, including continued privatisation, legal and regulatory reform, adoption of EU-friendly legislation and so on, raise grave doubts about the usefulness of current data for predicting borrower creditworthiness in, say, 2010.

Finally, IRB places enormous demands on banks and supervisors. Banks must create and test their models and show that they are an integral part of their credit underwriting and risk assessment practice. Supervisors must verify that the models provide a meaningful assessment of borrower and transaction risks as well as accurate and consistent risk estimates.

Rating and Weighting

It is unsure whether the bank and supervisory capacity to implement these technically challenging tasks will be on hand in SEE by 2006. While an early start would be welcome, it would be unrealistic and in fact unnecessary to attempt to implement IRB in 2006.

Another argument against rushing to embrace IRB is that the Standard approach already contains important improvements over Basel I. The main innovations in the Standard approach compared to Basel I are:

- use of external credit agency ratings to grade exposures to sovereigns (government debt) and rated corporates (company debt),

- removal of the OECD vs. non-OECD distinction for sovereigns,

- introduction of a 150% weighting category for below-investment grade sovereigns and corporates, and for unprovisioned past due claims,

- introduction of a 75% risk weight for retail claims,

- lower risk weights for retail and residential mortgages, and

- a 20% weight for some short-term commitments.

The use of rating agencies has been extremely controversial. However, for sovereigns, use of rating agencies will be a major advantage for non-OECD countries with investment-grade ratings, for example, S&P ratings above BB+. Sovereign exposures to these countries will require less capital.[8]

Rating agencies may make mistakes and ratings changes usually lag events. But despite these shortcomings, the advantage of the new proposal is a much more nuanced set of capital requirements. Unrated countries will not be at a disadvantage, but those with a below investment-grade rating will. Unrated sovereigns are weighted at 100%; below investment grade sovereigns at 150%. This creates a perverse incentive for a sovereign that does not expect to get an investment grade rating to avoid getting a rating at all (Svoronos 2003). A crisis or other event that leads to a downgrade below investment grade would additionally complicate a country's ability to return to international capital markets because it could not become unrated and would have to live with the 150% weighting. Of course, a country in such a situation would have difficulties accessing capital markets anyway, and increased capital costs from a heavier weighting might be only a minor component of the overall increase in borrowing costs.

Rating agency assessments for SEE corporates are likely to be largely irrelevant. Very few domestic companies are currently rated, and the prospects for substantial increases between now and 2006 or 2007 are low. If corporates are not rated, they obtain the standard 100% risk weight on unsecured exposures as in Basel I.

The Basel II Accord also offers more favourable treatment for local currency exposures to domestic banks and securities firms. Such exposures with original maturities of less than three months have a risk grade one notch above the domestic sovereign. In most cases, the domestic sovereign will be given a zero percent risk weight, so that exposures to banks and securities firms will carry only a 20% weight.

The 75% risk weight for retail claims recognises their substantially lower default rates. This portfolio, however, must be less than 0.2% of the bank's overall portfolio, and must not contain exposures to single borrowers of more than €1 million. Small businesses may be included in this "regulatory retail" portfolio, and those unrated small businesses that are not included will automatically receive 100% risk weights. Corporates rated below top ratings such as S&P A- to A+, will be weighted at 50%. Finally, the treatment of residential mortgages is more favourable. Risk weights of 35% are possible if loan-to-value ratios are low and loss histories are good.

---

[8] The credit ratings received by sovereigns from export credit agencies may also be used. Many commentators from non-G10 countries believe that these ratings provide a fairer picture of creditworthiness than those of external commercial credit rating agencies.

Risk, Disclosure and Timing

Two other major types of risk covered in the Basel II requirements would have to be adopted even by countries using only the simplest version of the Standard Approach.

- First, banks must provide capital for market risk, which covers the trading book, currency risk and interest rate risk. This requirement is not new, having been included in the enhancements to the original Accord, and should not create a problems for most supervisors and banks.

- Second, the Basel II Accord requires banks to set aside capital to cover operational risk, offering three choices for calculating the capital requirement. The Basic Indicator Approach is extremely simple: the capital requirements for operational risk are set at 15% of gross income. The Alternative Standardised Approach uses three settings (12, 15 and 18%) for different lines of business. The Advanced Measurement Approach requires that the bank have its own systems of monitoring and measuring operational risk. It is doubtful whether any SEE banks would be able to do this.

Furthermore, Pillar 3's disclosure requirements – intended to impose market discipline – can be implemented relatively simply, reinforcing Pillar 1 (capital requirements) and Pillar 2 (supervisory review). Basel II pushes banks to disclose key financial information (for example in the form of abridged balance sheets and income statements) more frequently, perhaps on a semi-annual or quarterly basis. They also push banks to disclose risk management methods. While the number of investors among the general public in SEE who are able to make use of such information is certainly small, their influence is potentially large. And disclosure requirements may well increase the quality as well as the transparency of banking operations.

To summarise, Basel II introduces a number of potentially useful refinements that can be adopted in SEE. While there is no obligation to adopt Basel II at the same time as the EU member states, SEE countries can choose to adopt the simplest options. The successful implementation of Basel II should strengthen investor confidence domestically and abroad. As long as the authorities in SEE are not overambitious and choose realistic options, Basel II may prove to be a benefit for them.

Admittedly, there may be pressures on supervisory authorities to implement Basel II in a more ambitious manner than recommended here. Ward (2002) worries that the international financial institutions, such as the World Bank and the IMF, will promote Basel II compliance through their regular policy consultations or through their Financial Sector Assessment Programmes (FSAP). However, this need not be harmful if conditions in each country are taken into account and appropriate timetables and menu choices are made.

Furthermore, foreign banks operating in SEE may be eager to use internal models, in part because the marginal costs of extending to SEE the models they are using in EU countries may seem small. While banking supervisors should certainly encourage banks to improve their risk management techniques, it is recommended that the banks be cautious about adopting these models blindly. Most reputable banks in SEE maintain substantially higher capital levels than the statutory minimum, so the use of models to set minimum capital levels should not be a source of friction.

Concluding Remarks

This article attempts to pinpoint the risks and opportunities connected with EU accession and Basel II for financial development in SEE. If SEE countries can make progress towards EU accession – a big if – the rewards in terms of increased political stability, greater investment confidence and improved access to resources should be substantial. However, these benefits must be viewed in the context of the attendant challenges and risks. Managing banking systems dominated by foreign banks and dealing with lending booms pose substantial challenges for bank supervisors and macroeconomic policymakers, as will the continued upgrading of banking supervision, especially if some version of Basel II is to be implemented.

SEE countries can take advantage of these opportunities and minimise risks by carefully tailoring their responses to their own financial development goals and their economic and political environments. There is no reason to adopt the most sophisticated regulatory or risk management approaches if the necessary preconditions for this are not in place. SEE countries should carefully consider how best to reach their goals. What appears to be the straightest and shortest way may not be that at all.

References

Avery, Robert and Allen Berger (1991): "Risk-Based Capital and Deposit Insurance Reform," *Journal of Banking and Finance* 15, pp. 847–874.

Barth, James, Gerard Caprio, and Ross Levine (2001): "Bank Regulation and Supervision: What Works Best?" World Bank Policy Research Working Paper 2725.

Basel Committee on Banking Supervision (1997): "Core Principles for Effective Banking Supervision," Basel Committee Publications Number 30, Basel, September.

Basel Committee on Banking Supervision (2001): "The New Basel Capital Accord: Consultative Document," Basel, January.

Basel Committee on Banking Supervision (2003): "Consultative Document: Overview of the New Basel Capital Accord," Basel, April.

Berger, Allen, Richard Herring and Giorgio Szego (1995): "The Role of Capital in Financial Institutions," *Journal of Banking and Finance* 19, pp. 393–430.

Berger, Allen, Anthony Saunders, J.M. Scalise and Gregory Udell (1998): "The Effect of Bank Mergers on Small Business Lending," *Journal of Financial Economics* 50, 2, pp. 187–229.

Berger, Allen, Leora Klapper and Gregory Udell (2001): "The Ability of Banks to Lend to Informationally Opaque Small Businesses," *Journal of Banking and Finance* 25, 12, pp. 2127–67.

Berger, Allen and Gregory Udell (2002): "Small Business Credit Availability and Relationship Lending: The Importance of Bank Organizational Structure," *Economic Journal* Volume 112, pp. 32–53.

Berger, Allen, Iftekhar Hasan and Leora Klapper (2003): "Further Evidence on the Link Between Finance and Growth: An International Analysis of Community Banking and Economic Performance," SSRN Financial Economics Network, July.

Berglof, Erik and Patrick Bolton (2002): "The Great Divide and Beyond: Financial Architecture in Transition," *Journal of Economic Perspectives* 16, 1, pp. 77–100.

Bernanke, Ben and Cara Lown (1991): "The Credit Crunch," *The Brookings Papers on Economic Activity* 2, pp. 205–239.

Boot, Arnoud and Anjan Thakor (1993): "Self-interested Bank Regulation," *American Economic Review* May, pp. 206–212.

Briault, Clive (2002): "Revisiting the Rationale for a Single National Financial Services Regulator," Financial Services Authority Occasional Paper Series 16, London.

Caprio, Gerard and Daniela Klingebiel (1997): "Bank Insolvency: Bad Luck, Bad Policy or Bad Banking," *Annual Bank Conference on Developing Economies*, Washington: The World Bank, pp. 79–114.

Carpenter, Seth, William Whitesell and Egon Zakrajšek (2001): "Capital Requirements, Business Loans and Business Cycles: An Empirical Analysis of the Standardized Approach in the New Basel Capital Accord," Board of Governors of the Federal Reserve, mimeo. Washington.

Catarineu-Rabell, Eva, Patricia Jackson and Dimitrios Tsomocos (2003): "Procyclicality and the New Basel Accord—banks' choice of loan rating system," Bank of England Working Paper 181.

Clarke, George, Robert Cull and Maria Soledad Martinez Peria (2001): "Does Foreign Bank Penetration Reduce Access to Credit in Developing Countries? Evidence From Asking Borrowers," World Bank, mimeo. Washington.

Cukierman, Alexander, Geoffrey Miller and Billin Neyapti, "Central Bank Reform, Liberalization and Inflation in Transition Economies – An International Perspective," Tel Aviv Foerder Institute for Economic Research and Sackler Institute for Economic Research Working Paper 00/19.

Demirgüç-Kunt, Aslı and Vojislav Maksimovic (1998): "Law, Finance and Firm Growth," *Journal of Finance* 53, pp. 2107–2137.

Demirgüç-Kunt, Aslı and Enrica Detragiache (2000): "Does Deposit Insurance Increase Banking System Stability? An Empirical Investigation," World Bank Conference on Deposit Insurance: Design and Implementation, Washington, June.

Eichengreen, Barry and Carlos Arteta (2000): "Banking Crisis in Emerging Markets: Risks and Red Herrings," in Mario Blejer and Marko Škreb, eds. *Financial Policies in Emerging Markets* Cambridge MA, MIT Press, pp. 47–94.

Fernandez de Lis, Santiago, Jorge Martinez Pages and Jesus Saurina (2000): "Credit Growth, Problem Loans and Credit Risk Provisioning in Spain," Banco de Espana, Servicio de Estudios Documento de Trabajo no. 0018. Madrid.

Galindo, Arturo (2001): "Creditor Rights and Credit Market: Where Do We Stand?" IADB Working Paper 448. Washington: Inter-American Development Bank.

Garcia, Gillian (1999): "Deposit Insurance: A Survey of Actual and Best Practices," IMF Working Paper WP/99/54. Washington.

Gavin, Michael and Ricardo Hausman (1996): "The Roots of Banking Crises: the Macroeconomic Context," in Ricardo Hausmann and Liliana Rojas-Suarez, eds. *Banking Crises in Latin America* Inter-American Development Bank, Washington 1996 pp. 27–63.

Goodhart, Charles (2000): "The Organisational Structure of Banking Supervision," Financial Stability Institute Occasional Papers 1, Basle: Bank for International Settlements.

Gourinchas, Pierre-Olivier, Rodrigo Valdés and Oscar Landerretche (2001): "Lending Booms: Latin America and the World," NBER Working Paper 8249, April. New York.

Hancock, Diane and James Wilcox (1997): "Bank Capital, Non-bank Finance and Real Estate Activity," *Journal of Housing Research* 8, pp. 75–105.

Jackson, Patricia et al. (1999): "Capital Requirements and Bank Behavior: The Impact of the Basle Accord," Basel Committee on Banking Supervision Working Papers Number 1, April.

Jonk, Annet, Jeroen Kremers and Dirk Schoenmaker (2001): "A New Dutch Model," *The Financial Regulator* 6, 3, December, pp. 35–38.

Kaminski, Bartolmiej and Manuel de la Rocha (2003): "Stabilization and Association Process in the Balkans: Integration Options and their Assessment," World Bank Policy Research Paper 3108, August. Washington.

Kim, Daesik and Anthony Santomero (1988): "Risk in Banking and Capital Regulation," *Journal of Finance* 43, 5, pp. 1219–1233.

Koehn, Michael and Anthony Santomero (1980): "Regulation of Bank Capital and Portfolio Risk," *Journal of Finance* 35, 5, pp. 1235–1244.

Kraft, Evan and Ljubinko Jankov (2004): "Lending Booms, Foreign Bank Entry and Competition in Croatia," *Journal of Banking and Finance* forthcoming.

Laeven, Luc and Giovanni Majnoni (2003): "Does Judicial Efficiency Lower the Cost of Credit?" World Bank Policy Research Working Paper 3159, October. Washington DC.

LaPorta, Rafael, Florencio López-de-Silanes, Andrei Shleifer and Robert Vishny (1997): "Legal Determinants of External Finance," *Journal of Finance* 52, pp. 1131–1150.

Levine, Ross, Norman Loayza and Thorstein Beck (2000): "Financial Intermediation and Growth: Causality and Causes." *Journal of Monetary Economics* 46, pp. 31–77.

Lindgren, Carl, Gillian Garcia and Matthew I. Saal (1996): *Bank Soundness and Macroeconomic Policy* Washington: International Monetary Fund. Washington.

Mann, Fiona and Ian Michael (2002): "Dynamic Provisioning: Issues and Application," *Bank of England Financial Stability Review*, December pp. 128–135.

Mehl, Arnaud and Winkler, Adalbert (2004): "The Financial Sector and Economic Development: evidence from Southeast Europe," in Ingrid Matthäus-Maier and J.D. von Pischke, eds., *The Development of the Financial Sector in Southeast Europe: Innovative Approaches in Volatile Environments*. Berlin: Springer.

Nenovsky, Nikolay and Kalina Dmitrova (2003): "Deposit Insurance During EU Accession," William Davidson Institute Working Papers Number 617, October. Ann Arbor MI.

Niinimaka, Juha-Pekka (2001): "Should New or Rapidly Growing Banks Have More Equity?" Bank of Finland Discussion Papers 16. Helsinki.

Peek, Joe and Eric Rosengren (1997): "The International Transmission of Financial Shocks: The Case of Japan," *American Economic Review* September, 87, pp. 495–505.

Peek, Joe and Eric Rosengren (1998): "Bank Consolidation and Small Business Lending: It's Not Just Bank Size That Matters," *Journal of Banking and Finance* 22, pp. 799–819.

Peek, Joe and Eric Rosengren (2000): "Collateral Damage: Effects of the Japanese Real Estate Collapse on Credit Availability and Real Activity in the United States," *American Economic Review* 90, pp. 30–45.

Rochet, Jean-Charles (1992): "Capital Requirements and the Behavior of Commercial Banks," *European Economic Review* 36, pp. 1137–1178.

Strahan, Philip and James Weston (1998): "Small Business Lending and the Changing Structure of the Banking Industry," *Journal of Banking and Finance* 22, pp. 821–845.

Svoronos, Jean-Phillipe (2003): "The New Basel Capital Accord: Using the Standardized Approach," presentation to FSI/BSCEE Workshop on Basel II, Zagreb, Croatia, May.

Taylor, Michael and Alex Fleming (1999): "Integrated Financial Supervision: Lessons of Northern European Experience," World Bank Policy Research Paper 2223, November. Washington.

Thimann, Christian, ed. (2002): *Financial Sectors in EU Accession Countries* European Central Bank, Frankfurt, July.

Tison, Michel (2003): "Challenging the Prudential Supervisor: Liability versus Regulatory Immunity," Universiteit Gent, Financial Law Institute Working Paper WP 2003–04. Ghent.

United States General Accounting Office (1985): *The Net Worth Certificate Program and The Condition of the Thrift Industry,* Washington: General Accounting Office.

Vives, Xavier (2001): "Restructuring Financial Regulation in the European Monetary Union," *Journal of Financial Services Research* 19, 1 pp. 57–82.

Wachtel, Paul (2001): "Growth and Finance – What Do We Know and How Do We Know It?" *International Finance* 4, pp. 335–362.

Ward, Jonathan (2002): "The New Basel Accord and Developing Countries: Problems and Alternatives," ESRC Centre for Business Research, Cambridge University, Working Paper 04.

Appendix 1: The Main European Union Banking and Financial Services and Directives

1. Second Council Directive 89/646/EEC of 15 December 1989 on the coordination of laws, regulations and administrative provisions relating to the taking up and pursuit of the business of credit institutions and amending Directive 77/780/EEC defines licencing procedures, minimum capital levels and supervision of credit institutions.

2. Council Directive 89/647/EEC on a solvency ratio for credit institutions aims to harmonise supervision and strengthen solvency standards among credit establishments in the Community.

3. Council Directive 86/635/EEC of 8 December 1986 on the annual accounts and consolidated accounts of banks and other financial institutions defines standard formats and contents of these reports.

4. Directive 94/19/EC of the European Parliament and of the Council of 30 May 1994 on deposit guarantee schemes defines guarantees provided to depositors and defines a minimum coverage level.

5. Council Directive 92/121/EEC of 21 December 1992 on the monitoring and control of large exposures of credit institutions limits the exposures banks may have to a single client.

6. Directive 2002/87/EC of the European Parliament and of the Council of 16 December 2002 on the supplementary supervision of credit institutions, insurance undertakings and investment firms in a financial conglomerate defines standards and procedures for the supervision of financial conglomerates.

7. Directive 2001/24/EC of the European Parliament and of the Council of 4 April 2001 on the reorganisation and winding up of credit institutions.

CHAPTER 6:

Implementing European Standards of Banking Regulation in Georgia

Merab Kakulia

Vice Governor, National Bank of Georgia

The sustainable development of the financial sectors in transition economies requires an institutional model that takes into account the standards established in advanced economies as well as the particular conditions in the countries concerned. Given their weak securities markets and underdeveloped insurance and pension systems, banking is the key to financial sector development in transition economies. In Georgia, for instance, 95% of financial sector assets are concentrated in the banking system; these assets are equivalent to 16% of GDP. Compared to advanced economies this seems rather modest, but it is in line with the figures reported by the other countries that emerged from the former Soviet Union.

The Banking Sector Regulatory Framework

The institutional framework of the banking sector in Georgia is modelled on international best practices and standards. Core banking supervision principles were incorporated into Georgian banking legislation in 1995–1996. For example,

- the National Bank of Georgia (NBG) was granted all powers necessary to supervise the banks.
- restrictions that unduly limit entry into the banking sector and the provision of banking services were phased out.
- enterprises operating in the banking sector now require a licence. The conditions for acquiring a licence include: meeting minimum capital requirements, fit and proper directors, an organisational framework for governance and a business plan.
- procedures are in place for:
  - opening a foreign bank branch,

- consultations and exchange of information with foreign supervisory authorities,
- revoking a banking licence.
* minimum internal control requirements are established.
* prudential standards of banking supervision include capital adequacy, credit limits and large exposures, open foreign exchange limits, etc.
* banks' ownership of nonfinancial entities is restricted.

The National Bank of Georgia (NBG) is committed to the permanent enforcement of prudential banking supervisory standards, with particular emphasis on Basel I capital adequacy standards, which were introduced in 1996. Reflecting the high-risk levels in Georgia, the capital adequacy ratio is 12%, exceeding the ratio specified in the EU Directives and Basel I standards. In general, an unstable economic environment generates higher levels of risk, forcing the National Bank to take a very conservative approach to capital adequacy and large exposures. According to the generally observed European standards, a credit institution's largest exposure should not exceed 10% of the bank's own capital and it may not incur large exposures totalling more than 800% of its own funds; in Georgia these figures are 5% and 200% respectively.

An important standard is currently being implemented: the minimum initial capital for banks must meet European standards. Since 1995, the required minimum start-up capital has been increased gradually. In 2000, this amounted to the local currency (lari) equivalent of only €2.2 million. In keeping with EU Directives, the NBG has resolved to raise the minimum to €5 million. These increases are expected to bring positive economic results; they will improve the soundness of the banks, promote the introduction of advanced banking technologies, upgrade the quality of banking services and enhance the branch network. Increasing the minimum capital requirement will protect the banking sector from the penetration of undercapitalised resident and nonresident banks. Banks now operating in Georgia are required to increase their minimum capital gradually – a process that is expected to continue through the end of 2008. These increases will stimulate new investments in banks to obtain sufficient capital, and facilitate mergers and acquisitions. Consolidation in the banking system will promote competition, as the remaining banks become bigger and better able to perform strongly in the market.

Strengthening the Supervisory Function

The important role of the Financial Sector Assessment Program (FSAP; a joint IMF-World Bank project) is to improve the supervisory function and efficiency of the NBG. The FSAP undertook a comprehensive analysis and evaluation of the existing legal framework for prudential supervision and generated a set of recommendations. This contributed to the implementation of the reforms that started in 1995. A number of new regulations were introduced as well as a series of changes and amendments to existing regulations. As a result, Georgian banking legislation took significant steps towards meeting the EU Directives and Basel I standards in 2001–2002:

- the National Bank's supervisory functions were strengthened: new instruments for problem bank resolution were introduced, making it possible to obtain information on bank owners and to restrict their control.

- licence application reviews became more strict; the review timeframe for applications was set at 3 months, compared with a 6 month limit under EU Directives.

- "Fit and proper criteria" were introduced for a bank's significant shareholders.

- the purchase of a significant share in a bank now requires the prior consent of the National Bank.

- internal control requirements were improved.

Policy Issues and Special Considerations

The Georgian authorities established a special working group comprising local and international experts to review and advise on harmonising Georgian legislation with EU standards. The group found that the legal basis for banking was essentially comparable with the European standard. However, three major areas of noncompliance were identified:

- requirements for "taking up and pursuit of the business of credit institutions" (Second Council Directive 89/646/EEC).

- principles and technical instruments for prudential supervision.

- deposit insurance.

These weaknesses can be examined from the following perspectives:

Fragmented Supervisory Authority

Under Georgian legislation, no single owner that is not a banking institution may hold more than 25% of a bank's stock, and there are therefore no bank holding companies. Efforts to lift this restriction have been hindered by political interests, but hopefully these can be overcome. If the restriction is lifted, the legislation will have to permit the supervisory authority to exercise supervision of financial holding companies on a consolidated basis. In this case, supervision would probably apply to holding companies only, because Georgian banking legislation does not consider leasing, investment banking and some other operations as banking activities. This impairs the National Bank's capacity to conduct consolidated supervision. For example, the securities market law specifies that securities brokerages are the only institutions that can undertake trading in securities, and these must be licensed by the National Securities Commission of Georgia. These activities are supervised, but not by banking authorities. American and European models somehow co-exist in Georgia; this is both inconsistent and inefficient. Amending legislation to address this discrepancy will be rather difficult given the current political climate.

Time Limits on the Review of Applications

The first and most important stage in prudential supervision is the review of bank licence applications, which involves a detailed study of information on shareholders and sources of funds, etc. During the review, supervisors obtain important documents, verify their authenticity and analyse their content. This is a very challenging process, especially when dealing with off-shore residents and complicated indirect shareholding schemes. It is therefore essential to take the time necessary to complete this examination in order to safeguard the system from criminal elements and money launderers. The same risks apply in change-of-control cases. To reduce these risks and to apply these principles properly, the time allowed for the review of bank licence applications should be increased from 3 to 6 months. For applications that involve changes of control in existing banks, the review period should be increased from 1 month to 3 months.

Incomplete Regulations on Ownership

Georgian banking legislation does not have a clear definition of "close links." Although the National Bank's prior consent is required before any party can assume a significant share (10% or more) of a commercial bank's capital, the authority of the regulatory body is nevertheless limited: the application of a resident individual or legal entity seeking a significant share can be rejected only on the basis of a court decision that the applicant is not fit and proper. The supervisory authority is thus unable to use the information available to it as a basis for declaring an individual or a legal entity unfit. This in turn enables the criminal world to directly or indirectly affect the activities of commercial banks. However, if the shareholder is nonresident, the National Bank may reject the application based on a criminal record presented by the competent authorities of the respective country.

Deposit Insurance: Coverage and Introduction

No deposit insurance exists in Georgia, but extensive efforts are being made to develop an appropriate institutional framework consistent with European standards. This model is governed by the following principles:

- deposit insurance will be mandatory for all banks registered in Georgia.
- deposits which are not considered under the EU Directive will not be subject to deposit insurance in Georgia.
- deposit insurance will cover, at least initially, only those deposits denominated in national currency.
- reimbursements for insured deposits in failed institutions will be paid within 3 months, with the possibility of a 3-month extension.

The EU Directives on deposit insurance require € 20,000 coverage, but this amount is rather high for Georgia. The recommendation by the IMF that deposit insurance coverage be three times GDP per capita, which is € 2,300 for Georgia, a coverage limit based on the IMF formula, is far more acceptable.

Irrespective of the mechanisms developed and the amounts insured, attention should be devoted to selecting the appropriate time to introduce deposit insurance. At least three preconditions should be met: the country should have a stable macroeconomic environment, good supervisory practices that are effectively enforced, and sustainable banking. From this perspective, it does not appear advisable to introduce deposit insurance in Georgia before 2006.

Outlook

Georgian banking legislation is basically in line with EU standards and requirements. Some areas of noncompliance have already been addressed. We are not under the illusion that it will be easy to bring about improvements in supervisory policy, but we are confident that the National Bank of Georgia, as the regulatory body, can successfully master the challenges ahead.

CHAPTER 7:

Issues Concerning Foreign Banks' Operations in Bosnia and Herzegovina

Peter Nicholl

Governor, Central Bank of Bosnia and Herzegovina

The prospect of EU accession has greatly helped to increase the role of foreign banks in SEE. To what extent will foreign bank entry help solve current financial system problems? Four aspects of foreign bank behaviour and its impact are explored here, illustrated by experience in Bosnia and Herzegovina (BiH).

Are the Operations of Foreign Banks Safe and Sound?

There is no single answer to this question. Foreign banks operating in BiH cannot be treated as a single group. As with the locally owned banks, the quality of the foreign banks varies considerably. This is largely due to the fact that bank entry conditions were relatively relaxed in BiH before 2000.

The BiH banking system is now dominated by five, predominantly Austrian-owned banks, which are generally considered "safe and sound." But the BiH banking supervision authorities will soon sign a Memorandum of Cooperation with the Austrian banking supervision authorities to ensure that we will be well-informed about the soundness of these banks. We have already signed such memoranda with supervisory authorities in Slovenia and Croatia and plan to do so with Italy, Serbia and Turkey in the near future.

A number of smaller foreign-owned banks from a diverse range of countries are operating in BiH. Some of them are small, even in their home countries, and some are relatively new institutions with little or no track record in BiH or in their domestic markets. One can therefore be much less confident about the safety and soundness of these foreign-owned banks.

The good foreign banks have already brought substantial benefits to the BiH banking system and economy. They have introduced new products and systems, and the better locally owned banks have followed their example. They are trusted by the citizens, who previously made little use of the banking system. As a result, the levels of bank deposits and lending have risen rapidly since 2001.

Will Mother Banks Stand Behind Their Operations if Problems Occur?

It is reasonable to assume that larger, long-established foreign banks will stand behind their operations outside their home countries. Some have been operating for more than 150 years and can claim that no depositor has lost money in their bank during that period. They will not undermine that track record lightly, and poor performance by their subsidiaries would certainly pose a risk to their reputations.

But this assumption received a jolt when the German BLB (Bayerishe Landesbank) failed to support its subsidiary in Croatia in 2002, preferring to sell the bank back to the Croatian Government for $ 1 and bear a loss of almost $ 100 million. This episode has made all supervisors in the region more cautious about relying solely on the support of the parent bank. BiH and all other countries in former Yugoslavia require foreign-owned banks seeking to enter the market to set up subsidiaries for this purpose and to meet both the minimum capital requirements (KM 15 million in BiH) and the Basel capital standards.

It is doubtful whether some of the smaller foreign-owned banks operating in BiH have the financial substance to stand behind their BiH operations if they faced a major financial problem. This is a concern, though such problems, should they occur, are unlikely to have systemic effects because of the small size of these banks within the BiH system.

Do Foreign Banks Have a Bias Towards Consumer Lending?

All banks in BiH currently have a "bias" towards household lending. This includes lending for house renovation, which is a legitimate area of major demand. The data indicate that foreign banks and locally-owned banks behave similarly in this respect.

Any such bias is understandable for the following reasons;

- It is generally easier for banks to collateralise household lending than business lending, using claims on salaries and personal guarantors. This is due partly to uncertain property rights and partly to inadequate collateral laws.

- The banks find it easier to exercise collateral for household lending than for business lending because the guarantor system is almost self-reinforcing: the borrower and the guarantors generally know each other well. The courts in BiH are extremely slow and have shown a tendency in the past to favour borrowers' rights over creditors' rights.

- The banks experience far fewer bad-debt problems with household lending than with business lending, due in part to the factors cited above, but also due to the cultural differences and attitudes between private individuals and people running businesses, particularly state-owned businesses.

- Bank deposits in BiH have grown very rapidly since 2001, but most are for very short terms. This restricts the ability to make medium and long-term loans, which has a greater impact on the business sector than on the household sector.

The way to reduce any such bias is to eliminate or reduce those features of the economic and legal systems that promote it. This is being done in BiH. The policy focus should be to extend and accelerate this process. A number of improvements are already underway in BiH.

- Better collateral laws and procedures are being developed, for example a Register of Claims on Moveable Property is expected to be in place in 2004.

- Specialist Commercial Courts are being established. This should expedite court procedures and improve the quality of rulings in commercial cases.

- A number of international agencies and donors are making medium-term credit lines available to BiH banks for on-lending, particularly to SMEs. In the past, some donors made direct lending facilities available to eligible SMEs. But with the substantial improvements that have taken place in the BiH banking system, most of these facilities are now going through BiH banks.

The desired improvements in the overall business environment will also have a positive impact. The whole reform effort, which aims to simplify and improve the regulatory and tax impacts on the private sector, will help reduce this "bias." Unfortunately, these reforms are moving very slowly in BiH.

Is Rapid Lending Growth a Prudential or Macroeconomic Problem?

The extent of financial intermediation in BiH is still very low in comparison with the countries of Eastern Europe, and the difference is even more marked if Western Europe is used as the yardstick. Given this situation, it is reasonable to expect bank deposits and bank lending to grow rapidly, which will have a largely positive impact on the economy and society. This is a signal that BiH really is undergoing transition and on the way to becoming a private sector, market-based economy.

However, very rapid rates of growth in bank lending can lead to prudential and macroeconomic problems. On the prudential side, there is concern that some banks may have neither the systems nor the management and staffing capacity to analyse the risks of the large number of projects they are considering financing. Their loan portfolios may therefore become more risky.

Most foreign owners of banks put considerable pressure on their managers in BiH to deliver high returns on equity (RoEs), as they view BiH as a risky environment. Most foreign-owned banks in BiH are meeting these targets. High RoEs are easily attainable because BiH is still under-banked, which does not necessarily mean that banks are taking higher levels of risk within the BiH market. However, the owners cannot expect to earn high RoEs indefinitely. If they continue to set high targets for their SEE subsidiaries, they will be able to sustain them over the medium-term only by taking increasing risk. This could develop into a major prudential concern.

On the macroeconomic side, rapid lending growth, particularly to households, generally leads to a strong growth in imports. In BiH, this is exacerbating an already large current account deficit.

Currently, the Central Bank of Bosnia and Herzegovina (CBBH) is not particularly worried about either of these potential unfavourable effects. The prudential condition of the BiH banking system today is considerably stronger than it was in the recent past. Moreover, the majority of the increased deposits and lending is concentrated in a few banks, most of which are substantial foreign-owned banks.

The current account deficit, though large at around 42% of GDP, is funded by a combination of official aid, remittances from Bosnians living abroad, and rising foreign direct investment. As a result, the CBBH's foreign reserves have been growing recently and, at € 1.3 billion, represent around 3.3 months of import coverage, which is a comfortable level.

In June 2003, the CBBH made major amendments to the structure of the reserve requirement imposed on commercial banks' deposits. The changes did not substantially increase the levels of these reserves at the time they were introduced, but the changes did make the instrument more effective as a means of constraining excess credit growth.

CHAPTER 8:

The Role of Foreign Banks in SEE

Mihai Bogza

Vice Governor, National Bank of Romania

Are the Operations of Foreign Banks in SEE Safe and Sound?

The expectation that foreign banks would provide more safety for their clients and for the financial system prompted the Romanian authorities to open the banking market to foreign investors from the initial stages of transition. It was also expected that the presence of foreign banks would foster competition, increase the number of staff with the skills required in modern banking and attract capital for economic growth.

Foreign banks are defined here as local banks owned by foreign capital. This includes banks owned by foreign banks, those owned by foreign individuals or nonbanks, those in which a foreign shareholder holds a majority stake, and those in which the shares are owned by a large number of foreign shareholders, none of whom controls the bank.

There is a marked difference in the ways these various categories of banks have performed in Romania since entering the market in the early-1990s. Foreign-owned banks in general appeared to be safer and sounder than banks with domestic capital only. However, in one case, the collapse of a bank owned by a Turkish nonbanking group almost turned the general public against the idea of stimulating foreign investment in the banking sector. In several other instances, minority foreign shareholders did not prevent imprudent management behaviour which ultimately led to the demise of the banks in question.

Banks owned by foreign banks performed much better. However, even within this category there was a marked difference between those whose parent banks were from the EU and those whose parent banks were based in other countries. While the former usually needed only limited correction from supervisors, chiefly relating to compliance with minor local regulations, the latter were a cause of serious concern in several cases.

Why did the Romanian authorities not take what now appears to be the obvious approach and allow only strong, well-regulated and prestigious foreign banks as shareholders in local banks? There are two answers to this question.

First, the Romanian market, in particular in the early-1990s, was not particularly attractive for those banks. With no local state-owned bank offered for privatisation in the initial stages of transition and the still unstable macroeconomic environment, many major European banks active in the region hesitated to invest in Romania before receiving clear signals that the situation was changing for the better. The Romanian authorities, on the other hand, could not afford to wait too long for the most desirable investors to make up their minds, and had to settle for what appeared to be the second best option.

Second, the standards set by the Romanian regulators did not discriminate between local and foreign capital. The admission standards were necessarily kept low for local private investors in the early-1990s, due to the overall scarcity of suitable funding sources. The regulators could therefore do little to control the entry of weak foreign investors. It was only after the system became more mature, with a sufficient number of established and sound market players, that the admission standards could be tightened up.

Will Mother Banks Stand Behind Their Operations in SEE if Problems Occur?

The best way in which major EU-based foreign banks in Romania have helped their subsidiaries is by enforcing good risk management principles, thus avoiding potential problems. However, there were complaints from the real sector that these banks limited their activities to low-risk products and did not do enough to help the economy. Foreign banks as shareholders seemed to monitor their subsidiaries well and maintain close contact with the Romanian supervisors.

Since no subsidiary of a foreign bank in Romania has failed so far, one can only guess what might happen should such an event occur. In recent years, there have been very few cases from which lessons could be learnt. The most significant seems to be the Argentinian crisis: at a certain point foreign parent banks refused to inject fresh capital into their struggling subsidiaries on the grounds that their losses were attributable to measures taken by the national authorities. In contrast, no depositor was negatively affected by the problems of Barings or Allied Irish.

While there is too little information to draw clear conclusions, the behaviour of foreign banks in dealing with problems in their subsidiaries can be summarised roughly as follows:

- They are likely to identify problems before these are serious enough to threaten the existence of the subsidiary as a going concern. They move quickly to fix problems.

- They can be expected to weigh the cost of their reputational losses against the cost of a bailout, should failure occur. Since reputation is one of their largest assets and their investments in Romania comparatively small, it can be assumed that they will fully support their subsidiaries.

- They are more likely to bail out their depositors fully if their subsidiaries fail as a result of their own mistakes, but are less likely to do so if their failure can be blamed, at least in part, on the local authorities.

However, each foreign bank adopts its own approach when dealing with ailing subsidiaries; for this reason, supervisors are called on to remain vigilant at all times.

Are Foreign Banks Biased Towards Consumer Lending?

Consumer lending is not the sole preserve of foreign bank subsidiaries in Romania; locally owned banks, too, engage in this activity. And quite a few foreign-owned banks in Romania are not currently active in the consumer credit segment. The factor that critically determines the level of engagement in consumer lending may be the number of branches a bank has: the larger the number, the more likely that the bank will engage in consumer lending. The reason for this is that this type of credit business involves investments in information technology (IT) systems, and the yield from this investment is greater if the distribution network is wider. In addition, consumer credit is a relatively standard, unsophisticated product that can be provided by less qualified staff in smaller outlets. In contrast, large loans are usually issued by bigger operational units staffed with experienced loan officers.

Developing consumer lending may be easier for foreign bank subsidiaries than for local banks because the former can take advantage of their parent banks' systems and experience. Nevertheless, this competitive advantage has not so far produced significant consumer loan portfolios for these banks in Romania.

The explosion in consumer credit that has taken place in Romania since 2001 seems to have been fostered more by improved macroeconomic stability than recent massive foreign investments in the banking sector. Most consumer loans are denominated in the national currency and carry a fixed interest rate, which requires a predictable and acceptably low inflation rate. Moreover, restructuring in the real sector has generated more labour market stability, thus improving borrowers' repayment prospects and making them safer as bank clients.

Is Rapid Lending Growth a Prudential or a Macroeconomic Problem?

Rapid credit growth appears highly desirable in Romania, where the level of banking intermediation is very low even by regional standards. However, the recent rate of increase in nongovernment lending has raised concerns. Year-on-year growth was 21% in 2001, 29% in 2002 and 49% in 2003. This growth has been driven primarily by consumer and mortgage lending.

In spite of this development, the banking system's main prudential indicators remained well below alarm levels. The capital ratio for the banking industry was

20% at end-2003, with nonperforming loans representing less than 2% of total loans. A stress test conducted in mid-2003 by an IMF-World Bank Financial Sector Assessment Program showed not only the system as a whole, but also the individual banks to be surprisingly resilient. Nevertheless, the central bank remained cautious, because lengthy legal procedures make foreclosure on collateral problematic, and the absence of a credit bureau and of a borrowing culture could lead to over-indebtedness on the part of individuals. In addition, the restructuring of the real sector has not yet been completed and corporate loans are therefore still riskier here than in a well-established market economy. To respond to these challenges, the central bank introduced a regulation on loan provisioning, requiring banks to increase provisions by almost 50%. This measure took effect on 1 January 2003.

The concerns on the macroeconomic side are even more serious, as aggregate supply in 2003 was unable to adjust to the increase in demand caused by credit growth and the marked increase in real wages. This resulted in a deterioration of the current account deficit to an estimated 5.8% of GDP, up from 3.6% in 2002. To address the problem, the central bank raised its intervention rate three times, in August, October and December, each time by one percentage point. As the central bank is a net debtor to the banking system, it is expected that increased returns on risk-free bank deposits with the central bank will provide an attractive alternative to granting loans.

The measures taken by the central bank were not welcomed by the banking community and the real sector, which argued that the rapid credit growth is to be expected given the very low level of bank intermediation. These critics maintained that the Romanian authorities should instead take measures to foster aggregate supply and to make better use of export promotion instruments. Debate on this issue continues.

CHAPTER 9:

The Impact of Basel II on Banking in Albania and Southeast Europe

Eris Sharxhi

Vice Director, Supervision Department, Bank of Albania

Risk management is certainly a timely topic – and one look at the news headlines shows why it matters so much. We have been reminded a number of times that when banks lack the commitment to manage risk prudently, they will fail in their responsibilities to their shareholders and to the public at large. The cost to society can be high and the impact on the economy devastating.

Sound corporate governance relies on a genuine commitment to taking appropriate action and to managing risk in whatever form it arises. Risk managers must provide timely, objective and accurate information to management. In turn, senior management and boards of directors need to ensure an atmosphere of transparency that promotes healthy and disciplined risk-taking.

Implications and Consequences of Basel II

It has become clear that the 1998 Accord and many of its amendments are outdated, overtaken by advances in the banking industry, the financial sector and the broader economy. To respond to current priorities and to improve the understanding and management of risk, the Basel Committee has formulated regulatory approaches that are designed to foster the soundness of the banking system and greater stability within the financial sector. This culminated in the drafting of a new proposal, known as Basel II, that is intended to be more attuned to risk, providing better alignment and calibration of regulatory capital and capital adequacy with the underlying economic risks that banks face.

Categorising debtors into a few risk "buckets" was certainly progress in 1988, but it caused significant gaps between the regulatory measurement of the risk of a given transaction and its actual economic risk, favouring high-risk loans at the expense of low-risk loans. This mismatch occurred because loans to firms were given a 100% risk weighting, regardless of their riskiness, with the consequence that capital requirements and allocations were set inaccurately to the disadvantage of many firms. The most troubling side effect has been the distortion of financial decision-making, which occurs when loans and investments are made on the basis of regulatory standards rather than on genuine economic criteria.

It is important to recognise that the new Accord is intended to apply to internationally active banks, which are highly developed and complex. However, it might also have implications for banking in emerging market economies, as discussed below.

Regulatory Disparities Between Multinational Banks and Local Banks

In principle, the three-pillar structure of the new Accord (capital requirements, supervisory review, and market discipline) provides a stringent mandate for regulators to strengthen bank supervision and encourages banks to become more sophisticated in risk management. The implementation of Basel II will eliminate a "one-size-fits-all" risk assessment methodology. Instead, it will offer a range of methods to evaluate risks, devoting more attention to the potential for loss. But the supervisory authorities in several emerging markets and many developing economies are concerned that Basel II sets a standard that they cannot meet.

Our greatest concern probably relates to the reliance on external rating agencies in the standardised approach to calculating minimum capital requirements. Domestic rating agencies are not well developed in many non-OECD countries,[1] while in most SEE economies, certainly in Albania, many small enterprises cannot afford to be clients of international rating agencies. Furthermore, the banking system in general features a group of small banks which are not internationally active. This suggests that, at least in the short term, most domestic credits will tend to end up in the unrated 100% category.[2] This could reduce the risk sensitivity of the new system relative to Basel I: better-rated SEE borrowers could borrow at lower cost from internationally active banks than from local banks. These international banks would apply their internal ratings based (IRB) analyses to determine lending terms and conditions, while the local banks would not have this degree of sophistication and hence would use the Standardised Approach. This would leave domestic banks at a competitive disadvantage when lending to high quality borrowers in SEE.

One of the most important objectives of Basel II is to encourage market discipline by developing a set of disclosure requirements. There is generally room in any market for such an approach, but it appears especially expedient in SEE countries, as it allows market participants to assess key information on risk exposures, risk assessment processes, and hence capital adequacy. However, while this may be beneficial in terms of increasing public pressure on banks to perform better through the adequate recognition and monitoring of risk, it might not have all the

---

[1] In Albania there are no domestic rating agencies.

[2] All the unrated borrowers will attract a 100% risk weighting under Basel II.

desired positive impacts. In the worst case, it could have some adverse implications, for example in Albania. Why is this the case? In general, the public is very sensitive to bad news and less so to positive developments. This holds true for Albania, where reactions to good and to bad news are much more asymmetric than in more developed markets, for instance in EU. The public in Albania takes bad news about the banking sector or individual banks extremely seriously and dismisses positive reports. This is due to a number of factors, such as the financial system crisis in 1997 and concerns about the low level of expertise in the banking sector. Unless we follow a step-by-step approach that generates more good news and builds confidence, measures to improve market discipline may be less effective than expected and produce suboptimal outcomes.

These and related issues call for an interim standard between Basel I and Basel II. This could deliver to domestic banks in emerging market economies some of the benefits of Basel II while incurring fewer costs. Furthermore, these countries should not be required to adopt the new standards: those that prefer to use Basel I rather than the standardised approach of Basel II should be free to do so. It would not be appropriate for the World Bank or the IMF to expect these countries to adopt Basel II overnight. Although the SEE countries intend to join the EU, the extent to which they are involved in the EU accession process varies greatly. EU banking directives are largely identical to Basel I or Bank for International Settlements (BIS) principles. EU directives will become mandatory as SEE countries join the EU, while Basel agreements such as Basel II are not likely to be mandatory except where they are embedded in EU directives. However, if the EU decides to make Basel II – either in full or in part – a prerequisite for accession, SEE countries will be faced with a challenging hurdle with no alternative course of action.

Challenges and Opportunities

Basel II poses three specific challenges: the location of supervisory authority, rating issues, and dynamic provisioning.

Supervisory Authority

Albania and the rest of the Southeast European countries host a considerable number of foreign bank branches or subsidiaries. Foreign branches and subsidiaries of banks from developed countries will naturally adopt the new system. Their head offices and parent organisations will implement Basel II and extend it throughout their network in order to maintain uniformity and competitiveness. However, where there is a high degree of integration in a banking group's risk management philosophy and the same risk management technique is applied consistently throughout the group, the host country supervisor might opt to rely entirely on the validation conducted by the home country supervisor, provided this takes adequate account of local conditions.

Conversely, where there is limited integration, the host country supervisor in SEE will probably be better positioned to lead the evaluation using internal rating based (IRB) models.[3] In this case, training will be required to prepare supervisory staff for working with the new rules, improving the capability of examiners to evaluate IRB approaches for consistency, integrity and accuracy and thus to measure risk properly. This new environment calls for better cooperation and coordination between home-country and SEE-country supervision in order to reduce the implementation burden on banks and to economise on supervisory resources.

Rating Issues

Stronger incentives are needed with a view to improving local financial systems generally and to developing the capability of the domestic rating industry to assess borrowers. This involves implementing some aspects of the standardised approach in a way that reduces the cost of intermediation and contributes to economic growth. Such an approach is valid as long as some borrowers can attract a better rating and, as a consequence, obtain a risk weight below 100%, while others attract a worse rating and weighting and therefore prefer to be unrated rather than badly rated. Encouraging the formation of domestic rating agencies might be the best option, but not without difficulty because rating agencies should satisfy a range of criteria and be subject to different constraints. These criteria call for objectivity, independence, transparency, disclosure and resources. These agencies must acquire experience, be free from external influence, produce publicly available assessments, meet requirements on the disclosure assessment models and approaches, have sufficient resources, and satisfy the validation or recognition criteria demanded by supervisory authorities in our countries.

Dynamic Provisioning

The new system challenges all banks to comply with the new framework if they wish to compete successfully and survive. Under this framework, banks should prepare to adopt a more dynamic and forward-looking approach to the evaluation of risk and provisions, since a risk sensitive approach creates a potential for pro-cyclicality.[4] This means that greater fluctuations in bank capital ratios are likely over the course of the business cycle.

---

[3] IRB application is difficult to apply in Albania and probably in SEE countries generally because it requires accurate and reliable data on at least a full business cycle, which in our case are insufficient, in order to produce sufficient and credible figures for IRB parameters such as LGD (loss given default) and PD (probability of default).

[4] According to Basel II, the assessment of the borrower's credit risk will be influenced by the performance of the economy. In the worst case, when the economy will be wholly in recession, banks will automatically have to increase the level of capital or shift towards less risky assets, putting the brake on lending and thus engendering a credit crunch and further recession.

Concluding Thoughts

Basel II is a logical and appropriate successor to Basel I. Its basic message is that all participants in the international financial system – banks, supervisory agencies and other market players – must become more discriminating in their evaluation of risk and better equipped to anticipate those problems that might turn into crises.

Basel II reflects the lessons of the distant past and the recent past, and points the direction in which the private and official sectors should continue to move. Adopting Basel II is a major, ambitious and difficult undertaking, and can be regarded as a work in progress. It is in our interest to help make it succeed. However, it is also in our interest to tailor it according to our situation, to follow a graduated approach, and thus avoid a superficial adoption strong on form but weak on substance.

Concluding Thoughts

CHAPTER 10:

Financial Stability in Southeast Europe – Basel II and the Challenges Ahead

Christian Fehlker[1], Arnaud Mehl[2], and Adalbert Winkler[3] *

[1] Financial Supervision Expert, European Central Bank
[2] Economist, European Central Bank
[3] Deputy Head of Division, European Central Bank

The financial sectors and supervisory authorities in the countries of Southeast Europe (SEE) face a double challenge. First, as these countries are going through a transition process and moving towards the market economy system in which financial intermediation occurs in accordance with the laws of supply and demand. At the same time, policymakers must set up a robust framework for economic and financial activity which also covers banking supervision. Second, on the way to reaching these objectives, SEE countries will become more integrated into the global financial system, putting additional pressure on policymakers to continue their reform efforts and posing new challenges for financial institutions. As these challenges are met, the nature of the tasks facing the SEE countries will gradually converge to that found in mature market economies.

In his paper, Evan Kraft addresses both challenges: first, describing the current state of SEE financial sectors and outlining key policy issues in their supervision and, second, focusing on external influences. These exogenous influences include the EU accession process and the Basel II reform. Kraft's analysis centres on policy issues relating to financial development in SEE. To summarise his conclusions, SEE countries should take advantage of the opportunities offered by accession and Basel II while simultaneously taking steps to minimise the potential risks. In so doing, SEE countries must carefully tailor their responses in order to achieve their own financial development goals within their economic and political environment.

We share these conclusions. However, even after compliance with international standards has been achieved, SEE countries, and indeed the more mature econo-

---

* The authors are grateful for helpful comments from Andrea Enria, Panagiotis Strouzas, Christian Thimann and Francesco Mazzaferro, as well as to Pierre van der Haegen and Mauro Grande for support in writing this paper. The views expressed in this paper are those of the authors and do not necessarily reflect those of the European Central Bank.

mies, too, must make a constant effort to preserve financial stability. Indeed, we suggest that the main challenge for SEE countries is not only to catch up but to remain compliant with the evolving international standards and best practices. This applies to all the dimensions of supervision: the preconditions, conduct and framework. We address each of these in turn.

Preconditions for Effective Supervision

Supervisors are faced with three immediate challenges that have a bearing on financial stability and which are unlikely to disappear even after compliance with international standards has been achieved.

First, supervisors are not the only guarantors of financial stability. Supervisors do not work in isolation nor do they have sole responsibility for maintaining the soundness of credit institutions. In fact, the primary responsibility for the soundness of any institution lies with its own management and supervisory board. Markets also have a key role to play as a corrective mechanism that exerts pressure on inefficient participants. It is indeed not the task of a supervisory authority to work against market discipline, as this would distort incentives and result in the suboptimal allocation of resources. Kraft rightly recognises that bank failures are not necessarily an indication of supervisory failure. The instrumental, albeit not unique, part played by supervisors lies in limiting risk-taking by banks and ensuring their adequate capitalisation.

Second, the environment in which economic activity occurs must be conducive to financial stability, and this is beyond the direct control of financial supervisors. The importance of the economic environment, which is duly taken into account in the internationally agreed standards established by the Basel Committee on Banking Supervision, has three main aspects:[1]

- Macroeconomic policies and developments. These have either a supportive or disruptive impact on financial stability, with implications for the effectiveness of prudential standards. Macroeconomic developments affect the inherent risk in existing bank exposures as well as bank earnings, and thus ultimately the banks' solvency. This impact is either direct, for example through interest rates, or indirect, for instance through asset quality or possible volatility in deposit volumes. In turn, the banks' lending behaviour may be pro-cyclical and thus amplify business cycles through the financial accelerator.

---

[1] The Core Principles also refer to crisis management issues as prerequisites for effective banking supervision, as dealt with in the following section. The Core Principles for effective banking supervision are found in Basel Committee on Banking Supervision (1997).

- Well-designed public infrastructure. While the design and effectiveness of the judiciary is clearly beyond supervisory control, public infrastructure includes an adequate body of laws combined with a proper credit culture, which form the basis for honouring and enforcing financial contracts. Elements which affect the quality of public infrastructure are, for example, the use and effectiveness of collateral arrangements, the position and protection of creditors in corporate bankruptcy proceedings, and transaction costs, including the time required to complete legal procedures.

- Market discipline. Effective market discipline requires adequate, reliable and timely flows of information to market participants, enabling them to make informed investment decisions. Moreover, financial incentives should reward well-managed institutions, and investors should not be isolated from the positive and negative consequences of their decisions. Market discipline is based on transparency, sound corporate governance and the absence of political influence on lending decisions.[2] These safeguards depend mainly on company law and its application to the whole economy. In this area, financial supervisors have a very limited input. High quality accounting standards are also a precondition for transparency and effective market discipline, as company information is published largely on the basis of these rules. Within the EU, a far-reaching reform is set to require listed companies to comply with the International Accounting Standards (IAS) from 2005 onwards. Supervisors and central banks have become increasingly aware of the complex interrelations between accounting rules and other disclosure standards for statistical and prudential purposes. Exploration of these links continues in a number of fora that include members of the accounting profession and the regulatory authorities mandated to develop these linkages.[3]

A third challenge is that financial sector development may render obsolete the existing supervisory framework: adaptation is constantly required in order for supervisors to maintain an effective framework and even more so to improve it. In fact, a framework carved in stone is inconsistent with the dynamic nature of the financial sector. Constant updates of supervisory arrangements are incorporated in current supervisory initiatives, such as the Basel II reform or the broader European Financial Services Action Plan. Kraft implicitly acknowledges this issue by first outlining financial sector development before turning to supervisory issues.

---

[2] However, in the aftermath of the Enron, WorldCom and Parmalat affairs, the role of private parties serving a prudential function, such as rating agencies and external auditors has come under increased scrutiny.

[3] See Enria et al. (2004) and ECB (2004) for an overview of work in this area and on the potential consequences arising from the far-reaching use of "fair value" accounting.

However, the challenge of maintaining a comprehensive and up-to-date framework in SEE, where financial markets are expected to grow strongly in depth and scope, is different from that in a mature economy such as the EU. As noted by Kraft, SEE financial systems are shallow, with low levels of intermediation and deposit mobilisation. By contrast, banking sector development over the past decade in the EU has been characterised by consolidation, financial product innovation, internationalisation and disintermediation. Cross-border and cross-sectoral linkages between the banking sector and other financial sectors have increased as banks have become more engaged in trading credit risk and have started to internalise securities transactions. At the same time, the overall level of competition has remained largely unchanged, and is considered to be relatively high in some European countries.

Finally, banks have reacted to difficult economic and financial market conditions by concentrating on their home markets and core activities, i.e. moving away from investment banking towards traditional lending and retail activities.[4] The vigilance of supervisors should assure that institutions remain stable in the face of such developments. In a benign environment, institutions might underestimate the inherent risk of their portfolios through the economic cycle and might face operational risks when coping with rapidly increasing exposure volumes. In more mature economies, banks' challenges tend to lie more in responding to supervisory practices and to the regulatory framework, facing ever-increasing complexities in financial intermediation.

The Conduct of Supervision

With regard to the conduct of banking supervision in SEE, two periods should be distinguished. Initially, the focus is on achieving compliance with international standards, such as the core supervisory principles or the recommendations of the Financial Action Task Force on money laundering (FATF), as mature economies in the EU have done.[5] Upon compliance, the second period will unfold, in which SEE and the EU will be confronted with similar challenges. Kraft points out that the overarching and uncontested principle on which banking supervision rests – both in emerging and mature economies – is the preservation of financial stability and the protection of depositors and other financial system customers. This objective will clearly not change as SEE countries comply with international standards.

A temporary challenge facing SEE is the necessity of applying the internationally agreed standards. There is international consensus on certain common principles with which supervisory authorities must comply if they are to be effective. These

---

[4] See ECB (2003a) and ECB (2003b) for a detailed analysis of developments in the EU banking sector and its stability.

[5] See FATF (2001) and FATF (2003).

principles, which have been established in banking, insurance and securities supervision, are common to all countries.[6] Moreover, these principles have gained recognition beyond the supervisory sphere; the IMF uses them as key inputs in its Financial Services Assessment Programme.[7] These principles include the independence of the competent authority, licensing requirements and ownership structure, prudential rules, supervision methods, information requirements and formal supervisory powers. An additional challenge is to prevent the international financial system being used for illicit purposes, such as money laundering or the financing of terrorist organisations. As early as 1990, the FATF established internationally agreed principles.[8] Moreover, depending on the degree to which the national financial system is integrated into the global economy, supervisors have to take international co-ordination into account, particularly with regard to the consolidated supervision of large, internationally active banking groups.

Upon achieving compliance with these international standards, a number of thorny issues, common to both the EU and SEE countries, will remain. These include:

Defining the proper supervisory focus. A distinction can be made between micro- and macro-prudential focus, reflecting the dual objective of banking supervision: financial stability and consumer protection.[9] The macro-prudential focus refers to measures that limit the economic costs of financial distress, including those that arise from moral hazard and described loosely as limiting "systemic risk." The micro-prudential focus pertains to limiting the probability of bankruptcy of individual institutions. It is well known that conflicts may arise between the micro- and macro-prudential aspects of supervision, i.e. between ensuring the soundness of an individual bank and preserving the stability of the system as a whole. For instance, keeping an individual bank in business may be deemed desirable from a micro-prudential perspective while, from a macro-prudential perspective, the bank's failure would be less worrisome, reflecting corrective market forces at work.

---

[6] The Joint Forum (2001a) compared the Core Principles of the three financial sector segments (banking, insurance and securities) and found broad consistency in the principles but a rather diverging focus across segments. Recent developments in insurance supervision in the EU (the so-called solvency II reform) align the supervisory approach with the Basel II reform by taking sectoral characteristics into account.

[7] See IMF (2002) for a summary of its experiences with the implementation of these Core Principles.

[8] The 40 Recommendations and 8 Special Recommendations of the FATF set minimum international standards that provide an enhanced, comprehensive and consistent framework of measures to combat money laundering and terrorist financing. The Recommendations cover all the measures that national systems should have in place within their criminal justice and regulatory systems and also specify the preventive measures to be taken by financial institutions and certain other businesses and professions. For further information see FATF (2001) and FATF (2003).

[9] See Crockett (2000) and Borio (2003) for details on this distinction.

Competition in banking may be good for efficiency but could be detrimental to financial stability.[10] Competition should create efficiency gains in financial institutions. However, it also creates the possibility that the weakest players may fail and be forced to exit the market, countering the micro-prudential objective of ensuring the soundness and stability of individual banks. Moreover, the international nature of banking activities requires international supervisory co-ordination in order to preserve a level playing field for banks. This ensures that no competitive bias arises due to divergent supervisory frameworks and the application of different supervisory methods, and thus avoids the risk of a "race to the bottom."

The allocation of supervisory responsibilities to one or more competent authorities. There is general agreement on the importance of supervisory independence and effectiveness. The Basel Committee, for instance, has named institutional and operational independence as its first Core Principle. However, there is no consensus on the institutional design of the proper supervisory framework. Several institutional designs are currently in use. The emergence of financial conglomerates and bancassurance, for example, is frequently considered a reason for creating a single supervisory authority to oversee banking, insurance and securities. Kraft also notes that the integration of financial services markets constitutes a main driving force behind organisational changes. The aim is to eliminate overlaps or gaps in the scope of supervision and to produce economies of scale, e.g. in data collection and processing.

The establishment of a single supervisor does not address all problems, however. Regulatory approaches vary substantially among the different segments of the financial sector. For instance, the underwriting risks in the insurance sector tend to be quite different in nature from the credit risks in the banking industry.[11] While some countries have left institutional structures and the allocation of supervisory responsibilities largely unchanged, others have already undertaken substantial reforms, and some are in the middle of the restructuring process. Reforms in the EU have targeted both the national supervisory structures and the mechanisms for cooperation among the authorities involved.[12]

Defining the role of central banks in supervision. The responsibility for financial stability does not lie exclusively with supervisory authorities. Central banks also have a major role to play in preserving financial stability, in part because of their information synergies,[13] and because payment and securities settlement systems may pose a threat to financial stability. Conversely, a stable financial system is a pre-

---

[10] For a general discussion on the relation between competition and stability in the banking sector, see Carletti and Hartmann (2003).

[11] See Joint Forum (2001b) for a detailed analysis of risks in the areas of insurance, banking, and securities.

[12] See ECB (2003) for an overview of the current setting and trends in the institutional arrangements for supervision in EU25.

[13] See ECB (2001) for a detailed analysis of arguments in favour and against the involvement of central banks in supervision.

requisite for the smooth transmission of monetary policy. Kraft also elaborates on the link between financial sector developments, its stability, and economic growth.

Establishing workable crisis management procedures. While supervisory authorities aim at maintaining the solvency and soundness of banks, their objective is not to avoid bank failures at any cost, but rather to avoid contagion and ensure that effective crisis resolution mechanisms are in place.[14] International standard setters have therefore moved to expand the preconditions for effective supervision to include crisis management. The Basel Core Principles require that supervisory responsibilities should include the efficient resolution of problem banks and the provision of an appropriate public safety net, including a lender of last resort and a deposit guarantee scheme. The Financial Stability Forum, in particular, has elaborated on the design of effective deposit insurance schemes.

In the EU, the responsibility for prudential supervision and for crisis management lies with the national authorities. This poses a particular challenge in light of the increasing integration of EU financial markets and the banks' cross-border activities. The effective exchange of information among central banks and other relevant authorities together with supervisory co-operation (to ensure appropriate and timely decision-making) are also key ingredients in controlling the severity of a crisis. Central banks play a principal role as lenders of last resort, and as such may be called on to provide emergency liquidity assistance (ELA). In Europe, ELA may be granted against collateral by national central banks to solvent institutions, while arrangements for co-operation are in place that include exchange of information with the European Central Bank.

The Supervisory Framework

The range of supervisory instruments is fairly comprehensive and includes licensing requirements, supervisory disciplinary powers, on-site and off-site supervision as well as quantitative and qualitative requirements for banks. In particular, capital adequacy requirements for banks have become a crucial cornerstone of supervision. The current Basel I framework, dating back to 1988, initially applied only to large internationally active banks. Its objective was to ensure an adequate level of capital on an internationally harmonised basis.[15] The Basel II reform has attracted attention throughout the world by making credit risk in banking a major compo-

---

[14] See The Committee of Wise Men (2000) on the "Lamfalussy procedure" as well as the Economic and Financial Committee (hereinafter EFC) (2001), EFC (2002) and the Working Group of the EFC (2000) for illustrative work on financial stability, integration and crisis management in Europe. See ECB (2002) for an overview of the arrangements for supervisory co-operation.

[15] In the EU, the framework was adopted as a directive, a legal requirement that applies to banks and investment firms of any size.

nent of supervision.[16] Kraft rightly elaborates on this reform, which is perhaps the most important in the pipeline.

It is still to early to make a comprehensive assessment of the consequences of the Basel II reform. Further work and information on the strategic re-orientation of banks is needed in order to address all the possible implications. Studies have shown that its impact on individual institutions will be substantial, leading to changes in minimum capital requirements as large as 50% of current levels.[17] These findings confirm earlier studies and thus raise concerns about the potential effects of Basel II on European businesses.[18] Another concern, relating to emerging markets in general and SEE in particular, is the impact on the cost and availability of credit. However, the most recent quantitative impact study suggests that capital requirements for sovereign lending will, on average, not change dramatically.[19] Furthermore, recent studies emphasise that there is not necessarily a close link between regulatory capital and the international banks' lending decisions and pricing policies.[20]

Outlook

Basel II is not carved in stone and will certainly see further modifications. Looking ahead, an agenda beyond Basel II is already on the horizon. It includes recognition of banks' internal credit risk models, including correlation effects, while the definition of capital (own funds) may also change. This agenda will largely be affected by market developments and by improvements in banks' internal risk management methods and capabilities. But before such methods can be incorporated in the capital framework, the supervisory authorities will have to be convinced of their reliability. In the immediate future, smooth implementation of Basel II will pose a key challenge to supervisory authorities, requiring increased

---

[16] Within the EU, a parallel reform is ongoing under the Financial Services Action Plan which closely follows the Basel II reform while taking EU concerns into account. See ECB (2003c) for a more detailed assessment on the basis of the third consultative paper issued by the Basel Committee on Banking Supervision.

[17] See Basel Committee on Banking Supervision (2003a and 2003b) for the most recent impact analysis. The European Council of Ministers at its meeting in Barcelona on 15–16 March 2002 requested *"a report on the consequences of the Basel deliberations for all sectors of the European economy with particular attention to SMEs."* This report was published in April 2004 and concludes that the overall impact of Basel II on inflation, growth and employment may be limited. The study is available from PriceWaterhouseCoopers (2004).

[18] EU-specific aspects of the reform concern the supervision of investment firms, the application of Basel II to small and medium-sized banks and to legal issues. Specifically, the new framework will be implemented using the "Lamfalussy procedure." See The Committee of Wise Men (2000) and EFC (2002a) for details.

[19] See Basel Committee on Banking Supervision (2003a) and (2003b) for details.

[20] See, for example, Hayes et al. (2002).

co-operation between home country and host country supervisors, especially as regards complex banking groups.[21] As for the SEE countries, catching up with international standards will, in all likelihood, mean chasing a moving target. International cooperation and technical assistance can make important contributions towards achieving this objective.

Literature

Basel Committee on Banking Supervision (1997), *Core Principles*, Bank for International Settlement, Basel.

Basel Committee on Banking Supervision (2003a), *Supplementary information on QIS3*, May 2003, Bank for International Settlement, Basel.

Basel Committee on Banking Supervision (2003b), *Quantitative impact study 3; Overview of Global Results*, May 2003, Bank for International Settlement, Basel.

Basel Committee on Banking Supervision (2003c), *High-level principles for the cross-border implementation of the New Accord*, August 2003, Bank for International Settlement, Basel.

Borio, Claudio (2003), "Towards a macroprudential framework for financial supervision and regulation?" *BIS Working Paper*, No. 128, Bank for International Settlement, Basel. http://www.bis.org/publ/work128.pdf

Carletti, Elena and Philipp Hartmann (2003), *Competition and stability: what's special about banking*, in: *Monetary history, exchange rates and financial markets*, Essays in honour of Charles Goodhart, Vol. 2, pp. 202–229.

Committee of Wise Men (2000), *Initial Report of the Committee of Wise Men on the Regulation of European Securities Markets* (the "Lamfalussy Report"). http://europa.eu.int/comm/internal_market/securities/docs/lamfalussy/wisemen/initial-report-wise-men_en.pdf

Crockett, Andrew (2000), "Marrying the micro- and macro-prudential dimensions of financial stability", Remarks before the Eleventh International Conference of Banking Supervisors in Basel on 20–21 September 2000. http://www.bis.org/speeches/sp000921.htm

Economic and Financial Committee (2001), *Report on financial crisis management*, ECONOMIC PAPERS, No. 156, July 2001, European Commission, Brussels. http://europa.eu.int/comm/economy_finance/publications/economic_papers/2001/ecp156en.pdf

---

[21] In recognition of the importance of this link, the Basel Committee has published high level principles for the cross-border implementation of the new Accord. See Basel Committee on Banking Supervision (2003c).

Economic and Financial Committee (2002), *Report on EU financial integration*, ECONOMIC PAPERS, No. 171, May 2002, European Commission, Brussels. http://europa.eu.int/comm/economy_finance/publications/economic_papers/economicpapers171_en.htm

Economic and Financial Committee (2002a), Report on financial regulation, supervision and stability, revised to reflect the discussion at the 8 October meeting of the Ecofin Council October 2002, European Commission, Brussels. http://europa.eu.int/comm/internal_market/en/finances/cross-sector/consultation/efc-report_en.doc

Enria, Andrea, Lorenzo Cappiello, Frank Dierick, Sergio Grittini, Andrew Haralambous, Angela Maddaloni, Philippe Molitor, Fatima Pires and Paolo Poloni (2004), *Fair Value Accounting and Financial Stability*, Occasional Paper Series, No. 13, April 2004. http://www.ecb.int/pub/ocp/ecbocp13.pdf

European Central Bank (2001), *The role of central banks in prudential supervision*, March 2001, Frankfurt am Main. http://www.ecb.int/pub/pdf/prudentialsupcbrole_en.pdf

European Central Bank (2002), "International supervisory co-operation", *Monthly Bulletin*, April 2002, Frankfurt am Main.

European Central Bank (2003), *Developments in national supervisory structures*, June 2003, Frankfurt am Main. http://www.ecb.int/pub/pdf/supervisorystructureen.pdf

European Central Bank (2003a), *Structural analysis of the EU banking sector, Year 2002*, November 2003, Frankfurt am Main. http://www.ecb.int/pub/pdf/eubksectorstructure2003en.pdf

European Central Bank (2003b), *EU banking sector stability*, November 2003, Frankfurt am Main. http://www.ecb.int/pub/pdf/eubksectorstability2003en.pdf

European Central Bank (2003c), *Comments of the ECB on the third consultative document of the European Commission on regulatory capital review*, December 2003, Frankfurt am Main. http://www.ecb.int/pub/pdf/eucapitaladequacycommentsecbcp3en.pdf

European Central Bank (2004), "The impact of fair value accounting on the European banking sector – a financial stability perspective", *Monthly bulletin*, February 2004, pp. 69 – 81. http://www.ecb.int/pub/pdf/mb200402en.pdf

Financial Action Task Force on Money Laundering (2001), *Special Recommendations on Terrorist Financing*, October 2001, OECD, Paris. http://www1.oecd.org/fatf/pdf/SRecTF_en.pdf

Financial Action Task Force on Money Laundering (2003), *The Forty Recommendations*, June 2003, OECD, Paris. http://www1.oecd.org/fatf/pdf/40Recs-2003_en.pdf

Hayes, Simon, Victoria Saporta and David Lodge (2002), "The impact of the new Basel capital accord on the supply of capital to emerging market economies, *Financial Stability Review*, December 2002, Bank of England, London. http://www.bankofengland.co.uk/fsr/fsr13art4.pdf

International Monetary Fund and World Bank (2002), Implementation of the Basel core principles for effective banking supervision, experiences, influences, and perspectives, prepared by the staff of the World Bank and the International Monetary Fund, 23 September 2002. http://www.imf.org/external/np/mae/bcore/2002/092302.pdf

Joint Forum (2001a), *The Joint Forum Core Principles Cross-sectoral Comparison*, November 2001, Bank for International Settlement, Basel. http://www.bis.org/publ/joint03.htm

Joint Forum (2001b), *The Joint Forum Risk Management Practices and Regulatory Capital Cross-sectoral Comparison*, November 2001, Bank for International Settlement, Basel. http://www.bis.org/publ/joint04.htm

PriceWaterhouseCoopers (2004), Study on financial and macroeconomic consequences of the draft proposed new capital requirements for banks and investment firms in the EU (MARKT/2003/02/F), April 2004, European Commission, Brussels. http://europa.eu.int/comm/internal_market/regcapital/docs/studies/2004-04-basel-impact-study_en.pdf

Working Group of the Economic and Financial Committee (2000), *Report on Financial Stability,* ECONOMIC PAPERS, No. 143, May 2000, Economic and Financial Committee, Brussels. http://europa.eu.int/comm/economy_finance/ publications/economic_papers/economicpapers143_en.htm

PART III:

Bankers' Perspectives – Dynamic Banking in the Changing Market of Southeast Europe

Introduction to Part III

What are the strategies and expectations of bankers in Southeast Europe (SEE)? What are the implications of competition among large foreign banks and much smaller domestic institutions? What progress is being made in creating a banking sector that provides a wide range of services accessible to the vast majority of households and formal firms? What can be done to create a large local cadre of professional banking staff? Will a combination of inexperienced borrowers, aggressive consumer lending and economic conditions create a credit bubble? These questions are important because finance links all sectors and has very broad social and economic impacts.

Bankers' Perspectives in Competitive Emerging Markets

Sylvia Wisniwski notes in her theme paper, "Bankers' Perspectives – Dynamic Banking in the Changing Market in Southeast Europe," that banking is among the most stable of all SEE sectors in terms of scope, depth and commercial dynamism. However, she cautions that a second phase of transformation is underway as competition intensifies, privatisation continues, and transparency and regulatory influence increase.

Southeast Europe has attracted many foreign banks. This influx began when governments in the region adopted a proactive approach to reform – tackling the insolvencies of the domestic banks and privatising them, sorting out fiscal problems and introducing and enforcing modern regulations. Other features that have attracted foreign banks include the opportunity to establish trade links with their home countries and a *carpe diem* effect – the chance to develop market potential while there is still little competition. But a handful of relics remain: for various reasons, investors have not readily come forward to take over large, dominant state banks, and these remain in public hands. However, IFC and EBRD assistance is intended to remove some roadblocks.

The structure of SEE banking sectors – in which the local banks are typically small – will change as a result of tighter regulation, the introduction of deposit insurance (that is costly to the banks), increased competition and progress on the privatisation front. These factors will fuel a second, more rapid wave of mergers and acquisitions, creating another investment opportunity for foreign banks. As a result, fees and margins will be more tightly squeezed, and the foreign banks will capture larger market shares. At the same time, the recent failures of a few foreign-owned banks in SEE have caused regulators to apply tighter standards.

The greenfield banks devoted to MSE (micro and small enterprise) clients continue to display great market potential and will be able to consolidate their market positions. Microenterprise lending remains underdeveloped, and demand is still relatively inelastic. However, this may change, as these lenders will be up against the commercial banks' aggressive pricing in the consumer lending market. Because deposit mobilisation tends to grow more slowly than loan demand and because the IFIs (official international financial institutions) face limits on the resources they can provide to these greenfield operations, the microenterprise banks may also face funding constraints. Interest rate sensitivity may lead some MSE lenders to curb their rapid growth in lending. But, the market conditions that would lead the commercial banks to move aggressively into lending to small and medium enterprises remain unclear.

Retail market potential remains attractive, especially as banks deepen their financial intermediation, moving away from simply investing customer deposits in government paper. Consumer lending is expanding rapidly and attracting new players. However, this could have a destabilising effect: an unexpected economic downturn could cause household liquidity to evaporate and the bubble might burst.

Leasing will become attractive as the appropriate regulatory frameworks are put in place. Housing finance is also expected to have great growth potential as suitable legal mechanisms are set up to facilitate the development of primary and secondary mortgage markets. Economic integration should create more trade finance. Fee income will be a driving force in banking strategy and competitiveness.

As banks expand, greater attention will be devoted to risk management. The management of operational risk will become more important as a result of recent bank failures and the influence of Basel II. Credit scoring will be used increasingly as appropriate models are imported and local databases are constructed. Double indexed loans (variable rate loans priced in euros in non-eurozone countries) solve some of the problems involved in making long-term housing loans, but they create a currency mismatch that could be crisis prone. Maturity mismatch is viewed with increasing concern in the region, but this is less problematic for foreign banks that are part of larger systems.

Trained staff are essential for the efficient operation of the financial system. Most bankers in SEE are trained on-the-job. Although about 30% of bank staff in the region have university degrees, there are no local professional banking qualifications or seasoned boards or institutes that offer local instruction. The number of staff is unlikely to grow because the increased demand for human resource capacity will be met through productivity increases. However, with continuing transformation in this sector, the training of bank staff will become more important.

Response Papers

A response paper by Per Fischer of Commerzbank discusses the role of foreign banks and of smaller domestic banks. Foreign banks have entered the SEE market in several ways, primarily by establishing local offices or subsidiaries, or by acquiring majority shareholdings in domestic banks. The author identifies three types of local banks: large state-owned institutions not yet privatised, banks with majority local ownership, and banks owned by foreign nonbank investors.

He foresees a declining role for local banks because the entry of foreign banks will lead to more vigorous competition, stimulating mergers or the acquisition of these smaller banks by larger ones. However, there will be exceptions: local banks that hope to survive must build on their market strengths, take advantage of modern banking expertise, employ professional staff, and expand beyond their national boundaries. Banking services will proliferate to include those commonly found in foreign banks' home countries. Micro and small scale lending is the province of specialised microfinance banks, which also compete with the larger banks for medium scale clients.

Mita Katic of Kulska banka, based in Voyvodina, indicates that the SME sector in Serbia and Montenegro is vibrant and strategically important, but still in a state of flux. The foundations of national economic development in the former system were based on large enterprises supported by large banks. This approach is giving way to the current reality in which small and medium-sized firms provide jobs and incomes in a liberalised economy. However, large foreign banks will continue to serve large enterprises in the region. Smaller domestic institutions such as Kulska banka are serving the SME sector. Technical support and funds for lending from official and private external sources have helped Kulska banka expand its operations serving small and medium-sized firms.

Evgeny Gospodinov describes the experience of Unionbank, Sofia, a Bulgarian bank that has carved out a market niche in a financial sector dominated by foreign banks. The strength of the local bank is due to its access to and understanding of local clients combined with other important characteristics such as flexibility, responsiveness, speedy service and confidentiality.

The banking crisis that ended in Bulgaria in 1997 stimulated competition between local and foreign banks. Policies were changed, foreign banks entered the market and traditional local banking was no longer viable. Innovation was required. Unionbank, assisted by foreign consultants, cultivated the SME lending market at an early stage and gained access to external medium-term financing. More recently, EBRD became an equity holder. Unionbank has rapidly embraced change and has profited from its pioneering approach.

Keith Flintham of Opportunity Bank in Montenegro, part of the Opportunity International Network, states that his bank's purpose is to improve the lives of disadvantaged people by assisting them in their business ventures. The micro and SME sector is Opportunity Bank's target group. This sector offers a number of market advantages over corporate lending: larger spreads, client loyalty developed through relationship banking, buoyant demand for loans (especially medium-term loans) and limited competition. Engagement in this sector also helps achieve positive economic impacts generally by promoting job creation and business generation. The micro and SME sector is growing as privatisation continues, and many microenterprises are expanding to become small businesses. Opportunity Bank foresees considerable opportunity for banking services and client development.

CHAPTER 11:

Bankers' Perspectives – Dynamic Banking in a Changing Market

Sylvia Wisniwski

Head of Bankakademie International, Frankfurt

Introduction

Comprehensive financial sector reforms in Southeast Europe (SEE) since the early-1990s have prompted the banking sector to expand very rapidly. Although the region witnessed several banking crises, banking can be considered among the most stable and advanced sectors in terms of scope, depth of reforms and business dynamic. Notwithstanding the progress made so far, the banking sector faces considerable challenges when it enters the "second phase of transformation."

Both internal and external factors will affect the further development of the sector. With regard to the former, increasing levels of competition and narrower interest spreads challenge the current composition of the banking sector and its product range. In addition, there is still more to do on the bank privatisation agenda. Among the external factors, the stability and association process in the run-up to EU accession offers new business opportunities. In addition, although the envisaged Basle II supervisory regime will most likely be only partially implemented, supervisory controls will be further tightened and transparency increased.

As always, a thin line separates the opportunities and the threats associated with the challenges that lie ahead. For the purpose of this paper, four major pieces of the puzzle that will determine where the banking sector is headed are scrutinised to provide insights into the areas considered most important.

The first section ventures a tentative exploration of the future structure of the banking sector. Section two focuses on possible product innovations associated with the envisaged second transformation. Risk management, a key function of banking, is the cornerstone of the third section. Finally, the human factor, which is critical for any change process, receives special attention.

A word of caution: the countries analysed for the purpose of this paper[1] differ greatly in their levels of financial deepening, real sector development and political

---

[1] The countries under consideration are Albania, Bosnia and Herzegovina, Bulgaria, Croatia, Kosovo, Macedonia, Montenegro, Romania and Serbia.

and economic stability. The task of framing general conclusions is therefore very challenging. The degree of uncertainty lends an element of crystal-ball gazing to this paper; however, the aim is to be thought-provoking – inviting readers to challenge the author's "predictions" and to reflect on the trends and events that will drive the banking sector in Southeast Europe (SEE).

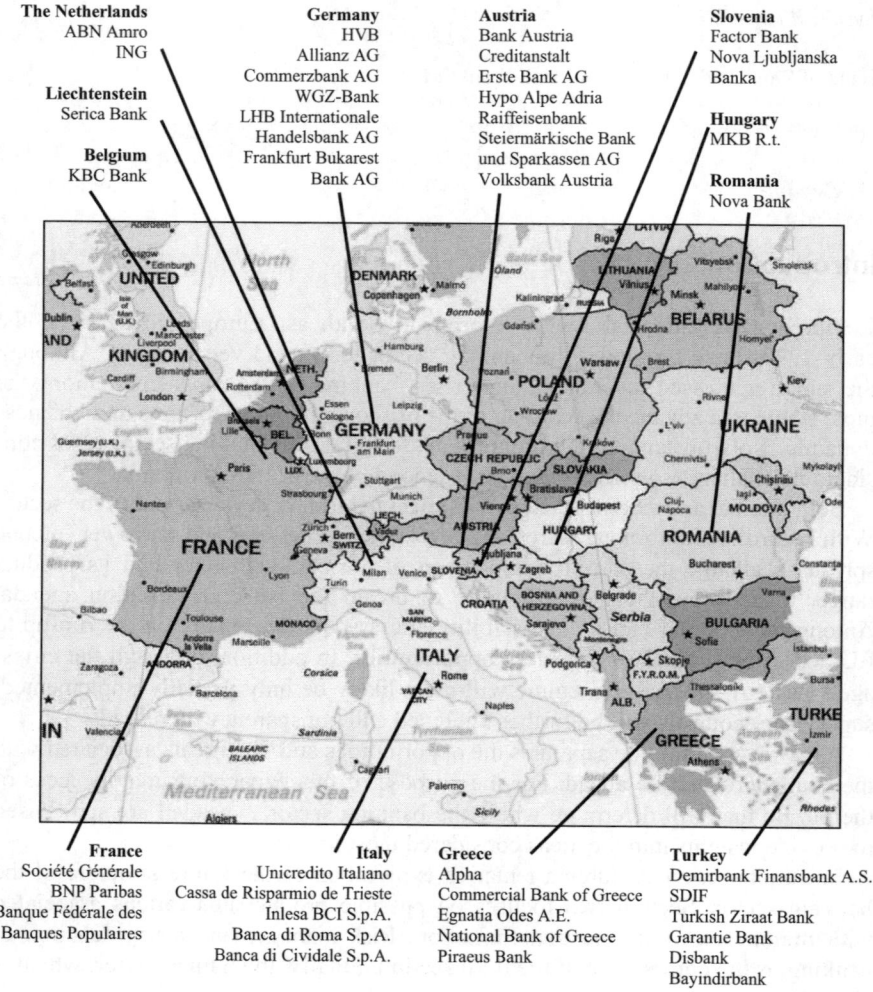

Figure 1. Participation of international banks in southeast Europe, by home country

Other Banks: United States: Citibank, AIG Inc., Diners Club International Ltd., Egypt: Misr Bank, Korea: Bank Daewoo.

Who Will Survive? Consolidation of Banking Sectors Dominated by Foreign Banks

Foreign banks[2] play a predominant role in the financial markets in Southeast Europe and in many transition countries. Since the early-1990s, they have been instrumental in consolidating the banking sector. As figure 1 shows, with their local branch networks and foreign direct investments, almost 50 different international banks are present in the region.

Three basic models have been pursued in foreign direct investments: 1) buying shares in an existing bank, 2) buying an existing bank, primarily through privatisation, and 3) setting up a new bank from scratch (greenfield bank, *ab initio* bank).

Two major factors are responsible for the predominance of foreign banks in the SEE market: first, deliberate government policy combined with the implementation of rigid bank regulations and, second, the market positioning and expansion strategies of – primarily – European banks.

With regard to the former, the privatisation of large state-owned banks was a door-opener for many foreign banks. In the early-1990s, Hungary and the Czech Republic offered majority shareholdings in state-owned banks to foreign strategic investors, and this pattern was adopted as a key strategy throughout the region. Governments in SEE realised that they were not in a position to restore the capital base of their mostly insolvent public banks and were forced to follow a similar approach. It is important to emphasise that foreign bank entry was neither spontaneous nor driven by Western banks, but rather a decision taken by governments in the region in view of their large fiscal deficits and decapitalised state banks.

The increasing tightening of bank regulations fuelled this process: experience in transition countries has shown that entry into the banking sector must be contingent upon meeting strict requirements. Entry barriers, particularly minimum capital requirements, should serve as a filter to select strong players in the market that are able to instil public trust in this war-torn and crisis-ridden region. As shown in the table below, minimum capital and capital adequacy ratios in Southeast Europe are often more rigid than EU standards.

Turning now to the second point, strategic location, several foreign banks have ventured into the SEE market as part of their regional expansion strategies. Italian, Greek and Turkish banks have entered due to the importance of cross-border trade and existing business ties. In addition, a small group of Western European banks, i.e. Raiffeisen Bank, Bank Austria/HVB, Volksbank Austria, and Unicredito, are present in more than five SEE countries and hold large market shares in the respective banking sectors.[3] Their aggressive market penetration strategy capitalises on the European integration process: many of the countries under consideration will join the European Union in the long run. Consequently, regionally oriented banks wish to position themselves as early entrants in a unified European banking market.

---

[2] Foreign banks are defined as commercial banks in which international banks own at least a 50% share.

[3] In Croatia, for example, Unicredito holds a 30% market share.

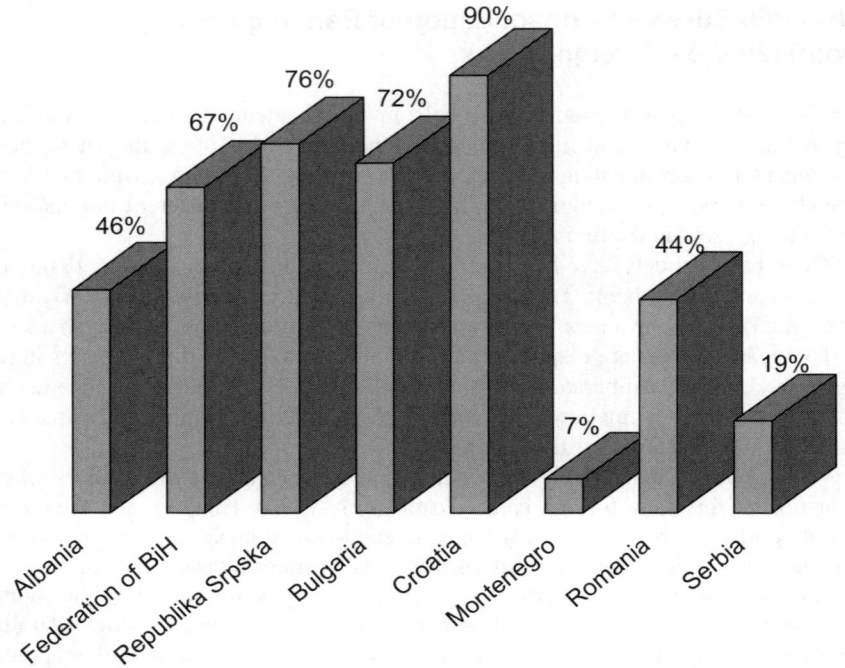

Figure 2. Foreign banks' share of total bank assets in SEE, 2002

Source: Banking Association of Albania; Bulgarian National Bank; Croatian National Bank; The Banker 05.04.04, page 85. Opportunity Bank/Montenegro. Larger foreign bank market shares are expected for 2003, especially for Serbia and Montenegro. In Bulgaria, the figure rose to 85%, as at the end of 2002 Bank of Austria bought Biochim and OTP Bank HK Savings.

There are also several factors that make foreign direct investment in the banking sectors of Southeast Europe attractive: first, these are virtually virgin markets with low levels of competition that generally results in higher interest margins and higher profits; second, these markets offer a new, attractive and broad client base for generic banking services; third, the rapid GDP growth that is envisaged and the estimated future growth potential it will create appears attractive in these transition economies.[4]

What Will the Future Bring?

Reform of the banking sector is entering into a second phase in several countries. These further steps will be taken with the mid-term prospect of EU accession and the long-term goal of compliance with the Basel II Accord. The two key issues on

---

[4] Focarelli, Dario and Alberto Franco Pozzolo (2003).

Table 1. Minimum capital requirements for banks in SEE, 2003

Country	Local currency	Min. capital requirements (in '000 of local currency)	Min. capital requirements (in '000 EUR^a)	Min. capital adequacy ratio
Albania	ALL	700,000	5,200	12%
Bosnia and Herzegovina (BiH)	KM	15,000	7,700	10%
Bulgaria	BGN	10,000	5,100	12%
Croatia	HRK	40,000	5,300	10%
Kosovo	EUR	5,000	5,000	8%
Macedonia	EUR	3,500	3,500	8%^{b}
Montenegro	EUR	5,000	4,300	8%
Romania	ROL	320,000,000	8,200	12%
Serbia	EUR	10,000	10,000	8%

Source: Bank of Albania, Regulations, Article 1 and Regulation on capital adequacy Chapter 2, Article 5; AR (annual report) 2002 of CBBiH, pp. 37, 92; Croatian Banking Law, Articles 15 and 65, Banking and Payments Authority Kosovo, Amended Rule 1 on Capital Adequacy Authorized under Section 13 of the Regulation & Rule 21 on increase in minimum capital of banks authorized under section 5 of Regulation 1999/21; Banking Association of Montenegro; Sándor Gardó (3/2003): Banking markets in central and eastern Europe (IX): Romania on a consolidation course. Die Bank: Zeitschrift für Bankpolitik und Bankpraxis. p. 3; National Bank of Serbia. Law on Banks and other Financial Organisations. The Law was published in "Sluzbent list SRJ" Nos. 32/93, 61/95, 44/99 and 3/02. Article 18, p. 6.

Note: (a) Exchange rates from *Financial Times* 20.10.03.

(b) For all banks executing activities stated in Art. 46 Banking Law, minimum capital is € 9 million and a capital adequacy ratio of 16% applies.

the agenda are the continuation of the privatisation process and the further tightening of legal stipulations that will propel further mergers and takeovers.

Privatisation of Banks

Privatisation of state-owned banks will continue and offer market opportunities to foreign banks. Further efforts will have to be made in some SEE countries either to privatise or resolve the few remaining public banks. In Macedonia and Croatia, the privatisation process is almost concluded, leaving only one or two banks with majority state ownership. In the Federation of Bosnia and Herzegovina (BiH), there are still six state-owned banks.[5] In Serbia and Montenegro, late-comers to bank privatisation, three of the currently 12 nationalised banks were put up for sale in 2003. In Montenegro, Montenegro Banka was privatised at the end of 2003 when Nova Ljubljanska Banka became the principal shareholder with 91.5% of

---

[5] Central Bank of Bosnia and Herzegovina, *Annual Report 2002*, p. 38.

total capital. This is to be followed by a similar tender for Podgorica Banka during 2004 where 76% of the bank's capital is still held by the state.[6] IFC currently holds 10% of Podgorica Banka's capital and actively supports the privatisation process with technical assistance.

Large state banks might stay on the privatisation agenda for some time. Despite considerable overall progress in bank privatisation, which is now in its final stages in almost all countries under consideration, the two biggest state-owned banks left in the region have been at the top of the privatisation list for several years without much success: Banca Comerciala Romana (BCR), representing 29.5% of total bank assets in Romania, and the Savings Bank in Albania with the largest branch network in the country and an estimated 58% deposit market share (end of 2003).

In Albania, after a lengthy restructuring process and several previous failures to privatise the Savings Bank of Albania, Raiffeisen Zentralbank Austria acquired 100% of the bank's shares in April 2004. Raiffeisen Zentralbank paid $ 126 million, representing 2.5 times the book value and is now the leading international bank in Southeast Europe.

In Romania, in contrast, BCR will remain on the privatisation agenda for some more time. It issued an invitation to strategic investors in 2002. Of the five potential investors, the three offering the most serious proposals withdrew in early 2003. Among the reasons were the overall economic slowdown in Europe and fears that the takeover would not run smoothly. Privatisation of BCR was a precondition for further assistance from the IMF and the World Bank. That the IMF subsequently offered a compromise solution was welcome news. This compromise foresees that the World Bank and the EBRD each take a 12.5% equity stake with the intention of selling the bank as the global environment improves over the next few years.

Restructuring the System – Again

A second and faster wave of bank mergers and acquisitions will involve a greater number of banks, opening up a "second business opportunity window" for foreign banks. Tighter bank regulations are expected to induce a second wave of bank mergers and takeovers. In mid-2003, for example, in addition to the introduction of new minimum reserve requirements, the Central Bank of Bosnia and Herzegovina obliged all banks to comply with the requirements of the Deposit Insurance System, which applies stricter rules than the bank law. In Romania, EU accession will require an increase in the deposit guarantee coverage from around € 3,000 to almost € 20,000 – an additional financial burden not all banks will be able to cope with. This will open a second business opportunity window for foreign banks to tap the SEE market or to increase their respective participation in these markets.

---

[6] IMF, Letter of Intent, Memorandum of Economic and Financial Policies, and Technical Memorandum of Understanding, July 11, 2003.

In addition to regulatory pressure, there are other reasons that contribute to the envisaged large number and pace of mergers and acquisitions:[7]

- commercial banks in SEE are small compared to those in Western Europe;
- competition in the domestic markets and from foreign banks is increasing;
- costs and interest margins of commercial banks in SEE are high compared to those in the European Union;
- mergers of foreign banks bring about mergers of their SEE subsidiaries;
- the poor financial performance and weak capital bases, particularly of smaller banks, require remediation that is often achieved through takeovers by sounder institutions.

Bank acquisitions have become common in the region and have strengthened the public's confidence in commercial banks as institutions that drive growth. One important factor that has contributed to the overall positive perception of bank mergers and takeovers is that, in general, weak local, national or regional banks have been absorbed by international banks, or existing foreign banks have been bought by even more prestigious international banks. This cascade effect is best illustrated by an example from Bosnia and Herzegovina: in December 2000, Universal Banka, a medium-sized national bank, was taken over by Zagrebacka Banka from Croatia. In early 2001, Universal/Zagrebacka Banka made an offer to purchase Komercijalna Banka, a small bank operating in the Tuzla area. Within a year, the Zagrebacka Group itself was taken over by an international consortium of Unicredito/Allianz.

Continuing mergers and acquisitions will lead to a higher degree of asset and capital concentration in the region. As the number of banks decreases, the market share of foreign banks will increase. This will lead to greater competition, squeezing interest margins, putting further pressure on loan portfolio quality and on operational efficiency.

Pressure on Growing Greenfield Banks

Greenfield banks serving small and medium-sized enterprises (SMEs) will strengthen their market position while facing considerable challenges. Small and medium-sized enterprise greenfield banks assisted by international finance institutions (IFIs) have attracted a sizeable number of clients. Given the small size of their transactions, their share of total bank assets is also significantly smaller. Despite these small transactions, the majority of the SME greenfield banks in the region have become profitable within the first 12 to 18 months of starting opera-

---

[7] These other factors were identified in many other EU accession countries in Eastern Europe that experienced a similar restructuring of their banking sectors. See Balcerowicz and Bratkowski (2001), summarising lessons from Poland.

tions.[8] The market potential in micro and small enterprise finance is still huge, and these banks are expected to expand massively and strengthen their market position.

Despite having achieved high levels of operational efficiency and showing very low loan loss rates, they face several challenges:

- The rapid growth of commercial bank consumer lending is often combined with a very aggressive pricing strategy that poses stiff competition to the SME greenfield banks. In addition, the SME market has become quite competitive in some countries.

  As noted in Bosnia and Herzegovina (BiH), ProCredit Bank (formerly MEB) has struggled to maintain a positive return on lending operations as interest margins have declined rapidly in an environment of increasingly stiff competition and pressure on interest rates. Reducing administrative cost levels at the same pace as interest rates decline poses a particular challenge when the bank must invest in its future by attracting and training new staff and expanding its branch infrastructure.[9]

- Another challenge consists in mobilising local deposits cheaply in order to sustain the continuous growth of the loan portfolio and to earn a comfortable interest margin. While the liquidity buffer of foreign-owned banks is provided by their parent banks, the SME greenfield banks benefit to a lesser degree from IFI contributions. However, the volume of funds that can be mobilised in such a way are small compared to those attracted by foreign banks.

- It has been noted that some SME greenfield banks are also exposed to interest rate risks (see table below). While ProCredit Banka Serbia, for example, is largely asset-sensitive, ProCredit Bank Kosovo is liability-sensitive. With the overall declining trend in interest rates in the region (see Annex 1), a negative impact on profitability could occur in the former case if the bank's net interest margin were reduced by locked in,

---

[8] The biggest success story is ProCredit Bank Kosovo (formerly MEB Kosovo) which doubled its equity within the first years of operation. This development was fostered by the bank's almost monopolistic position during the first months of 2000. In addition to ProCredit Bank Kosovo, its sister institutions in Bosnia and Herzegovina, Albania and Bulgaria have become profitable within 18 months of inception. Exceptions to this very positive picture are ProCredit Bank Romania (former Mirobank) and ProCredit Bank Serbia (former MFB Banka). In June 2003, ProCredit Bank Romania reported losses in its fifth year, while in Serbia, the bank made a loss in its third year of operation.

[9] In 2001, for example, ProCredit Bank (formerly MEB) generated a loss from lending (as a profit centre) due to interest rates that fell more rapidly than administrative costs (Maurer, Klaus and Sylvia Wisniwski 2004, pp. 195–221). This situation improved in 2002 when net income from lending again turned positive. Wisniwski (2003, p. 21, Table 10).

Table 2. Interest sensitivity of ProCredit Banka Serbia and ProCredit Banka Kosovo, 2002

Serbia

MFB/ProCredit Banka 2002

Dinars '000 000	Financial assets	Financial liabilities	Mismatch
0 – 30 days	3,573.3	1,867.2	1,706.1
31 – 180 days	121.8	784.5	-662.7
181 – 360 days	46.2	228.8	-182.6
31 – 360 days	168.0	1,013.3	-845.3
over 1 year	2.8	326.8	-324.0
Non-interest bearing	473,738.0	368.5	473,369.5
Total	**477,482.2**	**3,575.8**	**473,906.4**

Source: MFB Annual Report 2002, p. 56.

Kosovo

MFB/ProCredit Banka 2002

Dinars '000 000	Financial assets	Financial liabilities	Mismatch
0 – 30 days	91.5	218.9	-127.4
31 – 90 days	119.8	25.0	94.8
91 – 180 days	53.3	14.8	38.5
181 – 360 days	10.4	11.3	-0.9
31 – 360 days	183.5	51.1	132.4
over 1 year	11.3	6.3	5.0
Total	**286.3**	**276.3**	**10.0**

Source: MFB Annual Report 2002, p. 43.

more expensive long-term funds[10] while assets reprice in the short run at lower interest rates. Conversely, there might be a positive impact on the profitability of ProCredit Bank Kosovo if the overall declining interest-rate trend spreads to the Kosovar market.[11]

---

[10] Long-term funds are primarily provided by some of the shareholders: EBRD, KfW and IFC. Interest rates range from EURIBOR + 0.9% (EBRD) to 8.1% (IFC). Interest rates for funds provided by KfW and IFC are fixed at 6% and 8.1% respectively and have maturities through 2006/2007.

[11] One of the risks banks face is interest rate risk or the risk that market interest rates change and negatively affect the banks' interest revenues and expenses. Assets and liabilities are divided into those that are interest-rate sensitive, or change as market interest rate changes, and those that are not rate sensitive. A bank with an excess of interest-sensitive assets is considered to be asset-sensitive, while banks with a greater portion of interest-sensitive liabilities are said to be liablity-sensitive. If interest rates rise, banks that are asset sensitive tend to benefit in terms of greater net interest margins. In general, in banks that are liability-sensitive the same effect occurs if interest rates fall.

In summary, SME greenfield banks suffer from lower economies of scale and limited possibilities to pool and exchange liquidity within their network. One way to enhance their market position is to integrate the SME greenfield banks into a holding structure with a centralised risk management and treasury function. IMI, as one of the strategic investors in the SME greenfield banks in Southeast Europe, is considering creating such a centralised service facility.

In 2003, with the exception of the tough competition from consumer lending, SME greenfield banks did not perceive the rest of the banking sector as a serious threat, and microcredit NGOs even less so. They regard their primary advantages to be the speed of transactions, overall service quality, and lower interest rates compared to microcredit NGOs. However, large commercial banks that take a closer look at the SME markets could become serious competitors. Those owned by a foreign parent company have access to a large low-cost funding base and capital. SME greenfield banks have performed impressively in terms of growth and profitability. However, they will be challenged – as they already are in BiH – in increasingly competitive markets.

The Quality of Foreign Banks

Foreign banks are not always safe havens and can become troublemakers. There is no doubt that the large-scale presence of foreign banks has been instrumental in enhancing financial deepening in SEE countries. However, the impact of foreign banks is only as good as the quality of the foreign banks themselves. Problems in the foreign banks' home markets or institutional weaknesses of the parent bank may have a negative effect on their business strategy and future presence in the respective regional markets. The following examples illustrate possible contagion effects:

- *Croatia:* Bayerische Landesbank would probably not have sold its majority share in Rijecka Banka in Croatia so quickly in March 2002 if it had not also faced massive problems in Germany, its home market.[12] The sale might have occurred in a more orderly manner if Bayerische Landesbank had not incurred heavy loan losses with the Kirch media group, which led the European Commission to require immediate privatisation of the bank. In view of these events, staying involved in the Croatian market was not a real option. Rijecka Banka was later taken over by Erste Bank for € 50 million, fully recapitalising the bank.

---

[12] The German majority shareholder, Bayerische Landesbank, sold back its 60% stake in Rijecka Banka after discovering that a large part of the losses incurred by that bank were due to criminal mismanagement and fraudulent foreign currency trading. The bank's chief foreign currency dealer was arrested on 14 March 2002. Bayerische Landesbank sold its majority shares at a symbolic price of $ 1 to the Croatian state, which held a 25% share. See World Markets Research Center (WMCR), 19 March 2002, "Crisis Looms as Foreign Bank pulls out amid Corruption Accusations."

- *Romania:* Demirbank in Turkey was taken over by the Turkish Savings and Deposit Insurance Fund (SDIF) during the banking crisis in early 2000. At that time it was the fifth largest private bank in Turkey with considerable investments in subsidiaries in Eastern Europe and Central Asia. As part of the Demirbank group, Demirbank Romania, the 12th largest bank in Romania with 11 branches, also came under the control of the SDIF. In September 2001, the Italian bank Unicredito bought a 62.5% majority share of Demirbank Romania and increased its holding to 82.5% two months later. The bank is now named Unicredito Romania.

- *Romania:* In September 2000, rumours spread in Romania that Bayindirbank, the majority shareholder of Banco Turco Romano, had tried to transport funds illegally back to Turkey.[13] A massive bank run on deposits occurred in Romania, affecting primarily the Turkish-owned banks. In inter-government negotiations, the Turkish government was persuaded to stabilise Banco Turco Romano through a $ 25 million loan injection from Vakifbank, a partly state-owned bank in Turkey.[14] Despite all these rescue measures, the National Bank of Romania withdrew the licence of Banco Turco Romano in May 2002.

- *Albania:* In early 2000, Turkey's Kent Bank became the majority shareholder (60%) in the National Commercial Bank.[15] During the second banking crisis in Turkey in early 2001, Kent Bank was seized by the SDIF. Since then, SDIF has tried in vain to sell Kent Bank in Turkey and its subsidiary in Albania. Fears about instability were calmed when SDIF provided a $ 10 million loan to the Albanian bank. Depositors' sensitivity about bank stability was demonstrated in March and April 2002 when the Savings Bank and National Commercial Bank suffered $ 155 million in panic withdrawals fuelled by rumours about the two banks.[16]

To minimise the risk of financial contagion, bank regulators and supervisors in Southeast Europe might screen more carefully foreign banks intending to enter local markets. Cross-border supervision and the consolidated supervision of commercial banks that are financial conglomerates – which many foreign banks are – will quite probably be intensified.

---

[13] Persons associated with Bayindir Bank/Banco Turco-Romano were caught at the Bucharest airport with tickets to Istanbul and suitcases full of banknotes.

[14] Ercan Uygur (2001), p. 16. In the same paper, Rüdiger Dornbusch is cited as considering this event as precipitating the second financial sector crisis in Turkey.

[15] IFC and EBRD were part of this consortium, each contributing 20% of equity.

[16] Bank of Albania, Governor Shkëlqim Cani, Press Release, April 25, 2003.

What Is the Market Potential? Scale and Scope of Financial Services

Given the small size of the capital and insurance markets, commercial banks are and will probably continue to be the prominent players in the SEE financial sectors. During the early transition years, financial intermediation was rather rudimentary, with short-term savings and short-term lending operations constituting the core business. Investing in government securities was also attractive in some countries, giving the banks high-risk-free returns. However, with the consolidation of public budgets and tight fiscal controls, the interest paid on government securities has decreased, encouraging banks to look for new market opportunities.

Southeast Europe has been and probably will continue to be a market for retail banking. The primary range of products will therefore include typical retail services: consumer loans, standard savings products and noncash payment instruments.

Consumer Lending Is About to Bloom – at the Risk of Credit Bubbles

In the aftermath of war, there is strong demand on the part of private households for consumption goods and for housing renovation or expansion. This demand-side pressure matches the perception of many banks that private households are better borrowers than enterprises. Salaried employees have a constant stream of income, greatly reducing concerns about repayment capacity and collateral. Furthermore, the foreign banks active in SEE are universal banks with massive retail banking operations in their home countries. Providing standard mass products such as consumer loans is one of their strengths.

When corporate lending margins are falling and economic uncertainty is high, as in BiH in 2003, banks are keen to expand their retail market share. When competition is fierce, banks having well-established partnerships with distributors of retail goods might have a competitive edge.

In the long run, specialised consumer finance companies may venture into SEE, particularly into Romania, which has a sizeable market and population of 23 million. This happened in Poland, where major European operators now have a strong foothold in the market.[17] However, the market entry of Cetelem, Europe's leader in consumer finance, into Slovakia (a rather small market with 5.4 million inhabitants) implies the potential interest in the Balkan region.[18]

Overly aggressive credit expansion in consumer lending may evolve into a credit bubble. Consumer and housing loans as a share of the total loan portfolio have increased significantly in BiH and in Croatia. More than 40% of the total loan portfolio of the banking sector in Bosnia and Herzegovina consisted of con-

---

[17] Cetelem, a subsidiary of BNP Paribas (France), opened its first Polish branch in 1999. Other major European consumer credit companies operating in Poland are KBC (Belgium), Crédit Agricol (France). Two other international consumer finance giants, the US Household Finance (HFC) and Santander Consumer Finance, recently entered the market.

[18] Strategically, Cetelem is well positioned with branches in all important countries neighbouring SEE – Slovakia, Hungary, Greece, Turkey.

sumption and housing loans at the end of 2003. In Croatia, the figure was even higher with 48.3%. Even more distressing is the fact that despite efforts by the respective central banks to curb consumer lending in both countries, the share of household loans continued to rise in 2003.

Another very critical aspect is the level of indebtedness of private households as expressed by two ratios: total outstanding loans to households relative to total disposable income mass[19] and to GDP. As shown in Table 3, both indicators are at alarming levels. Even in countries known for being highly consumption oriented – the United States and Japan – total consumer credit as a percentage of disposable income in 2000 was slightly more than 100% and around 70%, respectively.[20] In 1990, the ratio was much lower, at 23% for Japan and 19% for the US.[21] The steep increase in consumer lending during the 1990s has been fuelled primarily by the intensive use of credit cards, something that is relatively new to SEE markets.

Apart from the possible negative impact on the current accounts of the SEE countries, more worrisome is the potential credit risk associated with consumer loans. Levels considered "safe" can backfire in a situation of massive lay-offs. Official unemployment is high and increasing in Croatia and BiH. A consumer loan crisis might be right on the doorstep.

Table 3. Development of consumer lending in BiH and Croatia, 1999–2003 (*percentage*)

Bosnia and Herzegovina (BiH)	1999	2000	2001	2002	2003
Household loans/Total loan portfolio	10	13	20	34	41
Total household loans/Total disposable income mass[a]	11	14	23	45	57
Total household loans/GDP	3	4	7	14	13
Unemployment rate (official)	39	40	40	41	41
Croatia	**1999**	**2000**	**2001**	**2002**	**2003**
Household loans/Total loan portfolio	36	39	41	44	48
Total household loans/Total disposable income mass[a]	25	27	35	47	n.a.
Total household loans/GDP	14	15	19	24	29
Unemployment rate (official)	19	21	22	22	20

Total disposable income mass is calculated here as average annual income per employee or household multiplied by number of employees or households. Note that disposable income might be underreported because of tax evasion.

Source: All data based on Central Bank statistics and the Central Statistical Offices of both countries.

---

[19] Total disposable income mass is calculated here as the average annual net salary multiplied by the number of employees registered in each country. Statistical data used for this calculation were taken from central bank statistics and from the Croatian Bureau for Statistics.

[20] Lafferty Group (2003), p. 4.

[21] Alexander, Arthur J. (1997), Figure 2, p. 6.

SME and Microfinance

SME lending is an attractive market that will expand, but microenterprise finance is still underdeveloped. If foreign banks buy local banks, will SME lending decrease because serving large customers is considered to be more profitable?[22] This possibility is hotly debated, but empirical evidence from Poland and Hungary shows that SME lending has increased.[23] Several factors contribute to the banks' interest in expanding credit to SMEs in Southeast Europe in the mid to long-term, if not now.

- The privatisation of SMEs is (almost) complete,[24] while the difficult task of selling large strategic enterprises is ongoing in all countries. Consequently, SMEs are the backbone of the local economies, and the private sector consists primarily, if not exclusively, of SMEs.[25]

- Even where progress has been made in attracting strategic investors to buy large enterprises, focusing bank business exclusively on these clients is risky. First, there is tough competition among the banks to pick the few "cherries." Second, many strategic investors arrive with an established bank relationship. Third, large enterprises may find it easier to finance themselves by issuing bonds and shares where the local capital market provides such opportunities. Finally, even if commercial banks could attract some big corporate customers, this strategy of "creaming the market" could not sustain their branch networks.

- Empirical evidence in many countries has shown that micro and small enterprises are less interest rate sensitive than large corporates. In addition, they are more loyal as customers: they stick with their "house bank" once a good personal relationship has been established.

All these factors contribute to making SMEs attractive customers for commercial banks. However, adjusting the loan products and lending technology to SMEs' socioeconomic characteristics in SEE is a challenge for many commercial banks.

Another critical question is whether microenterprises are being served by financial institutions, and where the current frontier lies between those which are served and those which are not. Analysis indicates that commercial banks are (still) positioned in the upper tiers of the MSME (micro, small and medium-sized enterprise) market, following a "cherry-picking" or "creaming-the-market" approach. This has occurred despite the significant growth of microfinance NGOs, particu-

---

[22] World Bank (2002).

[23] Balcerowicz, Ewa and Andrzej Bratkowski (2001), p. 24.

[24] The exception is Serbia, which is still heavily engaged in auctioning several thousand small companies.

[25] Directorate General for Economic and Financial Affairs (2003), see individual country reports. Commission of the European Communities (2003), p. 10.

larly in BiH and in Kosovo, and the creation of specialised microfinance banks such as Opportunity Bank and many SME greenfield banks that have expanded rapidly and continuously.[26] If microenterprise markets are tapped by traditional commercial banks, they are primarily served through the consumer lending window. However, as noted above, this might prove to be reckless in the mid term.

Leasing

With an appropriate regulatory framework, leasing services can become a fast-growing, promising business. In 1994, Romania was the first SEE country to issue a law on leasing. By 2003, there were 34 leasing companies, many of which are subsidiaries of foreign banks. In contrast, neither Albania nor BiH have a specific legal framework for leasing, limiting the incipient activities in those countries to financial leasing operations carried out through commercial banks.

Among the primary target groups are private households, particularly for car leasing, and small and medium-sized enterprises, for equipment leasing. In future, real estate leasing will play an increasing role in developed markets such as Croatia and Romania.

Housing Finance

There is large pent-up demand for housing finance, but the development of mortgage lending markets will take time. Establishing decent housing facilities is a priority for many families in Southeast Europe. Roughly 120,000 houses were damaged in Kosovo during the war in 1999. In Serbia, there are 90,000 displaced families that require new accommodation. In Croatia and Bosnia and Herzegovina, the war stopped in the early-to-mid-1990s. The reconstruction of demolished houses is largely complete, and there is now considerable demand for single family homes and apartments. In Albania, Bulgaria and Romania, several hundred thousand units are awaiting renovation or should be replaced owing to their poor condition or lack of basic utilities.[27]

The housing loan market has grown considerably throughout the region, except for Kosovo where it has only recently got underway. Evidence of this development can be seen in Croatia, where, at the end of 2002, 29% of all loans to households were used for housing purposes.[28] Several countries report increasingly stiff competition that is driving product innovation and reducing interest rates. However, only one specialised mortgage bank exists in the region: the Romanian Mortgage Loan Company (Ro-Fin), founded in early 2003 with

---

[26] Sylvia Wisniwski and Klaus Maurer, "Impact of Financial Sector Projects in Southeast Europe – Effects on Financial Institutions and the Financial Sector," in Ingrid Matthäus-Maier and J.D. von Pischke, eds., The Development of the Financial Sector in Southeast Europe – Innovative Approaches in Volatile Environments. Berlin: Springer, 2004.

[27] Hegedüs, József (2002), pp. 23–24.

[28] Merrill, Sally, Carol Rabenhorst and Paul Sacks (2003a), p. 3.

capital from Shorebank and USAID. Why has there been so little progress in developing more sophisticated mortgage markets and why is the outlook unlikely to improve in the short run?

- *Weak legal framework.* Except for Romania and Croatia, the basic enabling laws for a primary mortgage market are not in place. Even where laws that govern real property and the use of real estate as loan collateral formally exist, ownership rights are often unclear in practice due to incomplete registration records or the difficulties lenders face during foreclosure.

- *Banks show limited interest in using mortgage-backed securities or bonds.* Many banks are aware of the maturity mismatches in their balance sheets, but only a few show any concern. Despite the rapidly growing housing loan portfolio in the region, the advantages of mortgage-backed debt and off-balance sheet funding do not seem to be clear. Commercial banks seem to prefer long-term funding from external sources. In Croatia, banks state that they have more than sufficient liquidity, so that "turning around" the portfolio and increasing the return on equity through mortgage-backed securities does not seem attractive.[29] Finally, given the falling interest rates in mortgage lending in several countries, expanding the housing loan portfolio by selling other assets and using the cash for re-lending at lower rates is not an attractive option.

- *Secondary markets are in their infancy.* In most countries, the market for debt instruments is not highly developed. Although some countries, such as Romania and Croatia, possess the necessary capital market infrastructure, the primary market is dominated by treasury bills and a few corporate bonds. Moreover, some trading is done outside the stock exchange. At present, there seems to be little appetite on the part of local markets for mortgage-backed securities or bonds, the main reason being that commercial banks are the principal buyers on the primary markets. The only exception is Romania, where the seven licensed pension funds could be potential buyers of long-term bonds and securities. However, the asset allocation rules detailed in the Pension Act are defined very rigidly and limit the pension funds' capacity to hold mortgage-backed securities and bonds.[30] Despite this not very encouraging local market environment, the potential for selling mortgage securities off-shore should materialise when packages of sufficient size become available.

---

[29] Merrill, Sally, Carol Rabenhorst and Paul Sacks (2003a), p. 10.

[30] Merrill, Sally, Carol Rabenhorst and Paul Sacks (2003b), p. 11.

Fee-Based Business

Fee income will continue to be important. A significant portion of banks' total income is generated through fees and commissions. As the table below indicates, one-fifth to one-third of total income derives from fee-based business. Banks earn fees from originating loans, from international and domestic payments, and from off-balance sheet transactions such as letters of guarantee.

Table 4. Interest and fee income of selected banks, 2002

Country	Income				Share of total income		
	Total	Interest	Fee	Other	Interest	Fee	Other
BiH							
Gospodarska Banka (KM million)	9.8	4.8	1.7	3.2	49	17	33
Universal Banka (KM million)	36.3	23.8	12.2	0.3	66	34	1
Raiffeisen Bank (KM million)	92.1	57.9	26.8	0.1	63	29	0
Bulgaria							
United Bulgarian Bank (BGN million)	145.7	89.9	37.0	18.8	62	25	13
Bulbank (BGN million)	182.5	113.9	43.3	25.3	62	24	14
Croatia							
Nova Banka (HRK million)	413.5	268.7	65.3	79.5	65	16	19
Hypo Alpe Adria (HRK million)	800.2	660.8	67.7	71.8	83	8	9
Serbia							
Delta Banka (Din million)	2,823.4	1,931.1	709.9	182.4	68	25	6
ProCredit (Din million)	459.1	313.9	139.4	5.8	68	30	1

Source: Annual Reports 2002, income statements of the selected banks.

Table 5. Classification of fee income of selected banks, 2002

	BiH			Bulgaria		Croatia	Serbia	
Income	Universal Banka	MEB	Gospo-darska	United Bulgarian Bank	Bulbank AD	Privredna Banka	Delta Banka	ProCredit
Fee income from lending, guarantees and L/C*	30	39	10	0	23	43	9	42
Payment services	49	0	24	69	50	27	85	52
Credit & debit cards	0	0	0	17	10	21	3	0
Other fee income	21	61	65	14	17	9	3	6
Total fee and comission income	100	100	100	100	100	100	100	100

Source: Annual Reports 2002, income statements of the selected banks.
* Letters of Credit.

Table 6. Evolution of Maestro/Debit Cards in selected countries, 1998–2002

Country	Maestro/Debit Cards			Points of Acceptance			ATM		
	Q4 1998	Q4 2000	Q4 2002	Q4 1998	Q4 2000	Q4 2002	Q4 1998	Q4 2000	Q4 2002
Albania	0	0	0	0	0	0	0	0	0
BiH	0	3,462	12,000*	0	197	300*	0	1	10
Bulgaria	60,025	359,591	500,000*	134	656	1,000*	162	356	500*
Yugoslavia	0	0	n.a.	0	0	n.a.	0	0	n.a.
Croatia	740,040	1,700,560	2,580,000	41	7,517	16,900	151	677	1,200
Macedonia	0	1,961	10,000*	0	317	900*	8	12	30*
Romania	50,189	476,942	1,800,000	142	934	3,900	229	800	1,900
Slovenia	21,823	1,148,371	1,650,000	928	20,215	31,200	22	678	1,200
Slovakia	665,138	909,059	1,240,000	2,287	6,324	12,800	614	1,073	1,400
Czech Rep.	352,569	1,411,532	2,030,000	2,770	11,628	25,000	1,356	1,564	2,300

Source: Maestro – Internal figures.
* estimates.

Table 7. Evolution of Master Card/Credit Cards in selected countries, 1998–2002

Country	MasterCard – Credit Card			Points of Acceptance		
	Q4 1998	Q4 2000	Q4 2002	Q4 1998	Q4 2000	Q4 2002
Albania	0	0	0	0	0	0
BiH	0	0	0	0	0	0
Bulgaria	317	1,913	5,000*	360	820	1,000*
Yugoslavia	0	3,632	9,000*	0	282	500*
Croatia	136,080	123,424	230,000	20,839	33,969	44,000
Macedonia	2,843	4,663	9,000*	314	805	1,000*
Romania	8,340	78,813	180,000	5,773	7,041	6,000
Slovenia	162,695	217,488	270,000	22,448	30,510	32,000
Slovakia	12,009	31,790	130,000	2,732	7,134	12,000
Czech Rep.	327,749	596,227	680,000	19,844	29,408	40,000

Source: MasterCard International – Internal figures.
* estimates.

Noncash debit and credit card payments have expanded significantly in Bulgaria, Croatia and Romania, countries with more developed SEE financial sectors. Tables 6 and 7 show the increase in the number of internationally accepted Maestro Debit Cards. Local cards, issued in several countries, are not included in these tables due to lack of available data.

Despite this overall positive development, there is still large unmet demand for payment services. The level of market penetration of noncash payment instruments in Croatia is similar to that in Slovenia, Slovakia and the Czech Republic in Eastern Europe. In the other countries in Southeast Europe, a considerably smaller portion of the population use noncash payment instruments. In Romania, for example, only 1.8 million or 8% of the population use Maestro debit cards. In contrast, 80% of Slovenia's population are debit card holders. This gap between the two regions is even wider for credit cards. "Pay before" (e.g. travellers cheques), "pay now" (debit cards) and "pay later" (credit cards) services that are tailored to the convenience and risk profiles of specific market segments are therefore expected to expand further in the near future.

Regional Arrangements

Regional integration creates opportunities for trade finance and project finance. The European Union offers preferential trade arrangements to the region, allowing better market access that is expected to stimulate export opportunities. Furthermore, under the auspices of the Stability Pact's working group on trade liberalisation, Balkan countries are now concluding bilateral Free Trade Agreements (FTA) within the region. When fully implemented, these will boost intraregional trade, increase competition and create economies of scale. The increased level of trade integration is also raising expectations of increased foreign direct investment (FDI).

Even if these expectations are only partially fulfilled, many opportunities will be created in the financial services sector that will support regional integration.[31] Buyer credits, advance payments, the purchase of receivables in low-volume export business and standard letters of credit are major forms of trade financing that facilitate exports. Transactions involving the purchase of raw materials or goods for resale might require structured trade finance or commodity finance instruments. Finally, as donor contributions are reduced, there will be more and more demand for international project financing involving commercial funding.

Funding Strategies

Diverse funding strategies are likely to emerge throughout the region. The liability structure of the SEE banking sector is relatively simple (figure 3). Deposit mobilisation is expected to continue to expand provided the banking sector remains stable over the long term. Time deposits make up a significant share of overall deposits from the general public in countries that are economically stable and perform strongly, such as Croatia. In contrast, deposits in BiH remain primarily short-term.

There is still room for a greater diversity of savings products, such as savings certificates, savings plans, housing savings plans that integrate both savings and credit elements (building society plans) and other long-term instruments. Long-term funding instruments, for example bonds or securities, do not yet play a significant role in SEE but could develop when the framework conditions (e.g. country and institutional ratings) are in place.

---

[31] Bank Austria Creditanstalt (2003b), pp. 13–23.

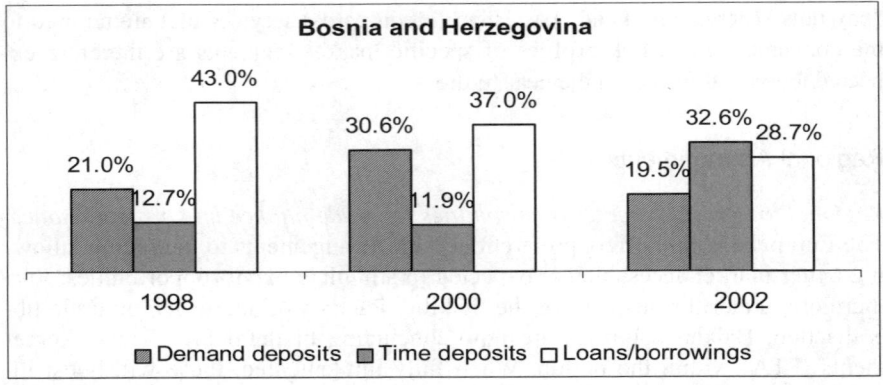

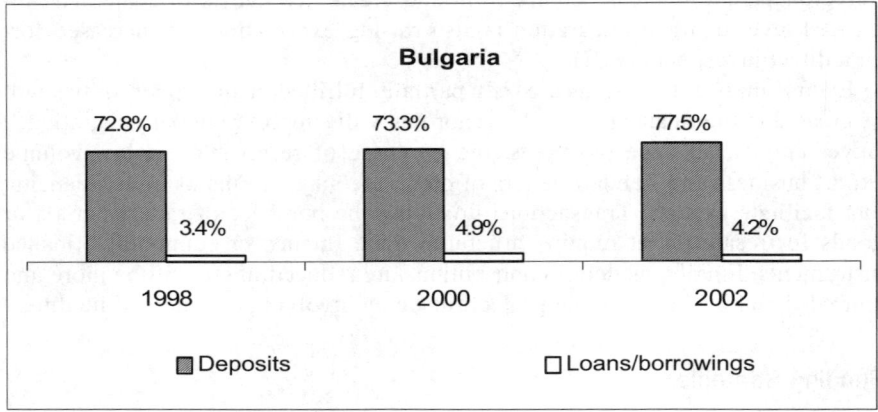

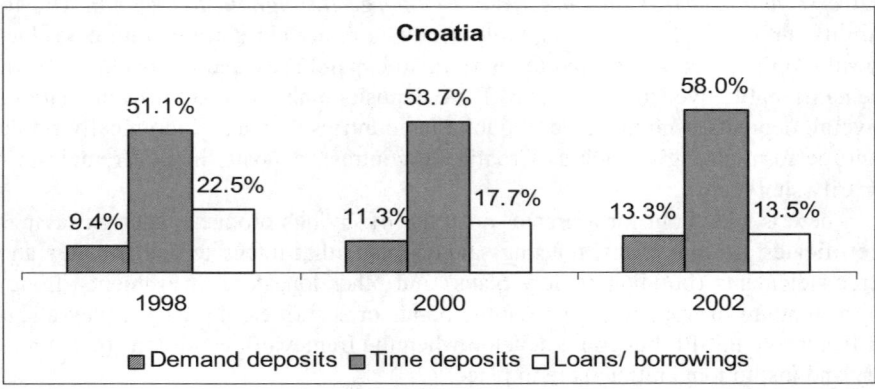

Figure 3. Liabilities of commercial banks in BiH, Bulgaria and Croatia

Source: CBBiH Annual Report 2002, p. 102; BNB Annual Report 1998, p. 148; 2000, p. 159; 2002, p. 169; Croatian National Bank Annual Report 2000 – 2002, p. 87.

Risk Management

The risk management of the banks has been fairly rudimentary throughout the region. This reflects the low level of market development and the limited technical skills and competencies in the banking sector. It also sheds some light on the degree of implementation of bank regulation and supervision.

Operating Risks

The EU accession process and Basel II will emphasise monitoring and mitigation of operational risks.[32] Many SEE commercial banks, particularly those under local ownership, exhibit weaknesses in internal control and audit. The fall of Rijecka Banka in Croatia serves as an example of how both a foreign majority shareholder, Bayerische Landesbank, and the Central Bank of Croatia were unable to identify fraudulent activities of a systematic nature conducted on a large scale. In addition to fraud, another "hot topic" is money laundering. Finally, the rapid expansion of ATMs, debit and credit cards and e-banking is evidence of the increasing importance of IT (information technology) systems. The associated technology risk is another form of operational risk (e.g. settlement failures).

On the path towards EU membership, assessing and mitigating operational risks will be high on the agenda of bank supervisors and commercial banks. An additional motivation for commercial banks to control operational risk is the reputational risk associated with the erosion of depositor confidence.

Credit Information Bureaus and Credit Scoring

The number and use of credit information bureaus will increase along with consumer lending. With rapid credit expansion, particularly in short-term consumer lending, borrowers' repayment histories become increasingly relevant in credit appraisal. At present, none of the SEE countries has a centralised facility to monitor repayment performance. However, in Albania and Serbia, initiatives have recently been started with a view to setting up such centralised facilities in close collaboration with the central banks.[33] In other countries, private credit informa-

---

[32] For a good summary of the Basel II approach to operational risk see Riskpartner (2002).

[33] In Albania, a donor project carried out by Deutsche Gesellschaft für Technische Zusammenarbeit (GTZ) GmbH in collaboration with Kreditschutzverband Österreich (KSV) is establishing an independent credit information bureau. In Serbia, a roundtable on setting up a centralised credit information bureau was organised in late 2002 by the National Bank of Serbia and the International Finance Corporation (IFC). The Banking Association of Serbia announced that such a facility would start operations in September 2004.

tion bureaus have emerged but still are the early stages of development. Microfinance institutions have been instrumental in developing some of these private initiatives, as in Kosovo and BiH.

Credit scoring will become part of credit risk management. As consumer lending loses its image as an "easy-going" business, commercial banks will screen clients with more care. In Poland, sophisticated scoring models have been developed to estimate the individual level of risk. These models are constantly updated and adjusted in response to changes in conditions. The development of comprehensive client databases has been the key to evaluating specific risks.[34] A similar development is likely in SEE. Foreign banks will probably lead the implementation of sophisticated risk-management tools because of their capacity to invest in IT systems and database development.

Variable Rate Euro Loans

Double-indexed loans might reduce exposure to interest rate risk but increase credit risk. Many banks lengthen their maturity structure in response to the high demand for housing loans while incurring foreign exchange risks. Nearly all these loans are both variable rate and indexed to the euro, so that they are double-indexed, which enables the lender to pass the foreign exchange risk to the borrower while increasing default risk. Most private households with housing loans do not generate income in hard currency. In some cases, family members living in Western Europe provide hard currency to offset this constraint. The importance of such transfers varies significantly throughout the region.

Maturity Mismatches

Domestic banks are more exposed to maturity mismatches and liquidity risks. Throughout the region, the banking sector's funding base is primarily short-term, creating widespread maturity mismatches. When the consumer lending boom comes to an end, and if the growth in housing loans continues, the maturity gap could become even larger.

The following tables show the maturity structures of a sample of domestic and foreign banks in Bulgaria, Bosnia and Herzegovina, and Serbia. Although not representative, they provide insights into some common features in the respective banking sectors.

---

[34] The Banker (2003).

Table 8. Maturity structure and liquidity gaps of selected commercial banks in Bulgaria, BiH and Serbia, end 2002

Bulgaria United Bulgarian Bank		BGN '000 000	
Time	*Financial assets*	*Financial liabilities*	*Liquidity gap*
0 – 30 days	1,072.7	1,196.6	-123.9
31 – 90 days	215.2	91.2	124.1
91 – 360 days	62.2	86.5	-23.9
31 – 360 days	277.9	177.7	100.2
over 1 year	301.1	11.8	289.3
Total	**1,651.7**	**1,386.0**	**265.6**

Source: Annual Report 2002, page 57.

Bulbank AD		BGN '000 000	
Time	*Financial assets*	*Financial liabilities*	*Liquidity gap*
0 – 30 days	1,215.3	1,060.3	155.0
31 – 90 days	161.2	152.7	8.5
91 – 360 days	334.5	174.7	159.8
31 – 360 days	495.7	327.4	168.3
over 1 year	1,011.0	821.1	189.9
Total	**2,722.0**	**2,208.7**	**513.2**

Source: Annual Report 2002, page 35.

Bosnia and Herzegovina Gospodarska Banka		KM '000 000	
Time	*Financial assets*	*Financial liabilities*	*Liquidity gap*
0 – 30 days	21.9	31.0	-9.1
31 – 90 days	7.0	10.3	-3.3
91 – 360 days	16.6	11.4	5.2
31 – 360 days	23.6	21.7	1.9
over 1 year	24.1	8.2	15.9
Total	**69.6**	**60.9**	**8.7**

Source: Annual Report 2002, obrazac br. 4 – Tabela C.

Table 8. (continued)

Raiffeisen Bank	KM '000 000		
Time	*Financial assets*	*Financial liabilities*	*Liquidity gap*
0–30 days	436.0	598.9	-162.9
31–90 days	146.6	118.8	27.8
91–360 days	101.1	57.3	43.8
31–360 days	247.7	176.2	71.6
over 1 year	274.0	148.2	125.8
Total	**957.8**	**923.3**	**34.4**

Source: Annual Report 2002, page 29.

Serbia Delta Banka A.D.	Din '000 000		
Time	*Financial assets*	*Financial liabilities*	*Liquidity gap*
0–30 days	16,111.7	20,994.5	-4,882.8
31–90 days	2,583.7	2,627.4	-43.6
91–360 days	6,130.5	644.0	5,486.5
31–360 days	8,714.3	3,271.4	5,442.9
over 1 year	3,106.2	183.1	2,923.2
Total	**27,932.2**	**24,448.9**	**3,483.3**

Source: Annual Report 2002, page 21.

ProCredit Banka	Din '000 000		
Time	*Financial assets*	*Financial liabilities*	*Liquidity gap*
0–30 days	1,906.1	2,238.3	-332.2
31–90 days	363.6	133.9	229.7
91–360 days	1,210.1	343.9	866.2
31–360 days	1,573.7	477.8	1,095.9
over 1 year	738.1	859.7	-121.5
Total	**4,217.9**	**3,575.8**	**642.1**

Source: Annual Report 2002, page 57.

The tables show that four out of the group of six banks have more short-term liabilities than financial assets falling due within 30 days. This indicates a potential liquidity shortage in the event that liabilities are not rolled over but are withdrawn on the due date. In terms of maturity mismatch and the associated liquidity risk, we must differentiate between foreign and local banks. Foreign banks[35] can manage their maturity mismatches through the liquidity back-up from their parent companies and their better standing in international money markets. This gives them a competitive edge over local banks,[36] which cannot draw on a secondary liquidity buffer and therefore might have to borrow funds on the international markets at much higher cost, assuming availability. Raiffeisen Bank Bosnia and Herzegovina, for example, cannot cover one quarter of its short-term liabilities (due within 30 days) by assets in the same maturity category. Given its parent bank liquidity back-up, however, it is probably in a more comfortable position than Universal Banka with a mismatch of more than 50%. ProCredit Banka Serbia may be in a similar position as its shareholders include Commerzbank, EBRD, FMO, IFC, IMI and KfW.

Increasingly stiff competition might tempt local banks to expand their credit business beyond prudent risk absorption capacities. Granting more long-term loans might be rational from a cost-efficiency perspective, but could negatively affect their liquidity by increasing the gap in the short-term category. Low repayment performance could make this even more threatening.

Interest Rate Risk

Management of interest risk might receive more attention with decreasing interest margins and more complex maturity structures. Interest risk management is at the bottom end of the priority list of commercial banks. Comfortable interest margins and the fact that banking transactions have been primarily short-term combine to reduce the level of risk. Interest risk will receive more attention in the future in countries where interest margins narrow and the maturity structures of assets and liabilities become more complex. Up to now, variable interest rates have been used to keep repricing gaps relatively small. However, over time, a variety of interest rate hedging techniques will be adopted in response to earnings pressure caused by volatile interest rates.

---

[35] Raiffeisen Bank, ProCredit Banka, Bulbank, and UBB. UBB was established in 1992 through the merger of 22 Bulgarian regional commercial banks. Its main shareholders are National Bank of Greece (89.9%) and EBRD (10%).

[36] Gospodarska Banka and Delta Banka.

Who Will Drive Financial Sector Development? Developing the Human Resource Base

The "people factor" is particularly critical in banking. Highly-skilled staff who understand the value of customer service are a core element of efficient and profitable banking. In comparison to many other transition economies, bank staff in SEE are highly skilled. The proportion who hold university degrees is rather high, at around 30%. However, despite the injection of "fresh blood" in the form of young, committed university graduates, many staff acquired their skills in the traditional Yugoslav banking system.

Except for Romania, Croatia and Serbia, the total number of bank staff is small. Due to the limited size of the sector, professional standards have barely developed.

Table 9. Number of bank staff, December 2002

Country	Number of bank staff
Albania	2,313
Bosnia and Herzegovina (BiH)	5,101
Croatia	16,051
Kosovo	1,944
Macedonia	4,569
Montenegro	951
Romania	43,602
Serbia	n.a.

Training Bank Staff

On-the-job and in-house training will continue to be the key instruments of staff development, while basic professional degrees will evolve later. In mature financial sectors, many bankers have professional degrees or qualifications. In Southeast Europe, these sophisticated and complex qualification systems will develop slowly, for several reasons:

- There is no local tradition of professional qualification in banking and finance.

- As a corollary to the first point, there is a lack of vocational training infrastructure. In the past, bank training was provided primarily by economic institutes and universities. Professional bank training institutes do not exist. Under the Stability Pact and within the framework of EU projects, various initiatives were started that aimed to set up bank training institutes from scratch in Albania, the Federation of Bosnia and Herzegovina, Republika Srpska, Serbia and Macedonia. These institutes are either still in their infancy or no longer in operation.

- As a result of reduced margins, cost-income ratios are closely monitored and cost-cutting is promoted. Therefore, commercial banks prefer in-house and on-the-job training as a cost-efficient alternative to external measures.

- Bank regulators do not require minimum professional qualifications for bank staff. "Fit" requirements are defined only for top managers, who generally hold a university degree.

Specialist Certifications

New, advanced professional degrees will develop along with product diversification and market growth. As was observed in many other transition countries, new professional degrees and qualifications evolve with new professions. One example is the mortgage lending segment, independent valuers – who generally gain certification after passing an examination – are critical for assessing the market value of real estate. Another example is the significance of the Certified Financial Planner (CFP) cachet, which has grown in response to the increasing importance of private banking. Moreover, developing stock exchanges require certified brokers or dealers. In summary, advanced professional qualifications that combine specific know-how with an ethics code will become increasingly relevant as markets mature.

Foreign Banks' Competitive Edge

Foreign banks' access to their parent companies' in-house training facilities gives them a continuous competitive edge over domestic banks. Foreign bank staff benefit from exchange programmes with the parent bank and are often sent abroad for training. Furthermore, these banks often have foreign managers who provide a day-to-day know-how transfer through coaching and their work with local staff.

Size of Workforce

Despite significant growth potential in this sector, the number of bank staff is not expected to rise significantly because the effect of growing markets will be offset by efficiency gains. Quite the contrary – the human resource base will be restructured. In the not yet privatised and transformed banks, older staff with limited skills will be let go through retrenchment, and young, motivated university graduates will be recruited. Efficiency gains are expected with an increase in the ratio of asset volume per staff member. However, restructuring will not be achieved easily or quickly.

Conclusions

The transition from a centrally planned to a market economy in Southeast Europe has resulted in the large-scale presence of foreign banks. This development is due to three factors: first, a deliberate policy to open up the banking sector to foreign direct investment in response to large public sector deficits that hindered the recapitalisation of ailing public banks; second, stronger bank regulation and supervision; and, third, the marketing and positioning strategies of international banks in preparation for the integrated European market.

In many countries, with the discussions on EU accession and the envisaged impact of Basel II, banking sector reforms have entered a second phase. This phase, with minor exceptions, will see the completion of bank privatisation. The further tightening of legal requirements will compel many banks, particularly smaller ones, to merge, providing a "second market opportunity" for foreign banks to strengthen their market positions. Overall, concentration in the banking sector is expected to increase. However, there will be room for specialised banks targeting specific market segments. The SME greenfield banks in most SEE countries, recently renamed ProCredit Banks, have significant potential for further growth, although they face many challenges. Of course, foreign bank presence is not a guarantee of success. These banks are only as good as their parent banks in their home countries. In several cases, the problems of foreign banks in their home markets have spilled over into Southeast Europe.

Market potential and product range will expand. Consumer lending is particularly attractive currently, albeit with the attendant credit-bubble risk which may result from imprudent lending in volatile markets. SMEs are perceived as an attractive client group. However, commercial banks accommodate only the upper tiers of the SME market, "picking the cherries" or "creaming the market." Microenterprises constitute a potentially large market, even where specialised SME greenfield banks and, in some countries, microcredit NGOs are the only providers of financial services. Leasing has expanded in several countries where the regulatory framework is conducive to this kind of business. There is substantial demand for housing finance, but the framework conditions are not well enough developed to facilitate the creation of mortgage markets. With the integration of regional markets, further business opportunities in trade and project finance are expected to develop.

Risk management, rudimentary to date, should become more sophisticated as a result of the EU accession process and Basel II. Particularly in credit risk management, new techniques and tools, ranging from increased use of credit information bureaus to credit scoring, are likely to be introduced in the short run. Liquidity risk arising from maturity mismatches is a problem in several countries. Foreign banks can generally cope with this better than domestic banks, using the liquidity buffers offered by their parent companies. Domestic banks may find themselves in an increasingly disadvantageous position.

Although the "people factor" is key to developing the banking sector as a service industry, professional standards are hardly developed due to the limited number of bank staff. As a general observation, commercial banks throughout the region invest little in staff training and professional upgrading. Besides on-the-job training and some in-house seminars, there is a lack of structured and systematic upgrading measures leading to professional degrees or qualifications. Only in a few niche segments are professional degrees likely to develop relatively soon. Foreign banks again have a competitive edge over their domestic competitors through their access to the in-house training facilities of their parent companies. With time, the existing human resource base will be restructured as veteran bank staff with limited skills are replaced by highly motivated younger employees.

References

Alexander, Arthur J. (1997): Consumer Credit in Japan since the Bubble Economy's End. Japan Economic Institute. Report No. 23, June. Tokyo.

Balcerowicz, Ewa and Bratkowski, Andrzej (2001): Restructuring and Development of the Banking Sector in Poland. Lessons to be Learned by Less Advanced Transition Countries. Center for Social and Economic Research Warsaw.

Bank Austria Creditanstalt (2003a): BiH – Schritt für Schritt in die wirtschaftliche Normalität. Osteuropa-Report Xplicit, September.

Bank Austria Creditanstalt (2003b): Investment Guide Bosnia and Herzegovina. Xplicit, September.

Bank of Albania (2003a): Governor Shkëlqim Cani, Press Release, April 25, 2003 (without title).

Bank of Albania (2003b): Meeting of the Supervisory Council of the Bank of Albania, Press Release, June 26, 2003.

Bank of Albania, Supervisory Council: Regulation for the granting of a license to conduct banking activity in the Republic of Albania.

Bank of Albania: Regulation on capital adequacy (Approved by Supervisory Council Decision no. 58 date 05.05.1999).

Banking and Payments Authority Kosovo: Amended Rule 1 on Capital Adequacy authorized under Section 13 of the Regulation.

Banking and Payments Authority Kosovo: Rule 21 on Increase in Minimum Capital of Banks Authorized under Section 5 of Regulation 1999/21.

Buch, Claudia M., Kleinert, Jörn and Zajc, Peter (2003): Foreign Bank Ownership: A Bonus or Threat for Financial Stability?

Bulbank A.D.: Bulgaria, Annual Report 2002.

Central Bank of Bosnia and Herzegovina: Annual Report 2002.

Commission of the European Communities (2003): Report from the Commission. The Stabilisation and Assocation Process for South East Europe. Second Annual Report. Brussels 26.3.2003.

Croatian National Bank: Annual Reports 2000–2002.

Croatian National Bank: Banking Law, Articles 15 & 65.

Delta Banka A.D.: Serbia, Annual Report 2002.

Directorate General for Economic and Financial Affairs (2003): The Western Balkans in Transition. Occasional Papers No. 1.

European Bank for Reconstruction and Development: Transition Report Update May 2003.

Focarelli, Dario and Pozzolo, Alberto Franco (2003): Where do Banks Expand Abroad? An Empirical Analysis. Economis & Statistics Discussion Paper No. 9. Università degli Studi del Molise. Facoltà di Economia. Campobasso.

Gospodarska Banka, Bosnia and Herzegovina: Annual Report 2002.

Hegedüs, József (2002): Housing Finance in South Eastern Europe. Metropolitan Research Institute Budapest.

Lafferty Group (2003): Credit Cards in Asia-Pacific, 2003–2005. A Lafferty Multi-Client Research Study.

Maurer, Klaus and Wisniwski, Sylvia (2002): Impact of Financial Sector Projects in Southeast Europe – Effects on Financial Institutions and the Financial Sector, in: Ingrid Matthäus-Maier and J.D. von Pischke, eds., The Development of the Financial Sector in Southeast Europe – Innovative Approaches in Volatile Environments. Berlin, Springer, 2004.

Merrill, Sally, Rabenhorst, Carol and Sacks, Paul (2003a): Developing Secondary Mortgage Markets in Southeast Europe. Assessment of the Mortgage Market in Croatia. Washington, DC.

Merrill, Sally, Rabenhorst, Carol and Sacks, Paul (2003b): Developing Secondary Mortgage Markets in Southeast Europe. Assessment of the Mortgage Market in Romania. Washington, DC.

ProCredit Banka, Serbia: Annual Report 2002.

Raiffeisen Bank, Bosnia and Herzegovina: Annual Report 2002.

Riskpartner (2002): Operational Risk as defined by Basle II. Luxemburg.

The Banker (2004): Eyes on the prize. April. Financial Times Business Ltd. London.

The Banker (2003): Lenders hatch cautious consumer credit plans. September. Financial Times Business Ltd. London.

United Bulgarian Bank, Bulgaria: Annual Report 2002.

Universal Banka, Bosnia and Herzegovina: Annual Report 2002.

Uygur, Ercan (2001): Krizden Krize Türkiye: 2000 Kasim Ve 2001 Subat Krizleri (Turkey – From Crisis to Crisis: November 2000 to February 2001), Discussion Paper 2001/1, Türkiye Economi Kurumu. Istanbul.

Wisniwski, Sylvia (2003): European Fund for Bosnia and Herzegovina (EFBH). Fifth Annual Evaluation 2003.

Annex 1

Table 10. Interest rates and interest rate spreads in selected countries (in %)

Country		1999	2000	2001	2002
Albania	Deposit rate (1 year)	9.1	7.7	7.7	8.5
	Lending rate (1 year)	25.8	23.7	24	14.5
	Interest rate spread	16.7	16	16.3	6
Bulgaria	Deposit rate (1 month)	3.3	3.1	2.9	2.9
	Lending rate (< one year)	14.1	11.5	11.1	8.7
	Interest rate spread	10.8	8.4	8.2	5.8
Croatia	Deposit rate	4.3	3.4	2.8	n.a.
	Lending rate	13.5	10.5	9.5	n.a.
	Interest rate spread	9.2	7.1	6.7	n.a.
Macedonia	Deposit rate	11.3	10.7	10	9.2
	Lending rate	20	19	19.2	17.7
	Interest rate spread	8.7	8.3	9.2	8.5
Romania	Deposit rate (average)	45.4	32.7	23.4	12.8
	Lending rate (average)	65.9	53.5	40.6	28.9
	Interest rate spread	20.5	20.8	17.2	16.1
Serbia and Montenegro	Deposit rate	13.1	8.3	4.1	2.6
	Lending rate	45.4	77.9	32.5	19.2
	Interest rate spread	32.3	69.6	28.4	16.6
Kosovo	Deposit rate (1 year)	n.a.	n.a.	2.68	2.68
	Lending rate (1 year)	n.a.	n.a.	15.03	15.6
	Interest rate spread	n.a.	n.a.	12.35	12.92

Source: EBRD, Transition Report Update May 2003, pp. 40 – 81.

Annex 2

Table 11. Interest rate gap, Bosnia and Herzegovina and Serbia 2002

Bosnia and Herzegovina Universal Banka		KM million	
Time	Financial assets	Financial liabilities	Liquidity gap
0 – 30 days	256.3	196.2	60.1
31 – 90 days	0.4	0.7	-0.3
91 – 360 days	1.7	0.7	1.0
31 – 360 days	2.1	1.4	0.6
over 1 year	6.7	30.0	-23.3
Non-interest bearing	49.7	58.3	-8.6
Total	**314.8**	**286.0**	**28.9**

Source: Annual Report 2002, p. 34.

Table 11. (continued)

Raiffeisen Bank	KM million		
Time	*Financial assets*	*Financial liabilities*	*Liquidity gap*
0 – 30 days	318.1	436.4	-118.3
31 – 180 days	146.6	118.8	27.7
181 – 360 days	101.1	57.3	43.8
31 – 360 days	247.7	176.2	71.6
over 1 year	274.0	89.0	185.0
Non-interest bearing	117.9	221.7	-103.8
Total	**957.8**	**923.3**	**34.4**

Source: Annual Report 2002, p. 26.

Serbia Delta Banka A.D.	Din million		
Time	*Financial assets*	*Financial liabilities*	*Liquidity gap*
0 – 30 days	13,110.3	1,996.1	11,114.3
31 – 180 days	5,369.2	3,453.3	1,915.9
181 – 360 days	3,928.2	285.0	3,643.2
31 – 360 days	9,297.5	3,738.3	5,559.2
over 1 year	1,286.6	102.6	1,184.0
Non-interest bearing	4,237.8	18,612.0	-14,374.2
Total	**27,923.2**	**24,448.9**	**3,483.3**

Source: Annual Report 2002, p. 21.

ProCredit Banka	Din million		
Time	*Financial assets*	*Financial liabilities*	*Liquidity gap*
0 – 30 days	3,573.3	1,867.2	1,706.1
31 – 180 days	121.8	784.5	-662.7
181 – 360 days	46.2	228.8	-182.6
31 – 360 days	168.0	1,013.3	-845.3
over 1 year	2.8	326.8	-324.0
Non-interest bearing	473.7	368.5	105.2
Total	**4,217.9**	**3,575.8**	**642.1**

Source: Annual Report 2002, p. 56.

CHAPTER 12:

Evolution of the Banking Sector in Southeast Europe – The Role and Business Strategies of Domestic Banks

Per Fischer

Senior Vice President, Commerzbank AG

Foreign banks play a dominant role in the financial markets of Southeast Europe (SEE), as they do in Poland, the Czech Republic, Hungary and Slovakia. Foreign bank penetration varies from country to country, accounting for 90% of total bank assets in Croatia (the highest proportion), 46% in Albania and 7% in Montenegro (the lowest proportion). It can be argued that indigenous banks, whether state or privately owned, play only a minor and increasingly marginal role.

With few exceptions, purely indigenous banks in SEE will either be transferred to foreign ownership or become niche players, as has happened in the larger EU accession countries in Central Europe. The few exceptions will be those indigenous banks that:

- quickly develop a strategy that builds on their local market strengths;
- catch up with contemporary Western banking expertise;
- recruit professional staff; and
- look for healthy expansion in markets beyond their own national borders.

How Did Foreign Banks Enter These Markets?

Foreign banks have a variety of strategies for entering SEE markets. Some set up regional offices or subsidiary banks as part of an overall regional strategy, maintaining their own name and brand. In these cases, Southeast Europe is part of a wider strategy, taking in the whole of Eastern Europe and the Commonwealth of Independent States (CIS). Spectacular examples of this strategy include Raiffeisen Zentralbank Österreich (RZB) and, to some extent, Hypo Vereinsbank (HVB). These banks started out by focusing mainly on corporate banking and then took very systematic steps to develop their retail and private banking business.

Other banks have gradually acquired majority interests in larger local banks, preserving the existing names. They bought their way in directly, by acquiring leading positions in extensive networks. They accepted the risk of dormant legacy burdens and the costs of the comprehensive integration processes that were necessary in areas such as risk control, IT and even corporate strategy. Notable examples include Unicredito, which acquired Zagrebacka Banka; Intesa Banca, which acquired Privredna Banka in Croatia; and Société Générale, which acquired BRD in Romania. Commerzbank pursued a similar strategy by buying BRE Bank in Poland. The respected and familiar name of BRE Bank was retained as a signal to the Polish market that the new owner respected the indigenous bank's thoroughly successful business concept.

Clearly, Western banks employ multiple market penetration models. In Central Europe, Commerzbank launched greenfield bank branches and took equity participations in seven microfinance banks, mostly in the Balkans.[1] RZB's acquisition of Banca Agricola in order to gain a foothold in the Romanian market was another approach. Market entry has not always followed a set pattern, nor does it have to do so: there is room for a broad spectrum of strategies.

The Situation of the Remaining Indigenous Banks

There are three categories of remaining indigenous banks:

- Large domestic banks under state ownership. Typical examples are Banca Comerciala Romana (BCR), long earmarked for privatisation and in which IFC and EBRD have 25% stakes, and the Savings Bank of Albania, also to be privatised. Serbia's Vojvodjanska Banka, which is large relative to its national market, needs restructuring. Factors specific to Serbia – restructuring and the Paris Club – mean that certain balance sheet risks will have to be spun off before such an investor can be found.

- Banks that are majority-owned by the indigenous private sector. There are several examples: Delta Banka and Komercijalna Bank in Serbia occupy a dominant market position in certain fields. Others are typical niche banks with a small market share, such as Istarska Kreditna Banka and Partner Banka in Croatia and Gospodarska Banka in Bosnia, which specialise in retail banking.

- Banks owned by foreign nonbank investors: these include Romania's Robank, Croatia's Nova Banka and Bulgaria's Hebros Bank.

---

[1] Jan Baechle, "Equity Participation in Microfinance Banks in Southeast Europe and Georgia – A Strategic Option for a Large Private German Bank?" in Ingrid Matthäus-Maier and J.D. von Pischke, eds., *The Development of the Financial Sector in Southeast Europe: Innovative Approaches in Volatile Environments*. Berlin: Springer, 2004. pp. 135–139.

Activities of the International Financial Institutions (IFIs)

The presence of the IFIs varies considerably in Southeast Europe. As minority shareholders, they play an important part in developing the region's financial sector. In some cases, they act as strategic investors in major institutions for a transitional period, or as minority shareholders until a strategic investor is found. They may also acquire equity stakes in smaller institutions as a platform for restructuring the balance sheet, transferring knowledge and integrating these institutions into Western markets in the absence of a strategic investor. The IFIs participate in microfinance banks whose specialised business model focuses on loans and funding for small and medium-sized enterprises.

Foreign Banks Set the Standard for the Development of Local Financial Markets

Foreign banks not only dominate markets in almost all Southeast European countries, they also set the standard in virtually every field of business. The major foreign banks operate a no-gaps business model, offering a full complement of corporate and private banking services, deposit business, card business and treasury services. They are also moving into leasing in countries that permit banks to do this, primarily Croatia and Romania. While the foreign banks show little or no interest in micro and small scale lending, they are increasingly wooing middle-range customers, intensifying competition with the ProCredit banks that specialise in serving micro, small and, to a limited extent, medium-sized businesses.

The development of domestic capital markets is an area of growing significance in Southeast Europe. Equally important is the possibility of financing local companies via foreign capital markets. Major foreign-owned banks have a clear advantage because they can tap capital market funding through their parent organisations. This is the point at which the level of development and privatisation of indigenous banking markets dovetails with the privatisation and restructuring of large corporations, providing opportunities for banking relationships at the high end of the market. But only those companies that already have a healthy balance sheet, functioning corporate governance structures and good credit histories will be able to access foreign capital markets via institutions owned by major foreign banks.

Business Models of Indigenous Banks That Are Not Foreign Owned

Large financial institutions, such as BCR, exert a dominant influence in many cases and command a strong market position in the provision of services to indigenous – especially state-owned – corporates. It is nevertheless debatable whether BCR will be able to survive in a fully competitive market.

As large companies are privatised, political patronage plays a diminishing role. Corporate customers increasingly demand intelligent product solutions coupled with good service. This poses a danger to local banks that fail to innovate. They will increasingly be forced into low-margin, bread-and-butter lending.

Indigenous banks that are state owned, privately owned or that have a mixed ownership structure can also assume a dominant position in serving private customers, as demonstrated by Komercijalna Banka in Serbia with its excellent track record in deposit-taking. To defend such positions, they must offer high-quality service, stay close to their customers, achieve economies of scale and subject their branch systems to rigorous cost-benefit analyses. In the future, these institutions will also face foreign competition in market segments which entail more complex operations, such as asset management.

In summary, to the degree that local markets open up, the standards in banking and finance will increasingly be set by foreign institutions. The indigenous banks that remain will have to adapt in order to preserve the positions they currently enjoy. For many, the focus on quality-based niche strategies will be essential.

Promising Strategies for Indigenous Banks Without Foreign Shareholders

Purely indigenous banks must begin by identifying, defending and building on their strengths in local markets. Strengths may include easier access to deposit business, healthy networking with local firms and with government and local authority organisations, or simply a deeper understanding of the market and the local mentality. To preserve these strengths, they must recruit professional staff who can develop intelligent products and modern forms of customer service.

One very useful option is to collaborate closely with a foreign bank in organising training programmes and technical assistance, e.g. to promote small and medium-sized firms. Although experience varies, all local banks have shown interest in technical assistance when offered by EBRD, KfW or IFC programmes.

If banks are to perform successfully, it is also important that they are free to determine their own strategy and to run their day-to-day business without political interference. Eastern Europe provides many examples of business leaders who have been able to ward off predation. However, this self-assertion makes them attractive to foreign banks, which have often acquired them, as in the case of Priorbank in Minsk.

OTP Bank in Hungary has thrived, using regional expansion to defend its market position. This example will be important for banks that pursue a universal strategy and strive to hold or gain a large share of the market. Whatever the case, it is safe to assume that as the EU expands eastwards, the financial and banking markets of the Balkan countries will converge into regional financial and banking markets. Cross-border banking will grow in importance.

Summary

The bottom line is that indigenous institutions can indeed survive. Depending on regulatory and political decisions, they will be exposed to different degrees of competitive pressure. As these markets open up, governments will have to lower the protectionist barriers designed to safeguard their own banking systems.

However, faced with the ever more powerful presence of foreign banks, domestic banks have one chance and one chance only: they must focus on their core competence, build on it, expand their business models, attain comparable or better levels of quality in the area of human resources, and install IT and risk management systems on a par with those of their foreign rivals. Depending on their business model, they must either expand beyond their own borders or concentrate on their niche segments in order to defend their home turf against foreign competition.

CHAPTER 13:

Financing Small and Medium-Sized Companies

Mita Katic

General Manager, Kulska banka a.d.

The majority of economists would agree that small and medium-sized enterprises (SMEs) are the most important factor in a country's economy. This is especially so in transition economies, where big systems that include large firms and major banks face significant problems.

Policy Changes and Structural Changes

In the past, huge economic entities formed the economic backbone of the former Socialist Federal Republic of Yugoslavia (SFRY), later the SRY. These economic giants were characterised by inflexibility – they were unable to react promptly to changing local and regional environments. Nevertheless, large companies were excellent clients for the banking sector, paying high interest rates, especially in the period up to 2000. With the onset of the economic transition process, the banking system had to cope with the accumulated debts of these companies, for which the banks themselves bore some responsibility. Some clients had been given loans without any assessment of their creditworthiness. This approach could not continue indefinitely; the consequences of such credit policies and procedures have since become abundantly clear.

It was therefore imperative to react at the first signs of change, yet only big banks could serve big networks, especially during the last ten years of the old system. With the changes in the region, most importantly the establishment of relations with economically strong European countries, the socialist countries faced a different economic environment. Since the early-1990s, their political and economic structures have gradually been adapting to the new environment; the pace of change varying from country to country. These changes were also felt in the Federal Republic of Yugoslavia, now Serbia and Montenegro, and have left their mark on the banking sector as well.

The economic reforms in Serbia and Montenegro are not yet completed. At a conservative estimate, only around one-third of the reform process is complete. The changes in the economic system are very pragmatic, but nevertheless painful. There are currently very few sound enterprises in Serbia and Montenegro, and creating more is proving difficult. Since 2000, the number of foreign banks in our market has grown to 12. These banks start with a much healthier capital base than the majority of domestic banks, giving them a distinct advantage. As a result, the domestic banks are facing increasingly stiff competition. To survive, they have had to choose a market-driven business policy. Aware that big regional banks will serve the larger players in the economies of Southeast Europe, domestic banks are left to find their clients among small and medium-sized companies as a way of slowly strengthening their economic position.

Kulska Banka Support for Microentrepreneurs and SMEs

Kulska banka a.d. was founded in Novi Sad in 1995. Since its founding it has had to adjust to significant political and economic changes. Kulska banka has oriented its operations towards small and medium-sized companies, which are one of the healthiest parts of our economy. The fact that Kulska banka was ranked thirteenth in asset size on a list of banks compiled by the National Bank of Serbia in mid-2003 can be taken as confirmation of the soundness of our business strategy. This result puts us ahead of some competitors founded by foreign banks or financial institutions.

Kulska banka is orienting its business more and more towards entrepreneurs and small and medium-sized enterprises, i.e. companies with up to 250 employees, total income of not more than € 10 million and assets valued at up to € 5 million. The importance of this category of companies is increasing as they continue to offer employment opportunities to the huge number of workers made redundant from socially-owned and state-owned companies.

The state is interested in supporting this sector. The Serbian Agency for Development of Small and Medium-sized Companies estimates that 370,000 persons or more are registered as owners of such companies, and that these owners have created jobs for 310,000 employees. It is estimated that more than 100,000 persons work in small and medium-sized private companies and in shops in the grey market without being on the official employment register. In total, small and medium-sized companies and private shops therefore employ around 800,000 persons.

The importance of small and medium-sized companies for Kulska banka is that they operate in strategically important activities, including manufacturing and various service sectors such as information technology, communications and tourism. According to Ministry of Economy and Privatisation figures, there were 66,218 small and medium-sized companies and only 742 big companies in Serbia in 2002. This is another important element that shaped Kulska banka's business policy. By issuing relatively small loans to a large number of small and medium-sized companies operating in a variety of business sectors, the bank diversifies its lending operations and reduces risk.

For very small amounts (€ 1,000 to € 2,000), the bank uses an extremely simplified micro-lending procedure developed in Kulska's retail sector and, as a means of attracting more clients, it is now offering payment services. However, the bank also makes larger loans: it is aiming for a minimum loan amount to small and medium-sized companies of at least € 10,000, as the costs of loan approval for small amounts exceed the benefits. Higher loan amounts lead the way to higher interest margins and are thus more attractive for the bank.

Under an arrangement with KfW in Germany and ING Bank in the Netherlands (guaranteed by KfW), Kulska banka grants long-term loans which vary in size between € 1,000 and € 50,000. These are among the bank's smallest corporate loans. The lending methodology adopted in the framework of cooperation with KfW through 2002 proved very successful. Based on information obtained from clients and potential clients, Kulska banka sees a demand for long-term loans of between € 100,000 and € 200,000 that should perform well. The bank also has an arrangement with Commerzbank in Germany which enables it to make long-term loans of € 750,000 or more. Through late 2003, Kulska banka had disbursed loans worth € 4.1 million, and its clients are servicing their loans regularly.

Outlook

The ongoing dynamic development of the private sector in Serbia is an indication that small and medium-sized companies will in future play an even more important role in the development of the economy. Kulska banka sees great opportunities for lending to this sector. The experience gained within the framework of co-operation with KfW showed demand for medium-term and long-term loans in this sector to be high; loan quality is also high. With the experience gained to date and the potential for growth in this market segment, Kulska banka is convinced that its strategic focus on financing and supporting small and medium-sized companies will continue to pay off.

CHAPTER 14:

The Business Strategies of Domestic Banks in the Long Run – SME Lending as an Attractive Market Segment

Evgeny Gospodinov

Executive Director, Unionbank, Sofia

Introduction[1]

Unionbank was established as a bank in 1994, and in 1999 it started lending to SMEs. This was the result of an innovative project in Bulgaria based on government and private agreements with IFIs (international financial institutions). Unionbank benefited from considerable technical assistance provided under two agreements, first and most importantly with IPC, Germany, and secondly with Bannock Consulting, UK. In 2000, Unionbank launched another project that was innovative for Bulgaria, featuring loans to grain producers and traders against warehouse receipts issued by licensed public warehouses.

The Bulgarian banking system is currently very strong. It has recovered from the severe crisis in 1996–97, after which a currency board was introduced. There are now 34 commercial banks in Bulgaria, only one of which is state owned. The share of bank assets owned by foreign banks is close to 90% (Table 1). An overview of the sector is presented in Table 2.

What Role will Domestic Banks play in the Long Run? What are the Most Promising Business Strategies?

Bank privatisation in Bulgaria ended with the purchase of DSK Bank, a savings bank, by OTP (Hungary's National Savings and Commercial Bank) in 2003. Bulgaria's banking market is dominated by foreign banks. In general, this has had a

---

[1] This paper reflects the personal views and opinion of the author and should not be associated in any way with the institution he represents. The paper deliberately aims to be provocative in order to stimulate discussion. It deals solely with the Bulgarian market and the author's personal experience as an executive director of CB Unionbank AD – a private bank with majority local ownership (consisting of 4 principal Bulgarian shareholders). In late-2002, the EBRD acquired a 15% equity stake in Unionbank.

Table 1. Bulgarian banking sector: asset distribution (as at June 30, 2003)*

Group	Number	%	Total assets BGN '000	%
Banks under foreign management and control	23	68	13,132,022	85.5
Locally owned banks	11	32	2,227,729	14.5
Total	34	100	15,359,751	100

* as per BNB Quarterly Bulletin – Commercial Banks in Bulgaria.

Table 2. Bulgarian banking sector: key statistics (as at June 30, 2003)*

Group	Number of banks	%	Total assets BGN million	%	Net loans to customers BGN million	%
Group 1	10	29	11,513	75	5,401	74
Group 2	18	53	2,967	19	1,391	19
Group 3	6	18	879	6	509	7
Total	34	100	15,359	100	7,301	100

Group	Deposits from non-financial institutions BGN million	%	Capital base BGN million	%	Net profit BGN million	%
Group 1	9,030	76	1,613	76	179	81
Group 2	1,998	17	476	23	32	15
Group 3	782	7	19	1	8	4
Total	11,810	100	2,107	100	219	100

Note: Columns may not sum to totals due to rounding errors.

The Bulgarian National Bank applies the following criteria to define the 3 groups:
Group 1 – first 10 banks in terms of assets,
Group 2 – all other banks,
Group 3 – local branches of foreign banks.

The Bulgarian lev (BGN) is pegged to the euro (€ 1 = BGN 1.95583).

positive impact, bringing new products, IT solutions, know-how and approaches as well as increased discipline and competition. The result is better quality services, lower prices and a stronger banking system.

However, the benefits are not only a result of active foreign presence: foreign ownership is not necessarily a guarantee for the success of a bank. In Southeast Europe, and especially in the Balkans, it is important to be in tune with the mentality of the customer, to speak to local clients in their language, and to be able to understand not only what they say but also what goes unsaid. Even at the current stage of IT development and with the mass usage of electronic banking services, most local customers need to know the banker on the other side of the counter.

The foreign banks may be divided into two major groups: first, those fighting predominantly for the business of large international corporations; second those also aiming to attract local customers. The second group poses the real threat to the local banks. The two groups can easily be distinguished by the nationality of their top managers, the first group being run mostly by managers from abroad, the second group by Bulgarian nationals.

However, even after Bulgaria has joined the EU and the domestic economy and the banking sector have become fully integrated into the global economy, local banks – with their flexibility, responsiveness and speed – will still maintain market share. Even the large local companies which tend to use the services of foreign banks would prefer to share their ideas with local banks when opportunities arise for specific business projects. When dealing with local banks, these clients need not be afraid that their ideas will be copied and used by a company in the home country of the foreign bank, or that the reply to the application will be delayed so that the foreign competitor will be the first in the market with the new idea.

But these are all medium-term considerations. In the long run, the economic significance of national borders will decline, and commerce and manufacturing will be viewed in a broader context rather than solely in local terms. The local banks will then have only few options: one is to merge – a difficult and time-consuming process given the interests of the different local owners. This option involves staying in the market, establishing and maintaining a significant presence and market share, and taking full advantage of the local label. The second option is to aim for business development, specialising in specific fields or products with a view to attracting the attention of a strong strategic foreign investor, either as a joint venture partner or as a potential purchaser of the business.

Regardless of the approach adopted, local banks are not advised to try to compete with foreign banks product range, pricing or profitability. They should aim to identify specific areas in which they have an advantage and where they thrive as niche players and service innovators. In addition, local banks are advised to market specific products and to offer a more personal and friendly approach to doing business, rather than providing customers with a cool and impersonal service.

How has Unionbank developed and what has it learned to date? From the outset, it was a small local bank, extremely conservative in developing its lending and investment activities and branch network. The mainstay of its business operations were foreign exchange (FX) transactions, trade finance and accurate, quick payments in local and foreign currency. Before the banking crisis of 1996–97, it was possible to operate profitably and develop the business on the basis of these activities. After the crisis, the currency board was introduced, reducing FX gains, and foreign banks started to penetrate the market and attract the best customers. The bank's owners had to decide whether to stay or to sell. Having decided on the former option, it was then necessary for the bank to find a niche.

At that time, all the banks were fighting to attract blue chip accounts, and no one paid much attention to SMEs. In 1999, Unionbank responded with a new service, and so became known as the "bank for SMEs." Little by little, lending volume grew, and between 2001 and 2003 the number of branches and offices expanded from four to twenty. Since 2002, although competition in the SME banking sector has increased without interruption, Unionbank has maintained its reputation as an effective and efficient service provider to the SME sector.

In 2000, Unionbank launched a pilot project for lending against warehouse receipts. Although a very large foreign bank introduced a similar service around the same time, Unionbank proved to be the more successful. Since 2002, despite the fact that other banks have followed our lead, Unionbank still holds more than 50% of the market.

The Market for SME Lending in Bulgaria and for Unionbank

SME lending is definitely interesting and profitable, especially for a smaller local bank whose strategy is to be a leader and innovator in this market segment. The most important preconditions for success are:

- the opportunity to be among the first to move into this type of business;
- access to external medium to long-term financing;
- access to technical assistance and professional advice;
- the will and discipline to follow professional advice, no matter how unorthodox it seems at first in the particular market context;
- at least 1 or 2 years' lead in building a market niche before a ProCredit Bank or MEB (microenterprise bank) enters the market.

Unionbank was fortunate to have met all the above preconditions when it started serving SMEs in 1999. As a result, it now has a significant competitive advantage over most local banks and has made great progress. The key data in Unionbank's development are summarised below:

- it entered the market when there were no major players and established a solid position and a name as a local SME bank;
- in the last 4 years its customer base – small and medium-sized companies in Bulgaria – has grown rapidly;

- it has benefited from state-of-the-art professional advice and has adopted a modern methodology for credit analysis and screening loan applicants;
- it has established new SME lending practices which provide a continuous income flow for the bank;
- the focus on SME business led to the establishment of credit relationships with institutions such as KfW, IFC and EBRD (which became a shareholder in 2002) and access to funds which were not available in the local market;
- the branch network has grown almost five-fold, bringing services closer to the clients;
- a graded or tiered credit approval system was established, and local loan committees with their own credit authority were set up in all branches, including the new ones;
- each branch was staffed so that it could operate like a small separate bank;
- the bank established a training system to qualify staff for special tasks;
- a bonus system was introduced;
- the bank was able to command higher interest margins because of its specialisation and service quality;
- the bank started an active advertising campaign, making it more widely known, not only among SMEs;
- many micro and small business clients now perform more solidly; they have continued their relationship with Unionbank, helping create a larger and more stable income base for the bank.

Although MSE lending has been an overwhelming success, it should be pointed out that Unionbank never designated microlending as its core business. One of the main reasons is the lack of additionality in this sector: the bank sees the borrower once a month on the loan due date and otherwise gains little additional business. Unionbank's experience shows that the lower "frontier" for SME lending in the Bulgarian market is about €3,000 to €5,000. The microenterprise banks are best suited to serve this market.

Conclusions

The author is in full agreement with the conclusions drawn in the theme paper.

CHAPTER 15:

Building a Market Niche Also Builds a Market – Opportunity Bank in Montenegro

Keith Flintham

Chief Executive Officer, Opportunity Bank, Montenegro

Opportunity Bank, Montenegro is part of the Opportunity International (OI) Network, a not-for-profit corporation established more than three decades ago, and specialises in the provision of microfinance. OI now operates in more than thirty nations worldwide. In countries where the political, economic, business and regulatory environment is considered acceptable, OI is establishing greenfield banking institutions or converting existing microfinance entities.

In Montenegro, OI's microfinance activities started in 1999. Following the resounding success in the market, Opportunity Bank was established in 2002 with 100% foreign capital. The bank opened its doors in Podgorica on 1 July 2002. Since then, branches have been set up in four other towns throughout the country.

Is SME Lending an Interesting Market Segment?

In order to answer this question comprehensively from the point of view of both Montenegro and Opportunity Bank itself, it is necessary to consider the unique aspects of Opportunity International. One of its key objectives is to improve the lives of disadvantaged people generally, by assisting them in their small business ventures. Initially, activities were largely restricted to the provision of microfinance to this target group, most often using a group lending methodology. The size and type of finance products continues to vary from continent to continent, and the differences between Europe and other regions are quite dramatic.

Whilst microfinance remains OI's dominant activity, it recognises that not all disadvantaged persons have the capability or ambition to set up their own micro businesses. For this reason, Opportunity provides active financial support to the SME sector, too, particularly in Europe. This sector's credit requirements are not fully met, and it plays a vital role in the transition economy while increasing employment prospects.

As well as being in line with Opportunity International's mission, SME lending is also perceived as an attractive segment for the following reasons:

- in comparison with the corporate market:
    - interest margins are higher
    - borrowers make mortgage security readily available
    - SMEs demonstrate greater loyalty to their (sole) bank
    - a loan officer is often able to obtain a better overall understanding of the client's business and to develop a closer working relationship;
- SMEs have historically been neglected by banks;
- there is significant demand for medium-term finance for capital investment;
- commissions and fees on payment and other services enhance the overall return on banking relationships;
- many loyal micro clients have transitioned into the SME sector;
- SMEs have a positive impact on the economy, benefiting banks at the macro level through an overall reduction of risk;
- client relationship management can be introduced, which is almost unheard of in the local banking community;
- quality services in line with international standards have a major impact on business generation.

Not unexpectedly, there are some drawbacks in the SME sector:

- an absence of reliable (audited) financial information;
- the business planning skills in SMEs are often poor;
- in some cases, a lower level of management expertise than in a larger corporates;
- the need for highly skilled and well-trained loan officers who have the ability to compensate for the deficiencies of the client in key business-skill areas;
- the credit assessment process for SMEs in this region has to be similar to microlending methodologies, which generally inhibits commercial banks that lack microlending experience.

The Market Potential for SME Lending

In Montenegro, the banking community has historically neglected the SME sector. Short-term finance was scarce and medium and long-term loans non-existent. The significant market potential for SME lending in Montenegro can largely be attributed to:

- the considerable unsatisfied demand as a result of the continuing reluctance of banks to lend to the sector;

- government policy aimed at reducing the size of the grey economy;

- more businesses being registered with the introduction of VAT;

- recent import regulations that have increased SMEs' demand for working capital;

- the number of micro clients that transition into the SME sector;

- the increase in the size of the SME sector as a result of privatisation.

Opportunity Bank's lending potential is significant in Montenegro for the following reasons:

- as a wholly foreign-owned bank, Opportunity Bank is generally excluded from the traditional Montenegrin mistrust of banks and is perceived as a "safe home" for clients' business, including deposits;

- the presence of foreign executives and banking experts increases client perception of the Bank's professionalism and strict adherence to confidentiality;

- all members of staff handling SME business relationships have received intensive training;

- credit assessment methodology has been developed specifically for Montenegro and other countries in the region;

- relationship management techniques have been introduced;

- the bank's high-quality services and its policies and procedures are in line with international standards and compare very favourably with other banks;

- many former micro clients grow into SME businesses, and their loyalty provides a basis for continuing banking relationships.

Definition of the Upper and Lower Sizes of SME Loans

In many developed economies, the question for banks moving down market is related less to the size of loans than to deciding which division of the bank should take responsibility for the client relationship. This is usually defined by a combination of the size of the SME in terms of turnover, capital and reserves, and the number of employees. The level of borrowing and bank services that an SME desires are considered by the bank in assessing the profitability of the client relationship and therefore the amount of relationship-management time that can be devoted to that client.

In Montenegro, Opportunity Bank initially adopted a relatively simple approach, setting the upper frontier at € 10,000, which was the maximum loan size in the predecessor microfinance organisation. However, this policy has since been reviewed to take into account, firstly, the extent to which a client requires nonlending bank services and, secondly, the estimated potential for a client to progress to full SME status.

As an example of this client-centred strategy, a new product has been developed that represents a prequalification stage for a full SME product. This product is designed as a bridge for micro clients that have the capacity to grow into small enterprises. It is very popular and is virtually unique in the market; Opportunity Bank is recognised as a strong supporter of these businesses in transition. These clients prove to be more loyal than many others and become more and more bankable each day.

As a criterion for evaluating the activities of Opportunity Bank and other commercial microfinance institutions, minimum loan size is not of major importance. What is important is that we create opportunity in the micro sector. Our smallest loan in Montenegro is generally not less than € 1,000, but in certain circumstances can be as low as low as € 500.

It is incorrect to state that microfinance services are underdeveloped in Montenegro because – apart from the major role that Opportunity Bank plays – some NGOs have micro portfolios. However, it is true that the micro sector is effectively ignored by other banking institutions.

PART IV:

Clients' Perspectives on Access to Financial Services for Micro and Small Enterprise in Southeast Europe

PART IV

Introduction to Part IV

Will the dynamic changes in the structure of the banking sectors in SEE create equally dynamic responses in the rest of the economy? Can the liquidity provided by banks and credit-granting NGOs trickle down and promote economic opportunity at the grass roots level? Outside the banking system, what nonfinancial barriers diminish the willingness to lend or discourage would-be borrowers? What steps are required to dismantle these obstacles?

Removing Barriers that Diminish Access to Finance

Sarah Forster's theme paper, "Clients' Perspectives – Providing More Effective Financial Services for Micro and Small Enterprises" discusses the range of financial services available to businesses – mostly micro and small firms which will drive economic growth in Southeast Europe (SEE).

Private business has grown rapidly since the early-1990s. In the decade up to 2001, the private sector's share of GDP in SEE rose from around 30% to over 60%, moving closer to the 89% level for the 15 countries constituting the EU prior to May 2004. However, the scale of enterprises varies greatly within the region: 76% of firms in Albania have only one employee, who is the owner. The vast informal sector also makes a significant contribution to overall economic activity, but this is not easily quantifiable. Enterprise growth is essential for overall economic growth, and funding from sources external to the firm is part of the formula for growth. However, there is little data on the scale and composition of demand for finance in SEE.

Generally, it is possible to rank the stages of company development within an industry by the types of finance used. But the boundaries of these stages are fluid and vary from industry to industry, and relatively few firms traverse the entire continuum. At the initial or seed stage, the firm is financed by its founders, their friends and families; at the top end, the company may obtain investment from its suppliers and tap sources of venture capital and the capital markets. External equity, apart from that provided by family and friends, is the most difficult type of funding to obtain, especially for small firms. The public policy objective should be to ensure that appropriate institutions are in place and capable of providing funding efficiently to enterprises of all sizes.

Immediately prior to the recent accessions, about 80% of SMEs (small and medium-sized enterprises) in the 15-member EU used commercial bank financing. Domestic credit to the enterprise sector equalled about 95% of GDP, whereas in SEE the credit/GDP ratio was around 15%. Commercial banks in SEE appear to favour lending to larger rather than smaller enterprises. The commercial banks tend to serve first those market segments that are easiest to cultivate, such as large firms and possibly consumer finance, penetrating other market segments only as competition in the original segments increases – causing the returns to earlier strategies to decline with competition and with increasingly marginal clients.

Virtually all MSE lending in the region has been funded by official donors. Their funds, in the form of grants and credit lines, are channelled to commercial banks, to fewer than a dozen microfinance banks and to about 45 NGOs. As of early 2003, outreach was estimated at 175,000 loans outstanding, amounting to USD 420 million. The NGOs served the largest number of clients: 112,000 active borrowers constituting a loan portfolio of USD 133 million. The microfinance banks served about 64,000 borrowers and had a portfolio of USD 288 million. These numbers are still growing quite rapidly.

The market niches created by these institutions can be broadly summarised as follows: few commercial banks appear interested in making business loans of less than USD 10,000; the average size of loans made by NGO MFIs is around 90% of per capita GDP, the figure for the microfinance banks is slightly more than 400%; about half of NGO clients are men, in contrast to the microfinance banks' ratio of around 80%; NGOs are particularly active in rural areas and small towns.

The microfinance banks benefit from strong initial investment and support. Their financial performance to date indicates that they will be sustainable. Their future depends on continued commitment by foreign investors, their ability to innovate and to meet client demand, and their capacity to attract deposits and external funding. The NGOs are in a different situation and can be broken down into 4 broad categories: commercially oriented NGOs with high growth potential that will probably become commercial institutions; those likely to remain operationally sustainable as development niche players requiring subsidy for growth; entities that are likely to merge or partner with stronger microfinance institutions (MFIs) or banks; and those unlikely to survive. In general, the MFIs are performing well and achieve high levels of portfolio quality.

MSEs searching for credit appear to find commercial bank loans difficult to obtain, reflecting demand- and supply-side barriers. The former include legal and registration problems, low levels of education and familiarity with financial practices, adverse market conditions and firm size. Among the supply-side barriers are loan decision-making processes, collateral requirements, term structures and currency mismatches.

Innovations by banks on the supply side include expedited decision-making, technical assistance, guarantees, better regulation and governance, and new products and delivery methods. Supply-side innovations by microfinance institutions and other MFIs include decentralised and timely credit appraisal and approval; cash flow lending rather than asset-based lending; client orientation and openness to change. As these institutions develop, funding is increasingly likely to become available through guarantees, leasing, factoring, insurance and also from savings and the reinvestment of profits by business owners. Further innovation could be forthcoming as a result of greater collaboration between commercial banks and other MFIs.

Response Papers

The response paper by Albrecht Mulfinger of the European Commission notes that failure to fund MSEs stifles economic growth and job creation. Numerous obstacles restrict or prevent MSEs in Southeast Europe from gaining access to financial services. Fortunately, as a result of privatisation, know-how transfer, donor support and foreign direct investment, the situation is improving. However, small firm size generally seems to be correlated with lower degrees of access, also in the former EU of 15 countries. Likewise, access tends to be more difficult in poorer countries than in richer ones.

The Charter for Small Enterprises is one effort by the EU which tackles the problems facing SMEs seeking finance. Other efforts include recommendations and agreements made by organisations and conferences focusing on the problem of access. A broad range of remedial actions is being undertaken by SMEs, by banks and by various levels of government, but much remains to be done.

Igor Brknovic, a Senior SME Expert, describes the SME loan market in Serbia. The former economic and political system supported neither microenterprise nor SMEs. However, with 99% of enterprises belonging in these categories, the government launched a strategy in 2003 to assist these target groups. In 2002, SMEs were estimated to account for about half of all employment; they produced one-third of all profits and owned almost a third of the fixed assets owned by businesses in Serbia. But SMEs have almost no access to commercial bank credit, in part because of the difficulty of providing acceptable collateral. Microentrepreneurs are not required to keep accounts and therefore can seldom provide the documentation required by banks.

In general, Serbian bankers consider SMEs to be nontransparent and difficult to evaluate: credit histories are not necessarily valid and collateral is usually inadequate. SMEs, on the other hand, believe that banks have an obligation to serve them – based on the precedent that applied to large firms in the former socialist banking system. They are critical of the banks, claiming that they do not keep information confidential, that business plans and other data are misused to their disadvantage, that bank procedures are cumbersome, and that credit analysis is inconsistent, slow and not suited to MSE operations. In this respect, ProCredit Bank, which specialises in lending to micro and small enterprises, is an exception.

Stefan Kossev provides a view of micro and SME finance in Bulgaria, where financing is hard to obtain. Even funding provided by donors does not always go to indigenous enterprises. Local firms therefore grow slowly.

Uninspiring levels of foreign direct investment tend to dampen the overall investment climate, and targeted efforts to improve the business environment do not include MSE promotion. Greater foreign investment is likely in Bulgaria as EU accession approaches, but EU regulations will probably be a burden for SMEs. As competition increases, many will go bankrupt or be bought up by international companies. Country risk and the failure of outsiders to understand local conditions add to the difficulties facing local firms.

The crisis of 1996–1997 destroyed both confidence in financial institutions and the bank balances of many Bulgarian enterprises. In the aftermath of this event, many entrepreneurs moved into the grey economy, making commercial bank credit almost impossible to obtain. ProCredit Bank addresses these problems to some extent, but there has been little interest in MSE lending by commercial banks. On a brighter note, leasing and factoring are common.

Christoph Freytag of ProCredit Bank Serbia demonstrates that there is more competition among microfinance banks and NGOs in SEE than commonly assumed. The indicators normally employed to differentiate between different types of lenders (such as minimum, average or range of loan size) are easily misinterpreted as the services provided by each type of lender are varied. Defining competition from a strategic standpoint requires a focus on similarities. This approach reveals that the SEE microloan portfolios of the NGOs and the ProCredit Banks are in the same range, that each have broadly similar rural outreach, and that loans to women as a proportion of total loans to real persons do not diverge as widely as might be assumed. In short, the ProCredit Banks and the NGOs serve virtually the same market, compete for much the same clients and achieve similar results in terms of outreach and target-group orientation.

The microfinance banks' superior performance in scaling up their operations is based on their ownership and their bank charters. The latter ensure regulatory and supervisory oversight and provide the capacity to mobilise deposits. These rapidly growing banks achieve profitability quickly and offer an expanding array of services. As their "credit technology" (that is, how client relationships are established and managed, including loan terms and conditions) is more appropriate for the MSE client group, the microfinance banks' portfolios in this segment are of better quality than those of the commercial banks.

GTZ – Deutsche Gesellschaft für Technische Zusammenarbeit GmbH – has for many years supported business development services (BDS). These nonfinancial services are intended to assist entrepreneurs and firms to produce better products and to operate more efficiently. Hayder Al-Bagdadi, Dirk Steinwand and Frank Wältring discuss a new strategy that provides BDS in response to demand oriented market signals rather than on a supply oriented basis. This new approach is based on a consensus among major donors, redefining their role as that of facilitating providers of these services. The providers include consultants, educational institutions, chambers of commerce, accountants and others in a position to advise. As a result of this reorientation, their relationship with their micro and small enterprise clients is now based on fees for services rendered. Free BDS, as offered in the past, required continuing subsidies and undermined the local consulting market or prevented it from functioning.

CHAPTER 16:

Clients' Perspectives – Providing More Effective Financial Services for Micro and Small Enterprises

Sarah Forster

Programme Director, New Economics Foundation

Micro and small enterprises (MSEs) make up the bulk of the private economy in Southeast Europe (SEE) and are the key drivers of job and wealth creation.[1] It is these businesses that will help SEE countries overcome their major economic and social challenges, which include widespread poverty and high levels of unemployment.

For MSEs to thrive and grow, entrepreneurs need a supportive environment and access to appropriate and affordable finance. Over the last decade, Southeast Europe has gone through a major transformation which has included financial sector reforms. This has led to the development of a private banking system and the deepening of financial services. But to what extent is the financial system providing effective services to micro and small enterprises? Are MSEs able to obtain the most appropriate source of finance applicable to their stage of development and likely future prospects?

This paper examines the performance of the financial sector from the MSE – or client – perspective in four parts, as follows:

- a brief overview of the MSE sector and the nature of MSE demand for finance.

- the current supply of finance, including loans, equity and other financial products.

- gaps in the supply of finance and current innovations to address both demand-side and supply-side constraints to effective financial services for MSEs.

- a discussion of some of the lessons from experience and recommendations for further deepening and broadening financial services to MSEs.

---

[1] Southeast Europe is defined here as Albania, Bosnia and Herzegovina (BiH), Bulgaria, Croatia, Kosovo, Macedonia, Moldova, and Serbia and Montenegro.

The countries of SEE have diverse cultures, histories, stages of transition and market characteristics. However, there are sufficient similarities in the enterprise and financial sectors across all countries to allow a regional analysis to be relevant. That said, finance providers need in-depth knowledge and a good understanding of the local market in order to develop effective financial services for MSEs.

The MSE Sector in Southeast Europe – The Demand Side

Private business activity has grown very rapidly throughout SEE since the collapse of state-controlled economies and the transition to more market oriented systems. In the early-1990s, the private sector accounted for less than 30% of GDP (gross domestic product). This rose to an average of 56% in 1998 and to more than

Table 1. Private sector share in GDP (2002)

Country/Region	*Private sector/GDP (percentage)*
SEE	
Albania	75
Bosnia and Herzegovina (BiH)	45
Bulgaria	70
Croatia	60
FYR Macedonia	60
Moldova	50
Romania	65
Serbia and Montenegro	40
Regional Averages	
SEE average (unweighted)	58
SEE average (weighted)	61
CEB average (unweighted)	76
CEB average (weighted)	76
CIS average (unweighted)	54
CIS average (weighted)	67
EU average	89

Source: EBRD, 2002.

Note: The private sector share of GDP is calculated using statistics from official and unofficial sources. The accuracy of estimates is constrained by data limitations, and estimates for SEE countries are rounded to the nearest multiple of 5. Weighted averages are calculated using the dollar value of GDP in each country.

60% in mid-2001 (Table 1).[2] However, this is still below the level of private sector activity in other transition countries in Central and Eastern Europe and the Baltic states (CEB), where about 76% of activity is private, and in the Commonwealth of Independent States (CIS), where private sector activity produces 67% of GDP. In EU countries, the private sector accounts for 89% of GDP.[3] The low level in SEE compared to CEB and CIS is due to the slower pace of privatisation.

Ubiquity

Micro, small and medium-sized enterprises (MSMEs) constitute the vast majority of businesses in SEE, with microenterprises (defined as having up to nine employees) dominating in most countries.[4] Notwithstanding the difficulties of doing business in the region, a strong spirit of entrepreneurship has emerged. However, the level of such development varies across the region. Enterprise density, defined as the number of MSMEs per 1,000 inhabitants, is highest in Bulgaria, which is comparable to the number in Hungary, but less than in the Czech Republic or Poland (Table 2). The lowest levels of enterprise density are in Moldova and in Serbia and Montenegro. In these countries, there is effectively an "enterprise gap" in terms of numbers, but in Serbia and Montenegro, enterprises are better developed with good market linkages (see later discussion).

The size and sectoral breakdown of enterprises across countries is linked to their impact on economic growth. In Albania, the majority of businesses are very small: 98% of MSMEs are microenterprises, and 76% have just one employee, the self-employed owner. Most operate in the local trade and services sectors or in the rural economy.[5] As drivers of economic growth, microenterprises are less effective than small and medium-sized firms due to their lack of market integration and supply chain linkages and, hence, their reduced ability to grow and add economic value. This is, in part, due to the weak business environment and low levels of infrastructure development and management skills.

In Croatia and the Federal Republic of Yugoslavia (FRY, now Serbia and Montenegro), MSEs are clearly the strongest sector of the economy and drive economic growth. Private ownership was allowed under the former Yugoslav regime, and these countries today have a larger pool of small private companies, many of which have acquired valuable business experience, some with excellent export links to Western Europe. These firms are concentrated in higher value added sectors. In FRY, for example, 57% of small and medium-sized enterprises are in construction and 11% in industry and mining.[6]

---

[2] *EBRD Transition Report, 2002.*

[3] *World Bank Development Indicators, 2002.*

[4] All enterprise definitions are based on EU standards.

[5] Southeast Europe Enterprise Development (SEED), *Small and Medium Enterprise Mapping of Albania, 2002.*

[6] SEED, *SME Mapping of the Federal Republic of Yugoslavia (Serbia/Montenegro), 2002.*

Table 2. Number of enterprises in southeast Europe (2000)

Country/Region	MSMEs	Micro only	% Micro	Large	MSMEs per 1000 inhabitants
SEE					
Albania	56,441	55,143	98	76	16.5
Bosnia and Herzegovina (BiH)	50,000	n.a.	n.a.	n.a.	14.7
Bulgaria	224,211	207,643	93	741	27.6
Croatia	59,907	47,368	79	529	13.7
FYR Macedonia	27,938	25,985	93	194	14.0
Moldova	18,898	15,138	80	2,525	5.2
Romania	306,073	270,843	88	1,991	13.6
Serbia and Montenegro	68,207	n.a.	n.a.	1,032	8.0
CEB					
Czech Republic	876,990	830,601	95	1,671	85.1
Hungary	275,671	249,388	90	1,030	27.4
Poland	1,762,982	n.a.	n.a.	3,071	45.6
Slovak Republic	60,310	48,662	81	610	11.2

Source: All data are from EBRD Working Paper No. 88 except for Bosnia and Herzegovina (BiH), which is from the Southeast Europe Enterprise Development (SEED) initiative based in Sarajevo. The original sources are survey data collected from national governments.

Informality

The informal sector is difficult to measure, but there is good reason to believe that as a proportion of GDP it is larger in SEE than in Western Europe and in the transition countries of CEB and CIS. Informal activities thrive in weak states where enforcement of the rule of law is patchy and barriers to entry are large.[7]

Table 3 presents estimates by Schneider (2000) of the size of the informal sector relative to GNP for SEE and selected CEB countries. The ratio in most SEE countries is about one-third. Moldova, the poorest country in the region, and FRY Macedonia have the highest levels of informal activity at about half of their respective economies, and Serbia and Montenegro, perhaps surprisingly, has the lowest at just under 30%.[8] The share of informal sector activity is much lower in

---

[7] EBRD, Working Paper 88. "Bridging the Gaps? Private sector development, capital flows and the investment climate in south-eastern Europe, 2003."

[8] In Albania, the share of informal activity is also thought to be much higher than these official estimates.

Table 3. The informal sector as a share of GNP in SEE and more advanced transition economies

Country	Informal sector/GNP in percent
SEE	
Albania	33
Bosnia and Herzegovina (BiH)	34
Bulgaria	37
Croatia	33
FYR Macedonia	45
Moldova	45
Romania	34
Serbia and Montenegro	29
CEB	
Czech Republic	19
Hungary	25
Poland	28
Slovak Republic	19
16 West European OECD Countries	18

Source: Schneider, 2002.

CEB, typically 20–25% of total economic activity, while the European members of the OECD average around 18%. When informal activities are taken into account, the level of private sector activity in SEE is close to the share in the more advanced transition countries.

Activity in the informal sector is a sign of entrepreneurial spirit, and by providing employment this sector also acts as a social safety net. However, the downside of a large informal sector is that it leads to a loss of government revenue and to unfair competition; it puts the formal sector at a competitive disadvantage. Providing incentives to bring informal enterprises into the formal sector should be a top priority of governments throughout the region. Some finance providers, particularly those targeting microenterprises, encourage informal microentrepreneurs to register their businesses as a condition for acquiring repeat loans. Other measures to encourage formalisation include offering tax incentives (such as a tax amnesty), making business registration simpler and less expensive, and providing business support, including financial and tax advisory services.

Rusticity

Rural economies in SEE are also very important, providing more than half of all employment in Albania and Romania. In Romania, a fifth of all enterprises are based in rural areas. There are also many small, start-up businesses in rural areas, as people formerly employed in state-owned enterprises or agricultural cooperatives turn to self-employment.[9]

Summary Characteristics

The characteristics of the MSE sector in SEE can be summarised as follows:

- the sector as a whole is underdeveloped compared to MSE activity in EU Member States, suggesting great latent potential for entrepreneurship and business formation;

- on average, businesses are very small, indicating opportunities for policies, finance and business support to encourage transformation of self-employment and microenterprises into larger firms that can contribute more to economic growth and employment generation;

- for the MSE sector to help lead economic growth, it is essential to create companies that generate higher value with greater market linkages;

- governments should provide incentives for informal businesses to register and become part of the formal economy so that these businesses can help build the tax base and fulfil the promises of social democracy.

MSE Demand for Finance

MSEs need finance to support their growth and development. Internal financing, including reinvestment of retained earnings, is typically by far the most important source for all businesses. However, external finance is of vital importance. External sources include:

- loans – short-term working capital to finance current assets, and longer-term investment loans for fixed assets and business development;

- equity – sources include informal equity/business angel, venture capital, share issues;

- other financial products such as guarantees, leasing, and factoring.

---

[9] Chaves, Rodrigo et al., *Financial Markets, Credit Constraints and Investment in Rural Romania*, World Bank Technical Paper No. 499, Washington DC: World Bank, 2001.

MSEs and households also want and use other financial services. Savings facilities are particularly important to businesses with lumpy and risky incomes, such as farming. Money transfers, insurance, consumer credit and housing finance are also useful for households and MSEs.

The demand for different types of external finance will differ depending on the nature of the business and its stage of development. Table 4 shows stages in a business's development and the possible financing sources at each stage. These stages are based on a venture capital perspective and particularly apply to high-growth businesses; other businesses may have less dynamic financing patterns, e.g. using only loan finance.

Table 4. Financing sources of MSEs by stage of development

Stage of business development	Types of Finance	Main sources of finance
Seed stage	• Informal equity • Loans if available and able to repay	• Founders, friends and family
Start-up stage	• Loans • Leasing for equipment • Informal equity • Formal equity – venture capital	• Founders, friends, associates and business contacts • Business angels • Non-bank microfinance institutions • Banks • Leasing companies
Expansion stage	• Loans • Formal equity – development capital • Leasing • Factoring	• Banks • Non-bank microfinance institutions • Venture capital funds • Leasing companies • Factoring companies
Replacement capital	• Trade investment • Venture capital • Share issue/IPO (initial public offering)	• Suppliers • Venture capital funds • Capital markets/stock exchange

Source: Adapted from "Guide to Risk Capital Financing in Regional Policy, October 2002," European Commission.

Little research is available on the demand for external finance among enterprises in SEE. Levels of demand are influenced by many factors including the cost of finance, market conditions that affect returns to the enterprise, and the degree of trust in banks and other financial institutions. Demand for equity finance is also strongly affected by entrepreneurs' fear of losing control of their business.

There are more data on demand levels in EU countries. In the UK, for example, it is estimated that 25% of microenterprises and 42% of small enterprises are actively seeking external finance at any given time.[10] Given the less promising market opportunities and growth prospects in most SEE countries coupled with the lack of trust in the banking system, the demand for finance among firms in SEE is likely to be lower. However, the experience of the microfinance banks and other specialised MSE lenders suggests that there is still a high level of demand, much of which is unmet (see following section).

In summary:

- limited data are available on the scale and composition of the demand for finance among MSEs in SEE;
- however, the experience of the microfinance banks and specialised nonbank microfinance institutions suggests that demand is considerable.

The Supply of MSE Finance

In EU countries, MSEs engage a diverse range of financial institutions, including commercial banks and companies offering leasing and factoring services. Commercial banks remain their most important source of finance: about 80% of SMEs turn to banks for external financing,[11] and many large commercial banks have specialised small business banking sections. Banks in the EU view business lending and other finance products as competitive and profitable markets. The situation in SEE is very different.

Commercial Bank Loans

Current patterns of loan finance in SEE countries suggest that MSEs are not likely to be favoured by commercial banks, most of which are not responding to MSE demand for loans.

- Total domestic credit to the enterprise sector in SEE amounted to an average of only 27% of GDP in 2001, compared to an average of 43% in

---

[10] Andy Cosh and Alan Hughes, *Enterprise Challenged: Policy and Performance in the British SME Sector 1999–2002*, ESRC Centre for Business Research, Cambridge, 2003.

[11] Of these, microenterprises experience a greater rejection rate in efforts to obtain bank finance than do small and medium enterprises.

CEB countries and 108% in EU Member States.[12] The private sector credit-to-GDP ratio is particularly low in some countries (less than 10% in Albania, BiH, Romania and Serbia and Montenegro). The highest level of domestic credit to the private sector is in Croatia, at 69% of GDP.

- Most commercial banks have neither demonstrated a commercial interest in lending to MSEs nor developed small-business lending as a core part of their operations. Few commercial banks, including those operating donor-funded SME credit lines (see below), have been prepared to put their own capital at risk in enterprise lending.

- Banks see greater opportunities in the retail banking sector. The entry and increasing dominance of foreign banks in SEE financial markets has accelerated this trend. For example, in Bulgaria, the local bank Varna specialised in MSE and SME lending. It was bought by Société Générale of France, and within two years its operations were reoriented to more profitable retail banking.

- Commercial banks that serve businesses typically favour larger firms with significant assets and older management. Some banks are still locked into cross-ownership with enterprises. In Macedonia, for example, large enterprises still consume the bulk of available credit – up to 70% – from some of the largest commercial banks.[13]

It is open to discussion whether the lack of MSE lending by commercial banks is a rational business decision by bank owners and managers or represents a real bias away from MSE lending. Evidence suggests that there are both demand and supply side reasons for this lack of entry by banks into MSE lending (discussed later).

What is clear is that MSEs and bankers typically have negative perceptions of each other. MSE owners have a distrust of banks, left over from the 1990s when a series of financial crises led to bank closures in many countries.[14] Trust in the financial sector is returning slowly, as indicated by increasing deposit levels, but time is needed for better networking between financial institutions and MSEs. Many entrepreneurs still consider banks as biased against lending to small businesses. Bankers, on the other hand, claim that they have funds to lend, but the problem is a lack of high quality MSE projects and enterprises.

---

[12] EBRD, Working Paper No. 88, with data from EBRD and IMF, International Financial Statistics.

[13] Southeast Europe Enterprise Development (SEED), *SME Mapping of FYR Macedonia, 2001*.

[14] Mehl, Arnaud and Adalbert Winkler, "The Financial Sector and Economic Development: Evidence from Southeast Europe" in Ingrid Matthäus-Maier and J.D. von Pischke, eds., *The Development of the Financial Sector in Southeast Europe: Innovative Approaches in Volatile Environments*. Berlin, Springer, 2004, pp. 11–41.

In the short-term, banks are likely to develop consumer-lending products before business-lending services, because demand and profit-making opportunities in this segment are seen as greater. Austrian banks, which have a large presence in the region, have already entered this market. Consumer lending has far lower transaction costs than business lending and provides greater opportunities for mass scale.

Such lending increases access to finance – also for entrepreneurs, who may use a consumer loan for business purposes. However, there are potential downsides. First, the aggressive marketing tactics of consumer lenders create a risk that households and MSEs will take on more debt than they can afford. Second, consumer lending may squeeze out the specialised MSE lenders, such as microfinance banks and NGO microfinance institutions (see below), that take a more analytical approach to business lending to ensure that businesses do not take on more debt than they can afford. In Poland, for example, the rapid rise of consumer lending quickly reduced the level of demand experienced by Fundusz Mikro, a leading microfinance institution.

Comparison of Institutional Models

To date, virtually all MSE lending in the region has been donor financed. Different donors have supported different institutional models to increase MSEs' access to finance.[15]

- Commercial banks (CBs) have introduced specialised lending services for MSEs with donor support from EBRD, EU, KfW and others. This approach is commonly referred to as "downscaling."

- Microfinance banks (MFBs) are fully regulated and mostly greenfield, for-profit commercial banks that offer a broad range of products and services targeted at MSEs. There are nine MFBs in the region, seven established by IMI (Internationale Micro Investitionen AG)[16] and two by Opportunity International.[17] Lead donor investors in the IMI-backed banks include BIO, DEG, EBRD, FMO, IFC and KfW.[18]

---

[15] Credit unions and financial cooperatives also have a strong presence in some countries in the region, such as Moldova and Romania. However, these typically provide savings and consumer credit, not business loans, and hence are not included in this paper.

[16] Claus-Peter Zeitinger, "Sustainable Microfinance Banks – Problems and Perspectives;" Jan Baechle, "Equity Participation in Microfinance Banks in Southeast Europe and Georgia – A Strategic Option for a Large Private German Bank?" and Syed Aftab Ahmed, "Strengthening Financial Sectors in Transition Countries: IFC's Contribution," in Ingrid Matthäus-Maier and J.D. von Pischke, eds., *The Development of the Financial Sector in Southeast Europe: Innovative Approaches in Volatile Environments.* Berlin, Springer, 2004.

[17] Keith Flintham, "Bankers' Perspectives – Dynamic Banking in a Changing Market" in Part III of this volume.

[18] DEG was bought by KfW and is now a subsidiary of KfW.

- Nonbank microfinance institutions are nonprofit, nonbank organisations that specialise in lending to the self-employed and microenterprises. This category includes nonprofit associations and foundations, as well as microfinance institutions (MFIs) registered as companies.[19] There are an estimated 45 NGO MFIs in the region. Lead donors supporting NGO MFIs include the World Bank and USAID.

In summarised form, Table 5 presents estimates that the microfinance banks and the leading NGO MFIs were providing loans to over 175,000 borrowers with a combined loan portfolio of US$ 420 million in SEE as of June 2003. (Complete data on the number and scale of commercial bank MSE lending were not available.)

Table 5. Lending operations of specialised MSE finance providers in SEE (June, 2003)

Type	Sample size	Active borrowers	Loan portfolio (US$)	Average loan size (US$)	Average loan size as percent per capita GNP
Microfinance banks	9	63,650	288,463,000	4,532	383
NGO MFIs	34	111,727	133,289,000	1,193	107
Total		175,377	421,752,000		

Source: Microfinance Centre for Central and Eastern Europe and the New Independent States (MFC), Poland.

These MSE financiers are expanding rapidly. (Annex 1 lists the ten largest.) Microfinance banks show the strongest growth rates: over 200% in terms of both clients and loan portfolio during 2001–2002. NGO MFIs experienced growth rates of 50–75%. This dramatic growth suggests that there is a strong market demand for micro and small business loans in the region.

With respect to *scale of operations*, microfinance banks have achieved the highest volume of lending in the SEE region, with an average of over 7,000 borrowers and a loan portfolio of US$ 32 million per bank, compared to an average of 3,000 borrowers and a US$ 4 million portfolio for NGO MFIs. In comparison, the averages for commercial bank lenders in Central and Eastern Europe and the NIS are fewer than 700 borrowers and a US$ 3 million portfolio.

However, NGO MFIs typically have the greatest outreach to poor clients and to women entrepreneurs. NGO MFIs' average loan balance relative to per-capita GNP (a recognised indicator of poverty outreach) was 87% compared to 416% for

---

[19] This group of institutions are not licensed to take deposits and are subject to limited government regulation depending on their legal form and microfinance regulations in the country concerned.

Table 6. MSE lending activities by institutional type in Bosnia and Herzegovina (June 2003)

Portfolio	NGOs	Microfinance banks	Commercial banks
No. of Institutions	15	1	5
Total no. of outstanding loans	64,087	8,299	281
Average no. of loans	4,272	8,299	56
Total outstanding portfolio (US$ million)	70.9	43.8	6.8
Average outstanding portfolio (US$ million)	4.7	43.8	1.4
Average outstanding loan amount	1,106	5,283	24,050
Average loan size as % per capita GNP	87	416	1,894

Source: Microfinance Centre for Central and Eastern Europe and the New Independent States (MFC), Poland; and KfW for commercial banks.

the microfinance banks.[20] Commercial bank MSE lending data were obtained only for banks in BiH, where the average outstanding loan size is about US$ 24,000, almost 1,900% of GNP per capita (Table 6).

Forty-nine percent of NGO MFI clients are women compared to 19% for microfinance banks (no data were available for commercial banks). NGO MFIs also have greater outreach to smaller towns and rural areas, with about 70% of lending operations in these areas, compared to 30% for MFBs and 25% for commercial banks.[21]

With respect to *profitability*, the microfinance banks, with the support of high levels of up-front investment, have achieved the best financial performance of any type of MFI. Five of the seven IMI-sponsored microfinance banks had a positive return on equity (RoE) in June 2003, as high as 34% in the case of MEB Kosovo.[22] The longer-term prospects for the microfinance banks differ depending on their country of operation. In countries with the least developed financial sectors, such as Albania and Kosovo, the microfinance banks have achieved a significant market share of depositors, providing a strong, locally mobilised funding base for growth. In countries with a more competitive banking sector, such as BiH, it is harder for these banks to achieve a significant deposit market share. Here, the future profitability of the banks will largely depend on their maintaining a competi-

---

[20] This figure refers to the entire operations of microfinance banks. On a stand-alone basis, their microenterprise lending levels of outreach are only slightly higher than those of the NGO MFIs. However, NGO MFIs clearly have a stronger focus on the smallest businesses.

[21] Forster et al., *The State of Microfinance in CEE and NIS*, CGAP, 2003.

[22] This high return is partially due to the unprecedented level of deposits mobilised by MEB Kosovo.

tive edge through customer service quality and product innovation, the continued commitment of foreign investors, and the ability of IMI and other sponsors to raise external financing.

The financial performance of NGO MFIs is more variable. They typically fall into four categories. First, those that have strong management, high growth potential and are likely to become commercially oriented financial institutions. The financially best performing NGO MFIs, such as Mikrofin in Bosnia, currently have adjusted RoE of between 10 and 20%. Second, those that are operationally sustainable and are likely to remain development oriented niche players, operating at a local or regional level or in particular niche markets (e.g. low-income women), but which may require continuing subsidy. The third category are promising candidates for mergers with stronger MFIs or banks, while the final category are unlikely to survive due to low levels of sustainability and weak management.

The small size of most commercial banks' MSE lending operations makes it doubtful that they can profitably make loans of less than US$ 10,000 without a radical restructuring of their business model. The microfinance banks have shown that such operations can be profitable with more decentralised, streamlined credit procedures. The question is the willingness of the commercial banks' owners and managers to invest in business lending as a core part of their operations and to adopt new business processes.

In terms of *portfolio quality*, all types of MSE finance providers are performing well. MFBs and NGO MFIs have portfolios at risk (PAR) of less than 3% past 30 days overdue, with many having less than 1% PAR.[23] Commercial banks' results are more variable, with an average PAR of less than 5%, but with some having PAR levels above 10%.

In terms of *impact*, the microfinance banks and commercial banks provide a broad spectrum of products and services to a broad range of MSEs, including micro, small and medium-sized enterprises. Their services include deposit-taking, providing working capital and investment loans, effecting money transfers, and in some cases supplying housing and consumer loans.[24] Such a range of services offered to businesses at different stages of development helps increase impact. However, NGO MFIs have more direct outreach to and therefore likely a greater impact on low-income households and more vulnerable groups, such as displaced persons and businesses owned by women.

Equity

Equity is the riskiest element in a business's financing structure and an important means of building a capital base and establishing a credit rating. In SEE countries, there is little availability of equity beyond the seed stage defined in Table 4.

---

[23] PAR (Portfolio at Risk) refers to the entire balance of any loan some part or all of which is overdue.

[24] These are not described in this paper, given the focus on business finance.

First, *equity markets* in the region are very limited. A few countries, such as BiH and Croatia, have stock exchanges, but with very few companies trading. Although such local stock exchanges provide an opportunity for small companies to obtain equity investment, the viability of stock exchanges in small countries with low levels of enterprise density is often tenuous.

Second, *venture capital funds* now operate in the region, but none focus on MSEs. Most seek investments of more than US$ 500,000 in larger firms with clear growth potential. Most funds have made investments in tens of companies at most. This reflects the limited funds available and low levels of awareness of these facilities among businesses. For those businesses that understand venture capital finance, many remain reluctant to attract investors, fearing loss of control of their business.

Venture Capital in SEE

A number of venture capital funds provide finance in SEE using donor funding from EBRD, KfW, IFC, and USAID:

- At the lowest end of the investment spectrum are country-level funds, as in Albania, Bosnia and Herzegovina, Kosovo and Macedonia. These typically provide minority equity investments of up to $ 500,000 in SMEs.

- Next up is the Small Enterprise Assessment Fund (SEAF), established in 2000 by the Community Development Venture Capital Alliance in the U.S. SEAF provides equity investment to high potential SMEs. Loan sizes range from $ 1 million to $ 3 million, with a minimum investment of $ 500,000.

- At the upper end of the venture capital market is the Southeast Europe Equity Fund, a $ 150 million private investment fund, sponsored and managed by affiliates of Soros Private Funds Management, which makes equity investments of between $ 5 million and $ 15 million.

This mirrors the views about venture capital among European firms. Venture capital finance is rare even in the UK, which has the most highly developed venture capital market in Europe. Venture capitalists (VCs) invest in about 1,100 start-ups a year, with an average investment of £ 5.8 million.[25] Many firms (often justifiably) think that VCs only look at a business proposition in terms of exit. "We are looking to grow a company, not be obsessed with 'when can I sell and get out.' VCs start at a very high figure – they won't look at anything less

---

[25] Global Entrepreneurship Monitor (GEM) Report, 2002.

than one million. They are too short-termist. And they tend to want lots of clear cut answers that are hard to give in a new business."[26]

For most MSEs, *grants*, typically made by NGOs in the region, are the only available form of equity. Some NGOs, such as Care International, take an integrated approach to MSE development, combining business grants, loans (available from an independent, specialised microfinance institution) and business support services, including efforts to develop market linkages between small and large firms. The mainstream microfinance movement typically has a negative attitude towards grants to enterprises, highlighting the greater sustainability and impact of loans on the enterprise and the lending institution. However, prudent use of grants to entrepreneurs with viable business plans can help capitalise businesses and get them started. The problem with many NGO grant programmes has been that they are targeted not towards potentially profitable businesses, but towards particular target groups, such as returning refugees, without sufficient consideration of the viability of the business.

Other Financial Products

A number of other financial products are also vital to business development:

Guarantees. The efficacy of guarantees for MSEs is a subject of debate. Well-designed guarantees can increase the flow of commercial bank lending to MSEs, particularly those with limited liquidity or insufficient funds for expansion. Currently, most guarantee schemes in the region are designed to encourage foreign direct investment in export businesses. There are only a few guarantee facilities for MSEs in the region, such as Open Society Institute's scheme in Bulgaria.

Leasing services. Leasing services are very valuable to MSEs because they allow companies to use equipment without having to borrow and meet onerous collateral requirements.[27] Leasing services are still very limited, due largely to the lack of a supportive legal and regulatory framework. Romania has a leasing law, while in most other countries work is still underway to resolve legal and accounting issues. Currently, leasing services focus primarily on vehicles, largely in the form of hire purchase from specialised vendors. With improve-

---

[26] Quote from a UK inner city business from *Secrets of their Success: Fast Growth Businesses in Britain's Inner Cities*, New Economics Foundation, London, 2002.

[27] See Linda Deelen, Mauricio Dupleich, Louis Othieno and Oliver Wakelin, *Leasing for Small and Micro Enterprises*, ILO Social Finance Programme, for guidance in the design and management of leasing schemes for MSEs.

ments in the legal environment, banks and specialised leasing companies are likely to develop financial and operating leasing.[28]

Factoring. Factoring, invoice discounting and related products have been growing fast in EU countries for many years. These products allow businesses to borrow against the value of their sales ledger and can help ease cash flow problems. Typically, their invoices are paid 30–150 days in arrears. Factoring companies are now well-developed in Central and Eastern European countries, such as the Czech Republic, Hungary, Poland and Slovenia. In SEE, factoring services are very common in Bulgaria, but not elsewhere. The Southeast Europe Enterprise Development (SEED) initiative[29] is one of the organisations exploring the feasibility of establishing factoring companies in the region. A feasibility study in BiH found that "micro and small businesses have very limited financing options and recurring needs for short-term finance which provide a great possibility for factoring."[30] As with leasing, improvements in the legal environment, as well as better financial information systems within businesses, are required for factoring to take off. When the legal environment is in place these services are likely to develop on a commercial basis without donor support.

Savings are also vital for business development, particularly for those with risky or lumpy investment cycles. Deposits have grown rapidly in the region; this is a very positive development, although domestic savings rates are still very low compared to EU countries. However, there is little information on the take-up and use of savings accounts by businesses. Greater marketing of savings products is in order, as well as the development of flexible savings products tailored to MSEs.

Insurance. Microinsurance is an area of innovation within microfinance, but it is yet to be developed in SEE. Some MFIs exploring this area are seeking to collaborate with commercial insurance companies in providing specialised business cover.

---

[28] Short-term or operating leases allow the lessee to use leased property for only a portion of its economic life. The lessee accounts for such leases as contracts, reporting the required rental payments as an expense. The lessor retains these items on its balance sheet. Financial leases allow the lessee to use the property for the entire economic life and the leased asset ends up on the lessee's balance sheet.

[29] SEED is a multi-donor initiative managed by IFC to strengthen small and medium-sized enterprises in Bosnia and Herzegovina, Albania, FYR Macedonia, and Kosovo.

[30] SEED, *Feasibility Study on the Establishment of a Factoring Company in Bosnia and Herzegovina*, October 2003.

Gaps in Supply and Innovative Remedies

Great progress has been made in deepening and broadening the SEE financial sector. However, access to finance for MSEs here is extremely limited compared to the EU Member States. MSE financing is also heavily reliant on donor funding.

In contrast to well-developed financial markets, SEE financial markets do not offer a full range of products. The main gaps in loan finance are found in the commercial banking market, in particular in the provision of longer-term loans, loans for start-up businesses, agricultural loans, and bank lending facilities in small towns and rural areas. In Moldova and in Serbia and Montenegro, even working capital for microenterprises is in short supply as there are few specialised microfinance providers. This is due to lack of a suitable legal environment in Serbia and Montenegro despite long-standing efforts to encourage the government to legalise lending by nonbank institutions.

Businesses in SEE typically face less favourable lending terms and conditions than those in EU countries. The typical loan term for an MSE is up to 2 or 3 years with annual interest rates of between 6% and 12%. Businesses in EU countries can obtain longer-term, cheaper loans, with interest rates currently around 5 – 7%. The inefficiencies that cause these higher rates make it hard for local businesses to compete with foreign firms. Many MSEs fear that they will be squeezed out as foreign competition increases.

Equity finance available to MSEs beyond the seed stage is very limited. Most venture capital funds seek investments greater than US$ 1 million and typically invest in medium-sized or large enterprises with high growth potential. Limited equity is available in the form of grants from NGOs, but the supply is diminishing with the decline in donor funding and NGO activity. There are also currently very limited leasing, factoring and insurance services in the region.

Commercial bank lending to MSEs is affected by demand- and supply-side factors that reflect overall low levels of economic development and the absence of developed and sophisticated economic and financial institutions. With respect to the *demand-side* barriers:

- Though progress has been made in streamlining business registration and taxation systems, many countries still lack a supportive business environment, and this inhibits business formation and growth.

- Weak and volatile market conditions further limit opportunities for business expansion and growth.

- Many businesses lack well-educated staff and management with skills and experience in running a business in a market economy.

- Many businesses are not considered investment-ready by banks. Reasons include poorly prepared business plans, lack of bankable projects, and financial reports that indicate limited profitability. (Profits are often under-reported to avoid taxes.)

- Businesses lack knowledge about the sources of finance available to them.

- Legal constraints to pledging real estate and moveable assets (equipment, machinery, inventories, livestock and accounts receivable) as collateral inhibit bank borrowing.

Efforts to tackle these constraints are evolving gradually, in most cases with donor support. A number of advances have been made: capacity-building for providers of business development services that can help increase the investment readiness of companies, information services to increase MSEs' knowledge of sources of finance,[31] and legal and regulatory reforms to allow moveable assets to be registered as collateral.

Now turning to the *supply-side* barriers:

- Banks' traditional, hierarchical approach to lending and decision-making. Cost-effective lending for MSEs requires rapid and decentralised loan approval. Many commercial banks have slow and complicated credit processes, with some banks reportedly taking up to six months to make loan decisions. Specialised microfinance providers typically make loan decisions within 1 or 2 weeks at the branch office level.

- Banks' reliance on collateral-based lending. Many banks require collateral worth between two and four times the amount of the loan. A shift from asset-based to cash flow based lending is required if banks are to provide effective services to MSEs.

- Most banks' deposits are primarily short-term, which inhibits their ability to provide long-term loans.

- Currency mismatches may also retard financial intermediation – banks may borrow in foreign currency but lend in local currency, often requiring the borrower to assume the currency risk.

- Banks lack customer orientation and are perceived to have a bias towards larger firms.

Innovations on the supply side have been developed within the microfinance sector. Innovators include investors and managers of commercial bank downscaling programmes, microfinance banks and NGO MFIs. There have been a number of positive results.

---

[31] See for example SEED's web-based information service: www2.ifc.org/sme/html/seed.html and www.seebiz.net.

- Introduction of decentralised lending policies and procedures.

- Technical assistance to develop banks' capacity in term lending, risk assessment, cash flow lending and more streamlined credit decision-making.

- Guarantees to diminish banks' risks resulting from the term mismatch between deposits and lending and to reduce currency mismatches. KfW has created credit guarantee facilities to address these mismatches.

- More stringent supervision and improvements in the governance of financial institutions to overcome insider lending.

- New microfinance delivery methods to increase outreach to the poor and to rural areas. For example, Prizma in BiH has developed a system of agents based in rural communities, and Constanta in Georgia has introduced mobile bank branches.

A key factor distinguishing banks from specialist microfinance providers, including MFBs and NGO MFIs, is that the latter typically take a "double-bottom-line" approach. They have a business mission (to seek financial returns) coupled with a social mission (to serve MSEs). In some cases there may be a trade-off between these two, with lower financial returns associated with reaching certain markets (e.g. rural areas) or client groups (e.g. start-up businesses owned by the unemployed). In order to adequately address the problem of gaps in financial markets, it will be necessary to look more closely at these trade-offs and their implications for subsidies.

Concluding Remarks

To date, only microfinance banks and NGO MFIs have demonstrated a commitment to and serious business interest in providing effective financial services to MSEs in SEE. These institutions have been the industry leaders in innovation, product development and customer oriented service delivery. Three factors have been key to effective MSE finance: decentralised, timely credit appraisal and approval processes; cash flow rather than collateral-based lending; and client orientation and openness to innovation.

While the performance of donor-funded MSE lending programmes is impressive, the challenge is to ensure that these financial institutions become integrated into the financial system. This requires a certain scale of operations and access to commercial sources of funding to sustain their operations as providers of MSE finance over the long term. Many of these institutions lack the sources of capital necessary to finance their growth.

Steps should be taken to support the growth of specialised MSE finance providers and increase their access to commercial capital. Useful measures include providing standby guarantee facilities to cover foreign exchange risks for those borrowing internationally and to cover the MFBs' term mismatches. Proposals to develop a specialised refinancing vehicle or investment funds for MFBs and nonbank microfinance providers in the region should also be investigated.

An even greater challenge is to engage mainstream commercial banks in lending and other means of financing MSEs. The microfinance banks and NGO MFIs have shown that there is a high demand among MSEs for loans and other financial products, and that these markets are profitable, with RoEs of between 10% and 30%. Commercial banks can learn from MFIs' lending methods when entering these markets. However, it has proved difficult to change the culture and mindset within the banks and to encourage them to embrace more customer oriented, decentralised delivery approaches.

MSE lending, particularly to the higher end of the market, is likely to become an attractive market segment for commercial banks as the private sector develops. In the short term it is important to encourage greater MSE lending by commercial banks and to improve the respective terms and conditions.

Greater cooperation and partnership among specialised microfinance providers and commercial banks could enhance the provision of effective financial services to MSEs. There is a wide range of mutually beneficial activities that can be arranged between banks and microfinance providers. These include graduating clients, sharing facilities, providing bank lines of credit to MFIs, offering cross-selling services, selling MFIs' portfolios to banks, and acquiring an MFB or NGO MFI as a subsidiary or specialised MSE lending department. Donors can help broker such relations through their funding of financial services for MSEs.

EU accession may lessen banks' incentives to lend to MSEs, given the increasing competitiveness of the financial sector and the new Basel Accords. In EU countries, there is already concern that with the introduction of credit scoring techniques and strong pressure on profits, commercial banks are reducing their small business lending, becoming more risk averse and centralised in their decision-making. EU countries, particularly the UK, have also seen mass closures of bank branches in rural areas. This has led European governments to take a more interventionist approach, providing incentives for banks to disclose information on their lending operations to small businesses and encouraging the provision of microcredit to MSEs by both banks and nonbank institutions.

SEE countries are advised to become informed about market developments in Western Europe and the role of banks and governments in MSE lending. EU Member States are likewise encouraged to take note of the experience gained in

SEE countries, where MSE providers have demonstrated greater levels of technical capacity, outreach, and sustainability. Such cooperation and knowledge-sharing could provide useful learning opportunities for all.

Increasing the competitiveness and investment-readiness of MSEs in SEE is also vital. A number of avenues could be explored.

- Improving the quality of business development services (BDS), particularly those focused on the strategic aspects of business operations, such as marketing, strategy and managing growth. Making this happen requires efforts to increase both demand and supply. Many MSEs have little awareness of how business support could help improve their operations. The quality of business support in the region also needs improving. Currently, there is little provision of high quality, affordable and strategically oriented services. Most providers focus on helping prepare business plans, and this is often of little use.

- Helping MSEs win government and donor contracts. Public sector procurement of goods and services is a major source of consumption and investment in all SEE countries, yet small, local businesses often find it difficult to win such contracts. Support is required to build the capacity of MSEs to secure public (and private) sector contracts. This will encourage the development of MSEs, which is vital for local development, and help local firms to supply goods and services efficiently. Models showing how small businesses can win contracts are available from the US and UK.

- Developing programmes to promote supply chain linkages. Foreign firms can help support the growth and development of local MSEs by linking them into their supply chains. Although this may require upfront investment in training and quality standards, it can reduce costs and increase profitability over time. Donors can play a role in development programmes that look beyond MSE finance towards more integrated approaches, building markets that integrate and strengthen the competitiveness of MSEs.

A strong, diverse and growing MSE sector is vital to the economic development and well-being of the SEE countries. MSE development should therefore be at the heart of development strategies across the region. Donors active in the region have agreed on three elements that are vital to any strategy aimed at developing effective financial services for MSEs: a focus on institution-building, a commercial approach, and a financial systems orientation. The foundations already in place should be the starting point for all donor efforts in the future.

Annex 1

Table 7. Top 10 MFIs in southeast Europe ranked by number of active borrowers (June 2003)

Name	Country	Year Established	Loan Outstanding (US$ millions) June 2003	No. of Active Borrowers June 2003
ProCredit Bank (formerly MFB Serbia)	Serbia and Montenegro	Apr-01	60.5	17,438
EKI WV	BiH	Feb-96	14.8	11,152
Partner Mikrokreditna Organizacija	BiH	Apr-97	12.7	9,995
ProCredit Bank (formerly MEB Kosovo)	Kosovo	Jan-00	55.1	9,954
ProCredit Bank	Bulgaria	Jan-01	52.1	9,095
PRIZMA	BiH	Jun-97	4.7	9,005
AGROINVEST	Serbia and Montenegro	Jul-99	9.3	8,940
ProCredit Bank (formerly MEB BiH)	BiH	Jan-97	43.8	8,299
Rural Finance Fund	Albania	Jan-92	7.2	7,319
ProCredit Bank (formerly FEFAD Bank)	Albania	Jan-96	44.4	7,041

Source: Microfinance Centre for Central and Eastern Europe and the New Independent States (MFC), Poland.

References

Chaves, Rodrigo, Sanchez, Susana, Schor, Saul and Tesling, Emil: *Financial Markets, Credit Constraints and Investment in Rural Romania*, World Bank Technical Paper No. 499, World Bank, Washington DC, 2001.

Cosh, Andy and Hughes, Alan: *Enterprise Challenged: Policy and Performance in the British SME Sector 1999–2002*, ESRC Centre for Business Research, Cambridge, 2003.

EBRD: *Transition Report*, 2002.

EBRD: Working Paper No. 88, 2003. *Bridging the gaps? Private sector development, capital flows and the investment climate in south-eastern Europe*, by Elisabetta Falcetti, Peter Sanfey and Anita Taci.

EU: Guide to Risk Capital Financing in Regional Policy, October 2002.

Forster, Sarah, Pytkowska, Justyna and Greene, Seth: *The State of Microfinance in CEE and NIS*, World Bank/CGAP, 2003

Global Entrepreneurship Monitor Report, 2002.

ILO Social Finance Programme: *Leasing for Small and Micro Enterprises* by Linda Deelen, Mauricio Dupleich, Louis Othieno and Oliver Wakelin, 2003.

Mehl, Arnaud and Winkler, Adalbert: "The Financial Sector and Economic Development: Evidence from Southeast Europe" in Ingrid Matthäus-Maier and J.D. von Pischke, eds., *The Development of the Financial Sector in Southeast Europe: Innovative Approaches in Volatile Environments*. Berlin, Springer, 2004.

New Economics Foundation: *Secrets of their Success: Fast Growth Businesses in Britain's Inner Cities*, London, 2002.

Schneider, Friedrich: *Size and Measurement of the Informal Economy in 110 Countries Around the World*, 2002.

SEED: *SME Mapping of Bosnia and Herzegovina*, 2001.

SEED: *SME Mapping of the Federal Republic of Yugoslavia (Serbia/Montenegro)*, 2002.

SEED: *SME Mapping of Macedonia*, 2001.

SEED: *Feasibility Study on the Establishment of a Factoring Company in Bosnia and Herzegovina*, October 2003.

World Bank Development Indicators, 2002.

CHAPTER 17:

Access to Finance: Issues and Opportunities in Southeast Europe

Albrecht Mulfinger

Head of Division in charge of Access to Finance, Enterprise Directorate General, European Commission

When considering access to finance, it is revealing to compare micro- and small enterprises (MSEs) in countries that experienced conflict after the disintegration of the communist system with MSEs in countries that made the transition more or less peacefully, such as Bulgaria and Romania. In the former war regions, GDP is still well below pre-war levels (60% in the case of Bosnia and Herzegovina), and the financial sectors still face difficult conditions. In some regions, ownership of real estate property is almost impossible to prove following the migration of much of the population. Under these conditions, and given the legal systems and their slow procedures, many new businesses or entrepreneurs cannot offer collateral.

The economic situation is slowly improving in Southeast Europe (SEE) due to:

- efforts to privatise the banking sector and large businesses; the increase in foreign direct investment (FDI); the transfer of know-how; support from the international private and public community, including international banks (EBRD, KfW, EIB), commercial banks (such as Commerzbank), foundations, and donors that provide technical assistance or support to microcredit institutions;

- the major contributions made by the EU public and private sectors to stabilise the region.

Political Efforts to Increase Access to Finance in SEE

However, insufficient access to MSE finance remains a major barrier to growth and employment. But this problem extends beyond SEE. Within the EU, there are major differences in the support policies for small and medium-sized enterprises (SME). In countries such as Germany with highly developed SME support policies that include financial and non-financial assistance, relatively more enterprises are created. These enterprises grow faster, create more jobs and remain longer in the market than those in countries with less developed SME support policies.

Nevertheless, between 15% and 20% of European SMEs regard insufficient access to finance as a barrier to growth. The percentage is surely much higher for business creators or start-ups, although they do not participate in the relevant surveys. In France, for example, 72% of business creators do not receive bank loans to start their businesses.

Compared to this benchmark, the situation is much more dramatic in the new EU Member States and candidate countries. In Poland and Turkey, some 45% of exporting SMEs (with up to 250 employees) complain about insufficient long-term finance and the cost of credit (Grant Thornton 2002 Business Survey). But it is well known that micro-enterprises in these countries and the EU are more undercapitalised than medium-sized enterprises and have real difficulties getting at least part of the external finance they seek.

Although only limited information is available on MSE support policies in SEE, the situation is clearly improving. Bulgaria and Romania agreed in May 2002 to participate, along with all the other candidate countries, in the European Charter for Small Enterprises, which was endorsed at the Feira European Council in June 2000. These two countries submitted their first reports in 2002. In May 2003, the Balkan states also agreed to adhere to the Charter exercise and the first reports are being implemented.[1]

The Charter reflects recognition at the political level that MSEs play an important role as providers of jobs and growth. In the words of the Charter, they are "the backbone of Europe's economy" and play an important role in promoting social and regional development. The Charter also recognises the importance of entrepreneurship.

The governments that adhere to the Charter agree to:

- strengthen entrepreneurship and innovation;
- create favourable legal, fiscal and administrative framework conditions;
- facilitate access to research and technology;
- improve access to finance over the lifecycle of an enterprise;
- promote good quality support services for small enterprises.

The Commission holds annual bilateral meetings on small enterprise support policies with the governments of the EU, candidate countries and now the Balkan states. The annual report for 2003, which also features the Balkan states, describes significant measures or new initiatives relevant to MSE development. The report is in the public domain, and the respective governments have given high priority

---

[1] The first Charter Report on candidate countries and national reports are available at http://europa.eu.int/comm/enterprise/enlargement/charter/index.htm

to ensuring its quality and substance. The reports and the discussions increase awareness and serve to identify gaps and strengths in MSE support policies, including access to finance. It is encouraging that this dialogue is taking place and that comparisons are now possible (for example, the financing of small enterprises in Croatia compares favourably with that in the other Balkan states). These activities and processes are part of the EU's overall policy to implement the Association and Stability Process (ASP) with the western Balkan states.

Market Failure in MSE Finance

Conditions vary greatly across SEE and the reports from these countries differ in substance and quality, making it difficult to construct a detailed picture at this early stage. More experience is required. In this context, input has been provided by the European Round Tables of Bankers, by SMEs in the candidate countries and from the results of the discussions with candidate countries on access to finance at the Maribor conference in April 2002. The main findings from these three sources can be summarised as follows:

- the supply of domestic loans to the private sector relative to GDP is much lower in candidate countries than in the EU: about 20% and 135% respectively according to the European Central Bank;
- banks give priority to internationally active enterprises and to their subcontractors;
- MSEs are not a priority for banks and have difficulties obtaining sufficient loans;
- banks are not interested in small projects because of the high administrative costs and the perceived high risks;
- leasing services are underdeveloped in SEE;
- factoring is often still unknown;
- credit insurance – if available – is too expensive for MSEs, and they may simply assume the risk themselves;
- high levels of collateral are required (150% or more of the loan value);
- venture capital, especially early-stage finance, is largely underdeveloped and not an option for MSEs;
- business angels rarely exist, except for family and friends;
- an equity culture is yet to emerge;

- there is a lack of guarantee mechanisms in some Balkan states, and where they exist they are rather small and provide low leverage, 1:3 compared to 1:10 and more in the EU;
- guarantees may be difficult to obtain quickly, and guarantors are slow in paying indemnities;
- interest rates are high for MSEs (18% and more), generally higher than for large businesses;
- there is an insufficient supply of medium- and long-term loans;
- MSEs encountering financing problems report a shortage of adequate business support services.

Whereas the banking sectors in Bulgaria and Romania have been stabilised and are becoming profitable, restructuring efforts in other Balkan states are still underway. The main advantages of the Balkan states are low wages and skilled labour. In labour-intensive production projects, these advantages often outweigh the weaknesses in infrastructure and legal systems, the vulnerability to fraud and insufficient access to finance.

The SEE countries export about two-thirds of their production to the EU. However, MSEs normally do not observe Community technical standards, hygiene and safety requirements and environmental protection regulations. Larger companies account for the bulk of exports. MSEs need to replace or modernise their plant and equipment and sales facilities. As the large majority of these firms are undercapitalised, they require external finance.

Based on the currently low levels of credit supplied to the private sector, it is expected to take at least a decade to close the gap, if not longer.

Challenges: What Needs to be Done?[2]

Action to improve access to finance may be taken at different levels and by institutions that fulfil a variety of functions. Change could be driven by a number of agents, for example SMEs, banks, various levels of government, donors, foundations or other bodies.

Action by SMEs

Bank credits are in short supply and the banks select only the best proposals. MSEs have to improve the quality of their projects. On the agenda are:

---

[2] The proposals provided here are the author's own; they do not necessarily reflect the views or policies of the European Commission.

- better and "investment-ready" business plans;
- greater transparency of MSEs through better financial reporting;
- introduction of e-businesses;
- improved business training in quality management in general and accountancy in particular.

Action by Local Banks

Banks should increase the share of MSEs in their loan portfolios. This would depend, however, on the banks being able to evaluate the full risk. In order to protect bank earnings and in anticipation of Basel II rules, banks and leasing companies will in any case tighten up their risk assessment of MSE clients.

Action by Local and National Governments or the EU

- develop SME support services in order to get the ball rolling;
- support the creation of incubators and technology-transfer centres;
- organise round tables with bankers and SMEs in order to increase mutual understanding;
- exchange information on best practices in MSE finance;
- support the creation of MSE guarantee instruments or improve the quality of existing instruments based on best practices within the EU in order to increase MSE collateral;
- consider support to microfinance institutions.

Action by Donors and Foundations

Given the insufficient supply of bank loans to MSEs and in rural areas, microcredit institutions play a useful role in reducing the micro-loan gap. In recognition of this fact, donors, foundations and the international public sector should give adequate priority to these enterprises in their support programmes.

Conclusion

It is widely recognised that MSEs play a major role in generating growth, competitiveness and jobs, and thus in improving social wellbeing. Improving the economic situation in SEE depends to a large degree on the interaction between the players in MSE finance and business support services, and on the supply of adequate external resources. There is still much to be done.

CHAPTER 18:

Nonfinancial Obstacles to SME Financing in Serbia

Igor Brkanovic

Senior SME Expert[1]

Owners and directors of small and medium-sized enterprises (SMEs), sole traders, representatives of SME associations and entrepreneurs all report that the basic obstacle to achieving more rapid development in Serbia is the lack of finance and modern mechanisms for its deployment.

The financial infrastructure that supports SMEs in Serbia is undeveloped. Up to now, SMEs and entrepreneurs have financed their operations out of their own resources because financial markets in Serbia were isolated and lacked the support of international financial institutions. The local financial sector in the former Yugoslavia was designed to support large scale, socially owned enterprises – otherwise known as the "Pillars of Development." Banks, especially large-scale socially owned banks, had a redistributive function imposed on them by the state, and they dealt solely with large-scale, socially owned enterprises. In addition, the Fund for Development of the Republic of Serbia disbursed its funds to the same target group. Capacity to repay the banks or the Fund was not a criterion for credit approval.

The former economic and political system did not support the development of financial instruments for SMEs. Cooperation with SMEs focused on a few selected companies, while sole traders were almost completely excluded from credit transactions with the banking sector. SME owners and citizens completely lost their trust in the banks and channelled their savings into the grey economy, to banks abroad, or kept their savings at home. Only payments effected through the National Payment Bureau functioned properly for SMEs.

Since 2001, the National Bank has been implementing reforms in the banking sector. The objectives are to establish market-based banking practices that boost the development of the real sector, stabilise the currency and gain the trust of citizens and SMEs. Bank balance sheets have been cleaned up, some banks have been closed, and strict control of loan use has been instigated to avoid the recurrence of

---

[1] The opinions expressed here are those of the author alone and do not reflect those of the European Agency for Reconstruction, European Union, the Government of the Republic of Serbia or Louis Berger S.A.

previous practices. In order to resolve the conflicts of interest inherent in the social ownership of commercial banks, ownership transfers were initiated. Several newly opened foreign banks are very active in the commercial and retail markets. Starting in 2003, payments are now made by commercial banks rather than via the National Payment Bureau. These activities have helped citizens regain their trust in the banks. In turn, this has led to an increase in savings deposited in banks and encouraged SMEs to redirect their funds into legal businesses and to establish relationships with banks.

One priority of the "Strategy for the Development of Small and Medium-sized Enterprises and Entrepreneurship in the Republic of Serbia 2003 – 2008" is to fund and develop SMEs and entrepreneurship.

Structure of the SME Sector in Serbia

The Serbian economy comprises about 270,000 economic entities, 1% of which are medium-sized and large-scale enterprises, with entrepreneurs and micro and small enterprises accounting for 99%.

The structure of the enterprise sector is overwhelmingly small scale: 96% of all enterprises are small, 3% are medium-sized and 1% are large scale. If sole traders are included, large-scale and medium-sized enterprises account for only 1% of the

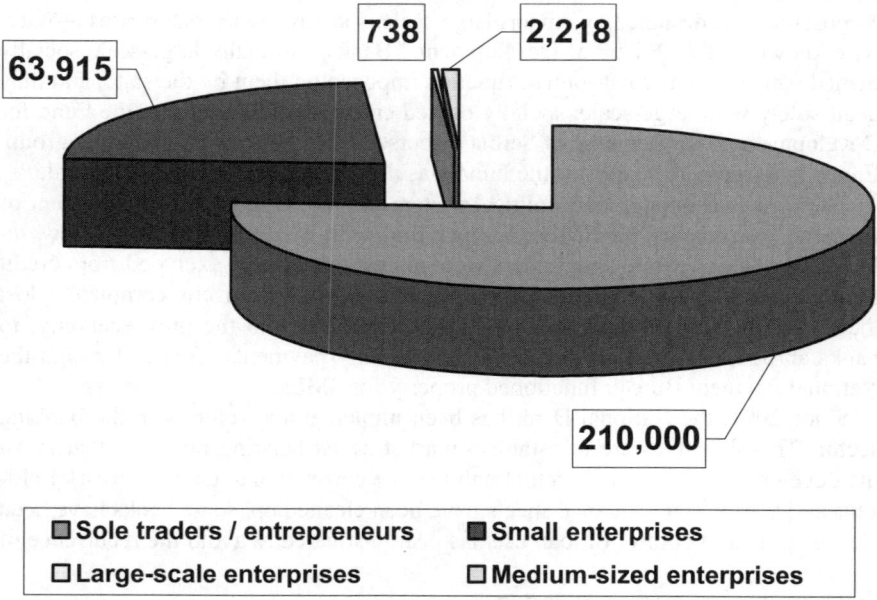

Figure 1. Size distribution of enterprises in Serbia
Source: Republic Development Bureau, Belgrade, October 2003.

total number of entities. The official definition of SMEs in Serbia does not include a micro category, but if micro enterprises are defined as having up to 10 employees, 99% of all small enterprises are actually microenterprises.

Basic characteristics of the SME sector in 2002:

- the average number of employees in the SME sector overall is 5, and 3 in the SME private sector;
- SMEs employ 51% of the workforce in Serbia;
- SMEs own 29% of the total fixed business assets in the economy;
- private SMEs produce 34% of all profits in the economy and 78% of total SME profits;
- SMEs incur 47% of the losses in the economy.
- SME structure and sources of finance:
- SMEs are basically financed through the private funds of their owners;
- undercapitalisation is common;
- current assets dominate SMEs' financial structure relative to fixed assets;
- the basic assets of many firms are obsolete and of little economic value;
- short-term borrowing increases the proportion of current assets relative to investment in long-term or fixed assets.

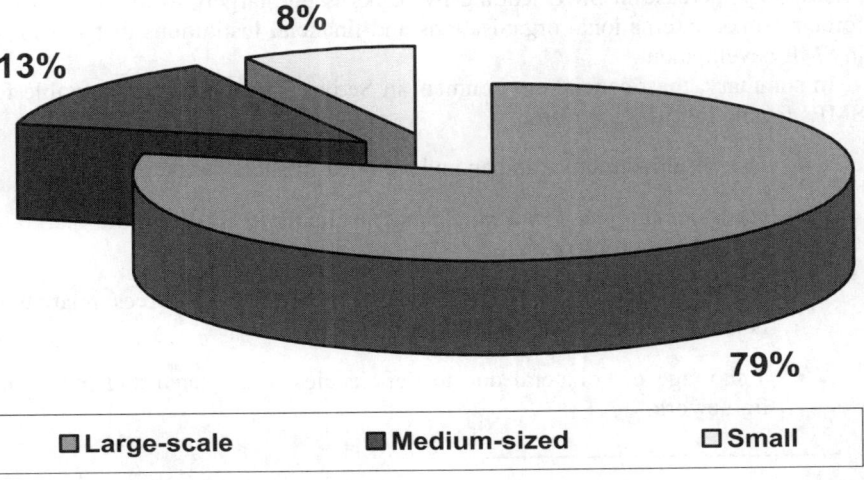

Figure 2. Enterprise capital in Serbia by size of firm
Source: Republic Development Bureau, Belgrade, 2002.

The distribution of capital by size of enterprise indicates a dominance of large-scale firms, followed by medium-sized and small enterprises. (No data are available on microenterprises.)

Structure of Priorities and Forms of SME Funding

SMEs seek forms of capital which are appropriate for funding their current operations and new investments: short-term for current assets, medium-term for equipment and technology, and long-term for land, buildings and infrastructure.

Recent experience indicates that SMEs seeking external funding have obtained credit mostly from buyers and suppliers, with only sporadic and very limited use of other sources and forms of funding. The reason is that the banks had few long-term sources of funding and hence no prudential basis for making term loans. Any such funds to be disbursed were channelled to a small number of large-scale enterprises at substantially reduced transaction costs. Another impediment is the absence of specialised financial institutions due to a lack of appropriate legislation for leasing and investment funds, coupled with the low level of confidence in the legal system which thus discourages direct foreign investment.

Entrepreneurs and SMEs, especially the smallest SMEs and business start-ups, have almost no access to formal financial markets. Access is limited by the insufficient provision of security for creditors. Two forms of security, deposit and mortgage, are used in Serbia, but neither is sufficient nor adequate for small-scale businesses. Small enterprises and sole proprietors often do not have any collateral. If they own real estate, it is usually not registered, and the deposit usually equals the size of the loan requested. The result is that any loans approved are made reluctantly and under far less favourable conditions than loans to large-scale enterprises. Any increase in SME lending by banks is due largely to the activities of foreign banks, international organisations and financial institutions that specialise in SME development.

In summary, the financial environment in Serbia is generally unfavourable for SMEs for the following reasons:

- lack of infrastructure and an undeveloped financial market;
- access to the few forms of finance available to SMEs in the market is limited and problematic;
- the financial market is small with very limited resources relative to potential demand in the SME sector;
- a shortage of collateral due to deficiencies in the legal and regulatory framework.[2]

---

[2] Problems include an overburdened companies registry, unreliable financial reports about companies' operations, unregistered real estate, and lack of registry for collateral, topped off by complicated, slow and uncertain court proceedings.

A particular problem is the legal status of the more than 200,000 entrepreneurs who are unincorporated sole traders. Not being legal entities, they are not obliged to keep accounts and to submit financial statements to the tax authorities. They are therefore unable to provide the documentation usually required by banks.

Banks' Perceptions of SMEs

SMEs and banks do not hold each other or their prospects for collaboration in high regard. When entrepreneurs are asked about the biggest barrier to their development, they cite a lack of funding and the impossibility of obtaining credit from banks. When banks are asked about lending to SMEs, they claim they have sufficient funds but that there are too few good SME projects. According to the banks, the problem is the small number of good and reliable clients with profitable projects and acceptable risks.

Bankers' perceptions of SMEs include the following:

- SMEs are not ready for banking relationships because they are not familiar with the procedures and operations of commercial banks;
- the financial information provided by SME loan applicants is not relevant: there is a huge gap between official business results and the data presented (which include activities and results from informal economic activity);
- the quality and performance of management is difficult to ascertain because the majority of SMEs are new and have no prior contacts with banks;
- credit histories are unreliable and the majority of SMEs do not have a credit history as they have never borrowed from a bank ;
- collateral is inadequate: entrepreneurs very rarely have legally registered fixed assets, and even fewer can provide registered immovables;
- lack of understanding and willingness on the part of SMEs to address the risks of their projects: SMEs expect the banks simply to approve the loan and not be further involved in their operations, decision-making and loan use.

The revolving fund donated by the European Agency for Reconstruction attracted over 1,300 applications by mid-2003, of which about 1,000 were rejected by the banks, largely for the following reasons:

- business plans were not realistic;
- lack of adequate collateral;

- financial data did not represent real performance; and
- debt burdens were already too high.

Of the approximately 300 applications considered by the banks, 140 were approved; the remainder were rejected because of insufficient collateral.

In contrast, ProCredit Bank deals with far smaller loans and shorter maturities, using an approach that is designed to overcome the problems facing sole proprietors and SMEs. It granted about 9,700 loans by mid-2003, disbursing about € 76 million. This suggests that entrepreneurs, micro and small enterprises can be very attractive partners for the banking sector.

SMEs' Perceptions of Banks

The main SME complaint is that the commercial banks do not do enough to support their business development. This attitude reflects the "socialist" view that banks are *development institutions* and obliged to fund SME development in much the same manner as they previously disbursed funds to the large-scale enterprises – the "Pillars of Development."

SMEs generally lack trust in commercial banks and are not ready to enter into open relationships with them. The reasons for this boil down to the following:

- lack of confidentiality regarding business information and profitable ideas: bank staff do not keep confidential information to themselves;
- SME participation in the grey economy is extensive.

Hence, the basis for cooperation and building mutual trust is yet to be developed.

SME complaints about the treatment they receive when applying for credit include the following:

Business plans:

- nonstandardised: almost every bank has its own methodology;
- some banks charge for evaluating business plans, even if the loan application is rejected;
- some banks collect business plans from SMEs to create a project portfolio that could qualify for some official credit line, which, if granted, is not used to fund the projects in the portfolio;
- some banks collect business plans to attract depositors, even though the proposals are not creditworthy or will not be funded because the bank's priorities lie elsewhere.

Evaluation of Credit Applications:

- slow, complicated and expensive;
- credit applications are often accepted and approved, but the loans are not issued because the bank has no funds available for lending;
- loss of time and money for SMEs.

Assessment of business and credit capacities:

- the same criteria and methodology are applied to large-scale enterprises and to SMEs, and banks are not helpful to entrepreneurs who are unfamiliar with the banks' requirements and expectations.

Collateralisation:

- movables are not accepted as collateral, not even the equipment which is to be financed;
- unregistered immovables are also not accepted, even when they are urban, legally registered and their ownership is undisputed.

NGO Micro Credit Operations

Donors provide significant amounts of funds for micro lending through NGOs that actively support SMEs and entrepreneurship among refugees, displaced persons, and vulnerable social groups. International NGOs are very interested in providing finance through nonbank institutions that serve micro and small business, especially for the self-employed and start-ups.

Local and international NGOs and other international organisations, such as UNCHR (United Nations High Commission for Refugees), have made several attempts to develop a legal framework for microfinance regulation, but without success. The only legal basis for microcredit is UNHCR's contract with the Government of Serbia regarding funding for refugees and displaced persons. Several microcredit NGOs work under this umbrella. The funds are disbursed and may also be repaid through the branches of commercial banks in which donors have accounts.

Summary

The obstacles to and potential for SME financing may be summarised as follows:

- SMEs are very important generators of economic development in Serbia. To establish an adequate environment for the rapid growth and development of this sector, the "Strategy for the Development of Small and Medium-sized Enterprises and Entrepreneurship in the Republic of

Serbia 2003 – 2008" was adopted in January 2003. One of the priority tasks defined in the Strategy is to provide finance for SMEs. Lack of funding is the greatest hindrance to development in this sector according to SMEs and entrepreneurs.

- In the past, the financial sector funded large-scale enterprises, which were considered the "Pillars of Development." The financial infrastructure based on this pattern is not able to serve SMEs.

- Despite certain regulatory improvements, the deficiencies remaining in the legal framework hamper the development of a new market that would fund SMEs. To overcome these barriers, a sound legal basis is needed for the provision of microfinance; for the establishment of regional credit, guarantee and investment funds; and for the creation of new financial instruments and schemes. Overcoming and removing regulatory barriers will facilitate public-private partnership financing in the SME sector.

- Measures and activities implemented to improve SME funding should take into account the objectives, models and sources of funding for potential and existing SMEs and entrepreneurs. Macroeconomic projections of the financing requirements for developing the SME sector are essential, as is information on the sources of funding.

- The banks lack long-term sources of funding, and their lending capacity is greatly limited by a lack of liquidity. Loan decision-making is still rigidly bureaucratic. Bank managements and employees are not trained to deal with SMEs. Banking is still oriented towards large-scale enterprises, and the pertinent decision-makers regard SMEs neither as an attractive target group nor a partner for long-term business relationships.

- Financial support for start-ups is insufficient. Because the banking sector is not able to fund start-ups, alternative sources of funding should be provided. For this, it is necessary to create specialised institutions, such as seed capital funds. Public sector institutions, NGOs and other providers should develop specific instruments and funding models.

SMEs are not sufficiently informed about the possibilities and procedures and thus not geared up to obtain external funding. Communicating and establishing working relationships with banks is a major obstacle for SMEs. A very small proportion of SMEs succeed in obtaining grants, equity and leasing services. As a general conclusion, it appears there is a high level of resistance throughout the SME sector to seeking direct forms of funding. From this perspective, SMEs require training in order to improve their ability to attract funding from a broad range of sources.

CHAPTER 19:

Constraints to Business Development in Bulgaria and the Case for Action

Stefan Kossev

Manager, Boliari EAD, Varna

Sarah Forster's theme paper covers many aspects of financial sector performance in the countries of Southeast Europe (SEE) from the micro and small enterprise (MSE) perspective. But within SEE, the differences in business environment and business development are greater than the similarities. The results reported here reflect the business activities in only some of the countries in the region.

This paper focuses on Bulgaria and the major financial constraints to starting up and developing micro, small and medium-sized enterprises (MSEs and SMEs). Most of these constraints are interrelated.

Understanding the Local Business Environment

In order to analyse business development in the region as a whole, a few general comments are in order concerning the problems facing the SEE countries as a group and the things they have in common. As their historical developments, traditions and customs differ, these countries have different starting points for transition. These factors influence the business environment and the inherent financial constraints. For example, the demand for finance cannot be estimated without taking into account the grey economy – and its impact is very hard to measure.

Unless the actual market situation in each country is understood, the constraints to business development cannot be addressed properly and effectively. Local experts should therefore be involved in each issue or problem to be examined, in particular to help ensure the provision of reliable data.

Contradictions in the Funding Process

Much donor financing is currently channelled to multinational companies or their subsidiaries that enter one or two countries in the region, such as Billa supermarkets in Bulgaria, owned by the German Rewe Group. This approach is presumably taken because local companies may be rather small or do not publish transparent financial statements. But even with an excellent strategic plan and a focused management team, it is very hard for a purely local enterprise to attract donor interest. It is thought that there are few opportunities for local micro and small enterprises (MSEs) or small and medium-sized enterprises (SMEs) to grow and eventually become competitive with international companies. According to this view, local firms' strategies should be to stay attractive as long as possible and to wait to be bought by an international company. However, international companies that enter the SEE market do not always perform well because they do not study the local market carefully enough, or because they simply copy their standard format without adapting it properly to on-site conditions.

Country Risk

With the EU accession process underway, country risk is expected to diminish, encouraging more MFIs to enter the market and improving access to finance for MSEs.

Bulgaria's country risk remains high, although EU accession is planned and the country's credit rating is improving. But there remains a reluctance to lend, and interest rates are high. Even big foreign banks are not willing to offer services other than collateral-based lending and are not willing to support the expansion efforts of Bulgarian companies. As a result, facilities offered to MSEs in the EU are not available to those in SEE.

Relatively little is known in the EU about Bulgaria and its business environment. The decision-making bodies at European financial institutions generally have a distorted view of the actual situation and do not focus on risk management and prevention. Lack of trust in the ability of local companies to run their businesses in the future or to manage expansion prevents positive decision-making.

Lack of Trust in the Financial System

In 1996–1997, the financial collapse in Bulgaria destroyed trust in financial institutions. More than 26 banks became insolvent. The collapse was a result of vigorous governmental interventions that supported political parties and financed state-owned companies that were no longer financially viable. At that time, many MSEs went bankrupt as their bank balances and working capital simply disappeared within several days. Most of the existing and newly registered MSEs then turned to their savings and the grey economy to finance their operations and in some cases their expansion. Trust is returning slowly, but the financial system's failure to allocate funds efficiently leads some businesses to remain outside the formal sector, where it is common practice to underreport sales and profits.

It will take time to improve networking between the financial institutions and MSEs, which because of their size continue to rely on friends and relatives for support and advice. Perceptions are expected to change over time.

The Bias of Banks and other Financial Institutions

Bank bias is very well described in the theme paper. Almost all the big local banks have been privatised and are now controlled by foreign investors. Their preferred clients are large companies and prosperous individuals. The bias against MSE lending is illustrated in the following example: Varna, a Bulgarian bank specialising in MSE and SME lending, was bought by Société Générale BF, France. Within two years, most of the MSE and SME clients had been "chased out." Emphasis shifted to more profitable retail banking, and there were no resources available or trained staff to provide the services desired by the former clients. In contrast, ProCredit Bank performs well as a specialised MFB. It has rapid decision-making processes.

The banks' bias is reflected in collateral-based lending: SMEs or MSEs seldom have many free assets acceptable to lenders. Most banks are reluctant to participate in a company's expansion using cash-flow lending approaches because they consider the risk to be very high. Within any given timeframe, the banks prefer to grant loans for bigger projects which have a sufficient degree of collateral backing, rather than for several smaller projects that might produce rapid business expansion.

Government Policy, Legislation and Administrative Constraints

Administrative constraints have a great impact on the availability of finance. In Bulgaria constant changes in legislation are the norm, and this leads to confusion in the market. Factors that hinder SMEs and MSEs include:

- a lack of significant improvement in the investment climate and a dearth of incentives for long-term domestic investment and the introduction of new technology; even foreign direct investment is decreasing;
- underdeveloped infrastructure;
- an incomplete legal basis for SME activity, including licensing and certification;
- an abundance of supervisory bodies with overlapping functions;
- insufficient government protection from large foreign competitors;
- illegally imported goods with false declared values, resulting in low duties and retail prices that are below the cost of local producers;
- destruction of Bulgaria's historically strong industries during the transition period that began in the early-1990s.

The main focus of the current government is to attract large strategic investors for the companies yet to be privatised. This also results in a lack of attention to and support for SMEs. A draft law to encourage investment is being prepared; it aims to provide an investor-friendly climate, tax and infrastructure subsidies as well as investment incentive packages. But most of the incentives are for projects larger than € 5 million, which again leaves MSEs with almost no support.

More incentives are needed for the priority sectors of the local economy, especially tourism, the service sector, hi-tech manufacturing and agribusiness. If the financial constraints are not reduced as EU regulations come into force, doing business in Bulgaria will remain an expensive and sometimes financially unrewarding undertaking.

Domestic Funding

Domestic funds are an important determinant of investment in most industrial economies. This is not the case in Bulgaria.

Local banks tend to lend to related parties, or may even set up a joint venture with an entrepreneur simply as a vehicle for lending, sometimes using funding received from European donor institutions. Many loan agreements specify interest rates that are twice as high as those in the EU and with shorter loan tenors. Furthermore, it is widely accepted that the role of local financial institutions is primarily to help local businesses.

The rather narrow equity markets should be developed. The Bulgarian stock exchange has been operating for several years. At the beginning of the transition period there was a surge of company listings, including some state-owned companies being privatised, but after privatisation these enterprises were de-listed. The regional stock exchanges find it hard to compete with the large well-established European exchanges. However, the local exchange can play a significant role in the development and expansion of MSEs.

Small companies cannot be listed on European exchanges, but they can be attractive on local exchanges and can bring benefits. Advertising within the country or region in order to obtain capital is much cheaper and much more effective because of local awareness, giving some companies a better sense of their market value. In Bulgaria, there are no real benchmarks for company valuations, and all valuations are disputed. This hampers restructuring efforts, buyouts and mergers.

Guarantees are not very common in Bulgaria. Due to the risks involved, banks are reluctant to offer guarantees, demanding collateral instead. Guarantees also tend to be expensive, almost equal to the normal lending rate in the EU.

Leasing services are available but expensive. Factoring is very common (contrary to the claim in the theme paper) in the wholesale sector, for example, because it provides liquidity quickly. However, banks that offer factoring services sometimes require collateral, which limits the demand and the scope for employing this instrument. A supportive legal and regulatory framework should be established for factoring.

Expected Impact Following EU Entry

The EU accession process and the corresponding changes in legislation are expected to have a positive impact on the economic environment and investment activity in Bulgaria. It is believed that Bulgaria's accession, scheduled for 2007, will attract more foreign investment from European companies that want to expand into the Balkan states. However, many SMEs will be exposed to increased competition and may not survive because of their inability to comply with EU regulations. Some will no longer be able to sell their products even within Bulgaria. If new EU oriented regulations come into force that increase the cost of services and production without providing corresponding business development incentives, local SME performance will deteriorate.

During the accession process, efforts should be made to provide MSEs and SMEs with funding to increase their operational effectiveness. Governmental support is needed in the shape of more incentives for business development. It is also essential to provide further training for SME owners in order to enhance their managerial skills.

Conclusion

Research suggests that SMEs and MSEs generate more jobs per unit of investment than larger firms, and they have greater social impact, reinvest in the local community and respond flexibly to changes in economic and market conditions. For these reasons, government support in the form of favourable legislation and the creation of a better business environment is important. Trust and cooperation between SMEs and MSEs on the one hand, and the financial sector on the other, should be encouraged. In addition, priority should be given to the simplification of administrative procedures.

CHAPTER 20:

Degrees of Competition in Serving Target Groups – They May Be Closer than You Think

Christoph Freytag[1]

IPC GmbH

Comparing the performance of the ProCredit Bank[2] network, NGOs and commercial banks in providing financial services to micro and small businesses is always difficult. Difficulty arises because ProCredit Bank's concept does not fit in easily with (neo)classical criteria.

The concept of NGOs offering target groups certain services that are not provided by the market is understood perfectly well, as is the justification for the public funding of such activities. The provision of microfinance via donor-financed NGOs is justifiable because profit-driven, market-based private financial intermediaries do not offer credit to low-income households, rural borrowers, or other groups who are perceived as similarly unattractive. Without intervention, the microfinance market is left to informal lenders and is probably crucially underserved.

The concept of a traditional private, profit-driven bank is even better understood. It is not necessary to repeat the long list of reasons or excuses frequently put forward by banks when asked why they do not lend more money to micro and small businesses. In a nutshell: the banks expect to earn little or nothing in this sector.

As the ProCredit Banks are both target-group and profit oriented, part publicly and part privately owned, an assessment of these institutions requires a more differentiated approach.

---

[1] During 2003 the author was General Director of ProCredit Bank (Serbia).

[2] The ProCredit Bank network in Southeast Europe previously consisted of Micro Enterprise Bank (Bosnia), Micro Enterprise Bank (Kosovo), FEFAD Bank (Albania), Microfinance Bank (Serbia), ProBusiness Bank (Macedonia), Miro Bank (Romania) and ProCredit Bank (Bulgaria). Since August 2003, all these banks have changed their name to ProCredit Bank, demonstrating a common mission and similar ownership structure. IMI (Internationale Micro Investitionen AG) is a shareholder in all banks, and IPC (Internationale Projekt Consult GmbH) has provided management services to all these banks since their creation.

Comparing Like with Like: Outreach

In terms of target-group orientation, it is not possible to compare NGOs and ProCredit Banks on the basis of their total loan portfolios. This is because ProCredit Banks lend not only to micro businesses, but also to small and medium-sized enterprises (SMEs). However, data for the ProCredit Banks and NGOs serving the region yield interesting comparisons.[3]

- The micro loan portfolios of the ProCredit Banks have an average loan amount of € 1,549, compared to $ 1,193 for the 34 NGOs in the region.

- The average number of borrowers at the 34 NGOs is 3,286, and 70% of these are in rural areas. This means that, on average, each NGO has 2,300 borrowers in rural areas; whereas at ProCredit Bank Serbia, 2,663 out of a total of roughly 23,000 borrowers are farmers. Thus, the fact that an NGO is very often focused on rural areas does not necessarily mean that it serves more rural borrowers than an MFB (microfinance bank) does.

- Female microentrepreneurs account for 49% of all borrowers at NGOs, compared to 19% at MFBs. But if legal entities are excluded, a different profile emerges by comparing female sole proprietors to the total number of sole proprietors who have taken loans. The proportions range from 24% in Serbia to 39% in Bulgaria.

Thus, NGOs and ProCredit Banks in the region serve virtually the same market, they address basically the same client group, and they achieve very similar results in terms of outreach.

The Institutional Basis of ProCredit Banks' Scale

The survey cited in the theme paper states that ProCredit Banks perform better than NGOs with regard to scale of operations, sustainability and impact. However, the reasons for this are not given. The key to better performance is likely due to several factors: ProCredit Banks are licensed, set up like commercial banks and subject to supervision and regulation; they are partly privately owned, giving them a strong incentive to grow, to operate sustainably and to achieve an impact. This entrepreneurial approach is reinforced by investor expectations that these institutions will generate a profit and maintain target-group orientation.

Although the degree of success achieved by the ProCredit Banks in financial intermediation varies from country to country, the younger banks in particular

---

[3] The region is Southeast Europe; the ProCredit Bank network covers Bosnia and Herzegovina, Serbia and Montenegro, Kosovo, Macedonia, Albania, Moldova, Bulgaria and Romania.

(with a larger share of private equity from the start) have clearly succeeded in mobilising deposits, in utilising the domestic money market and even in tapping the emerging domestic capital markets.

ProCredit Bank Serbia ranks sixth in the country by volume of private savings, just ahead of the national savings bank. Financing from international institutions (IFIs) accounts for less than 25% of the bank's balance sheet, in spite of a 50% mandatory reserve requirement on hard currency savings from private customers. ProCredit Bank Bulgaria, a latecomer in a fairly advanced financial sector in which foreign banks compete strongly, has raised deposits amounting to 50% of its loan portfolio, and has pioneered by issuing a mortgage bond in domestic currency. It also attracts funds from local banks and institutional investors to finance its activities. Here, too, the share of funding from IFIs is less than 25% of the balance sheet total.

So, even in competitive markets, ProCredit Banks can succeed in mobilising domestic resources and channelling them effectively to the target group. In less competitive environments, such as Albania or Kosovo, ProCredit Banks' deposit volumes have more than funded their loan portfolios. The case study cited in the theme paper focused on Bosnia, a market where a substantial volume of donor grants and loans was committed, and this clearly has an impact on the current structure of the credit supply. How will the composition of the Bosnian credit market evolve over the next decade?

As a result of their structure and funding strategies, the younger ProCredit Banks (founded in 2001) have reached break-even more quickly. Those now in their third year of operations achieve respectable returns on equity of around 10%. Most of these institutions are now operating independently of technical assistance. Of the nine ProCredit institutions operating in Eastern Europe, only the two most recently founded – in Romania (2002) and Macedonia (2003) – did not break even in 2003.

The lesson here is that the institutional setup of a bank, combined with private equity participation from target-group oriented investors, provides a basis for future opportunities and growth.

Institutional Basis of ProCredit Banks' Scope

The institutional setup of a bank can enable it to explore and develop additional target-group- oriented business opportunities which are not accessible to NGOs. ProCredit Banks generate additional income by offering domestic and international payment services, documentary credits, payment cards, POS (point of sale) terminals and ATMs (automatic teller machines). They finance receivables, grant credit lines and overdraft facilities. They have introduced related lines of business, such as housing and housing improvement loans. To the degree that micro and small business owners develop successfully, they also become increasingly attractive as private customers. Today, and more so in the future, the more affluent owners of small and medium-sized enterprises (SMEs) offer further opportunity for ProCredit Banks to develop savings products.

The house bank concept, with a clear orientation towards the target group of micro, small and (in the future) medium-sized companies, offers additional potential for growth and sustainable profits.

Strategic Prerequisites for Successful MSE Relationships

The results of donor attempts to provide loans to micro and small enterprises (MSE) via commercial banks have been mixed. Generally, commercial banks prefer to serve small and medium-sized businesses rather than the micro segment. In terms of loan volume, recovery and outreach, the commercial banks' performance tends not to be very impressive if the use of their own funds is factored in: "partner banks" receiving donor financing tend not to expand their MSE portfolios beyond this funding source. Even the sustainability of these programmes may be questioned.

Very often, problems centre on the inability or unwillingness of the partner bank to exercise real ownership of the MSE lending activities. Exercising real ownership means making a fundamental strategic decision to integrate micro and small businesses into the overall strategy of the partner bank and to give these activities (at least a certain) priority. Such a decision has consequences for the bank's organisational structure and business policy which go far beyond merely recruiting a few loan officers. Every single department must understand the specific requirements for efficient MSE lending and this will usually mean that existing policies have to be changed. There are very few cases in which bank owners have made this decision and have fully followed through with implementation.

In this context, ProCredit Banks play an important role as market makers. In a number of markets, other banks have begun to replicate the ProCredit Banks' procedures and products, or have even attempted to headhunt whole teams of loan officers in order to improve their own MSE lending. Clearly, ProCredit Banks increasingly enhance the status of micro and small businesses in the eyes of the financial community, demonstrating that they are viable businesses that provide opportunities for engaging in profitable banking relationships. The importance of this demonstration effect should not be underestimated.

Competition, Debt Capacity and the Range of Services

Commercial banks entering the MSE market with alternative, "less risky" instruments pose a potential threat. The boom in consumer finance and leasing products in some markets is clearly a challenge to a ProCredit Bank and even more so to NGOs. Consumer loans *can* replace micro loans. Leasing *can* replace term loans to SMEs. But, commercial banks take a less analytical approach to MSEs when they rely on highly standardised and usually insured consumer lending facilities and on asset-backed financing arrangements such as leasing.[4] In both cases – consumer lending and asset-backed deals – the banks neglect to determine repayment capacity in markets where borrowers have little or no experience with formal credit. This omission translates into lost opportunities for borrowers with greater debt capacity, and dangers for those who borrow beyond their sustainable limit. In several SEE countries there are no credit bureaus, and here in particular, the risk of banks enticing MSEs into overindebtness is clearly real.

ProCredit Banks follow a policy of relationship banking rather than transaction banking. Time will tell whether a ProCredit Bank can compete in an environment where the structure of the credit supply is changing. At the moment, we can safely say that the ProCredit Banks' market presence, with a great number of established business relationships, will enable them to maintain a strong position. In any case, their institutional setup will allow them to react more flexibly to the changing environment than the NGOs, which typically offer one kind of product.

Outlook

The points made in this paper clearly support the approach chosen by IMI and those institutions that have adopted a similar strategy. The institutional setup of a bank is best suited to serve MSEs; NGOs enjoy no specific competitive advantage in terms of target-group orientation. The second key to the success of the ProCredit Banks is clearly their public-private ownership structure. This efficiently combines the financial strength and mission of donors and IFIs with the expertise and profit orientation of private investors.

We strongly advocate the further commercialisation of microfinance. Bringing microfinance out of its niche as an exclusively donor-financed activity is clearly in the best interests of MSEs. We believe that by continuing to pursue this strategy, substantial private capital will become available to increase the supply of credit to MSEs. Whenever and wherever IMI and like-minded investors tap these funds, the justification for public intervention stated at the beginning of this paper becomes increasingly obsolete. But let us not rush ahead too quickly. There is still a long way to go in Central and Eastern Europe, and there are a vast number of micro and small businesses that can be increasingly empowered through financial services.

---

[4] In some cases, we observed suppliers of consumer finance that, due to their (leaner) cost structure, are prepared to factor higher default rates into their profitability calculations. They are not concerned about their social responsibility as a lender nor worried about deterioration in the markets.

CHAPTER 21:

A New Approach to Business Development Services in Southeast Europe

Hayder Al-Bagdadi,[1] Dirk Steinwand,[2] and Frank Wältring[3]

[1] Junior Project Manager, Financial Systems Development Section,
[2] Head of Financial Systems Development Section,
[3] Economic Advisor, Private Sector Promotion Section,
Deutsche Gesellschaft für Technische Zusammenarbeit GmbH – GTZ

In the last decade, the importance of encouraging enterprise development services has received increasing attention in the development community. This rekindled interest is due to the role these services play in the private sector in general. Access to consultancy services increases enterprise competitiveness by bringing about improvements in a number of areas: training, management, product development, standards compliance, efficiency, research and development, market information, supply linkages and marketing. Micro, small and medium-sized enterprises often lack access to these services, which, when offered, are usually provided by the public sector with financial support from donors on a subsidised and supply oriented basis. Consulting services are generally provided directly to enterprises; there is little emphasis on integrating or supporting institutions and private-sector service providers active in this market.

With the benefit of hindsight, the weaknesses of these often ineffective and unsustainable approaches have become apparent. Many services collapsed after the donors phased out their financial support. These poor results were due to insufficient demand orientation and the failure of both donors and the private sector to create a market for these services in developing countries. In response, discussion within the donor community led to the establishment of criteria for developing business support services. The Guidelines of the Donor Committee for Small Enterprise Development[1] were the result of efforts by large international donors to learn from their experience in providing these services.

---

[1] Since 1979, the Committee of Donor Agencies for Small Enterprise Development has provided a forum for multilateral and bilateral donors to exchange information and to coordinate activities in the area of small enterprise development. It encourages consistency among donor programmes by distilling lessons of experience into common principles

The Learning Processes of the International Donor Community

The search for solutions within the donor community was multifaceted. Most donors worked with public institutions, NGOs or directly with the private sector. The public institutions had difficulty determining the real demand among enterprises due to insufficient knowledge, lack of specialisation at the field level, and changing circumstances in the market. NGOs faced these problems, too, and often applied a paternalistic approach in supporting the target group. In addition, it was costly to create the necessary infrastructure and to staff offices. Services were often provided free of charge or on a subsidised basis, which obscured the real demand. In many cases, this market distortion made it impossible for private providers to compete with services funded by donors or the public sector.

The Principles of the Business Development Services (BDS) Approach

The Guidelines of the Donor Committee for Small Enterprise Development contain the following recommendations for enterprise support services:

- the role of donors is to assist service providers, not to support target enterprises directly;
- the approach must be demand and not supply oriented in order to increase the outreach, utilisation and benefits of BDS; and
- the services should be financially sustainable in the long run and not subsidy-driven.

The overall goal is to expand the market for BDS and so create an institutional framework based on market principles that enable client enterprises to improve their competitiveness.

Matching BDS Demand and Supply in SEE

The BDS approach aims to match the supply and demand for enterprise support services more efficiently. As most economies in SEE have a socialist history, it will take some time to establish effective BDS, due to institutional weaknesses, lack of experience with market mechanisms and unfamiliarity with these services.

The potential demand for BDS appears large; however, the supply of these services is growing very slowly. The weaknesses are the result of:

---

for assistance. The first draft of the Guidelines on BDS was produced in 1997 (see http://www.gtz.de/wbf/doc/BDS_SME_1997.pdf).

- market distortions due to weak, decentralised policy decisions and bureaucratic blockages;
- insufficient knowledge on the part of public sector providers about the conditions of micro, small and medium-sized enterprises;
- existing public BDS that fail to provide the services most useful to members or clients;
- the image, based on their former political relations, of institutions (such as chambers of commerce) that provide BDS to various sectors;
- the time-lag in recognising the importance of services, and the quality of the assistance provided;
- the generally low level of enterprise incomes and entrepreneurs' doubts about the costs and benefits of BDS services;
- the high cost structures of many service providers and the reluctance of donors to cover these costs.

The Donor Guidelines are therefore important in setting the direction for future approaches in SEE. In this context, the BDS approach should be seen as a learning process based on the experience gained in private-sector promotion and on the aim to improve the effectiveness of donor intervention and donor cooperation.

GTZ's Business Development Services in SEE

GTZ is focusing on different targets in the region, especially on private-sector development and vocational training and upgrading, including management training for businesses and chambers. Projects are being implemented in various fields:

- training and upgrading for employees, entrepreneurs, consultants, and chambers;
- support for chambers in adopting a demand-orientated approach towards their members;
- assistance for local approaches within cities and regions;
- export promotion and the training of replicators;
- organisational development in chambers, especially branch offices;
- strengthening specific business services within different institutions;
- capacity-building for demand oriented service approaches;

- analysis of the BDS market based on demand and supply studies, mainly on behalf of chambers.

The Contribution of BDS in SEE

A distinction can be made between operational and strategic business services. *Operational services* are useful for improving day-to-day operations, such as information and communications, the management of accounts and tax records, and compliance with labour laws and other regulations. In many countries in the region, a commercial market for operational services already exists, and companies are willing to pay for them.

Strategic services help enterprises address medium and long-term issues in order to improve their performance. These services include advice in marketing, strategy and engineering. Such "high-end" services are already provided to some extent; however, due to local circumstances, consultants often lack the international and market experience that would improve the quality of their services. Donors should therefore concentrate on strengthening the capacity of providers to deliver high-quality strategic services.

Improving BDS

Many BDS providers try to expand the range of their activities instead of focusing on specific core competencies. To become more market oriented, it is necessary for BDS providers to reprogramme their activities, offering products and services that can be easily identified in the market. As well as defining service and product profiles and creating the services themselves, this evolutionary process requires organisational and institutional adjustments. In their role as facilitators, donors can support BDS providers by developing new services, promoting good practices, building provider capacity and encouraging quality and transparency in the BDS market.

The marketing of services and products is of major importance. Many BDS providers currently fail to market their services directly and proactively to the target client group. They seek to deliver services as contractors to donors. Hence, BDS providers need to integrate marketing tools fully into their business operations. Donors can support this process by not providing services directly, and especially not free of charge – this being the worst case. The broad provision of free services undermines the local consulting market. The resulting negative effects are visible on both the supply and demand sides. Private sector BDS providers are crowded out, and an expectation is created that knowledge-based services are, in principle, free of charge. To avoid these market distortions, it is essential that donors coordinate their activities.

PART V:

Looking Ahead – Public-Private Partnerships in the Financial Sector in Southeast Europe

PART V

Introduction to Part V

Can public-private partnerships, most commonly found in the development and operation of infrastructure projects in the US and UK, be used to promote the expansion of finance for small and medium-sized enterprises (SME) in transition economies and developing countries? If so, how can the responsibilities of public sector and private sector investors be structured in ways that will achieve superior returns, especially in dynamic situations such as SME finance in Southeast Europe?

Structuring PPPs to Promote Finance at the Bottom End of the Market

In the theme paper "Looking Ahead – Opportunities for Public-Private Partnerships (PPP) in Financial Development," Professor Harry Schmidt and his co-author Nina Moisa define PPP as an arrangement in which private *capital, management* and *ownership* are used to provide what are typically regarded as public services. PPPs are an institutional form that, when properly designed, enables the public sector to obtain leverage by enlisting private parties in ways that reap the advantages of private economic activity, i.e. initiative, experimentation, innovation and reduced costs.

For PPPs to work, the incentives of all parties must be aligned with the project's objectives. Achieving alignment is a complex task that requires fine-tuning. Alignment requires that contracts are workable and enforceable, and that they allocate risks and rewards efficiently. Contracts also allocate property rights. However, no contract is ever complete in the sense of covering all eventualities, and the challenge of PPPs is to maintain productive activity in situations that were not foreseen in contracts. Conflicts will inevitably arise, and the procedures for dealing with them are important if contract objectives are to be realised. Effective contracts lower the cost of resolving conflict.

Participation in ownership by the private party is a first step towards aligning interests. Ownership is defined not solely in terms of property rights, but rather in a functional or economic manner defined in terms of the right to make residual decisions, which should reside with those who have residual claims. Residual decisions are those that are not defined in contracts, which means that residual decision-makers bear some risk. If the designated residual decision-maker or claimant has only limited capacity to provide capital and take risks, others will become residual claimants and hence residual decision-makers.

As situations change over time and in the course of a project, the likelihood of contract renegotiation increases. Those who have made the most specific investments incur the largest sunk costs and have the most to lose in renegotiation. This party should therefore be assigned ownership rights as a counterweight.

One problem that inevitably arises in PPPs is moral hazard, which is the temptation for the private party to cut costs and thus reduce the quality of service delivery beyond a point that is beneficial for the realisation of project objectives. This is most likely in areas where behaviour is nonverifiable and therefore not specifically enforceable by contract. Many countermeasures are available that diminish these risks. One is the value of reputation and trust accumulated through repeated satisfactory collaboration, which creates incentives to behave in a way that continues the prospects of partnership.

Summarising, the economic objective in structuring PPPs is to assign residual decision rights to the party who will use them to make decisions that add the most value to the project. This party must have a long-term perspective.

PPPs are often set up to implement infrastructure projects. A more recent development is to exploit the advantages of PPPs in the finance sector, and specifically for micro and small enterprise banks. This is illustrated by the highly successful case of the micro and small enterprise banks affiliated to IMI (Internationale Micro Investitionen AG, an investment company that invests in the ProCredit banks). The interests of the investors and consultants that establish and manage these banks are aligned in a number of ways: by enhancing the role of reputation, making payment dependent upon performance, ensuring that the consultant has an equity share, and defining as clearly as possible the grounds for intervention by the public party and the possible sanctions that can be used to check the actions of the private party, in this case IPC (a consulting firm that founded IMI and that executes IMI projects).

Potential conflicts include a) IPC's dual role as investor and as contractor providing management services to the IMI banks, and b) balancing the development objectives and the commercial objectives of these banks. Giving the private party a majority ownership interest appears to be the best solution in this case because the trust and reputation it has earned are consistent with residual decision making. An unusual twist is that the private party, IPC, claims to be the more concerned about the development mandate – serving the target group of micro and small entrepreneurs – while the public sector investors in IMI and the network of banks are more concerned about commercial performance. Although this supposition could be contested, the IFIs will (in line with their mandates) at some point exit IMI, while IPC has no intention of doing so and presumably has a longer-term interest. This divergence or complementarity of roles is common in PPPs and is managed by ownership rights, which protect the private party, and strict governance structures, which protect the public party.

Could the PPP concept be applied more widely, for example in the leasing sector? Leasing provides a strong form of property right, and a PPP leasing company could be socially useful in environments in which property rights are otherwise defective. However, if setting up a leasing operation provides high private returns, the case for a PPP is weakened because private providers should move in spontaneously. This contrasts with the SME sector, where high start-up costs must be offset by subsidies in order to achieve acceptable private rates of return. Housing finance is similar to leasing in many respects, and PPPs also have potential in this sector. Although PPPs for public housing finance appear to pass the test of high social returns and low financial returns, but they should be compared to alternatives.

Response Papers

A response paper by Klaus-Eckhard Hartmann of Deutsche Investitions- und Entwicklungsgesellschaft mbH (DEG) describes the fundamental strengths and weaknesses of public sector investment in financial sector development. Public sector investors are often prepared to accept a high level of risk, but their funds are in short supply and therefore should be used strategically as a basis for attracting private funding. The supply of private sector funds is vast, but private sector investors are almost always risk-sensitive. The trick is to match project risk with the risk tolerance or appetite of the investors. This is accomplished by constructing hierarchical divisions or "risk ladders" that provide choices for investors. When funding a project, the public sector may assume a disproportionate amount of risk, commensurate with its catalytic role. This consequently diminishes the amount of risk assumed by the private investors. This remaining risk is also laddered, allowing private investors to assume different levels of risk according to their own objectives.

The risk-bearing hierarchy includes equity and different types of loan finance, and the ratio between equity and debt is a critical factor for managing risk and distributing it accordingly. Other factors that have to be considered in any project involving both private and public sector investors include currency risk.

DEG structures financial sector projects and provides management expertise. It employs several different models based on the types of institutions being formed or assisted, and also provides guarantees or standby arrangements that can promote development by transferring risk.

Ira Lieberman of The Open Society Institute summarises the use and evolution of cooperation arrangements involving public and private sector participants. Such arrangements are generally found in relatively large infrastructure projects. They can take the form of contracting out agreements, concessions or PPPs (a term that Lieberman uses more broadly than the definition provided by Schmidt and Moisa).

Challenges frequently arise because of the incompleteness of contracts, including means of dealing with *force majeure* in the form of economic crises. Political considerations relating to the pricing of services may make cooperation impossible in sensitive areas such as water and electric power. Corruption is also a problem. Finding off-shore jurisdictions in which the private parties feel comfortable and which are beyond local conflicts of interest, is critical for productive dispute resolution. In contrast, cooperation in microfinance has worked much more smoothly, beginning with donor engagement of NGOs as implementing agencies and then moving towards support for for-profit institutions with emphasis on sustainability.

As the interests of the contracting parties may diverge over time, instability remains a threat. This can be triggered by the scarcity of private partners' funds as operations expand or by the public sector partner's desire to exit when it perceives that its development mandate has been achieved. Lieberman advises that partnerships should have a defined life with clear procedures for parting and exit.

Helen Alexander of IMI notes that credit technology was an early focus of IPC's consultancy work with microfinance institutions that were oriented towards sustainability. However, as it became clear that the institutions, not the technology, were the barriers to serving the SME target group, this concern was slowly eclipsed by a focus on ownership and governance. Microfinance organisations with no owners, such as NGOs, were inefficient, while institutions with real owners, such as commercial banks, sought short-term profits. These lessons led IPC to create IMI, with the objective of forming new institutions that would be regulated, serve a specific target group and accept local deposits. Official international financial institutions (IFIs) and other investors joined IMI and furthered its agenda.

As of early 2004, IMI's public sector and private sector owners held nearly equal shares, and total equity exceeded €43 million. The total equity of the 18 IMI institutions worldwide was €134 million, much of which was held by the public sector investors in IMI (IFC, KfW, FMO and BIO), joined by EBRD and others that invested in the network but not in IMI. In 2004 and 2005 these investors will swap their shares in the individual banks for shares in IMI, which will become a holding company, a network of banks with essentially one owner. IMI shares are more liquid than those of the 18 banks, and this consolidation will help pave the way to an IPO that will permit exit by public sector owners that have a development mandate.

The network has been profitable overall, with a return on equity (RoE) of 10% in 2003, during which four institutions that were formed between 2001 and 2003 had not broken even. In early 2004, network institutions had about 320,000 loans outstanding with a combined portfolio of €700 million. Sixty percent of these loans were for amounts of less than €1,000. By mid-2004, monthly disbursements amounted to €70 million, comprising 40,000 loans. Funds for the expansion of the network have been provided primarily by IMI's public sector owners and by EBRD, but their exposure limits are being reached. Deposit-taking is essential, but is by nature slow in most markets.

The key to IMI's success is governance and ownership, and its close ties to IPC as the manager of the IMI banks. IMI has been fortunate in two respects, first, in not being forced by its public sector owners to include local shareholders in its ventures and, second, in having investors with a long-term perspective. A level of trust has been developed that greatly facilitates unity of purpose and economy in governance. The eventual exit of public sector investors creates the challenge of finding a new investor base. IMI plans to take a two-pronged approach by attracting a small number of like-minded, large private investors and also a multitude of small private investors in order to safeguard IPC's leadership role and IMI's target-group orientation.

Syed Aftab Ahmed (chapter 26) provides perspectives on the highly successful IMI public-private partnership in which IFC has played a decisive role as a public investor. He notes that both the private and public investors in this PPP share a common enthusiasm, but in varying degrees, for financial returns as well as for the creation of benefits of another kind, in this case sustainable, expanding financial services for micro and SME clients. In addition to working for these results, both types of investors are "patient" but attach different priorities to exit, that is, to the time horizons of their investments.

Ahmed explains that the effort to counteract market failure that animated investment decisions in the past has been displaced by concern for governance, for creating commercial structures in which incentives are aligned to produce financial results as well as benefits of another kind. In this sort of venture, it appears that investors subject to the discipline of capital markets may have an advantage over other investors who are not so disciplined or who are primarily motivated by eleemosynary ideals.

Subsidies for starting up commercial micro and SME financial institutions are required, and these figure in the effort to align incentives of the public and private parties. Ahmed provides examples of the dynamics of PPPs as they develop and mature. One is that renegotiation, as detailed by Schmidt and Moisa, can lead to conflict. Ahmed concludes that there are really three bottom lines for PPPs with objectives such as those of IMI: financial returns, other forms of desired impact, and governance.

Klaus Glaubitt and Haje Schütte (chapter 27) call for public-private partnerships to promote financial sector development in Southeast Europe, where immature financial sectors will not be modernised by private actors alone. Glaubitt and Schütte argue that as long as public actors respect the principle of subsidiarity and design their interventions in ways that will not lead to market distortions, there is a rightful, catalytic place for public actors in financial sector development. They support their thesis by presenting original data comparing the performance of the microfinance banks of the IMI network – classified by the authors as public-private partnerships – with those of local commercial banks that KfW supports through refinancing lines. The comparison favours the microfinance banks. Glaubitt and Schütte conclude that the incentives of these institutions are better aligned with the project's objectives than are those of the commercial banks assisted by KfW.

Michael Jainzik and Doris Köhn (chapter 28) examine the basis for partnership in the creation and proliferation of microfinance investment funds as a vehicle to advance development goals by attracting private investors through satisfactory financial and social returns.

After defining microfinance investment funds and reviewing their benefits for both private investors and MFIs, Jainzik and Köhn identify and compare two major approaches in microfinance fund investment. The network approach caters to the MFIs' interests and the outsider approach to the investors' perspective, but it is the network approach that offers unequalled in-depth "insider" knowledge of risk, returns and procedures and thus may possibly serve as a superior investing strategy for new investors in microfinance. In comparing these two approaches, Jainzik and Köhn also discuss the risks and returns of funds versus stand-alone MFI investments, and detail the Global Microfinance Facility to illustrate how a microfinance investment fund may be modelled to suit risk tolerances of various investors.

Finally, Jainzik and Köhn define the useful role of development finance institutions in the initiation of microfinance investment funds, citing unique experience and informed risk perception as the key to their staying power in difficult markets. In the conclusion to their paper, Jainzik and Köhn frame a set of open questions for microfinance investment funds to be revisited as the funds and actors gain experience and document results. Questions of risk, market timing, accountability, ratings, and best-practice scenarios will be analysed in-depth at the 2004 KfW Financial Sector Symposium.

CHAPTER 22:

Public-Private Partnerships for Financial Development in Southeast Europe

Reinhard H. Schmidt[1] and Nina Moisa[2]

[1] Professor, Wilhelm Merton Chair for International Banking and Finance

[2] M.Sc., PhD Candidate, Johann Wolfgang Goethe University Frankfurt

Public-private partnership (PPP) is a new term with clearly positive connotations. Who could be against drawing private sector initiative and capital into undertakings which have always been areas for public policy and service? And who would not approve of partnerships?

However, beyond that, not much is clear at all, which inspires this paper. It is not always clear what a PPP really is, or, more specifically, what the precise meaning of the term is and what the specific institutional arrangements of a PPP are.

- Does PPP designate *any* organisational form that involves the private sector alongside the public sector?

- Is it restricted to forms of cooperation that exhibit elements of partnership, a concept which itself needs clarification?

- Is PPP confined only to the rather well-defined concept that has emerged in the UK and the US during the last two decades; for example privately financed, operated and owned toll roads and prisons?

For the sake of clarity, "public private cooperation" (PPC) is used here to denote common undertakings of public and private sectors that involve some element of partnership but not necessarily private ownership. PPPs are a subset of PPCs, with the distinctive feature of partial or complete private ownership of the facilities which provide the services in question.

The introduction of the term PPP into development policy suggests that the public and the private sectors act as partners, and that this is a new and hopefully good idea for addressing and solving real problems. However, close cooperation between public and private sectors is not at all new in development policy or in financial sector policy. Any merit of the new concept can lie only in its emphasis on partnership and ownership, the potential and limitations of which are certainly worth exploring.

This chapter complements earlier parts of this book by focusing on the organisational aspects of cooperation between the public and private sectors in financial sector development in Southeast Europe (SEE). In the next section, we discuss the conceptual, theoretical and empirical foundations of the PPP concept, emphasising the aspects of ownership and partnership. The terms PPC and PPP are defined, and then the economic rationales for having a partnership and of allocating ownership rights in a certain way are explored. The British and North American experience with PPPs is then discussed along with some elements of economic theory which suggest why this institutional arrangement has recently gained wide acceptance.

Is the experience gained in projects in industrialised countries directly relevant to financial sector development in SEE? There are many aspects in which they differ greatly, which suggests that the discussion of the roles of public and private parties in SEE financial sector development should begin on a more general level. Accordingly, an investigation of where the (foreign) public and private sectors collaborate in PPC is provided. The scope for PPC is indeed large, whereas with a few exceptions, that for PPP is quite limited. The most important exception is micro and small business or small enterprise (MSE) finance, as suggested by a case study. A discussion of lessons learned so far explores their applicability to financial sector development more broadly.

Public-Private Partnership: An Overview of Concepts, Theory and Experience

Concepts

In order to address the key concepts upon which PPPs are based we must first define the term. This is most important because of a) the complexity and subtlety of interactions within PPPs, b) the meaning and definition of ownership as the central functional feature of PPPs, and c) the nature of partnership within a PPP structure.

Defining a PPP

A PPP is an arrangement in which private capital, private management and private ownership provide what are traditionally public services. This structure has been developed in the context of privatisation, and a PPP can be regarded as a form of semi-privatisation or privatisation with a heavy dose of regulation.

According to the relevant literature,[1] a PPP is a long-term relationship between a private party and a public entity or authority. The cooperation is based on an agreement or a contract in which she agrees to offer certain services either to him[2] or to private persons who pay for these services in full or in part.

---

[1] See the two collections of papers on PPPs edited by Vaillancourt Rosenau (2000) and Osborne (2000).

[2] In what follows, we use the female form for the private party and the male form for the public party.

The definition of PPP may also be explored within the broader concept of public private cooperation (PPC). Consider "contracting out" for example, a PPC arrangement in which the state or a state agency buys or builds a facility, which is then used by some private agent to achieve the state's purpose. In contrast, a PPP that would serve the same purpose would be structured so that the state buys the services from the contractor, who for this purpose first builds and later owns the relevant facility. The fact that private partnership and ownership seem to be essential features of a PPP requires an economic explanation of these two concepts.

Any PPC or PPP agreement must be designed so that the private partner is willing to enter into the agreement. The net present value of the stream of uncertain future payments and possible other benefits to her must be positive. A PPP agreement also determines which services the contractor is supposed to provide, and typically also imposes limitations concerning what she may do with the facility. However, these contract stipulations should not undermine the basic economic logic of the PPP, which is that it is mainly the contractor who benefits if she finds ways of "doing her job better," whatever this may mean in the specific case. Since ownership is the distinguishing feature, "doing her job better" has to do with the way in which the relevant facility is created, maintained and used.

From the state's perspective, the purpose of establishing a PPP is to provide some public service. Most real-life cases involve services which are not complicated and rather well established. This simplifies the contractual obligations that determine what the contractor will actually do and makes it easier for the public partner first to monitor performance against contractual obligations and second to appeal to courts if these obligations are not fulfilled.

Ownership

Ownership is the next concept to be defined and explained. Ownership has three aspects: risk-bearing, decision-making and renegotiation.

From a narrow economic perspective, an owner is the party who retains the surplus or profit from some economic endeavour after all relevant contractual and legal payment obligations have been met. She or he or it is a "residual claimant." This definition suggests that the essence of ownership is to bear risk. In order to make the promise to bear risk credible, an owner is expected to provide "up-front money."[3] This is why ownership typically requires commitments of risk capital. The theory rests on the implicit assumption that the allocation of risk and of the obligation to contribute equity is agreed in a set of contracts which specify who will get what under *all* conceivable circumstances. In other words: the contracts are complete and perfect. If this condition is fulfilled the party with the highest risk tolerance should be the owner in the sense of being the residual claimant and risk-bearer.

In this theoretical world of complete contracts everything is agreed beforehand, which means that decision rights do not feature as an aspect of ownership. In the

---

[3] See Fama and Jensen (1983).

real world, however, and in recent economic theories of ownership based on property rights, contracts are regarded as notoriously incomplete (Hart 1995). Decisions not fully prescribed by contracts and laws are called "residual decisions." The party who has the right to make these decisions is a "residual decision-maker" or an owner in an economic sense.

This definition of ownership based on residual decision rights squarely poses the question of who should have ownership. It suggests that residual decision rights should be assigned to residual claimants and risk-bearers because they have the strongest motive to make good, value-increasing decision. If others had these rights, their incentives would cause them to make decisions that would produce less value and inflict a loss on the residual risk bearers.[4]

But this argument, which makes the allocation of risk bearing the determinant of the allocation of decision rights, provides only a partial and possibly even misleading solution. There is also, or even more so, the reverse relationship between cause and effect. The first question should, at least in some cases, be that of who should be assigned the residual decision rights. The answer would then determine who should bear risk, keeping in mind, of course, that a certain amount of risk-bearing capacity is necessary for an owner. The answer to the premier question is that the allocation of residual decision rights or ownership rights should be determined by the availability of information and the incentives to acquire it. This is important because pertinent information is an essential prerequisite for making good, value-increasing decisions, whereas incentives alone are simply not enough to generate good decisions. From a purely economic standpoint, it would be optimal if the *incentives* to make good decisions, which are created by having to bear risk, were closely connected with the *ability* to make good decisions, which is based on knowledge and information.

The third aspect of who should have ownership has to do with renegotiation and the protection of wealth and incentives to make valuable investments. Any long-term cooperation is based on a contract which determines who has which decision rights and which financial claims under the conditions foreseen in the contract. However, contracts are necessarily incomplete and situations are likely to arise that are not covered by the contract. In these cases, it is important for both sides to be able to *jointly* revise and renegotiate the contract. In other words, it is rational to have some flexibility. However, flexibility creates the opportunity for each of the parties to one-sidedly start renegotiations. Each side can be expected to do this unilaterally if it feels that by renegotiating it can improve its own position, even if this is only to the detriment of the other party. Such behaviour would be considered unfair by most people, even though it may be within the limits of what is legally accepted.

---

[4] See Ricketts (2003), who discusses various theories of ownership, and quoting Robertson and Dennison, defines "capitalism's golden rule" as the allocation of decision rights to those who bear risks and therefore have the strongest incentives to make value-increasing decisions.

When one party starts to renegotiate, the other party is threatened. If this other party has ownership rights it can to some extent counteract the threat, which reduces the temptation for the first or "unfair" party to begin renegotiation. What does this imply for the allocation of ownership? Are there any considerations to suggest which party should have protection from the threat of renegotiation which ownership affords? Surprisingly, there are general answers to these questions: the party that needs protection most is the party that has undertaken or can undertake project-specific or relationship-specific investments. Specific investments can be extremely valuable for the project, and thus *both* parties will have an interest in ensuring that these investments are undertaken.

However, in many cases these investments are unobservable and therefore unsuited for coverage in a contract. This weakens the bargaining power of the investing party in the case of a contract renegotiation while increasing the incentives for the other side to renegotiate. This course of events is foreseeable. Rational agents avoid getting into a weak bargaining position, which they can do by *not* undertaking specific investments. Thus, the incompleteness of contracts discourages valuable specific investment. Ownership is a remedy in this case, since by protecting the weaker party it encourages specific investment, and therefore it makes sense *for both parties* to allocate ownership rights to the party which is in the best position to make valuable specific investments. Since these investments may not be observable and hence not subject to contract, the party best in a position to make these investments is the weaker party. Thus the economically efficient allocation of residual decison rights in a world of incomplete contracts *systematically* strengthens the weaker party.

Partnership

Now turning to the definition of partnership: not only undertaking specific investments is dangerous; giving away ownership rights is also dangerous. Residual decision rights and a share of residual claims for one party also enable and encourage that party to take decisions which do not maximise the value of cooperation for all parties, but rather only to him- or herself and at the expense of the other. This would also constitute "unfair behaviour." In the end, both sides have some power over the other, and both sides are exposed to the temptation of "opportunistic" behaviour (Williamson, 1985) or simply unfair behaviour. This mutual dependence can cause cooperation to break down. The risk inherent in cooperation can never be completely precluded, but the opportunities and incentives for unfair behaviour can be limited through various devices and features of cooperation such as trust, a commitment to a common cause, a long history or period of cooperation, a reputation in a relevant market or public arena, and various formal rights including that of terminating the contract and the cooperation.

An arrangement is called a partnership if and only if the opportunities and the incentives to take decisions that hurt the interest of other parties, including the renegotiation of the underlying contract for opportunistic reasons, are limited in some way. Behaving as a partner may appear inconsistent with strict egoistical rationality from a short-term perspective. However, over the longer term, cooperative behaviour can have enormous economic benefits.

What is the relationship between the three concepts – public-private partnership, ownership, and partnership from an economic perspective – which we have just defined and explained? In reality, decisions must be made as the future unfolds in order to make a PPC or PPP successful. Therefore, residual decision rights must somehow be allocated. Almost always the optimal distribution of these rights will be unequal, and this can lead to conflicts. Ownership rights can provide at least partial protection in such conflicts. However, any unequal distribution of ownership rights creates other negative incentives. Partnership weakens these negative incentives and thereby reduces the need to protect oneself, and it also reduces the importance of ownership. In a way, complete ownership and perfect partnership are substitutes, while limited or *attenuated* ownership rights and certain elements of partnership tend to complement each other. Therefore it is appropriate that the PPP concept includes ownership and partnership.

Motives for Creating PPPs

In general, by teaming up, the public sector partner can augment and combine its strengths with those of the private sector, which comprise creativity, dynamism, entrepreneurial spirit, an efficiency orientation, flexibility and access to private finance. Mobilising these resources can reduce costs and improve performance.

However, this involvement also implies the transfer of decision rights to private parties and, as a consequence, some loss of public control. With this loss of control, there is a danger that private contractors might reduce the quality and quantity of the services which they provide, and that they might boost their profits by increasing their reimbursable costs. Therefore, the potential benefits of a PPP must be substantial if they are to outweigh the negative effects resulting from the reduction of public sector control.

It seems that the benefits of combining the strengths of the public and private sectors in the delivery of a public service could also be achieved merely by buying private services (or contracting out). As such, the benefits do not offer an economic justification for PPPs. But as contracts are always to some extent incomplete, PPPs offer scope for benefits that contracting out would not assure, since neither the costs nor the quality of services can be fully determined in advance and fully contracted. Requiring that the private party contributes financially to the project and shares risks and benefits over a longer time tends to align the incentives for the private party with the financial success of the project. First of all, this means that the private party has an incentive to minimise the costs of providing the service. Furthermore, private financial involvement can be an effective way to enforce "whole-life costing," thus introducing at the initial setup phase a long-term perspective on the costs of design changes (Spackman, 2002).

However, there is also a downside to giving a private party strong incentives and decision rights. A purely financially motivated private contractor (with a short time horizon) lacks the incentive to improve service quality and even has an incentive to lower it provided that it is cheaper to offer services with lower quality. In principle, the public side can try to counteract this incentive by imposing detailed quality-related performance requirements. But compliance is costly to monitor, difficult to measure and hardly enforceable in court.

Surprisingly, these arguments are not those which dominate the political debate about PPPs. Rather, a common political motive for the private financing of public services is the presumed opportunity for off-budget public financing and for avoiding macroeconomic and budgetary constraints. Even leaving short-term considerations of political feasibility aside, this would be a valid argument only if public financing faced constraints which do not apply in the case of so-called private financing initiatives (PFIs). There is no evidence that this is the case in reality (Spackman, 2002).

The Economics of PPPs

Taking a theoretical approach to analysing the potential benefits of a PPP as an institutional form is a recent development. In contrast to a "conventional" contractual relationship, the standard way of modelling a PPP assumes that a government agency contracts a private party to provide a service and the private party in turn builds, owns and operates the necessary facility. In a conventional setting, the public agency contracts two private parties; a builder-contractor who sets up the facility and an operator-contractor who uses the facility to provide the service. What are the benefits of combining the roles of these two private parties in a PPP? The advantage of this arrangement lies in the bundling of the different steps of service provision and the resulting change in incentives for the private contractor. If contracts are incomplete due to nonverifiable investments in the construction phase, the PPP structure produces incentives which lead to less costly or more efficient service provision in the operating phase, and this is more desirable from the perspective of the government agency.[5]

In a "preliminary" model, which compares PPP with the conventional contracting of two separate private parties, Hart (2003) shows that a PPP (or having only one private contractor for both functions) can be a better choice from the government perspective if the quality of the services is observable while that of the facility is not. In the case of two separate private parties, the builder would not make an unobservable costly investment in the building phase which both increases service quality and lowers the cost of providing the service. In Hart's model, conventional contracting is advantageous if the quality of the facility can be clearly specified and observed by the government agency and the quality of service cannot, whereas a PPP is desirable only if the service quality can be specified and enforced.

---

[5] See Hart, 2003. The same effect can be explained by reference to an asymmetric information distribution in general, as shown by Bentz, Grout and Halonen, 2003.

This model is indeed preliminary since it does not take into account the aspects of long-term cooperation and reputation, which seem to be of paramount importance in reality. A common finding of PPP practitioners is that the key success factor in this partnering is a trusting relationship between the participating parties, a factor which can only be modelled in a multi-period setting.

Practical Experience with PPPs

The British and North American experience with PPPs is substantial, but objective evaluations of the economic costs and benefits are scarce, and the performance record of PPPs seems mixed. Many optimistic predictions for the potential cost savings of PPP tend to leave out important cost components such as the drafting of contracts, monitoring and adapting the regulatory framework. In addition, the quality of the services or products provided by a private contractor is often hard to evaluate, but also likely to decrease over time because of her incentive to cut costs if quality is hard to verify. On the other hand, many benefits of PPPs, such as innovative design, access to new technologies, better contract design and management, may be substantial but cannot be easily integrated into a formal evaluation. Comparison with purely public sector service provision is often impossible and leaves room for speculation.

Vaillancourt Rosenau (2000b) evaluates the success and failure of PPPs in the US and Canada and also comes to the conclusion that they can improve cost performance in several sectors, but only to a limited degree. Long-term performance is hard to evaluate and its tendency to decline may offset any short-term savings. She also finds that there are surprisingly few authentic, fully integrated partnerships: "minimalist partnerships" or "partnering at a distance" in fact are the rule, and these do not combine the respective strengths of the public and private sectors to any great extent. Based on the findings of several evaluations, she recommends PPPs only if cost considerations clearly speak in favour of this arrangement, if there are few externalities and if the timeframe of the arrangement is short. If this is not the case, and especially if service quality is hard to specify in advance and at the same time very important, the benefits of PPPs are limited.

In the UK, many evaluations of Private Finance Initiatives (PFI) as a specific form of PPP paint a slightly more positive picture of the value provided by private sector involvement. In a study based on surveys of authorities and contractors responsible for managing 121 PFI/PPP projects, the British National Accounting Office (2001) came to the conclusion that "value for money" is secured only through careful project and relationship management.

Nevertheless, there is little systematic evaluation of PPPs in the UK. Many studies are based on the individual perceptions of the authorities and contractors involved rather than objective long-term comparisons. According to Spackman (2002), the true balance between the benefits and costs of PPPs in the UK is still an open issue.

PPC and PPP in Financial Sector Development and Microfinance

Financial sector promotion comprises the entirety of efforts (from abroad) aimed at strengthening the financial sector of a (partner) country. Its normative basis is the conviction, now widely shared, that it is beneficial for a country and its inhabitants to have an efficient financial sector.

It is now also widely accepted that foreign public institutions may have a role to play in the development of the financial sectors in developing and transition economies. However, the principle of subsidiarity also applies across borders. This principle says that (foreign) public intervention is justified only when the social rate of return of a project is higher than the private rate of return, and when the social rate of return is above the relevant cost of capital while the private rate of return is below.[6]

Established Forms of PPC in Financial Sector Development in Southeast Europe (SEE)

This section briefly examines three important classes of private actors in the financial sector of developing and transition countries, especially in SEE. The question is whether projects in which these foreign or local actors cooperate with certain foreign public entities qualify as PPCs or even PPPs.

Private Consultants

The first of these three classes are private consultants. Various foreign public entities use foreign private consultants in three types of financial sector projects in SEE (and elsewhere). Type one: projects that seek to strengthen financial regulation and supervision and the relevant legal framework for financial institutions. Type two: downscaling projects which aspire to motivate and equip existing local banks to lend to MSE clients. Type three: projects that aim to strengthen institutions, and promote institution building and institutional transformation.

In all three types of financial sector projects, contracts between the respective (foreign) donor and his consultant are drawn up and include terms of reference. However, these terms of reference should not be mistaken as complete descriptions of what the donors really expect from their consultants. The "real contracts" are incomplete: donors expect the consultants to contribute as much as possible to achieving certain objectives. But what is possible and what the specific objectives are is not known in advance and therefore difficult to define. Moreover, in all three cases there is the possibility, or even the likelihood, of conflict between the consultant and the institution at which she works and which she is more or less expected to transform, and of conflicts with influential incumbents in these institutions.

---

[6] With explicit reference to PPP, this point is made by Stiglitz and Wallsten (2000).

This situation requires flexibility, mutual commitment and trust on the part of the donor and his consultant and a great deal of ongoing communication: the main ingredients of a partnership. In some projects, it is extremely difficult to measure performance over the short term. These characteristics indicate that this relationship between donors and consultants is indeed a PPC and should be handled as such. However, in none of these projects can the private partner have ownership of some relevant facility, so these relationships are not PPPs as defined here.

Investments in Private Banks by Foreign Public Institutions

The second class of projects which may qualify as PPCs or PPPs are investments made by foreign public institutions in local private banks. International financial institutions (IFIs), such as the EBRD and the IFC as well as bilateral aid donors such as DEG or FMO, have invested in many local banks in SEE,[7] including subsidiaries of big banks from Western countries. In some of these cases, the local private partner banks have also received loans and technical assistance from the foreign donors/investors. In only a few cases are the local banks specifically committed to serving special groups of clients (such as MSEs) and to developing the national financial system. However, facilitating the provision of financial services in a professional way and on a permanent basis through these public foreign investments may already be a valuable contribution to financial sector development.

At first glance, these foreign public investments seem to qualify as PPCs because any equity investment constitutes a long-term relationship, which almost by definition entails at least some elements of a partnership. However, in most cases the foreign public investors seem to be largely inactive minority shareholders and the partnership features do not seem to be strong, which would not permit them to be classified as PPCs. At first glance it may also seem that these investments may have characteristics of PPPs because the local partners own the facilities, in this case banks that provide the service. But it is an open question to what extent the foreign investors expect the local banks in question to provide public services in the traditional sense, another defining characteristic of PPP. Moreover, on a normative or political basis, some of these investments violate the principle of subsidiarity. In fact, several of the IFIs which invest in banks in SEE see themselves less as donors and more as investors. They may not be concerned about subsidiarity because they simply find it attractive in purely financial terms to invest in profitable banks in this region.

Foreign Support for NGOs

The third group of projects that may qualify as PPCs or PPPs are those entailing foreign support for private not-for-profit and nongovernmental organisations (NPOs or NGOs) which make very small loans to clients who are assumed not to

---

[7] The relevant information is readily available from the websites of the donor/investor organisations. For details see Part III of Matthäus-Maier and von Pischke 2004.

be bankable on a commercial basis. Many of these NGOs are permanently dependent on subsidies, which mostly come from foreign public donors, so that in effect these NGOs/NPOs provide a social service on behalf of the foreign funding organisations.

Due to the way in which they are funded, executed and monitored, NGO-based credit programmes are clearly PPCs. They also qualify as PPPs by performing what is rightly considered a public sector function and because they own the respective facilities.[8] Due to the legal form under which they are established NGOs/NPOs do not have an owner. This suggests that the PPP discussion does not fully apply to them, and therefore they are not considered further. However, with only minor adaptations, many arguments provided in the remainder of the paper also apply to credit-granting NGOs in SEE.

To sum up, as in many other regions, there are numerous forms of (foreign) public and private sector cooperation in SEE financial systems. However, none of the three main types of cooperation we have analysed conforms to the general view of what constitutes a PPP. There may be no relevant facility in which the private partner can have ownership, or there are foreign public investments in otherwise privately owned institutions with only a very limited element of partnership and no more than traces of public services, or the private partner is not a for-profit institution. Some forms of cooperation qualify as PPC, and there is certainly more room for PPCs in the foreign support for financial sector development in SEE. However, the scope for PPP is limited except in one case, which is explored below.

PPP as an Institutional Form for Commercial Micro and Small Business Finance

The proposition presented in this section is that MSE financing is an area in which PPP plays an important and fruitful role. The relationship between the private and public actors involved entails many elements of partnership; the relevant facilities are the institutions that provide financial services, and the ownership of these institutions needs to be determined and ultimately allocated to the private side; and the services provided are considered to be in the public sphere.

The Arguments for PPPs

Why might there be a role for foreign public institutions in MSE finance? The standard answer for any public service applies: the provision of basic banking operations can be considered an important public service that enhances social welfare and because private formal sector initiative does not currently offer this ser-

---

[8] Classification as a PPC and/or PPP is not a value judgement. It does not imply an answer to the question of whether the external funding of permanently subsidy-dependent NGO-based credit programmes is advisable from a development policy perspective. For a critical view of these programs see Schmidt and Zeitinger (1996).

vice.⁹ Indeed, as in many other developing and transition regions, the MSE sector in SEE is grossly underserved or even plainly ignored by local banks and by most of the foreign banks which have recently made inroads into the region (Mehl and Winkler 2003). Thus, the government is called on to act. The national governments in SEE as well as purely commercially oriented private investors are either not aware of the importance of a sound financial sector or they lack the required know-how and funding. It therefore falls upon foreign governments, acting via multilateral and bilateral aid organisations, to step in. This role is part of their political mandate. Foreign public sector activity can jump-start private initiatives by providing temporary subsidies, loans and equity, or by taking an active long-term role in the financial sectors of SEE countries.

However, the long-term involvement of the state, and especially of foreign public entities, should be examined with some reservation based on the principle of subsidiarity: the lack of local public and purely private initiative is not a sufficient condition for foreign public involvement. There is the possibility that private initiative and market forces alone, without any form of state involvement, will move to serve this banking market in SEE too, as it has already for some other formal financial services. But if this happens at all, which is questionable, it will not be soon. As with local banks, those from Western countries which have recently entered the SEE markets are targeting a market segment that is wealthier than the MSEs. Waiting until purely private banks start to serve the MSE sector would imply a politically unacceptable long-term loss of employment and growth opportunities.

Why is the private sector needed, and what role can it play? The answers depend on the timeframe. In the short term, it can obviously provide management and know-how. Foreign donors/investors would hardly be in a position to set up and run a local financial institution from a distance, and purely local management is typically too close to the local establishment to run a bank with the social orientation which most foreign donors believe is desirable.

Over the medium to long term, the private sector has to become the main source of debt and equity capital. Foreign private debt (or credit) is needed to fund lending operations of the recently or soon-to-be created MSE banks. Local loan demand from MSEs is expected to grow fast. The mobilisation of local deposits may not keep pace with local loan demand, and even the largest official international and foreign donors/investors face funding constraints that could delay or preclude their providing more funds to an MSE bank.¹⁰

Any serious attempt to ease the financing problems of the MSE sector presupposes the existence of the relevant financial institutions. Until quite recently, such institutions did not exist in most SEE countries. They have to be created, and this

---

⁹ The provision of basic financial services for the general public is a problem in many countries, and therefore assuring these services is often considered a function of the state.

¹⁰ This does of course not preclude the possibility that local deposits are sufficient to fund local lending. But empirically this seems quite unlikely, especially in view of the requirement that lenders match maturities in order to limit the risk exposure of an MSE bank.

requires equity. Since it seems unlikely that sufficient local equity can be mobilised, and since it is questionable whether local private interests and local public and private institutions are the most appropriate owners of MSE banks in SEE, there is an indispensable role for foreign equity.

The main argument in favour of the provision of medium to long-term foreign equity by private sources is that the alternative organisational setup is too weak: i.e. a local bank owned by public donors and investors and managed by foreign consultants. Such an institution would face exactly those incentive problems which led to the development of PPPs: foreign consultants (who are not owners) can be expected to cut costs at the expense of service quality[11] and to withhold effort and investments which could strengthen the banks over the long term but diminish short-term performance. Finally, frictions would result if residual decision rights resided with foreign public donors/investors while the private consultants had the better access to the relevant information. Therefore, the ultimate reason why private equity is essential is because it complements the private management of the banks. However, the arguments based on incentives and transaction costs presented above also suggest that these private owners should be sufficiently competent to play an active role in the management and control of the banks.

Three crucial questions arise: are there potential private owners for specialised MSE banks in SEE? Would they find it financially attractive to invest in these banks, and under what conditions? And would they have sufficient capital to fulfil the role of an active and developmentally oriented owner?

The next section argues that there are private parties which can become owners and also manage the banks. They are not established foreign bankers but rather development finance experts who have developed a framework that makes MSE financing attractive enough to warrant investment if supported by start-up subsidies. However, the funds of these potential private owners are quite limited. At present there is not enough private debt and equity capital available to fund all of the MSE banking projects which experienced contractors *and* public donors/investors would consider worthwhile. There is growing recognition that properly designed and well-managed MSE banks can be commercially attractive is gaining adherents, but it is not yet widespread. There is simply no perfect capital market for shares in MSE banks. At least for an interim period public funding is required as a complement or even a substitute. Taken together, these arguments lead to an institutional setup which is a genuine PPP.

Alternative Institutional Arrangements

We have argued that PPP is an appropriate organisational form for MSE banks in SEE. However, a closer look at incentives, conflict and contract designs is required to complete the case. The standard PPP model assumes that the public partner has a dual interest – in financial results and in the quality of the service

---

[11] In the present context, the extent of target-group orientation would be one proxy for service quality.

in question. The private partner, on the other hand, is mainly or exclusively motivated by financial considerations. The standard literature recommends the use of a PPP only where the public partner is in a position to make sure that the quality and quantity of services are adequate from a public service perspective. The best way of assuring quality is to monitor. Therefore, PPP seems advisable only if service quality can be monitored precisely and at low cost by the public partner and if failure to meet contract terms can be remedied in court. However, these conditions are not currently fulfilled in the area of MSE financing, because all the relevant activities are so innovative that performance requirements cannot be easily defined. Thus, the standard concern in all PPPs that there are incentives and opportunities for those involved to reduce service quality seems to apply in this case too.

Private ownership alone is not a perfect solution to this incentive problem, and it may not even be the best solution. This suggests a re-examination of the relevant alternative design option with strong PPC features. The alternative would be a contracting-out arrangement with a consulting or management contract and strong performance-related incentives.

How well can a PPC which is not a PPP function? To answer this question, let us first consider the role of reputation. Except for initial engagements, donors/investors select consultants based on their experience with them. This is common practice and creates incentives for the consultant to perform in accordance with the long-term interests of the donor/investor. However, the likelihood of good performance being rewarded by contract extensions and future contracts is uncertain. No donor or investor organisation could commit itself to automatically entering into repeat contracts because that would jeopardise its options in the future and might create an impression of impropriety. Thus, the reputation mechanism cannot work perfectly.

The same applies to performance-related incentive systems. These work only if success can be measured accurately. If the donor/investor expects performance along several dimensions, only some of which can be precisely measured, the incentives cannot be very strong. This means that the incentives will either have to be rather weak, or the incentive system will have to leave out some performance dimensions. Those left out would probably be related to the developmental aspects, inducing a kind of behaviour which is not in the interest of the donors.

By design, consulting and management contracts also transfer important decision rights to the consultant. However, final decision rights are invariably tied to legal ownership. Thus the partial transfer of rights can benefit the project and the parties who jointly undertake it, but it cannot fully eliminate the incentive problems of cooperation between a public partner interested in financial and developmental results and a private partner who is only financially motivated. Some conflict of interest remains even though optimal incentive devices and contractual features may be in place.

Ownership Once More and the Commitment to Developmental Objectives

The arguments presented so far suggest that contracting out can be somewhat similar to a PPP, but cannot be a superior alternative to a PPP with a private ownership component. At the same time, there is not yet any reason to assume that it would be inferior. This leads to the third aspect of ownership introduced earlier: incentives to create value and how they are shaped by the allocation of ownership rights.

In contracting out, a donor/investor will retain the right to monitor the consultant working on his behalf and to take remedial action if he feels, rightly or wrongly, that the consultant is underperforming. After all, poor performance due to lack of effort or competence on the part of the consultant is a real possibility, and most donors would want to have recourse if they are unhappy with the consultant. Given the problems of assessing performance correctly and of enforcing performance through legal means alone, the only relevant sanction in practice is to terminate or not renew the contract or to bar the consultant from future contracts.

The Problem of Sanctions

However, this raises an important question: what are the likely consequences of giving the less informed party the right to apply this sanction? Remember that in the case of the creation of MSE banks in developing and transition countries the output must be innovative, effort is difficult to observe and performance depends strongly on external factors. Thus the sanction can be applied only on the basis of subjective assessments which may or may not be correct. As explained above, the possibility of the less informed side imposing sanctions on the better informed side is dangerous for both parties, because sanctions can be used inappropriately or even opportunistically. A rational consultant-manager would anticipate the inappropriate application of the sanction and adjust her behaviour accordingly.

The impact of an inappropriate use of the sanction to terminate a contract or not to renew it, to withhold future contracts or award future contracts only under less favourable conditions, is straightforward. Termination will destabilise the project. Even if this is anticipated only as a possibility, it has negative effects. A consultant who fears the imposition of largely arbitrary sanctions is under pressure to undertake activities which the donor/investor likes to see in a project and which he can easily observe, rather than those which she finds optimal for the project. But even judicious adjustments do not eliminate the threat to the consultant: she still has to worry that she might not be able to reap the benefits of the sound but unobservable investments that she undertakes. If these investments are costly, there is an incentive to avoid them. Thus, the possibility of inappropriate sanctions being imposed shortens her time perspective and reduces the financial and developmental value of the project.

The impact of an opportunistic application of the sanction is even more problematic. Its direct and indirect consequences are largely the same as in the case of inappropriate use, except that it also discourages communication. But this is exactly what could occur if the donor-investor is strongly motivated by financial considerations.[12] Consider the following scenario in a contracting-out arrangement: a donor/investor offers the consultant substantial financial incentives based on observable performance but, because of observability problems retains the right to cancel the contract "at will." In financial terms, this right is a call option for the donor/investor which, if performance is unexpectedly good, he may exercise opportunistically in order to avoid paying the substantial financial award to the consultant.

Moreover, the threat of terminating the contract is also a way of forcing the consultant to renegotiate the "constitutional contract" underlying the joint project. As noted above, the fear of renegotiation would prevent the consultant from undertaking specific and possibly very valuable investments, since these would weaken her future bargaining position. This highlights the fundamental difference between contracting out and PPP. PPP includes private ownership in the relevant facilities as a critical element; ownership protects the consultant by making renegotiation less attractive for the other side. At the same time value-increasing activities, observable or not, become more attractive for the consultant. This reinforces the conclusion that private ownership is a very important element of a PPP.

This section has so far largely disregarded an aspect emphasised in the standard PPP literature: the private consultant may not be genuinely interested in the nonfinancial or developmental aspect of the project which she executes. If this objective holds and since it is indeed difficult to monitor service quality, private ownership can even exacerbate the conflict of interest, and a PPP with private ownership holds little promise.

However, if this fundamental assumption of a conflict of interest were relaxed, it would ease the conflict and strengthen the conventional mechanisms used to provide incentives and further align interests. Reputation could play a larger role, incentive systems could be designed in a more effective way, and the risks perceived by a donor/investor of transferring residual decision rights would be reduced.

Finance *and* Development

The assumption that private ownership distorts incentives can be relaxed if a public donor/investor succeeds in finding and hiring consultants who are interested not only in their own financial success but also in the developmental side of what they are doing. In reality this is not only a possibility, it even seems to be the rule for those who implement MSE finance projects. The typical private partners in these development projects are either "fanatics" who attach great emotional value to the development side of their work, or not-for-profit organisations. For these

---

[12] Most IFIs have always been both donors and investors at the same time. However, an emphasis on the role as investor or even investment banker seems to have gained in importance recently in a number of IFIs.

two groups of private partners, the incentive to take advantage of the public partner is weaker than for a purely financially motivated private partner, and therefore the concerns or reservations of the public partner are also weaker.[13]

What does this imply for the importance of ownership? If interests are very similar, this can lead to a cooperation of "like-minded" or real partners. The common interest in the PPP project and its success can outweigh those conflicts of interest which are nevertheless present. Residual decision rights can be assigned to a) the party which has the best information and the expertise necessary for taking appropriate decisions, b) the party on whose effort the project success depends the most and who also has the most to lose if the project and the cooperation failed, and/or c) those who can make the most value-enhancing investments. This will often be the consultant. But of course, adequate checks and balances are required so that she cannot abuse her power. This implies that a PPC is the optimal form of collaboration because of the not-for-profit or other non-commercial orientation.

Under ideal conditions, ownership is unimportant. However, in real-life PPCs, there may be harmony at some times and conflict at others. Ownership is important as a safeguard if conflict arises because it is a determinant of bargaining power. It is not surprising that conflicts can be a consequence of failure or bad performance, in which case the conflict is largely about who is to blame. But it can also be the negative consequence of very good performance, in which case the conflict may be about who can claim which part of the resulting benefits.

These considerations show that for very sound economic reasons the standard PPP model in the narrow, technical sense of the term is relevant for MSE financing in SEE. This is not only an area in which public and private parties can and should cooperate, but one in which the private side should be in the driver's seat and have an ownership position.

IMI as a Case Study in PPP

This section briefly describes the case of IMI (Internationale Micro Investitionen AG), a PPP active in SEE financial sector development. IMI is an investment and holding company and the strategic investor in nine MSE banks in SEE. IMI banks, most of them now trading under the common name ProCredit Bank, operate in Albania, Bosnia and Herzegovina, Bulgaria, Kosovo, Macedonia, Moldova, Romania, Serbia and Ukraine.[14] In contrast to the PPCs discussed in the last section, IMI combines all characteristics of a PPP:

---

[13] Similar considerations also apply the other way round: private development consultants may be most interested in working for donors/investors who have a professional understanding of the business requirements of the partner and of the project, and a long-term interest in the developmental side of project success.

[14] The institution in Moldova is an exception since it is not a bank but a finance company. There are nine other IMI-affiliated banks in other parts of the world, but they can be left out of the present discussion.

- Private and public sector institutions jointly undertake a sizable and complex project;

- the project is in a field which was until quite recently regarded almost exclusively as a domain of (foreign) public sector activity;

- the project would not have been possible without the full cooperation of public and private sector agents;

- it presupposes trust and partnership on a continuous basis;

- ownership plays an important role at several levels.

"The IMI project" arguably represents the essence of a PPP better than any other financial sector project in SEE and illustrates the potential of PPPs, as well as some of their difficulties and limitations. This case shows why public and private partners are needed and why partnership and ownership are equally important.

Background and Origin

The largest private investor and the strategic investor[15] in IMI is the private German consulting firm Internationale Projekt Consult (IPC). Over the past 20 years, IPC has earned a good reputation in development finance, setting up, restructuring and strengthening microfinance institutions. IPC has been very successful in its work for various donor agencies because of its clear focus on the dual requirement of financial viability and developmental impact of the local institutions with which it worked as a consultant. Its success also rests on its firm conviction that only formal financial institutions can achieve these goals.

IPC-supported institutions were among the first to demonstrate that, with start-up assistance from donors, microfinance can indeed become self-supporting and even profitable. However, there was another lesson from IPC's earlier work. The transformation of an existing institution such as a credit-granting NGO or a conventional bank into a formal MSE bank typically created resistance (as described in general terms in the last section). IPC felt that this resistance, and occasionally lack of support from donors in these conflicts, was a problem of all "upgrading" projects. Their role as a consultant did not give them enough power to do what they (and most of the donors/investors) regarded as being in the long-term interest of the MSE target group, which was to create stable MSE banks.

In this situation, IPC seized the opportunity to become a shareholder in a new microfinance bank that it launched and then managed. After the Dayton Accords, a group of multilateral and bilateral IFIs (international financial institutions) decided to create an MSE bank in Bosnia. One of these, the International Finance Corporation (IFC), convinced the others that a financial investment by the con-

---

[15] In various "Summaries of Project Information" on the International Finance Corporation (IFC) website, IPC is described as the strategic investor.

sultant should be used as an incentive. Although IPC management felt that putting their reputation at stake would be a sufficiently strong incentive, they welcomed the chance to become co-owners because this combination of roles would strengthen their position and help them realise their vision of creating viable MSE banks in SEE.

The model worked well, and it was suggested that it should be replicated in SEE. But this would have outstripped by far the financial capacity of IPC. This led to the founding of IMI. In a way, IMI was intended to leverage IPC's options to become a shareholder in MSE banks in SEE and elsewhere.

The Concept

IMI was set up in 1998 as a joint stock corporation under German law. The first private shareholders were IPC, the Dutch DOEN Foundation, a Bolivian foundation and a group of IPC staff members. The public sector was represented by the German DEG and later by the Dutch development bank FMO, the IFC, the Belgian development organisation BIO and KfW. To this day, IMI's equity is almost equally divided between private and public shareholders.

As far as its owners are concerned, IMI is clearly a PPP, the founder and main owner of IPC is also the chairman of IMI. This concentration of power seems delicate because IMI mainly invests in new banks which are launched and managed by IPC staff. The expatriate staff are to a large extent paid through technical assistance (TA) contracts with donors, which typically have a two year term, and later through management contracts between the banks and IPC. The double role is the basis for the very close cooperation between IMI and IPC, but it creates a conflict of interest[16] and requires a counterweight to the concentration of power.

The balance is redressed in a number of ways, first through the internal rules and regulations of IMI. All investment decisions are taken by the IMI supervisory board, on which all shareholders are represented. The second counterweight is the ownership structure of the banks in which IMI invests and which IPC manages. In most of the banks, some of the IFIs which hold shares in IMI are also shareholders, which implies that the banks themselves are also PPPs. The third counterweight derives from the fact that the creation of a new MSE bank requires technical assistance and also access to long-term funds in order to be economically feasible. TA typically comes from IFIs such as the EBRD, which are not IMI shareholders. Thus, there are three locks to which different parties hold the keys. The IMI board, the investors in the new banks and the TA donors would all be in a position to stop any new bank project if they felt that its primary purpose was to give additional management contracts to IPC.[17]

---

[16] "Conflict of interest" is sometimes used in American English to infer abuse. The correct definition describes a situation in which abuse could occur, but without any implication that it has occurred.

[17] For an up-to-date account of IMI see Schmidt and Von Pischke, 2004.

Assessment of IMI Performance

With these three checks, IPC is under extreme pressure to perform well. This pressure was an intended effect of having made a commitment and of having installed a powerful incentive mechanism. The network of banks and the partnership between IMI, IPC, the IMI shareholders, the outside investors in the banks and the local MSE banks themselves have performed very well – much better than some investors expected.

All IMI-related banks in SEE are growing rapidly and following their business plans without losing their MSE client focus. The average loan size in Eastern Europe is stable at around € 5,000, much lower than the average of almost all other banks in the region. Most IMI-affiliated banks no longer receive TA. The time required for a bank to cover all of its costs was shorter than anticipated, as was the time taken to recover the initial losses following its establishment. As of mid-2004, the SEE network of banks employed some 2,500 people, had total assets of approximately € 750 million and a loan portfolio of € 400 million.

In purely financial terms, IMI's record is good. Its equity has increased from about € 1 million to close to € 45 million at the end of 2003. The ex post rate of return on an investment in IMI, the most important figure for those who considered IMI purely as an investment, is now close to 10%. The return on equity (RoE) of the SEE portfolio is above 10%; IMI's target over the medium term is 15%. Even if all the TA contributions were treated as equity, the RoE of IMI's portfolio in SEE would still be only slightly below 10%. All of these figures are based on book values. Economic or market value may be greater because a network of vibrant MSE banks generates potential for future development impact and future profits. One can compare these figures to the corresponding performance of the stock market in general and to bank stocks in particular. But it may be more appropriate to compare IMI's performance with other endeavours to support MSE financing in transition and developing countries. This comparison shows that those who hold the three keys have no reason to complain, whether their specific interest is primarily financial or developmental.

Assessment of IMI as a PPP

In a genuine PPP both the private and the public partners are needed. At IMI, the private partner is needed to manage the banks: IPC staff possess know-how, experience and work within incentive structures that cannot be transferred to or replaced by public institutions. IPC employees are bound together in the IPC value system and under its leadership, and have the expertise to make the MSE institutions work. Secondly, IPC and IMI jointly control the network. They exercise tight control, stricter than would be possible based only on the formal ties between IMI shareholdings and IPC's management contracts. This control is based on the bank managers' close personal links to IPC.

But IPC and the group of IPC staff who are also investors in IMI are not the only private investors. The DOEN Foundation plays an especially important role.

DOEN has always been very clear about its interest in the permanence of IMI's developmental mission.

Why are the public partners needed? The most obvious reason is that without them, IMI's ambitious expansion and that of the network could never have been financed. In the medium or long term, it is hoped to attract outside private investors and to replace those public investors who can play only a transitory role in keeping with their corporate objectives. Second, the public shareholders have political influence in the host countries, and they use it occasionally when it seems necessary to protect IMI banks. So each side has strengths which they apply in the common interest.

To sum up, IMI really is a PPP. It can thrive only as a partnership. As in any partnership, there are drawbacks and difficulties. One is exit, the eventual sale of some bank participations to third parties. The private side, including IPC management, seem to be less concerned about exit possibilities than are some of the investors on the public side. At least in part, the latent conflict over exit results from the unexpected success of IMI and its network of banks. If they were less successful, nobody would even think of finding a buyer for an MSE bank.

A second latent conflict, which may also have its roots in the unexpected degree of success, concerns the division of roles between IPC, IMI, and the IMI shareholders in their capacity as shareholders of the banks. To meet the challenges of the next decade, control over the banks and the coordination among them need to be tightened even more. This requires a concentration of ownership at the level of the banks. One possibility would be for the public IMI shareholders to swap their shares in individual banks for additional IMI shares. However, it is still unclear what this would imply in terms of the control of IMI management and the protection that IPC and its staff would need for the extensive relationship-specific investments they have made. The latter consideration might explain the interest of IPC owners, managers and staff in maintaining a strong ownership role and clear strategic leadership in IMI.

One concern of some of the public partners is that too much control may be given away and conflicts of interest may arise. The private partners do not want their specific investment to lose value and thus seek a strong ownership role that provides protection and needs to be complemented by a strict governance regime. These concerns of the two parties are characterised by the features of any PPP (as described in the literature) that are crucial for success or failure. Each side has learned to appreciate the legitimate concerns of the other.

Conclusions Regarding IMI

To sum up, IMI is an example of a genuine, successful PPP. This holds for the positive aspects of the partnership, which have clearly dominated so far, and also for the negative. The success of this PPP opens the way to recommending PPP as a general model for organising development aid activities. However, there is one fundamental difference between IMI and the standard account of a PPP. The literature on PPPs normally assumes that the public partner cares more about the nonfinancial aspects of the project than the private partner and that the latter is motivated primarily by financial benefits. In IMI's case, this does not hold: both sides share a strong developmental commitment, and this may be the most important factor in explaining the stability of the partnership and the success of IMI. But if this like-mindedness or the similarity of the public and the private sector regarding objectives and values were indeed essential to the success of the IMI network, caution is called for in recommending PPP as a broadly applicable model. It works only with private and public partners who, besides being competent, are financially and also inherently motivated to be successful.

Applying PPP and PPC Concepts More Broadly to Financial Sector Development

What does all this suggest for the potential of PPP in financial sector development generally? There are certainly many areas in which the SEE financial sectors require further efforts to become more modern and efficient. However, many of these areas and functions are already adequately covered by purely private initiative, sometimes backed by public support as discussed above. Could it apply to regulation and supervision? Could PPPs improve the supply of credit to small and medium-sized firms through leasing and factoring? Other possible areas are municipal finance and housing finance, especially for socially oriented housing. Do these activities lend themselves to the organisational form of a PPP or at least for PPCs, as defined earlier, and should foreign public agencies play a role?

Regulation and Supervision

Regulation and supervision generally provides a clear-cut case for foreign public intervention because the service has the character of a public good and its importance is generally underestimated by local governments. Investments in improved regulation and supervision are almost certain to fulfil one condition that justifies foreign intervention: their social value is much higher than their private value, which might even be negative in purely financial terms. As in the past, it seems plausible that public entities use private contractors, and it is desirable that the relationship between the public principal and the private agent is characterised by mutual trust and understanding. Thus, this is a case for PPC.

The only reservation about foreign public intervention in regulation and supervision might arise from a political consideration: why should foreign public entities and not local governments or local public agencies hire, monitor and fund the required foreign experts? This question is beyond the scope of this paper, and regulation and supervision are not a case for foreign-dominated PPPs in the narrow sense of the term, since there are no facilities in which a foreign party could acquire ownership.

Leasing

The other cases are less straightforward. Take leasing. Leasing is an attractive business proposition, especially in a region like SEE where creditor rights are notoriously weak on paper, in practice, or both. Leasing bestows property rights on the lender that are stronger than in other forms of lending. This is why many foreign banks have entered this field, usually with some success. From a foreign or a development oriented perspective the private introduction of leasing in SEE countries might appear to take too much time. However, this is not necessarily the case. The social value of introducing leasing more rapidly in SEE might be higher than the private value – a necessary condition for legitimate public intervention and also a condition which is almost always fulfilled in the context of financial sector development. But it is not apparent that the other necessary condition would also be fulfilled, i.e. that the private rate of return is below the rate required for private investment and that investments in leasing are likely to produce negative present value for competent investor-entrepreneurs.

This assessment is supported by the fact that leasing exists and functions in almost every social environment. Therefore, public intervention is not needed: market forces will probably work effectively and rapidly. We should note that this assessment of leasing stands in strong contrast to MSE financing. MSE financing is indeed in extremely short supply in many countries, including the US, UK and France. So we conclude that PPP might be an appropriate form of foreign public intervention in the field of leasing, but hardly justifiable from a development policy standpoint.

Municipal Finance

As the next field, we briefly look at municipal finance as a possible area for PPPs Scepticism is required because concepts of what foreign donors could do in this area do not yet seem to be developed. The first step is to devise concepts and to acquire know-how. If these were available, caution would still be called for in using a PPP with foreign public and foreign private partners to create a municipal finance institution because making a municipality repay a loan as agreed in a loan contract is more politically sensitive and therefore much more difficult to enforce than making a small business person repay her loan. And the organisational form of a PPP is not an easy one. There is already the built-in conflict between the foreign public and private partners. If this is combined with the political dimension of lending to municipalities, it may simply be too much.

However, this should not preclude experimenting with various forms of PPCs to test the ground, to develop concepts and expertise, and to tap the market for private capital. For example, could a foreign public entity provide a guarantee for bonds issued by a local municipal bank which is managed by a foreign consultant-manager who might also be paid by the foreign entity?

Housing Finance

The high social value of an efficient housing finance system is generally accepted all over the world by researchers, politicians – and homeowners. It also seems that housing finance, especially for less well-to-do people, is an area in which private activity is not well established in many parts of the world. In almost every country, there is some form of public intervention in this field, be it the large-scale lending activity of the CDC in France, the public guarantee for the huge government-owned and controlled housing finance organisations in the US, or the tax privileges for housing finance in Germany. This could indicate a systematic market failure and therefore a case for public intervention.

For SEE countries, these considerations apply with even greater force: market forces unassisted by the public sector are not likely to fill the gap in supply in the near future if ever (see the cases of France and the US). Moreover, an organisation would have to be set up that someone would have to own and manage. Most likely, private actors are better suited than public actors to setting up and running housing finance facilities, and for reasons explained above these private actors should also have a substantial share of ownership. Thus, the conditions are fulfilled for using a PPP as an appropriate organisational form to implement a sound project. However, whether it is really advisable to create PPPs with foreign public owners and possibly also foreign private partners to support housing finance in SEE is a different question. In order to provide a positive answer, we would need a thorough investigation and some evidence to show that in developing countries a) a housing finance development PPP is better than not having any housing finance, and b) that a PPP is better than other forms of foreign support, such as subsidies for housing finance.

These considerations cover all the areas in which the concept of a PPP might be applicable. The short look beyond current practice shows that housing finance is the one field in which PPP might be feasible. It does not come as a surprise that this field is in many respects quite similar to MSE finance.

References

Bentz, A., Grout, P. and Halonen, M.L. (2003): Public-Private Partnerships: What Should the State Buy? CMPO Working Paper 01/040.

Fama, E., and Jensen, M.C. (1983): Separation of Ownership and Control; in: Journal of Law and Economics, Vol. 26, pp. 301–326.

Grout, P.A., and Stevens, M. (2003): The Assessment: Financing and Managing Public Services, in: Oxford Review of Economic Policy, Vol. 19, pp. 215–234.

Hart, O.E., (1995): Firms, Contracts, and Financial Structure; Oxford: Clarendon Press.

Hart, O.E. (2003): Incomplete Contracts and Public Ownership: Remarks, and an Application to Public-Private Partnerships, in: Economic Journal 113 (March 2003), pp. C69–C76.

Matthäus-Maier, I., and von Pischke, J.D. (eds.) (2004): The Development of the Financial Sector in Southeast Europe, Berlin: Springer.

Mehl, A., and Winkler, A. (2003): The Financial Sector and Financial Development: Evidence from Southeast Europe, in: Matthäus-Maier and von Pischke, eds., pp. 11–41.

NAO (2001): Managing the relationship to secure a successful partnership in PFI projects, Report by the Controller and Auditor General, HC 375, (London) 29 November 2001.

Osborne, St. P. (ed.) (2000): Public-Private Partnerships: Theory and Practice in an International Perspective, London and New York: Routledge.

Ricketts, M. (2003): Alternative Explanations for Changes in Ownership Structure, Journal of Institutional and Theoretical Economics, Vol. 159, pp. 688–697.

Schmidt, R.H,. and von Pischke, J.D. (2004): Networks of Microfinance Institutions: A Contribution to Financial Sector Development, Finance and Accounting Working Paper 126, University of Frankfurt, published in a French version in Technique Financière et Développement No. 74, pp. 18–31. Schmidt, R.H., and C.-P. Zeitinger (1996): Prospects, Problems and Potential of Credit-granting NGOs, in: Journal of International Development, Vol. 8, pp. 241–258.

Spackman, M. (2002): Public–Private Partnerships: Lessons from the British approach, in: Economic Systems, Vol. 26, pp. 283–301.

Stiglitz, J.E., and Wallsten, S.J. (2000): Public-Private Technology Partnerships: Promises and Pitfalls, in: Vaillancourt Rosenau, Pauline (ed.), (2000a), pp. 37–58.

Vaillancourt Rosenau, P. (ed.) (2000a): Public–Private Policy Partnerships, Cambridge and London: MIT Press.

Vaillancourt Rosenau, P. (2000b): The Strengths and Weaknesses of Public–Private Policy Partnerships, in: Vaillancourt Rosenau 2000a, pp. 217–241.

Williamson, O.E. (1985): The Economic Institutions of Capitalism; New York: The Free Press.

CHAPTER 23:

Replicable and Transparent PPP Models for Financial Sector Development

Klaus-Eckhard Hartmann

Director, Head of Structured Finance, Deutsche Investitions- und Entwicklungsgesellschaft mbH (DEG)

The basic objective of public-private partnerships (PPP) is not merely to complement private and public efforts but to proactively enhance them. Enhancement occurs when:

- one partner contributes something which the other does not have, and/or
- one partner's input leverages the other partner's input or makes it possible in the first place.

What Are the Specific Strengths of the Two Partners?

The *public sector* uses budget funds that contain a grant element (GE). The "weakness" of the public sector is that these funds are available only to a very limited degree.

Public funds containing a GE that are provided to developing and transition countries are typically in the form of:

- technical assistance (100% GE)
- financial assistance (100% GE)
- financial cooperation including loans with soft conditions (GE between 25% and approximately 80%)
- guarantees (limited GE)

In comparison, the *private sector* has almost unlimited resources but invests only when the risks involved appear justified by the expected returns in the form of dividends, capital gains and interest. If a financial institution cannot obtain adequate risk-adjusted returns and the capital market can do no better, public-sector resources can be used to reduce the risk of a private commitment and/or to increase its return.

Private funds for development are available to an almost unlimited degree – as long as the private sector's conditions are met. This makes it possible to adopt a strategy of using public funds to produce maximum leverage for the mobilisation of private funds.

Bottlenecks in Financial Sector Development

- Equity capital is totally exposed to the risks of the business; raising equity capital can therefore be problematic. This is especially true in developing or transition countries, where the success of financial institutions is often uncertain. On the other hand, equity is the precondition for raising debt based on an acceptable debt-equity ratio.

- Mezzanine finance is quasi-equity. In part, it can be treated as equity when determining the debt-equity ratio, also producing a leverage effect. However, mezzanine finance is exposed to correspondingly high risks, and its supply is consequently also tight.

- The ability to raise debt is limited by the debt-equity ratio of the financial institution, i.e. by its equity.

    - Long-term debt facilities are often not available on the domestic markets in developing and transition countries for a number of reasons: the banks do not have long-term deposits and hence would have maturity mismatches if they made term loans; the bond market is not developed; pension funds and similar financial intermediaries do not exist or do not invest their funds in long-term instruments.

    - Foreign long-term debt can be a burden on the balance of payments because debt has to be serviced in foreign currency. Moreover, currency risks are always a burden for those who have to service the debt. Saddling the end-borrowers with this risk is generally acceptable only for big borrowers who are familiar with and can manage the risk – and even then only if they have an export orientation that creates a natural hedge in the form of foreign currency revenues.

- Institution-building: setting up a microfinance institution is often expensive relative to the size of the loans and the capacities of the institution's microfinance clients. Imposing these costs on the clients through interest charges and fees would be prohibitive. In such cases, the institution requires start-up subsidies.

- Human resources: setting up a financial institution often requires foreign management with the required skills. However, expatriate management is disproportionately expensive, although often indispensable until local management has been recruited and trained. Some microfinance institutions, for example, cannot cover the full cost of the expatriates and are dependent on technical assistance.

Examples of Successful Models

The following models address some of the issues mentioned above and demonstrate how public and private funds can purposefully complement each other and provide transparency.

DEG / DFI Model

DEG (or a similar DFI – development finance institution) invests funds from the German federal government budget in a revolving facility (or in equity) that can then be used *inter alia* to promote financial sector development in developing or transition countries.[1] Based on this equity, DEG produces leverage by raising funds on the capital market and combining them with its own resources. As a simple illustration: the combination of DEG's equity capital (provided by public sources) and debt capital (provided by market resources) produces a leverage factor of 2; DEG's financial contribution covers on an average up to one-third of the respective investment, thereby mobilising a further two-thirds or more from the private sector, resulting in an additional leverage factor of 3. Thus on a conservative basis, DEG's equity actually produces a leverage factor of about 6.

IMI / IPC Model

IPC is an international consulting firm that establishes and manages microfinance institutions. IMI – which has had the same management as IPC – is an investment company that provides equity to microfinance institutions. Together, IPC as a partly publicly financed manager of microfinance banks, and IMI as a partly privately financed equity investment vehicle, fostered the start-up of a network of privately run microfinance institutions.[2]

---

[1] Volker Neuschütz, "Institutional Development and Commercialisation – Optimal Exit for Equity Financiers," in Ingrid Matthäus-Maier and J.D. von Pischke, eds., *The Development of the Financial Sector in Southeast Europe: Innovative Approaches in Volatile Environments.* Berlin: Springer Verlag, 2004. pp. 101–111.

[2] Syed Aftab Ahmed, "Strengthening Financial Sectors in Transition Countries: IFC's Contribution"; Claus-Peter Zeitinger, "Sustainable Microfinance Banks – Problems and Perspectives," in Ingrid Matthäus-Maier and J.D. von Pischke, eds., *The Development of the Financial Sector in Southeast Europe: Innovative Approaches in Volatile Environments.* Berlin: Springer Verlag, 2004. pp. 71–77, 125–134.

Emerging Markets Fund Model

An emerging markets fund for infrastructure in sub-Saharan Africa, for example, can be established by a group of public and private-sector investors to provide long-term debt finance for projects which – due to the risks involved – could not attract long-term loans on a purely commercial basis. A hypothetical structure that adequately mitigates the risk for commercial banks could take the following form:

	€ million
Equity (donor group)	80
Subordinated loans (development finance institutions – DFIs)	70
Senior debt (commercial banks)	150
	300

If this hypothetical investment turned out badly, the three parties would be affected quite differently. All of the equity could be lost before any of the subordinated loans and senior debt would be affected. The combination of public funds with a high GE (donor group equity, first loss tranche) and DFI funds (mezzanine finance, low GE, second loss tranche) enables commercial banks to make senior debt available, creating multiple leverage. Further confidence could be created by placing this fund under private management and by providing management incentives for good performance.

Local Currency Loans, Long-Term Liquidity Line Model

In this hypothetical case, an African commercial bank is unable to offer long-term finance for SMEs because it does not have long-term resources, although it does have sufficient local currency deposits to provide short-term liquidity.

Raising a long-term loan in foreign currency would not be feasible because the bank would have to pass the exchange risk on to its end-borrowers or bear the risk itself. Using its short-term deposits to fund long-term loans would create a maturity mismatch.

Any solution that would allow the African bank to lend its own short-term local currency funds on a long-term basis would have to offer protection against the liquidity risk. This can be achieved by providing a long-term standby facility that would be disbursed only in an emergency. Donors often provide such guarantee facilities.

Conclusion

Public funds with a high grant element are in short supply and therefore are highly valued. Accordingly, they should be used strategically and should never replace private capital. If the risk/return ratio makes it impossible for the capital market to finance financial sector development by setting up or expanding financial institutions, the use of public funds is appropriate. Public funds should be used to mobilise complementary private funds, achieving as high a leverage effect as possible. However, it is vital when structuring such collaboration that the interests of both public and private investors are balanced or can be synchronised to the satisfaction of all parties.

CHAPTER 24:

Using PPPs to Facilitate Transactions in Financial Markets

Ira W. Lieberman

Senior Economic Advisor, Open Society Institute

Public-private partnerships (PPPs) have been utilised in a variety of circumstances and have evolved over time. PPPs have often been associated with infrastructure, transport, energy and natural resource investments as both greenfield investments and privatisation transactions in transition economies.[1]

Concessions and Contracting Out

PPPs are used by governments that are constitutionally unable or otherwise unwilling to alienate or divest natural resources such as oil and gas, minerals and metals, forest and water. These governments may invite entry by private firms into these sectors through long-term concession agreements or intermediate-term contract management agreements. PPPs in the form of concessions are set up to build toll roads and bridges, to privatise marine ports and airports; separate contracts are employed to attract ancillary service establishments to these facilities.

PPPs are used in the power sector when the state lacks the budgetary resources to expand generating capacity. Various mechanisms have been employed to mobilise private-sector finance for the construction of power plants. The assumption is that a public or state-owned utility will remain in place to purchase this power through an off-take agreement. In Turkey, for example, various types of concessions have been set up for this purpose, such as build-operate-and-transfer agreements (BOTs) or build-operate-and-own agreements (BOOs).[2]

---

[1] For an extended discussion of PPPs through privatisation or greenfield investments in the CEE, CIS and SEE, see Ioannis Kessides, Ira Lieberman and Dirk Sommer, "Privatization and Private Participation in Infrastructure and Energy in ECA Countries: Is There a Need for a New Paradigm," World Bank, ECA Region, Infrastructure and Energy Department, 1993.

[2] Off-take agreements are often referred to as take or pay agreements. For example, the state owned utility or the government agrees to purchase a specified amount of generated power or electricity at a given price or else pay that amount to the BOT facility, as if it had purchased the given amount. This creates guaranteed revenue for the BOT facility which then encourages the private investor to make the investment.

These types of PPPs are found most often at the national level, but increasingly they are being set up at the municipal level in transport, garbage collection, water supply and sanitation. Concessions are important where local capital markets remain constrained. The concession holder, often a major multinational firm or a large domestic private group, can raise long-term financing for the concession in the form of bonds and syndicated loans in external capital markets.

Concessions of 20 to 30 years' duration confer quasi-ownership rights on the private stakeholder that provides technical and management expertise and financing. Contracts, on the other hand, are usually medium-term (5–10 years) and include the provision of management and technical expertise, but not normally financing. The state or municipality, as owner, is expected to provide financing. Contracts often offer significant incentives based on benchmarked performance measures, including some percentage of equity or ownership earn-out.[3] Contracts, in contrast to concessions, are further removed from real ownership and are therefore more problematic.[4]

PPPs in Financial Services

Microfinance and SME (small and medium enterprise) finance offer examples of PPPs that have worked well. The issues they raise are illustrated by the very successful case of IMI. In microfinance, PPPs have evolved to include:

- donor funding of NGOs that have pioneered in difficult markets such as Opportunity International[5] in Southeast Europe (SEE) and the CIS (Commonwealth of Independent States), or FINCA and Mercy Corps in Central Asia;

- donor support for capacity-building (e.g. CGAP – Consultative Group to Assist the Poor);

---

[3] There are many different potential formulas for an equity earn-out, but essentially this implies that the contract manager is given an incentive to earn a share of the ownership in the facility based on meeting contractual performance criteria or benchmarks. The percentage of equity earn-out may vary, for example between 10% and 20%, and usually the earn-out is over the life of the contract.

[4] See Mary Shirley, *Bureaucrats in Business: The Economics and Politics of Government Ownership*, World Bank and Oxford University Press, 1995 for a discussion of the relative merits of concessions, contracting out and contract management.

[5] See Keith Flintham, "Building a Market Niche also Builds a Market: Opportunity Bank in Montenegro" in Part III of this volume.

- donor funding with management contracts (e.g. EBRD and IPC in the CIS);[6] and

- IMI, in which the private participant enjoys both ownership and management rights (described below).

Some NGOs, notably parts of the Aga Khan Group in Central Asia and Pakistan and the Open Society Institute (OSI) in Central and Eastern Europe and SEE, have largely used their own resources to operate microfinance and SME financing facilities and have engaged in PPPs to a limited degree only. An interesting feature is that some NGOs, such as FINCA, Save the Children and Opportunity International, fund their start-up operations through donations from private contributors and then rely on donor mezzanine financing for capacity-building and expansion.

IMI (Internationale Micro Investitionen) has provided a pattern for transforming their operations into formal financial institutions, which has inspired several other microfinance networks to establish similar structure (e.g. Opportunity International) or to start their own investment vehicles to scale-up their efforts (e.g. CARE through MICROVEST, ACCION International in Latin America and Africa, and most recently OSI). In SEE, IMI's banks have challenged small and medium-sized commercial banks. Based on interviews in Croatia and Bulgaria, these banks consider microenterprise and SME as increasingly important niche markets. IMI has not only inspired new forms of PPPs, but has begun to engender real private sector competition. In order to compete successfully in the long run, IMI's banks have evolved to become full service banks with a focus on SME and micro lending.

In Latin America, ACCION International has successfully converted many of its affiliates into banks; it has raised two different equity funds and a guarantee fund, and it has participated in PROFUND, the first microfinance investment fund in the region. In all cases, this has been achieved with a significant mix of public and private investment. ACCION's public-private partnerships have worked well because of the trust it has built up with public institutions and its commitment to good management and governance. These appear to be the essential ingredients of such PPPs.

In SME finance, the Small Enterprise Assistance Fund (SEAF) has pioneered venture capital or private equity investments in SMEs in Central and Eastern Europe, the CIS and SEE. Originally created by CARE in Poland in 1990, SEAF is an NGO that has expanded successfully, using a combination of private and public capital. Like IMI and ACCION, SEAF's governance and management are first rate, and it has created trust through its performance over the last 12 years of transition in the region.

---

[6] See Elizabeth Wallace, "EBRD's Micro and Small Enterprise Lending Programmes: Downscaling Commercial Banks and Starting Greenfield Banks," in Ingrid Mattäus-Maier and J.D. von Pischke, eds., *The Development of the Financial Sector in Southeast Europe: Innovative Approaches in Volatile Environments*. Berlin: Springer, 2004. pp. 79–87.

Cooperation and Conflict in Structuring PPPs

Private sector and public sector collaboration has produced a range of outcomes; PPPs may work better in some sectors than in others, based on the underlying degree of flexibility of the public and the private partners, on the environment in which PPPs operate, and on situation-specific conditions that create or destroy trust between the partners.

Infrastructure and Energy Concessions and Contracts

Many concessions and contract arrangements have worked well and meet the state's objective of modernising facilities (such as ports or airports) and operating municipal utilities. However, concessions and contracts are a second best solution to outright private ownership. It is difficult to draft concessions or contracts to protect the interests of the various stakeholders, which results in dispute and renegotiation. Detailed regulations are often drafted into contracts, and this is difficult to get right. There is a need for simple procedures to facilitate contract adjustment.

Often, the PPP fails to meet investor expectations because governments simply renege on their contracts when faced with the political and social difficulties of raising tariffs to contractually agreed levels. In Turkey, BOTs have often been perceived as corrupt, and the state has been left with very high priced off-take agreements: public policy goals were met but at a very high cost. If trust within the PPP is lacking, the relationship can quickly turn sour. External investors may not have much confidence in local regulators and courts, and contracts increasingly contain international arbitration clauses that provide for dispute resolution on neutral ground in countries with trusted legal traditions.

The recent crisis in Argentina illustrates what can happen when trust breaks down. Foreign concession holders in utilities (e.g. water) had entered into tariff agreements with the government based on the Argentine peso's one-to-one peg to the US dollar. When the government floated the peso during the crisis, the exchange rate slid rapidly to 3 pesos to the dollar. Utilities with large external debts denominated in dollars were unable to adjust tariffs to compensate for the massive devaluation. They also incurred losses because of the inability of their clients to pay for services, and so moved rapidly towards bankruptcy. Virtually all concession holders were forced into workout agreements that included long-term rescheduling.

Micro and SME Finance

PPPs in microfinance have, on balance, worked well. Initially, donors, as public institutions, financed the expansion of microfinance throughout the world in partnership with NGOs. As the sector has evolved, public intervention has grown more sophisticated. The IFIs (international financial institutions) have formed partnerships with leading private investors to form banking groups (e.g. IMI) or investment funds such as PROFUND, which have invested in commercialised MFIs throughout Latin America. PPPs increasingly accept that MFIs should operate as regulated financial institutions that generate profit and provide their investors with a reasonable return. Most of these MFIs also mobilise savings. For legal and prudential reasons, NGOs are not normally able to do this.

Structuring PPPs to Create Sustainable Financial Institutions

Microfinance PPPs dedicated to sustainability have increasingly evolved into formal, regulated, financial institutions. This development was driven by a number of factors: first, the realisation that this is the only way to meet the virtually unlimited worldwide demand for greater access to financial services; second, increasing recognition that the poor desire savings as much as they desire credit; third, formalised MFIs have to offer a variety of products and services in order to compete in the long run. Moreover, to remain sustainable, they have to become more efficient and not rely exclusively on very high real rates of interest. Finally, these new forms of PPPs have to be able to raise funds readily at a competitive cost in domestic and, potentially, in international capital markets. This is particularly true in SEE, where a very competitive banking sector has emerged in countries such as Croatia, and Bulgaria. In order to provide micro and SME finance, PPPs will have to compete largely as commercial banks that provide a full range of services.

Strengths and Weaknesses of PPPs in Micro and SME Finance

The strengths of PPPs seem clear. Both public and private investors in this sector have recognised the importance of upscaling. In the absence of sufficient private sector interest or conviction, these investors have assisted this sector in successfully planting its seeds throughout the world. They have done this in part through PPPs, while avoiding the worst problem of SME finance – the involvement of host governments. The negative side is that PPPs are not a stable solution for the long-term development of the sector. For microfinance to remain viable in the long term, the domestic private financial sector will have to be engaged, supplemented by international investors. The question is whether or not PPPs will be able to attract the necessary investments. On balance, there seem to be good chances of success.

The Major Risks for PPPs in Micro and SME Finance

In all partnerships there is a danger that the partners' interests will diverge over time. This is particularly true when private institutions join with public institutions whose objectives and goals are likely to shift over time, regardless of the performance of any given cooperative arrangement or transaction. Microfinance is currently the "flavour-of-the-month," but next year that may not be the case. In addition, public entities may see their role as seeding a sector, such as microfinance, in a particular country for a period of five years or so, and then exiting. But, microfinance may be the entire livelihood and only line of business of the private partner, who may not be contemplating exit for some time.

Finally, MFIs financed through PPPs may be subject to external political and economic shocks, such as financial crises. The public partner may move to bail out the MFIs concerned, but the private partner may not have the capital base to support an injection of emergency funds. In other cases, the public partners may want to expand the PPP very rapidly and again the private partner may not have the means to follow up. The private partner may object to diluting his or her share. The risks of divergence probably increase over time.

Summary

Public-private partnerships are a tried and tested method by which governments, public sector institutional investors and state-owned enterprises seek to draw private capital into markets or to institutions that have difficulty attracting such capital, largely due to the perceived risk. These partnerships have been successful in utilities and infrastructure investments and, most recently, in finance, especially microfinance. However, PPPs are likely to be unstable over time, as the partners' interests may diverge. For example, in seeking to inject more capital into an institution, the private partner may not have the financial strength to match the reserves of public investors and may therefore resist dilution. Alternatively, the public investor may want to re-deploy its capital after a relatively short investment period, for example 5 to 7 years, while the private partner may wish to stay in and build up the institution over the longer term. PPPs should be supported, but it is advisable that PPPs have a defined life and that the partners have a clear path to separation and mutual exit.

CHAPTER 25:

Sustainable Microfinance Banks – IMI as a Public-Private Partnership in Practice

Helen Alexander

Manager, Internationale Micro Investitionen AG

Internationale Micro Investitionen AG (IMI) has been highlighted as a good example of a public-private partnership. This paper explains the IMI model, laying out the basis for its success and highlighting some of the challenges lying ahead.

Internationale Projekt Consult (IPC) has worked as a microfinance consulting firm since the late-1980s. It has advised NGOs, cooperatives, municipal savings banks and commercial banks in projects sponsored by development organisations. The specialised credit technology developed in these projects, based on credit to individuals rather than groups, quickly proved successful. However, in most cases, IPC found that the institutions, not the technology, were the barriers to serving the SME target group.

Ownership and Governance

Many institutions had no real owners in the true sense of the word, and they consequently developed little, if any, interest in efficiency. Where institutions did have real owners, these were so interested in short-term profits that the necessary long-term investments were not undertaken. NGOs generally fell into the first category, while commercial banks generally fell into the second.

These experiences ultimately convinced IPC that ownership and governance are the essential factors that determine success or failure. This realisation led IPC to invest its own money in microfinance institutions.

In 1998, IPC founded IMI, the first private company established to invest exclusively in commercially oriented microfinance banks (MFBs) worldwide. By MFBs, we mean institutions which:

- are subject to supervision by a banking supervisory authority and have to adhere to banking legislation;
- have a clear focus on lending to micro and small enterprises; and
- attract local deposits, which helps the MFB to become more independent from international credit lines.

IMI's founders were originally private investors: IPC, IPC Invest (composed of IPC staff) and two foundations – the Netherlands-based DOEN foundation and ProCrédito, a Bolivian entity. Later they were joined by various IFIs (international financial institutions). The shareholder structure in early 2004 was as follows:

Table 1. IMI shareholder structure as of March 2004

Public/Private	% share	Equity holding (€ million)
IPC	19.4	8.4
IPC Invest	7.2	3.1
DOEN	15.6	6.7
ProCrédito	6.0	2.6
Private	**48.2 %**	**20.8**
KfW/DEG	14.3	6.2
IFC	15.8	6.8
FMO	14.4	6.2
BIO	7.3	3.2
Public	**51.8 %**	**22.4**
Total	100.0	43.2

Source: http://www.imi-ag.com

IMI is clearly a partnership between public and private parties, each block having roughly equal representation. No one shareholder owns more than 20%. The driving entrepreneurial force in the group is IPC.

In March 2004, IMI's capital was invested in 18 microfinance institutions in as many countries. Ten of them operate in Southeast and Eastern Europe, 5 are in Latin America, and 3 in Africa. Table 2 gives an overview of the investments in IMI banks. The individual banks are also founded on the principle of partnership between the public and private parties.

The IFC, the KfW Group and FMO also hold shares in individual microfinance banks, in addition to their stakes in IMI. IMI and these three shareholders hold a majority of the shares in almost all 18 of the MFBs. Plans are underway to consolidate ownership of these institutions under IMI. IMI will acquire the shares of these three institutions, which in exchange will receive more shares in IMI. Following the consolidation, IMI would be the majority owner of each of the individual MFBs. Recognising the synergistic effects of having one network under one owner, all the banks either have or are being rebranded ProCredit Bank. IPC provides the management services to all of the banks.

Within a few years, IMI will go public in order to increase its equity and to offer an exit option to international investors. Going public would also demonstrate

Table 2. Ownership structure of IMI institutions, March 2004 (amounts in € or US $ million)

Country	Equity* (€/$ million)	IMI	IFC	FMO	KfW group	Others
		%				
Eastern Europe						
ProCredit Bank, Georgia ($)	12	39	16	-	10	35
ProCredit Bank, BiH (€)	9	34	23	-	8	35
ProCredit Bank, Kosovo (€)	13	16	16	16	16	36
MIRO Bank, Romania ($)	11	12	19	7	21	41
Microenterprise Credit, Moldova (€)	1	39	15	-	-	46
ProCredit Bank, Albania (€)	8	15	20	-	25	40
ProCredit Bank, Serbia (€)	11	16	16	16	16	36
ProCredit Bank, Ukraine ($)	16	20	20	-	20	40
ProCredit Bank, Bulgaria (€)	13	21	19	-	20	40
ProCredit Bank, Macedonia (€)	6	26	16	17	21	20
Latin America						
Caja Los Andes, Bolivia ($)	13	69	-	-	-	31
Financiera ProCredit, Nicaragua ($)	5	81	-	-	-	19
Financiera Calpiá, El Salvador ($)	15	25	15	15	15	30
Sociedad Financiera Ecuatorial ($)	7	69	-	-	-	31
Micro Credit National, Haiti ($)	2	25	20	-	-	55
Africa						
NovoBanco, Mozambique ($)	2	25	13	13	-	49
Sikaman S&L, Ghana ($)	2	35	25	20	-	20
Angola, NovoBanco ($)	5	43	14	-	-	43
Total (€) 134.1**						

* As of March 2004
** exchange rate €/$ 0.8215

Source: http://www.imi-ag.com

beyond all doubt that microfinance is commercially viable. In this respect, consolidating ownership under IMI provides shareholders with greater liquidity for their shares than would a sale of shares in individual banks in their local markets.

Financial Performance

These institutions have performed well. The MFBs – most of which have been in operation for less than five years – are already earning a profit, as shown by the latest annual RoE figures in Table 3. That the institutions have been able to achieve profitability so quickly is in part due to the generous technical assistance they received in the establishment phase, primarily from the U.S. government (some of which via EBRD) and the government of the Federal Republic of Germany.

Outreach

At the end of March 2004, the outstanding combined loan portfolio of the MFBs in the network was € 700 million, comprising some 320,000 individual loans. By the end of 2006, IMI banks will have half a million borrowers and an outstanding loan portfolio of over € 1 billion. As of March 2004, 96% of their loans were for amounts of less than € 10,000, and 60% of all loans are for amounts of less than € 1,000.

Table 3. Return* on equity of the 18 banks in 2003

Bank	Start date	RoE**
Caja Los Andes, Bolivia	1995	25.5%
Financiera Calpiá, El Salvador	1995	14.7%
ProCredit Bank, BiH	1997	4.5%
ProCredit Bank, Georgia	1999	16.7%
ProCredit Bank, Albania	1999	8.2%
ProCredit Bank, Kosovo	1999	34.0%
Financiera CONFIA, Nicaragua	2000	64.7%
Micro Credit National, Haiti	2000	7.5%
Micro Enterprise Credit, Moldova	2000	28.6%
NovoBanco, Mozambique	2000	-14.1%
ProCredit Bank, Ukraine	2001	4.0%
Sociedad Financiera Ecuatorial, Ecuador	2001	17.9%
ProCredit Bank, Bulgaria	2001	12.5%
Micro Enterprise Bank, Philippines***	2001	-4.9%
ProCredit Bank, Serbia	2001	1.0%
Sikaman SLC, Ghana	2002	-1.4%
MIRO Bank, Romania	2002	-11.9%
ProCredit Bank, Macedonia	2003	-9.2%
Average return on equity for all IMI investments in 2003:		**9.9%**

* annualised, after tax, includes impact of local currency devaluation ** in EUR or USD
*** divested in 2004

Source: http://www.imi-ag.com

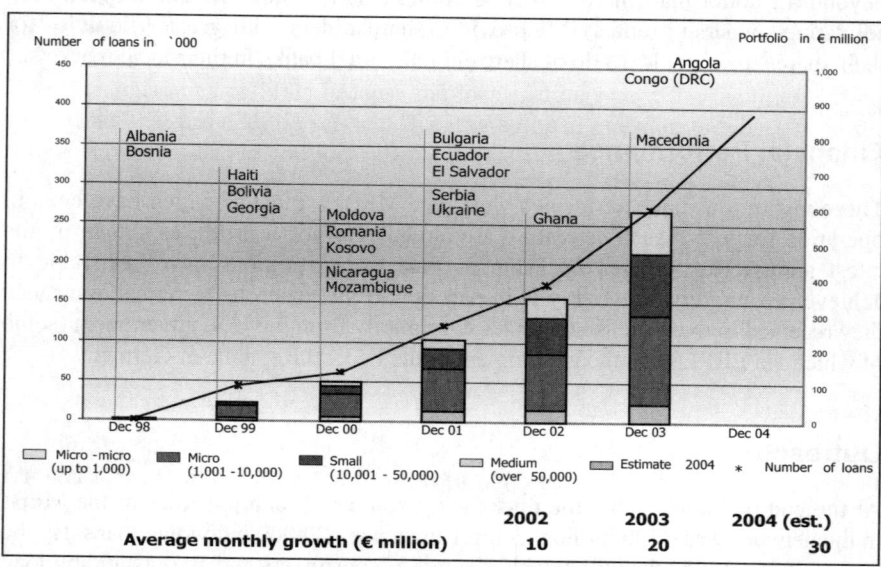

Figure 1. Portfolio growth and composition: four loan size categories, 1998–2004
Source: http://www.imi-ag.com

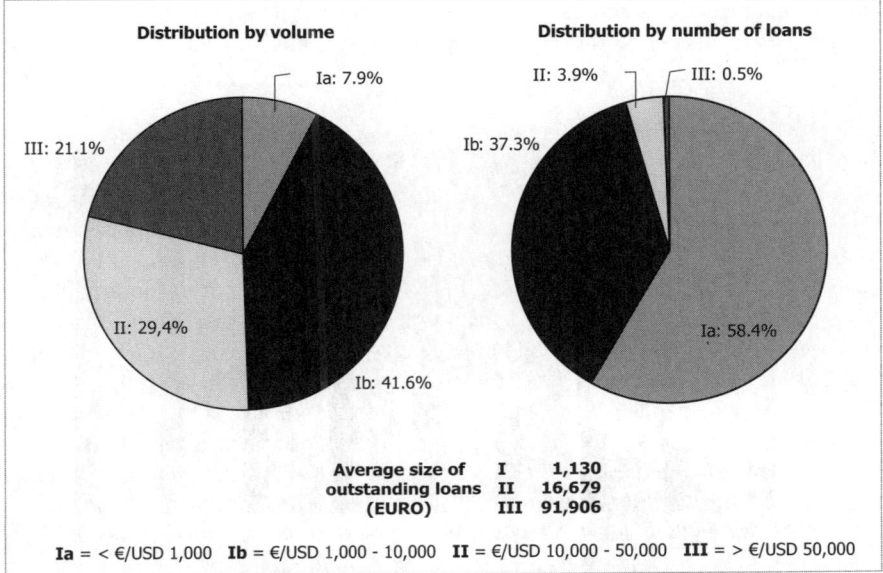

Figure 2. Composition of the combined portfolio of all institutions in which IMI invests (March 2004)
Source: http://www.imi-ag.com

As of mid 2004, some 40,000 loans amounting to more than € 70 million were being disbursed monthly, responding to a market that others have ignored.

The MFBs issue loans based on meticulous and labour-intensive analysis, but without applying the rigid requirements normally set by traditional banks, such as certified accounts, a business plan and excessive collateral. Precisely because of this information-based rather than asset-based approach to lending, the MFBs' portfolio quality is very high – considerably higher than at most other banks – as the arrears rates illustrate. In March 2004, the arrears at all of the IMI banks, expressed as the portfolio at risk for more than 30 days, was only 1.06%, and the figure for Eastern Europe was below 0.6%. Write-off rates are much lower than 0.5%, also indicating excellent portfolio quality.

Managing Growth

The results have been good, but when institutions grow this quickly certain constraints emerge.

It becomes much more difficult to obtain funds to maintain this growth, even at market terms and conditions. Commercial banks are at best willing to provide short-term money market lines to IMI banks, but are not willing to extend maturities beyond 365 days. IMI's public sector partners have been important allies in provid-

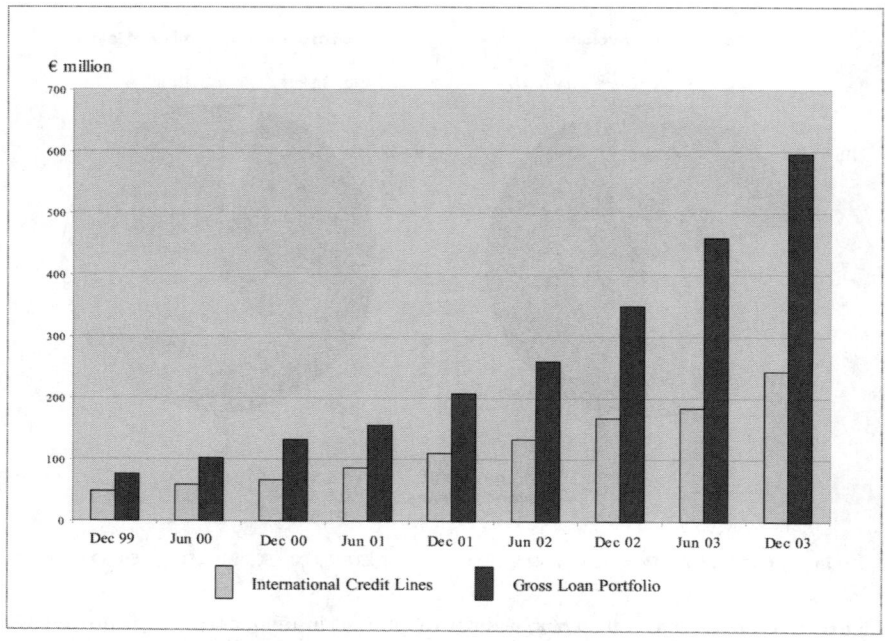

Figure 3. The IMI banks: IFI credit lines vs. gross loan portfolio, December 1999 to December 2003
Source: http://www.imi-ag.com

ing commercial long-term finance to date, having financed about half of the increase in the growth of the loan portfolio (Figure 3). But the additional amounts they can now offer are limited, since their internal credit risk ceiling usually demands that lending to any institution does not exceed 100% of that institution's equity.

Is deposit-taking a viable alternative? To develop sustainable sources of finance, IMI banks have to develop their deposit bases. This requires them to offer a range of savings products and banking services – in other words to develop a fully-fledged commercial banking approach. All IMI institutions are now undergoing this transition.

Our combined customer deposit volume is in line with our outstanding loan volume. Although some countries have surplus deposits (especially Kosovo), regulatory requirements preclude use of excess liquidity at one bank to fund lending at another. Thus, the goal is to build a successful deposit business in all of the countries in which IMI operates. This will not be easy: it cannot be assumed that MFBs which are only three or four years old and lend primarily to small enterprises will quickly be able to attract large volumes of deposits from larger enterprises or from households, i.e. from wage and salary earners. Deposit growth is determined by the reputation a bank builds, and by the extent to which it expands its branch network. Both take time.

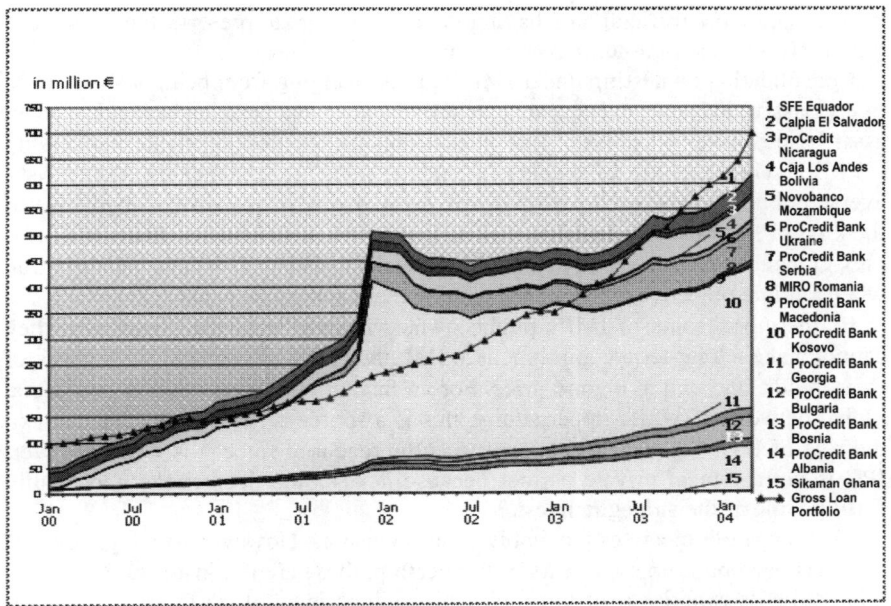

Figure 4. The IMI banks: combined deposit volume vs. gross loan portfolio, January 2000 to March 2004
Source: http://www.imi-ag.com

How to Explain This Success?

Many assume that our success is due primarily to sound credit technology and the "demand" of the disadvantaged entrepreneurs that the MFBs serve. These elements do play a role, but not by any means the most important one.

The key to our success has been ownership, sound governance and good management. Ownership has been particularly important, and the privilege of having dedicated shareholders, who take a long-term view and think in social terms, has been invaluable. Likewise, the driving entrepreneurial force of IPC, which has full management responsibility for all the IMI institutions, is also a critical component. IMI has not had to make too many compromises – either to development policy rituals such as requiring local shareholders or to short-term profiteers.

IMI has been able to set clear goals and priorities and to inspire very good managers to implement the corresponding strategies.

Outlook

Ownership, sound governance and good management will remain IMI's key challenges. The banks are now successful, growing very rapidly and becoming more commercial. Finding the balance between commercial and development priorities is becoming more difficult, and having the right owners to preserve the mission of the MFBs over the long-term ever more important.

Consolidating ownership under IMI requires changing from being a small, relatively passive investor, to becoming an active owner of a banking network with an asset base of over €1 billion. This puts strains on the public-private partnership (PPP). Having a group of owners, including some understandably highly risk-averse public owners, each with a nearly equal share, is not always conducive to the kind of fast business decision-making needed to succeed when running a complex global business in rapidly changing financial markets. This is particularly true when a prime objective is to balance development and profit goals.

Furthermore, some of IMI's public owners have a "catalytic" mandate. They cannot make a long-term commitment to IMI; they have to keep exit at the back of their minds, and exit at a good price. For an institution whose mission is to run a global network of MFBs in perpetuity, this is a source of tension. In this context, the role of IPC – as the driving private entrepreneurial force – is key. However, IPC is not a typical private partner because it lacks the deep pockets to readily fulfil its role as the strategic investor.

This range of objectives inevitably creates tensions. However, as a high level of trust has been built up over years of partnership, these are not insuperable. Nevertheless, IMI's experience makes it clear that a high level of trust, open communication and a common, deeply held sense of vision are essential for a PPP if the "rules of the game" are to be successfully renegotiated as a successful business develops.

"Going public" will be an important part of the development of IMI as a PPP. IMI plans to go public in a way that attracts private investors with a particular profile. Two investor target groups will be cultivated. IMI will look for shareholders to invest between €500,000 and €5 million and who are prepared to accept modest returns (5% per annum), while enjoying long-term security and the expectation of significant development impact. IMI will also look for ways to open up the shareholder structure to a large number of smaller investors. Ultimately, IMI will seek a listing on a public stock exchange. Attracting a large number of private investors who are inspired by the concept, including many "socially responsible greens," is part of IMI's development mission. Having small investors also means that IPC's leadership role is retained. Additional patient private capital will preserve IMI as a successful PPP over the long term.

CHAPTER 26:

Opportunities for Public-Private Partnerships in Financial Sector Development

Syed Aftab Ahmed

International Finance Corporation

Long-term public-private partnerships (PPPs) in development finance are made possible by aligning the financial interests of private capital with the interests of public capital that seeks to create benefits of another kind. In the case of microfinance, the second benefit is financial sector development oriented towards the small end of the financial market, where micro and small businesses reside. This, however, does not mean that the private investor has no interest in the second benefit or that the public investor is willing to sacrifice financial returns completely to achieve the second benefit. In fact, the public investor does seek adequate financial returns, and the private investor views the development of financial markets as a necessary precondition for achieving its own financial objectives. Accordingly, the financial return on investment, private and public, has a direct co-relation with the objective of developing the target microfinance market. Absent this clarity and unity of vision, the partnership will not endure.

Financial Objectives and Development Objectives

The financial objective of a private investor seeking to achieve these sorts of results is to realise adequate financial returns. "Adequate" returns have no specific definition other than that they are positive. Probably the least demanding investor's financial criterion would be a return equal to the rate of inflation, while others might consider a yield equal to that of a government security as their target return on investment.

But the rate of return on an investment is only one aspect of what investments have to achieve in order to provide sustainable results. For example, investors are sensitive to the length of time required to achieve a desired financial return. Investors seeking to maximise their returns will generally prefer a quick return because risk increases as time horizon lengthen. In general, more things can go wrong over a long time period than over a short time period.

In contrast, investors who want to create benefits of another kind may be "patient investors" who are willing to receive no or lower dividends in the short-term and who are willing to watch their money work for a decade or more before seeking an exit that will provide an overall better than average reward. For this strategy to succeed, the benefits of another kind – in this case, development impact in the financial sector – must also be achieved by the time of exit. The development mandate must be fulfilled to realise the goals of the patient investor. Interestingly, this means that the two benefits are not mutually exclusive: the expected financial rewards will not accrue unless the small end of the financial market has been developed and profitably served.

The apparent conflict in time horizons can be managed by enlisting parties having somewhat similar degrees of patience. Public-private partnerships are a means of resolving this structural issue. In the case of micro and small enterprise finance, there are currently few, if any, opportunities to combine high returns, early exit, and sustainable financial institutions. However, public sector investors who are patient and private investors with a longer time horizon can collaborate effectively when the creation of sustainable target-group oriented financial institutions serves their common objectives.

The Role of Start-up Subsidies

Whether because of market failure or for other reasons, the reality on the ground is that sustainable institutional capacity for the delivery of credit and other financial services to the target group is either absent or very limited in almost all developing countries. The creation of sustainable institutional capacity for the target group therefore by definition has to be subsidised: there would be little microfinance capacity as we know it today if no grants were available.

Properly structured subsidies act as credit enhancements that boost the quality of the investment proposal. Credit enhancement makes it possible to attract investors who will provide equity funding and loans to the institutions that are to be created at the small end of the financial market. By altering the risk profile of the investment proposal, subsidies provide an initial building block and a basis for negotiations among potential partners.

In the absence of subsidy, even the most patient investors are deterred from investing in greenfield microfinance institutions in developing countries. This is because individual micro loans are tiny. Hence, the micro loan portfolio initially grows one tiny micro loan at a time, much more slowly than the portfolios of other new financial institutions such as, for example, commercial banks. Slow growth in lending translates into slow growth in income, lengthening the time required for a new microfinance institution to break even in the absence of subsidy.

Therefore, in addition to the high project risk, which is inherent in all projects that aim to introduce a new product line in uncertain markets in developing countries, the length of time required for a microfinance operation to breakeven is almost twice as long as for commercial banks. Hypothetical breakeven time horizons without subsidy could extend to 8 years for a new microfinance institution, but even 4 years would deter most investors. Subsidies allow us to shorten this breakeven period to acceptable time frames, permitting benefits of another kind – development impact – to occur sooner and in greater volume.

The use of subsidy to attract development oriented investors also has a subtle and even controversial element, which is governance. A working hypothesis is that investors who are subject to the discipline of capital markets are more likely to provide better guidance for the development of commercial microfinance institutions than those who are not so disciplined, but rather those who are motivated primarily by charitable objectives or for whom development impact, however measured, outweighs the quest for an adequate return on investment.

At the current stage, the majority of funding for the development of commercial microfinance is provided by public sector entities. On this basis, the corollary to the working hypothesis would be that for each dollar provided, equity investors are more productive contributors in this respect than those providing only funds for on-lending, and that commercially oriented investors are more valuable in this respect than charitable supporters. At the same time, these public sector investors can collaborate productively with others based on a core set of common objectives that can be structured as public-private partnerships. One example of this collaboration is the global IPC/IFC partnership in the field of commercial microfinance.

IFC's Role and Contribution

IFC raises funds by selling its bonds in capital markets. It is, therefore, subject to the disciplines of capital markets and provides leadership in the development of commercially oriented microfinance institutions. For IFC, while financial returns are a precondition, development impact is paramount and always plays a role in every IFC investment decision. IPC (Internationale Projekt Consult GmbH) is a patient private investor that provides technical assistance through specific initiatives and also as a board member of institutions in which it invests.

Paradigm Evolution – From Market Failure to Ownership

Twenty or so years ago, the question that every development finance practitioner asked was, "What can we do to prevent or overcome market failure in financial markets?" Investments were made in development finance institutions, usually state-owned, that were meant to fill gaps attributed to market failure. Market failure, an economic concept, is said to occur when two conditions apply. The first is that information is insufficient for the production of economically efficient outcomes, such as the delivery of credit and other financial services to micro and small enterprises. The second is that private incentives are inconsistent with the public good, such as when banks do not lend to micro and small entrepreneurs.

Public sector programmes executed by state-owned institutions were designed to overcome these perceived deficiencies.

After years of hard work, it was concluded that this economic concept was not of much help. It appeared that the definition of market failure is so broad that it can be applied to almost any economic endeavour in which the price system operates. It was found that government institutions often have woefully inadequate incentive structures that fail to create viable institutional solutions to perceptions of market failure. In sum, efforts to improve welfare by overcoming market failures all too frequently led to non-market failures based on poorly structured interventions.

Our response to these disappointments has been to focus more narrowly and more precisely. Our fundamental project design question is, "What does it take to build a strong financial institution that can compete in a sustainable manner in financial markets?" The underlying premise is that innovation is required to achieve results where few have been achieved before. The innovation may be entirely original, but more often it involves applying and modifying successful efforts achieved elsewhere.

The critical ingredients required to create strong, sustainable financial institutions are knowledge and technology, incentives, capital, and technical support. Know-how is the most important feature. We tap know-how by developing long-term relationships with competent strategic investors and technical assistance providers. These relationships often take the form of public-private partnerships.

Incentives are also crucial for every party involved in a joint endeavor. IFC, as a lead investor, has increasingly focused its attention on structuring incentives that will help strategic private investors perform at their very best. In 1996, IFC implemented an innovative concept by requiring that the management consultants hired to operate the Micro Enterprise Bank of Bosnia and Herzegovina also act as strategic investors. This aligned interests, serving all parties – investors, service providers and clients – quite well. In fact, this initiative planted the seeds of IMI, which was formed in 1998.

The other ingredients for building effective institutions are demonstration and strong capital. Demonstration means that models exemplifying best practice are created and then replicated. For demonstration to work, innovation must be continual, which requires incentives. Capital enables good models to expand and innovate. But innovation always creates risks, and another role of capital is to bail out projects that suffer setbacks but have the potential to overcome shock.

At last development finance has a strong model in which consultants have incentives that go considerably beyond fulfilling the letter of their contracts. Real world problems in volatile environments can be handled more proactively. We as investors now have a tool that gives us more confidence that situations that are not covered in consulting contracts, or that are covered only partially or ambiguously, will be resolved in a more productive manner. Of course, the incentive for a private partner must focus both on short-term and long-term financial benefits, and now, through PPP, we provide such incentives and more.

Managing Success

IFC's experience with IMI has been positive: this PPP has yielded the desired results. IFC's catalytic role is exemplified by the growing number of similar investment vehicles that owe some of their inspirations, if not all, to IMI. The success of PPPs as vehicles for development finance is becoming apparent, creating a virtuous circle of development at the small end of financial markets. It is fair to say that this began in Southeast Europe, where it has flourished.

Corporate governance has become much more important as new insights into the incentives of various parties in a partnership become more refined. This adds a new dimension to our financial market skills. At the same time, we may be victims of our own success. Conflicts of interest consume more attention: the alignment of interests we so confidently introduced in 1996, linking a management consulting firm with an investment company dedicated to creating greenfield microfinance banks, are now perceived as conflicts of interests.[1] As we move forward, we are identifying and meeting challenges that concern the separation of the roles of consulting firms and investment companies. Questions to ask ourselves include:

- Should a consulting firm, closely related to an investment company, be considered impartial?

- How long should a consulting company manage a new microfinance institution?

- How can conflicts of interest that arise from successful investment be managed in ways that do not disrupt the operations of the new microfinance institution that has been created? What operating principles can be designed, agreed and implemented?

We are now moving to address these issues in the context of IPC and IMI as the leaders in this area. The results should make it easier for IMI to attract investors and also make it easier for IFC and other IFIs to exit investments at some propitious time, possibly going public through an IPO (an initial public offering of shares on a stock exchange).

We may also be victims of our own success in other ways. The rush to establish institutions for micro and small enterprise finance might lead to unrealistic expectations. New entrants or critics of our efforts might underestimate the requirements for success. Also, the inherent time horizons or stages of growth in creating sustainable microfinance institutions test the degrees of patience of the various stakeholders.

---

[1] In American usage, conflict of interest is often interpreted as a situation in which abuse has occurred. The correct legal meaning of the term is that a situation exists in which abuse might occur. The context usually involves one party that plays a dual role within a single structure in which another or numerous other parties also have an interest.

Finally, we have created more work for ourselves. Rapidly growing loan portfolios, such as those in the IMI network that grew by €40 million during March 2004, far outstrip growth in deposits. Funding through credit markets is required for further growth. Capital is also required to provide a cushion for the risks in these portfolios and to conform to regulatory requirements. With success, more capital is required – not less. This paradox requires, for the moment, a strong continuing public sector presence that will eventually permit the partnerships to "go private" by going public.

We began by discussing the double bottom line: financial returns and development impact. But an additional bottom line has become of overwhelming importance to us in our quest to create sustainable microfinance institutions at the small end of the market: in investment, ownership matters.

CHAPTER 27:

Public-Private Partnership – Results in the Banking Sector in Southeast Europe

Klaus Glaubitt and Haje Schütte

Vice Presidents, KfW Bankengruppe

The Role of Private Public Partnerships in the Banking Sector

Public-Private Partnerships (PPPs) – also referred to as Private Sector Participation (PSP) – in transition and developing countries are often heralded as a paradigm shift in development policy. Many consider this new approach to be the most remarkable recent innovation in cooperation (Richter 2003, p.7). At international conferences, PPP is championed by bilateral and multilateral donors and government officials as a promising new development strategy.

But what does PPP represent and why do we need it? The majority of the world's population do not participate significantly in the formal sectors of the economy that provide infrastructure, social and financial services. This is due to scarce public funding, inefficiencies, political influence in the allocation of services, a lack of knowledge and incentives in the public sector and risk perceptions of the private sector. In the search for remedies to these market and nonmarket deficiencies, governments all over the world are approaching the private sector in an effort to bridge the knowledge and finance gap. This is happening in all areas in which the state believes its withdrawal is politically acceptable and can result in improvements in public welfare. The same reasoning holds true for development cooperation, in which the PPP concept has become a prime topic.

The main reasons for PPP are to mobilise private sector capital and to improve operational efficiency in service delivery. This implies that the state concentrates on its core functions of regulating the framework for economic activity while production and service provision lie in the hands of the private sector. Experience shows that this division of labour creates efficiency gains. This is especially true for government-owned facilities in transition and developing countries, which are not efficient and not in a position to mobilise sufficient investments funds. However, as the mixed track record of initial PPP investments in these countries shows, strong institutions in both the public and private spheres are indispensable for the direction of investments and activities to those areas that are most appropriate for the PPP approach.

By its very nature, the provision of financial services is not a public task, but one that is better undertaken by the private sector. This widely-held view might lead us to conclude that there is no room for PPPs in the financial sector or, more specifically, in the banking sector. On the other hand, enhancing efficiency by addressing market imperfections and fulfilling development mandates are well-defined public tasks. Consequently, if market imperfections exist in the financial sector and public action can be taken in ways that do not lead to market distortions, PPPs can help improve the provision of financial services.

This is the rationale behind the international discussion on PPP: the state should provide the economic and regulatory framework and – on a selective and temporary basis – public funds for promotional activities. However, the principle of subsidiarity should be applied, using the private banking sector as a means to achieve socially and economically desired ends. This permits appropriate targeting while efficiently filling a gap in the financial market.

If we accept that market inefficiencies in the financial sector justify setting up partnerships between the public and private sectors, there remain nevertheless a number of crucial and difficult questions: how can the private sector be brought on board? How can partnership be structured to improve the efficiency and effectiveness of financial service provision and to prevent distortions in the market? And finally, which specific tasks can be carried out efficiently by PPPs?

Market Distortions in the Banking Sector in Southeast Europe: A Reason for PPP

Despite significant progress, the banking sector in SEE still exhibits distortions and has not yet completed the transition to the market system. These distortions are due to:

- **A weak legal framework and deficient contract enforcement:** shortcomings in the banking laws applying to credit for micro and small and medium-sized enterprises (as in Romania) mean that creditor protection and foreclosure procedures are inadequate. Deficiencies in banking supervision create inefficiencies and delays, raise the costs of enforcing contracts and make outcomes uncertain.

- **Poorly functioning or nonexistent capital markets:** nonexistent or fragmentary securities markets and a lack of institutional investors, such as insurance companies and pension funds, as well as weak leasing and mortgage finance undermine the sustainability of the banking sector. An efficient banking sector is complemented by functioning capital markets. This role cannot be assumed by the international community in the long run: bilateral and international finance institutions have neither the intention nor the capacity to act as the main source of refinancing for the banking sector, except possibly as a temporary stimulant.[1]

---

[1] The absence or poor functioning of capital markets in SEE makes it at best problematic to attempt to calculate benchmark interest rates that could be applied for project evaluation

- **The high degree of uncertainty caused by discriminatory measures against micro and small enterprises (MSEs):** SEE governments tend to underestimate the economic benefits of MSEs, especially microenterprises. This is reflected in business registration systems that are often cumbersome, and tax treatment that is frequently inconsistent and unpredictable.

- **Non-transparent modes of operation:** this obstacle makes it difficult for banks to play their proper role in the evaluation and management of credit risk, especially in the small and medium enterprise (SME) sector.

These weaknesses show that economic development in the region is being hampered not only by the absence of capital markets but also by legal, administrative and regulatory impediments. Such deficiencies add to the cost of providing financial services to SMEs and also increase risk premiums.

From a banker's perspective, two factors contribute decisively to market distortions in the banking sector:

- **Asymmetric information for credit decision making:** in theory, if resources are to be allocated efficiently, all market participants must have the same information. In reality, this is not the case. The distortions in the banking sector in transition countries make it extremely difficult and costly for banks to obtain information on the creditworthiness of potential SME clients. Most banks therefore tend to exaggerate the risk of serving SMEs. Consequently, banks ration credit by charging higher interest rates or even refraining from lending to that target group altogether.

- **Insufficient legal basis for collateral and weak enforcement:** in the transition countries in Southeast Europe, laws governing the use of property as collateral often exclude moveable assets, such as machinery or livestock. Moveable assets often account for a greater share of the assets of smaller firms than of larger companies, and this has a particularly negative impact on SMEs' access to financial services. In addition, enforcement procedures are often inefficient.

The factors mentioned above add to transaction costs and prevent private commercial banks from providing financial services to micro, small and medium-sized enterprises (SMEs) to the extent they would in less distorted markets. The perception of high risks in transition countries is reflected in relatively high interest rate margins or spreads and high real interest rates (Table 1).

---

purposes. However, some evaluators have used estimates from the fragmented capital market of Ukraine to impute benchmark rates for Albania, Bosnia and Herzegovina, Georgia, Moldova, Ukraine and Kosovo. These fragile derivations have then been used to impute the implicit subsidy components in the profitability of microfinance institutions in these countries. In the absence of local capital markets or Eurobond issues that generate a benchmark, these estimates are misleading and unacceptable for policy purposes or as a basis for structuring financial support for these partner institutions.

Table 1. Nominal interest rate margins (in percent) in selected transition countries, 1999 – 2003

Country	1999	2000	2001	2002	2003
Albania	8.67	13.80	11.93	6.77	5.90
Armenia	11.50	13.49	11.79	11.54	13.95
Bosnia and Herzegovina (BiH)	15.22	15.83	11.80	8.17	6.85
Bulgaria	9.57	8.42	8.23	6.58	5.92
Georgia	18.83	22.58	19.50	22.02	22.99
Macedonia	9.05	7.75	9.38	8.80	8.03
Moldova	7.99	8.91	7.76	9.32	6.74
Ukraine	34.25	27.81	21.29	17.42	10.92

Source: Calculations on basis of IFS databank.

While nominal interest rates tended to decrease between 2000 and 2003, spreads remained high (for example 10.92% in Ukraine in 2003), reflecting distortions or inefficiencies in the markets. This creates an opportunity for the public sector to engage in promising partnerships with the private banking sector and so improve the provision of financial services to microenterprises and SMEs. If successful, such interventions positively influence price-setting by creating competition among private financial institutions providing services to this client group. With public sector functions now focused on eliminating market imperfections and on creating a level playing field for competition among private financial institutions, official support should be limited to improving framework conditions and to providing refinance for the private financial sector.

In view of the limited capacities of the local public institutions in SEE, the international donor community has played a major role in successfully reducing market distortions, thereby improving access for microenterprises and SMEs to financial services offered by private commercial banks.

PPP Projects in the Banking Sector in Southeast Europe

In SEE, the main activities of German financial cooperation projects focus on improving the quality of financial institutions and providing refinance for lending to micro, small and medium-sized enterprises. These activities are consistent with the German Ministry for Economic Cooperation and Development's objectives for the financial sector, which aims at "developing functioning financing systems and institutions" (BMZ 2004, p.3). The goal is to create sustainable access to banking services for weaker sections of society. In transition countries, two principal strategies are followed by KfW Entwicklungsbank:

- Cooperation with existing local banks (downscaling approach)
- Cooperation with newly founded banks (greenfield approach)

In almost all countries in SEE, KfW implements both the greenfield and downscaling approaches to foster competition. The KfW Group together with the IFC, IMI, EBRD and the Dutch FMO have founded 10 greenfield microfinance banks, 7 of which have attracted additional equity investment from Commerzbank AG, a private commercial bank (Table 2).

Table 2. Ownership structure of the eastern European ProCredit institutions (February 2004)

Bank	Equity (€M)	IMI %	kfw	IFC	COMMERZBANK	EBRD	FMO	Others %
ProCredit Bank, Georgia	12	39.0	10.0	16.0	3.0	20.0	-	12.0
ProCredit Bank, BiH	9	33.6	7.7	23.1	12.5	23.1	-	-
ProCredit Bank, Kosovo	12	16.7	16.7	16.7	16.7	16.7	16.7	-
Microfinance Bank, Romania	11	11.9	20.8	19.0	20.8	20.8	6.5	-
ProCredit Bank, Albania	8	15.0	25.0	20.0	20.0	20.0	-	-
ProCredit Bank, Serbia	10	16.7	16.7	16.7	16.7	16.7	16.7	-
ProCredit Bank, Ukraine	15	20.0	20.0	20.0	-	20.0	-	20.0
ProCredit Bank, Bulgaria	13	20.8	20.0	19.2	20.0	20.0	-	-
ProCredit Bank, Macedonia	5	31.0	25.0	19.0	-	25.0	-	-

Source: http://www.imi-ag.com

In addition to taking an equity stake, Commerzbank provides training facilities, offers access to their international payment systems and refinances SME loans made by the various banks. The strategic investor is IPC (Internationale Projekt Consult GmbH) which was also the founder of IMI. Hence, the dynamic private entrepreneur heading a German medium-sized enterprise is the driving force for implementing the financial network in SEE. Given their mixed ownership structure, these banks are true PPP ventures.

Ranked by loan size, the bottom 75% of loans outstanding from these ProCredit institutions at the end of 2003 had an average loan amount of less than € 6,500. This is significantly below the € 10,000 ceiling for average micro loans as defined by CGAP[2] for Eastern Europe. This result is even more impressive when the number of loans is considered: the bottom 93% of all loans have an average size of less than € 1,600.

Thirty-five partner banks are supported by KfW in SEE through downscaling (see Annex 1). The downscaling approach entails cooperating with an existing

---

[2] CGAP = Consultative Group to Assist the Poor

local private bank, changing or developing its management skills, building its commitment to SME finance and training loan officers in SME lending skills. Downscaling requires significant technical assistance, especially during the early stages when special SME credit departments are being established in these banks. The average loan amount is slightly higher than that of the greenfield banks in the PPP network, thus again fulfilling the CGAP requirements for microfinance.

Results of PPP Projects in the Banking Sector in SEE

KfW evaluations and those carried out by FMO and IFC covered PPP banks between 1998 and mid-2004. These projects are rated as highly successful. This reflects the capacity of the ProCredit institutions to achieve high growth in terms of loan numbers and volume, high portfolio quality and financial sustainability. The average growth rate in loan numbers amounts to 33% from 1999 to 2002 while the portfolio-at-risk indicator remained at around 1% in 2003, reflecting the excellent quality of the portfolio (see Annex 4 for data for 2000–2002).

When comparing the results of the PPP projects with those of the downscaling projects, the assessments indicate that the PPP projects are more successful in establishing a continuous and efficient vehicle for providing financial services to SMEs.

The comparison applies the usual rating criteria of the microfinance industry (CGAP, 2003): portfolio quality, efficiency, financial management and profitability. The results of the statistical test of a sample for the period from 2000 to 2002 (see Annex 3 and 4) are as follows:

Table 3. Summarised results of the statistical test comparing Greenfield banks with downscaling

Year	Portfolio quality		Efficiency		Financial management			Profitability		
	PAR	PFG	PER	OXR	FXR	DER	CAP	ROA	RoE	PFY
2002	L1	H10	X	H5	X	X	X	X	X	X
2001	L5	X	X	X	X	X	H5	X	X	X
2000	L5	H5	X	X	L10	X	X	L10	X	H10

Key for assessment variables:

PAR = portfolio at risk
PER = efficiency of employed staff
FXR = funding expense ratio
CAP = capital adequacy
RoE = return on equity

PFG = portfolio growth
OXR= operating expense ratio
DER = debt equity ratio
ROA = return on assets
PFY = return on portfolio

Source: Makarenko, 2004.

Table 3 shows how PPP projects performed in relation to downscaling projects. L stands for significantly lower averages for PPP projects compared with those of financial institutions supported through a downscaling scheme. H represents significantly higher averages and X means no significant differences between the two groups. The numbers 5 and 10 indicate the level of significance: 5 denotes an accuracy of 95 out of 100 results, and 10 denotes 90 out of 100.

Three of the ten variables show no significant differences. With regard to portfolio quality and growth, PPP projects perform better than downscaling projects. This is due to more appropriate credit technology, efficient repayment monitoring and strict measures for dealing with clients in arrears.

Experience also shows that the policy for writing off arrears differs between the two groups of institutions. The managements of local private banks refinanced under the downscaling approach tend to be reluctant to establish adequate provisions or write off non-performing loans on a timely basis in order not to diminish reported profits. Consequently, the return on equity for the downscaling banks is higher than might be expected. The reverse holds true for the financial performance of the PPP banks. The higher growth rate of the portfolio of the PPP projects may be explained by their greater willingness to take risks. Another reason is that PPP projects have succeeded in decreasing their transaction costs substantially. A positive factor that improved the performance of some downscaling projects was investment by foreign banks. Examples include Eksim Bank in Serbia and Euromarket Banka in Montenegro. The mixed results presented in Table 3 indicate that a more detailed analysis of the performance of the two groups is required.

Technical Assistance and Sustainability

The PPP projects in the SEE banking sector require substantial subsidies in the form of technical assistance (TA) during their first three years of operation. This TA (Annex 2, page 3) specifically targets the training of young people in appropriate lending methodology, sound risk management and diligent client monitoring procedures. On average, the subsidy equals around 9% of the total equity of approximately € 75 million of the ProCredit network in SEE. TA is the basis for venturing into the microfinance business successfully. More than 2,000 people, mostly women, have been trained so far. As a rule the PPP banks have become profitable within 4 to 5 years of operation. On average, PPP banks achieved an RoE of 11.0% in 2003. The RoE is expected to increase provided that the flexible concept on which the PPP projects operate continues to be in place.

"Graduation," defined as consistently building clients' debt capacity, will feature high on the agenda. Debt capacity is created by the continuous adaptation of services to client potential and aspirations: providing larger and longer term loans as the debt capacity of clients' businesses increase, even when it outgrows micro credits. Accommodating clients in this way does not constitute "mission drift" because micro credit will remain the banks' core business segment. Staying with a client as his or her enterprise grows beyond the micro scale is good banking and good business. The PPP banks are designed to be flexible, allowing them to adapt swiftly to changing environments. These banks are not destined to be niche players in the banking sector. They have already comfortably achieved their intended objectives and have demonstrated their efficiency and effectiveness.

In general, the downscaling projects (Annex 1) imitate the business approach of the PPP banks. The performance of the management and staff of downscaling banks begins with a steep learning curve. With some exceptions, sustainability has not yet been reached: the microfinance and SME business of these banks in general still relies on technical assistance. In addition, there is an apparent lack of firm commitment to the target market, which is reflected in the scant attention paid to microfinance and SME operations in corporate strategy statements. The ability to develop appropriate financial products and services and to allocate the institutions' own financial resources to microfinance and SME business also lag compared to the PPP banks. Taken together, these factors indicate that the downscaling banks have not yet reached the point where they can continue SME lending without donor support. In general, the management of these partner banks are easily persuaded to take up other lucrative business activities to the detriment of their microfinance business.

Though cooperation between the public and private banking sector and IPC, as the private strategic investor, it has been possible to address the key transition challenge of creating access to microfinance services. As a result, the PPP banks have helped to create an environment conducive to SME and micro lending. It is a best practice model which demonstrates that targeting small enterprises can be a commercially viable strategy. The performance of the PPP banks has convinced some local and foreign banks to reorient their business plans towards SME and microenterprises. In addition, the presence of PPP banks has increased competition in the market and led to a reduction in interest rates.

These results are unique: PPP projects in other sectors seldom lead to more competition. For example, most privatised water utilities generally retain their monopoly position. The efficiency gains accruing to the private investor are rarely passed to consumers in the form of lower water charges.

The PPP banks have had a positive structural impact by greatly improving sector conditions. They have made a major contribution to the economic transition process, even if social and political emergencies have in some cases had a detrimental effect on the overall business climate.

The Key Success Factors for PPP Banks

The reasons for the overall success of the PPP banks in the financial sector are as follows:

- **Professionalism and efficiency:** experienced private investors can reduce transaction costs. Furthermore, a PPP can draw on the know-how and services provided by the private investors and benefit, in particular, from the dynamic strategic investor. PPP banks do not directly improve the efficiency of services delivered by public agencies as sometimes stated in the literature (von Gleich, p. 71). Instead, gains in efficiency and effectiveness are generated at the level of the individual banks.

- **Mobilising additional capital:** the equity capital required to found a new bank can be provided by a private commercial bank or other private investors as shareholders. At the same time, it is also necessary to mobilise savings, although this may prove difficult. Except in Albania and Kosovo, the PPP banks must continue and intensify their efforts to attract more savings. Experience indicates that in the face of vigorous competition and due to the cost of mobilising savings, PPP banks require up to eight years to attract sufficient local savings to cover their strongly growing appetite for refinancing. Private investors have successfully helped to bridge this refinancing gap.

- **Risk sharing:** all the projects in question were implemented in highly risky environments. The country risk for SEE as a whole is rated as M 16^3 on the 20-point scale used by the international rating agencies (M 1 being the least risky rating). This country risk rating makes the majority of private investors unwilling to invest in SEE. However, the PPP structure makes possible an efficient allocation of risks. The public finance institutions share the risks, reducing the exposure of the private investors to an acceptable level.

- **Transparency and good governance:** the PPP bank model offers a high degree of transparency in line with EU rules and regulations, facilitating supervision by banking authorities.

- **Sustainability:** PPP banks reach sustainability within a short period. The economic survival of the institutions is underpinned by their capacity to make profits on a consistent basis.

Evolution of PPPs and KfW's Role

The IFIs hold the majority of shares in the various PPP banks. However, the diversity of the overall ownership structure means that the various shareholders have different levels of commitment to development objectives. The essential stakeholder objective of KfW (German Financial Cooperation) is to help the PPP banks fulfil their developmental role. By far the most important task is to guarantee that the core business segment is maintained as the banks expand.

Various PPP banks have been transformed into a network of ProCredit banks. The IMI fund has assumed a new strategic role and function based on the synergy of the network. IMI is part publicly and part privately owned and qualifies as a

---

[3] The country risk of Germany is rated M 1; Bosnia and Herzegovina is rated M17.

PPP initiative in its own right. It offers exits for shareholders in the individual PPP banks that no longer need direct public support. The role of financial cooperation within IMI differs from that within the individual PPP banks because it is centred on the strategic network of ProCredit ventures. KfW's prime role is still to underpin the network's commitment to the target group while at the same time ensure "graduation" as defined above. In other words, in order to support the development of a sound micro and SME structure and ensure the sustainability of the PPP banks, it is necessary to "follow the client" and provide larger and longer-term loans as businesses grow. In contrast, "fundamentalists" in microfinance tend to adopt a static concept which limits individual lending amounts to USD 10,000 in SEE. This approach also fails to allow for inflation and effectively reduces the real value of the lending limit over time.

In the pursuit of developmental objectives, PPPs are neither a panacea nor a substitute for other development approaches. For the transition countries in SEE, PPPs are a highly successful vehicle that reach the poorer sections of the society while at the same time helping to stabilise the financial sector.

In SEE, cooperation between public sector and private sector owners of the PPP banks has created a win-win situation: access to a new market for the private partners and surplus value for development cooperation.

Literature

BMZ (2004): Financial Sector Concept, Bonn.

BMZ (1998a): Gemeinsam Entwicklung gestalten. Partnerschaften zwischen privater Wirtschaft und öffentlicher Entwicklungszusammenarbeit, Bonn.

CGAP (2003): Microfinance Consensus Guidelines: Definitions of Selected Financial Terms, Ratios and Adjustments for Microfinance, 3. Auflage, Washington, 2003.

Makarenko, Alexander (2004): Downscaling versus Greenfield-Ansatz: Eine vergleichende Analyse von Mikrofinanzinstitutionen in Transformationsländern, unveröffentlichte Diplomarbeit, Passau.

Richter, Judith (2003): "We the Peoples" or "We the Corporations?" Critical reflections on UN-business "partnerships", in: IBFAN/GIFA, www.ibfan.org.

Schmidt, Reinhard H. (2004): Public-Private Partnerships (PPP) in Financial Sector Development, in this volume.

Schmidt, Reinhard H., Terberger, Eva (1999): Grundzüge der Investitions- und Finanzierungstheorie, Wiesbaden 1999.

Von Gleich, Albrecht (2003): Entwicklungspartnerschaften mit der Wirtschaft (PPP) – Erfolgsmodell der deutschen Entwicklungszusammenarbeit?, in: Nord-Süd aktuell, S.65 – S.72.

Annexes

Annex 1: KfW Downscaling Projects in Southeast Europe

Downscaling Approach
Financial Institutions in Eastern Europe
Key Figures as at 31 December 2003
(in EUR million or USD million)

Armenia	Currency	Foundation date	Total assets	Gross loan portfolio	Average SME loan (€ '000)	Deposits	Equity	RoE*)	TA	PaR**)
ACBA	EUR		25.2	16.7	4.8	5.5	7.7	9.6%	0.7	0.0%
Anelik Bank	EUR		20.7	9.8	4.8	7.7	3.2	39.1%	0.7	0.0%
Armeconom Bank	EUR		26.9	12.5	8.5	17.6	4.3	38.6%	0.7	0.0%
Converse Bank	EUR		36.0	12.9	4.5	27.3	4.8	17.5%	0.7	0.9%
Ineco Bank***)	EUR		9.6	6.5	0.9	5.2	2.5	20.9%	0.1	0.0%
Total in EUR			118.4	58.4	4.7	63.3	22.5		2.9	

*) After profit tax, including impact of local currency devaluation
**) Portfolio at Risk related to loans granted under the downscaling programme only
***) Figures as at August 31, 2003

Azerbaijan	Currency	Foundation date	Total assets	Gross loan portfolio	Average SME loan (€ '000)	Deposits	Equity	RoE*)	TA	PaR**)
Bank of Baku	USD		13.3	10.2	3.7	5.2	2.8	14.11%	0.45	2.5%
Bank Respublika	USD		19.0	10.4	11.3	8.0	3.0	26.64%	0.45	0.6%
Para-Bank	USD		11.2	7.4	9.9	4.5	2.5	2.60%	0.45	0.1%
UniBank	USD		22.9	14.6	8.9	10.3	6.1	9.74%	0.45	0.1%
Total in EUR			52.9	33.9	26.9	22.3	11.5		1.4	

(FX-Rate: 1 USD = 0.7967 EUR)

*) After profit tax, including impact of local currency devaluation
**) Portfolio at Risk related to loans granted under the downscaling programme only

Bosnia and Herzegovina*)	Currency	Foundation date	Total assets	Gross loan portfolio**)	Average SME loan (€ '000)	Deposits	Equity	RoE***)	TA	PaR****)
Raiffeisen Bank BH	EUR		582.9	389.9	18.3	483.8	41.9	28.6%	0.45	5.84%
Universal Bank d.d.	EUR		181.2	137.2	16.4	127.3	17.5	2.7%	0.45	3.55%
LT Gospodarska Banka	EUR		53.7	32.2	17.7	36.1	11.4	5.2%	0.45	4.50%
UPI Bank d.d.	EUR		112.8	57.3	17.5	86.5	14.2	6.9%	0.45	1.94%
Zagrebacka Bank BH d.d.	EUR		353.1	160.9	21.8	279.1	28.3	18.9%	0.45	10.63%
Volksbank BH d.d.	EUR		92.5	41.8	9.0	59.8	15.0	-5.1%	0.45	0.00%
Others*****)									1.25	
Total in EUR			1376.2	819.3	16.8	1072.6	128.3		3.95	

*) Data as at June 2003
**) Total Customer Loan Portfolio (excluding loans to financial institutions)
***) After profit tax, including impact of local currency devaluation
****) Portfolio at Risk related to loans granted under the downscaling programme only – overdue loans (over 30 days) as % of outstanding loans
*****) BH Banka, Kristal Banka, Kommercijalna Banka)

Kosovo	Currency	Foundation Date	Total Assets	Gross Loan Portfolio	Average SME Loan (€ '000)	Deposits	Equity	RoE*)	TA	PaR**)
Bank for private Business	EUR		33.5	27.9	17.0	29.1	7.2	0.00%	0.23***)	9.39%
Total in EUR			33.5	27.9	17.0	29.1	7.2		0.23	

*) After profit tax, including impact of local currency devaluation
**) Portfolio at Risk related to loans granted under the downscaling programme only
***) European Agency for Reconstruction

Macedonia	Currency	Foundation date	Total assets	Gross loan portfolio	Average SME loan (€ '000)	Deposits	Equity	RoE*)	TA	PaR**)
Moznosti***)	EUR		7.5	7.1	2.2	0.7	5.2	6.0%	0.04	n.a.
Export Credit Bank	EUR		31.8	17.1	11.8	12.1	12.2	6.1%	0.49	0.85%
Tutunska Banka	EUR		220.5	120.9	40.0	100.4	36.1	17.7%	0.49	2.11%
Total in EUR			259.8	145.1	18.0	113.2	53.5		1.02	

*) After profit tax, including impact of local currency devaluation
**) Portfolio at Risk related to loans granted under the downscaling programme only
***) Cooperation started in March 2004

Montenegro	Currency	Foundation date	Total assets	Gross loan portfolio	Average SME loan (€ '000)	Deposits	Equity	RoE*)	TA	PaR**)
CKB Bank	EUR		93.4	61.2	8.1	32.9	12.4	12.0%	0.374	4.0%
Euromarket Banka	EUR		28.9	13.9	26.7	8.8	7.9	6.0%	0.366	8.1%
Opportunity Bank	EUR		17.1	13.0	5.1	3.7	6.4	6.1%	0.211	3.0%
Total in EUR			139.4	88.1	13.3	45.4	26.7		0.951	

*) After profit tax, including impact of local currency devaluation
**) Portfolio at Risk related to loans granted under the downscaling programme only

Romania	Currency	Foundation date	Total assets	Gross loan portfolio	Average SME loan (€ '000)	Deposits	Equity	RoE*)	TA	PaR**)
Banca Commerciala Carpatica	EUR		69.5	41.8	7.5	41.5	12.2	5.1%	0.89	0.25%
Banca Romaneasca	EUR		160.5	87.6	9.1	77.4	20.5	3.2%	0.70	0.50%
Volksbank Romania	EUR		148.1	108.6	5.8	53.0	9.2	6.4%	0.12	2.73%
Banca Romana Pentru Dezvoltare	EUR		1741.1	1042.2	11.0	1292.7	243.7	24.7%	0.06	n.a.
Total in EUR			2119.2	1280.2	8.4	1464.6	285.6		1.77	

(FX-Rate: 1 USD = 0.7967 EUR)

*) After profit tax, including impact of local currency devaluation
**) Portfolio at Risk related to loans granted under the downscaling programme only

Serbia*)	Currency	Foundation date	Total assets	Gross loan portfolio	Average SME loan (€ '000)	Deposits	Equity	RoE**)	TA	PaR***)
Eksim Banka	EUR		112.8	47.5	47.9	77.4	10.0	14.6%	0.32	0.0%
Komercijalna Banka	EUR		642.3	365.9	80.9	480.9	82.3	2.2%	0.32	5.7%
Kulska Banka	EUR		121.4	95.9	45.0	46.3	67.4	5.2%	0.32	1.6%
Zepter Banka	EUR		97.9	60.9	39.1	71.2	16.9	7.7%	0.32	8.8%
Total in EUR			974.4	570.2	53.2	675.8	176.6		1.28	

*) unaudited figures
**) After profit tax, including impact of local currency devaluation
***) Portfolio at Risk related to loans granted under the downscaling programme only

Ukraine	Currency	Foundation date	Total assets	Gross loan portfolio	Average SME loan ($ '000)	Deposits	Equity	RoE*)	TA	PaR**)
Aval Bank	USD		1862.0	1270.0	4.0	1399.0	170.0	2.2%	n.a.	1.4%
Forum Bank	USD		220.0	138.0	4.0	129.0	26.0	1.4%	n.a.	0.5%
Nadra Bank	USD		542.0	333.0	3.0	258.0	38.0	1.7%	n.a.	0.1%
Privat Bank	USD		1846.0	1367.0	3.0	1432.0	179.0	11.4%	n.a.	0.1%
Total in EUR			3561.2	2476.1	2.8	2563.8	329.0		n.a.	

(FX-Rate: 1 USD = 0.7967 EUR)

*) After profit tax, including impact of local currency devaluation
**) Portfolio at Risk related to loans granted under the downscaling programme only

	Total assets	Gross loan portfolio	Average SME loan (€ '000)	Deposits	Equity
Total in EUR for all Partner Banks:	8635.0	5499.3	20.9	6050.1	1040.9

Source: KfW Bankengruppe

Annex 2: Results of ProCredit Banks in Southeast Europe

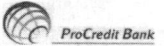

ProCredit Institutions in Eastern Europe
Key Figures as of 31 December 2003
(in EUR or USD million)

	Currency	Foundation Date	Total Assets	Gross Loan Portfolio	Deposits	Equity	RoE*
ProCredit Bank, BiH	EUR	1997	50.7	44.4	10.6	9.2	4.5%
ProCredit Bank, Georgia	USD	1999	61.7	47.3	17.7	11.7	16.7%
ProCredit Bank, Albania	EUR	1999	103.0	47.4	80.3	7.8	8.2%
ProCredit Bank, Kosovo	EUR	1999	276.0	66.6	256.1	12.3	34.0%
ProCredit Bank, Ukraine	USD	2001	72.1	59.4	13.7	15.1	4.0%
ProCredit Bank, Bulgaria	EUR	2001	94.9	78.5	38.0	13.3	12.5%
ProCredit Bank, Serbia	EUR	2001	103.5	74.3	54.7	10.3	1.0%
MIRO Bank, Romania	USD	2002	33.1	26.8	5.2	11.4	-11.9%
ProCredit Bank, Macedonia	EUR	2003	10.5	7.5	1.8	4.5	-9.2%
Total in EUR (exchange rate 1 USD = 0.7967 EUR)			805.5	452.2	478.1	95.6	

* After profit tax, including impact of local currency devaluation

Composition of the combined portfolio of the Eastern European ProCredit Institutions by three loan size categories (02/2004)

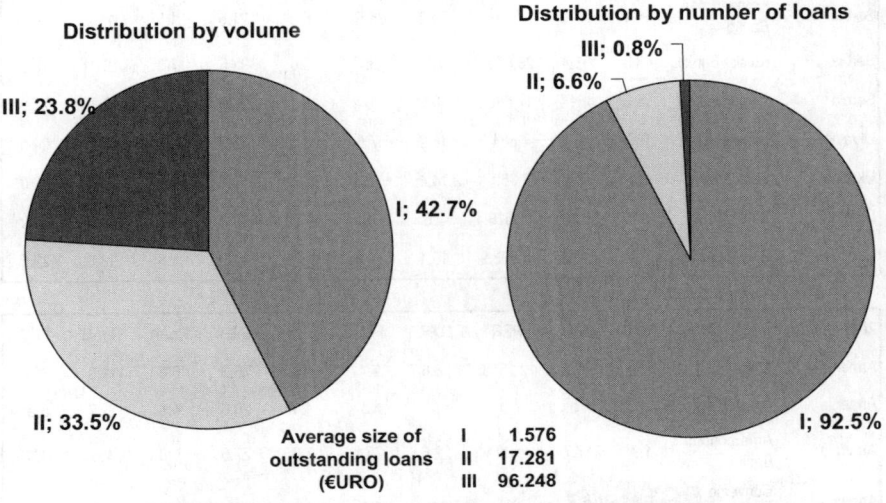

Average size of outstanding loans (€URO)	I	1.576
	II	17.281
	III	96.248

I = €/USD 10,000   II = €/USD 10,000-50,000   III = >€/USD 50,000

Annex 3: Indicators for Downscaling Projects and PPP Projects

2002		PaR	PFG	PER	OXR	FXR	DER	CAP	RoAA	RoAE	PFY
Armenia	ACBA	3.0	72.8	12,290.2	14.5	6.9	1.9	17.0	3.0	15.8	21.6
Armenia	Analik Bank	0.4	n.a.	14,857.0	n.a.	n.a.	5.3	22.9	6.3	37.4	20.2
Armenia	ArmEconom Bank	4.2	n.a.	n.a.	n.a.	n.a.	n.a.	n.a.	3.9	38.0	n.a.
Armenia	Converse Bank	12.9	25.6	6,848.2	7.3	6.7	6.7	26.7	2.0	20.5	12.9
Bosnia and Herzegovina	LT Gospodarska	5.6	32.9	n.a.	15.1	3.7	5.3	27.0	0.9	5.4	13.6
Bosnia and Herzegovina	Raiffeisen Bank	3.0	120.4	28,094.0	9.6	5.0	14.7	11.1	1.9	33.5	18.7
Bosnia and Herzegovina	Universal Banka	16.7	142.2	32,593.5	9.1	3.9	9.9	10.0	0.0	1.9	12.5
Bosnia and Herzegovina	Zagrebacka Banka	8.0	89.1	31,883.5	10.6	4.7	12.2	15.4	1.6	21.2	12.4
Bulgaria	Eurobank	6.0	144.1	n.a.	14.2	8.4	10.0	19.0	2.6	27.4	18.4
Kazakhstan	Kazkommertsbank	3.9	18.8	16,899.3	4.5	7.4	7.6	17.7	3.5	28.9	16.1
Kazakhstan	TuranAlem Bank	1.7	17.0	14,996.3	6.7	8.4	10.4	14.3	2.6	28.6	18.4
Macedonia	Tutunska Banka	2.3	48.1	33,770.8	8.9	5.9	3.0	40.8	3.0	12.4	19.5

2002 (continued)		PaR	PFG	PER	OXR	FXR	DER	CAP	RoAA	RoAE	PFY
Romania	Banca Romaneasca	1.8	67.9	22,047.4	26.7	18.5	5.7	34.0	2.4	15.2	37.0
Serbia	Komercijalna Banka	44.4	171.9	n.a.	15.3	5.5	6.8	21.6	1.5	11.7	18.7
Serbia	Kulska Banka	48.8	36.4	26,840.9	7.7	3.4	0.6	91.6	7.3	121.1	25.3
Serbia	Zepter Banka	15.3	181.2	17,680.8	19.9	10.4	5.0	35.9	0.0	0.1	27.0
Ukraine	Bank AGGIO	0.7	46.7	7,684.2	18.0	7.6	3.1	43.7	4.4	16.6	24.5
Ukraine	Bank Aval	0.1	92.7	7,360.1	14.4	12.4	10.2	12.1	2.0	25.1	29.0
Ukraine	Bank Forum	0.9	53.0	11,528.4	7.6	11.0	7.1	19.7	1.9	14.0	23.2
Ukraine	Privatbank	9.3	46.3	5,803.9	16.1	13.8	13.8	11.2	1.3	18.8	22.4

2001		PaR	PFG	PER	OXR	FXR	DER	CAP	RoAA	RoAE	PFY
Armenia	ACBA	1.2	35.2	12,154.6	18.6	7.4	1.5	76.2	5.6	12.9	21.4
Armenia	Analik Bank	1.3	n.a.	n.a.	n.a.	n.a.	4.4	26.6	4.5	22.7	n.a.
Armenia	ArmEconom Bank	1.9	17.7	n.a.	22.6	20.1	7.3	27.6	0.8	1.6	36.5
Armenia	Converse Bank	6.8	n.a.	n.a.	n.a.	n.a.	n.a.	n.a.	n.a.	n.a.	n.a.
Bosnia and Herzegovina	LT Gospodarska	8.3	26.9	n.a.	13.9	4.1	5.1	31.8	1.8	11.5	21.7
Bosnia and Herzegovina	Raiffeisen Bank	2.2	106.7	19,710.2	10.7	4.8	20.5	12.1	1.2	18.0	20.3
Bosnia and Herzegovina	Universal Banka	12.5	36.8	29,334.3	14.2	6.1	-13.3	-15.21	-22.6	-1,416.9	14.5
Bosnia and Herzegovina	Zagrebacka Banka	6.3	12.3	23,991.4	11.3	4.7	12.5	20.4	1.3	15.9	11.5
Bulgaria	Eurobank	4.5	40.7	n.a.	19.9	7.6	8.4	30.5	1.8	13.8	20.4
Kazakhstan	Kazkom-mertsbank	2.3	92.2	15,868.0	5.1	7.7	7.0	16.6	3.4	26.2	13.9
Kazakhstan	TuranAlem Bank	0.4	92.7	13,747.6	25.3	13.5	9.5	13.1	1.3	0.1	30.6
Macedonia	Tutunska Banka	4.4	16.7	21,728.66	6.6	6.3	3.6	44.2	3.0	12.5	21.9
Romania	Banca Romaneasca	1.8	41.8	n.a.	32.7	19.1	4.8	35.5	2.1	11.6	38.2
Serbia	Komercijalna Banka	56.0	n.a.	n.a.	n.a.	n.a.	n.a.	n.a.	n.a.	n.a.	n.a.
Serbia	Kulska Banka	32.4	n.a.	n.a.	n.a.	n.a.	n.a.	n.a.	n.a.	n.a.	n.a.
Serbia	Zepter Banka	8.9	n.a.	n.a.	n.a.	n.a.	n.a.	n.a.	n.a.	n.a.	n.a.
Ukraine	Bank AGGIO	0.5	113.4	6,465.4	25.3	13.5	2.4	61.7	4.8	14.0	30.6
Ukraine	Bank Aval	0.3	94.5	7,509.0	21.4	18.5	13.7	15.7	3.5	56.3	42.0
Ukraine	Bank Forum	0.6	97.6	8,406.6	7.4	12.4	5.8	23.1	5.3	33.0	27.6
Ukraine	Privatbank	12.9	103.5	6,901.3	17.3	16.1	13.2	13.8	1.5	19.6	24.2

2000		PaR	PFG	PER	OXR	FXR	DER	CAP	RoAA	RoAE	PFY
Armenia	ACBA	1.7	n.a.	11,443.2	n.a.	n.a.	1.1	89.1	n.a.	n.a.	n.a.
Armenia	Analik Bank	2.9	50.0	n.a.	43.7	13.7	3.8	46.3	n.a.	n.a.	22.8
Armenia	ArmEconom Bank	4.5	n.a.	n.a.	n.a.	n.a.	6.8	27.6	0.4	2.9	n.a.
Armenia	Converse Bank	1.0	n.a.	n.a.	n.a.	n.a.	n.a.	n.a.	n.a.	n.a.	n.a.
Bosnia and Herzegovina	LT Gospodarska	13.4	45.9	n.a.	17.8	6.3	5.8	32.0	n.a.	12.7	26.8
Bosnia and Herzegovina	Raiffeisen Bank	0.4	97.8	23,799.0	12.5	6.8	7.4	23.6	2.4	20.0	27.4
Bosnia and Herzegovina	Universal Banka	10.3	23.0	32,690.5	11.8	7.8	13.5	13.4	n.a.	1.5	19.9
Bosnia and Herzegovina	Zagrebacka Banka	7.2	n.a.	n.a.	n.a.	n.a.	10.2	18.0	n.a.	n.a.	n.a.
Bulgaria	Eurobank	9.8	40.8	n.a.	22.7	n.a.	5.2	40.0	1.4	9.1	22.0
Kazakhstan	Kazkommertsbank	3.8	0.3	15,260.7	6.8	10.5	n.a.	23.6	3.7	24.6	19.8
Kazakhstan	TuranAlem Bank	0.7	100.2	12,873.6	12.7	9.0	7.8	15.8	n.a.	n.a.	22.9
Macedonia	Tutunska Banka	4.0	53.2	24,661.2	6.5	7.4	2.9	49.7	2.8	10.5	13.5
Romania	Banca Romaneasca	n.a.	n.a.	n.a.	n.a.	n.a.	n.a.	n.a.	n.a.	n.a.	n.a.
Serbia	Komercijalna Banka	66.9	n.a.	n.a.	n.a.	n.a.	n.a.	n.a.	n.a.	n.a.	n.a.
Serbia	Kulska Banka	28.0	n.a.	n.a.	n.a.	n.a.	n.a.	n.a.	n.a.	n.a.	n.a.
Serbia	Zepter Banka	3.8	n.a.	n.a.	n.a.	n.a.	n.a.	n.a.	n.a.	n.a.	n.a.
Ukraine	Bank AGGIO	0.4	33.2	n.a.	33.4	22.8	1.4	111.7	4.9	12.0	n.a.
Ukraine	Bank Aval	0.2	54.7	5,931.0	25.5	21.7	17.4	15.2	0.7	6.2	35.1
Ukraine	Bank Forum	3.2	n.a.	n.a.	n.a.	n.a.	n.a.	n.a.	n.a.	n.a.	n.a.
Ukraine	Privatbank	22.6	74.6	6,961.3	29.8	31.6	10.1	25.7	2.4	26.4	n.a.

Source: own calculations

PaR: Portfolio at Risk; PFG: Portfolio Growth; PER: Efficiency per Employed Staff; OXR: Operating Expense Ratio; FXR: Funding Expense Ratio; DER: Debt Equity Ratio; CAP: Capital Adequacy; RoAA: Return on Average Assets; RoAE: Return on Average Equity; PFY: Return on Portfolio.

Annex 4: Indicators for PPP Projects

2002	PaR	PFG	PER	OXR	FXR	DER	CAP	RoAA	RoAE	PFY
ProCredit Albania	1.8	88.0	16,463.1	12.3	1.0	8.4	26.9	2.2	19.3	16.85
ProCredit BiH	0.6	93.9	22,424.1	15.2	2.8	3.4	29.2	5.2	23.2	23.56
ProCredit Bulgaria	0.1	420.0	10,627.0	14.3	4.8	5.5	21.8	0,9	3.7	19.28
ProCredit Georgia	2.8	22.2	11,948.0	14.7	7.3	3.5	29.3	1.1	5.8	27.99
ProCredit Kosovo	0.4	175.9	28,433.5	36.2	21.4	21.8	57.0	2.0	58.3	27.23
MEC Moldova	0.8	n.a.	7,803.9	15.5	5.2	7.6	n.a.	0.0	0.3	n.a.
MIRO Romania	0.5	142.7	10,680.2	16.2	3.6	0.5	163.6	-5.6	-8.6	16.93
ProCredit Serbia	0.1	411.0	22,593.6	26.8	7.4	5.6	15.1	-3.0	-32.2	25.22
ProCredit Ukraine	0.5	155.8	7,549.8	12.6	4.8	2.3	37.4	7.2	13.2	24.51

2001	PaR	PFG	PER	OXR	FXR	DER	CAP	RoAA	RoAE	PFY
ProCredit Albania	1.6	7.01	18,442.2	16.7	9.2	7.5	43.4	2.2	18.4	19.26
ProCredit BiH	0.7	63.1	19,519.3	18.3	1.3	3.6	37.5	8.0	35.2	24.33
ProCredit Bulgaria	0.0	n.a.	14,365.8	n.a.	n.a.	0.7	110.7	-4.1	-6.8	n.a.
ProCredit Georgia	1.4	113.0	10,738.3	12.9	8.0	5.9	18.0	1.1	7.6	26.67
ProCredit Kosovo	0.1	163.0	16,933.5	64.9	23.7	36.8	102.4	3.0	83.3	29.44
MEC Moldova	2.4	n.a.	5,955.8	14.9	n.a.	4.1	n.a.	-1.1	-4.1	n.a.
MIRO Romania	1.1	n.a.	n.a.	n.a.	n.a.	n.a.	n.a.	n.a.	n.a.	n.a.
ProCredit Serbia	0.0	n.a.	13,927.3	n.a.	n.a.	6.4	75.3	n.a.	n.a.	n.a.
ProCredit Ukraine	0.4	n.a.	6,426.1	n.a.	n.a.	0.9	85.9	-3.1	-4.6	n.a.

2000	PaR	PFG	PER	OXR	FXR	DER	CAP	RoAA	RoAE	PFY
ProCredit Albania	1.7	100.0	13,582.2	13.7	8.0	4.6	39.8	2.1	12.5	28.92
ProCredit BiH	0.6	59.5	7,256.1	6.8	1.7	3.0	35.3	5.8	20.9	32.95
ProCredit Bulgaria	n.a.	n.a.	n.a.	n.a.	n.a.	n.a.	n.a.	n.a.	n.a.	n.a.
ProCredit Georgia	0.9	80.5	7,761.3	10.6	5.3	6.8	18.2	0.1	1.0	n.a.
ProCredit Kosovo	0.0	n.a.	14,530.7	n.a.	n.a.	14.5	223.3	n.a.	173.0	n.a.
MEC Moldova	0.4	n.a.	10,005.0	24.6	3.5	1.6	n.a.	-4.1	-8.8	n.a.
MIRO Romania	0.7	n.a.	n.a.	n.a.	n.a.	2.5	n.a.	-13.8	n.a.	n.a.
ProCredit Serbia	n.a.	n.a.	n.a.	n.a.	n.a.	n.a.	n.a.	n.a.	n.a.	n.a.
ProCredit Ukraine	n.a.	n.a.	n.a.	n.a.	n.a.	n.a.	n.a.	n.a.	n.a.	n.a.

Source: own calculations

PaR: Portfolio at Risk; PFG: Portfolio Growth; PER: Efficiency per Employed Staff; OXR: Operating Expense Ratio; FXR: Funding Expense Ratio; DER: Debt Equity Ratio; CAP: Capital Adequacy; RoAA: Return on Average Assets; RoAE: Return on Average Equity; PFY: Return on Portfolio.

CHAPTER 28:

Microfinance Investment Funds – An Innovative Form of PPP to Foster the Commercialisation of Microfinance

Doris Köhn[1] and Michael Jainzik[2]

[1] First Vice President Europe, KfW, Frankfurt, Germany
[2] Project Manager, KfW, Frankfurt, Germany

Microfinance has experienced tremendous growth and success as an effective tool for the alleviation of poverty. The establishment of specialised microfinance investment funds could promote financial sector development through the creation of new capital and new professional resources, and through diversification of risk. This could enhance sustainability and mitigate volatility, while helping microfinance institutions in developing and transition countries to raise capital on their home markets.

Such microfinance investment funds are usually formed through the participation of private and public institutions that constitute an innovative form of Public-Private Partnership (PPP). Microfinance investment funds are a bit different from the usual PPP because it is not a question of private investors "doing the job better" than public entities, as Schmidt and Moisa (2004) have put it. Rather, we see it as a complementary relationship where public and private partners jointly establish services that otherwise would not exist.

The Basis for Partnership

Linking microfinance institutions (MFIs) with international capital markets is receiving increased attention. MFIs are actively seeking new forms of refinancing, while capital market investors are becoming aware of a rising industry that may offer business opportunities for so-called socially responsible commercial investors. While earlier literature on microfinance hardly considers the possibility of refinancing from private sources, recent publications reflect growing interest.[1] During the last decade, MFIs have become more mature and eligible for capital market transactions, in terms of both size and the quality of their operations. A

---

[1] See for example Forster, Greene and Pytkowska 2003, which provides a checklist of minimum criteria for MFIs seeking access to commercial refinancing (pp. 87–90).

number of MFIs have already received refinancing from the market (Forster et al. 2003), and many more are hoping to do so.

The flow of private capital into the microfinance industry is critical for upscaling and outreach. It is even more essential because 1) public resources available for microfinance are limited and much lower than the demand,[2] and 2) private capital enhances the sustainability of MFIs by imposing commercial standards of operational quality. MFIs must acquire capital from the private capital market in order to grow, and microfinance investment funds can be a means for this to occur.

Two groups of international capital market participants may be willing to invest in microfinance. First are the institutional investors: banks, insurance companies and pension funds. Second are individual investors, including small investors and very wealthy high net worth individuals, both of whom may already invest in ecologically or socially rated and quoted investment funds.

"Big" players in capital markets mobilise substantial financial resources. Their overall positive impact also includes an important institutional capacity, as their established distribution channels and marketing expertise in retail or private banking could link individual investors and microfinance investment funds. Thus, not only is there an opportunity for banks and insurance companies to invest their own capital, but also a role for financial institutions that distribute products for a fee. As far as we know, financial institutions have not yet been invited to play such a role, but we are convinced that with further maturing of the microfinance industry and microfinance funds, such possibilities will soon appear.

A second important institutional capacity is accumulated financial and distribution knowledge. Institutional investors critically review proposed fund structures, investment proposals and investment products. Thus, the involvement of institutional investors would create a higher quality of funds and investments: designing funds so that they are suitable for private investors can be accomplished only through collaboration with experienced financial institutions.

Microfinance Investment Funds Are Attractive Vehicles for Refinancing Commercial MFIs

Why microfinance investment funds? Why are private investors not investing in MFIs directly? Why is private investment in MFIs scarce, although they are profitable and have huge growth potential?

---

[2] Although the scarcity of financial sources is usually mentioned (Schmidt and Moisa 2004), some experts fear that the demand may be lower than an expanding supply, making the funds compete to serve the small group of suitable MFIs (Ivatury and Reille 2004). Judging according to present market conditions, the authors tend towards the first position, since the second has not yet been proved. However, in the medium run, the increasing presence of funds will benefit the most efficient and professional MFIs. At the same time, competition would also affect funds. In the longer run, only a limited number of professionally and efficiently managed funds would be able to survive.

Microfinance investment funds are becoming a sustainable option for the long-term financing of MFIs while offering attractive investment opportunities to investors. Apart from financial return, investors may also seek a reputational cachet through investment in microfinance. Given any set of expectations for financial return and risk, investment in microfinance may be considered superior to ordinary investment because of its developmental character.

Microfinance investment funds make investments in microfinance more attractive than stand-alone investments in individual MFIs. For example, they should appeal to investors seeking diversification. Rather than investing a significant amount in one institution, an investor in a microfinance investment fund enjoys diversification.[3] By spreading the investment over various countries, investment funds can mitigate high country risks. Investment funds can also invest in countries where institutional investors are deterred by ratings and necessary equity provisions. For example, highly indebted poor countries (HIPCs), despite their having to restructure debt, may offer good business opportunities for MFIs.

Microfinance investment funds can realise economies of scale that a single investor cannot. Market research, due diligence analysis, establishment of control mechanisms, monitoring, recovery costs in cases of default, and other related activities can be executed efficiently by the fund manager. This saves money and time, and is vastly preferable to having single investors bear these costs. Taking into account the still relatively small investments into still relatively small MFIs, these transaction costs are likely to be prohibitive and possibly prevent investment in MFIs altogether unless they are shared by a number of investors placing large amounts via fund allocation.

The expansion of private investments in MFIs through investment funds provides opportunities not only for investors, but also for MFIs and development finance institutions. From the MFIs' perspective, tapping (international) capital markets offers a multitude of advantages (Chu 1999):

- Diversification of funding sources as a key element of risk management
- Cheaper funding than through savings mobilisation
- Lengthening the weighted maturity of the capital structure
- Gaining access to "virtually unlimited funds (the world's savings)" to remove funding constraints.

---

[3] If numerous MFIs sell bonds, private investors may achieve some diversification but with the associated transaction costs. As far as the authors know, some MFIs issue bonds in the domestic market. We know of no international issues. Term deposits in MFIs are usually not a convenient alternative for an international private (individual) investor. Domestic markets where MFIs are present offer only limited vehicles for raising capital because of high interest rates, low savings rates, poor capital markets, and investor preference for short-term investments. These conditions engender interest and incentive for MFIs to participate in international capital markets.

The first three of these points refer primarily to the efficiency and effectiveness of the MFIs' operation, while the fourth point tackles constraints on outreach. In a survey of the microfinance industry in Eastern and central Europe and the CIS countries, about 60% of the MFIs organised as nongovernmental organisations (NGOs) or nonbanks and 50% of the microfinance banks listed lack of funding as the factor most likely to stand in the way of their realising their growth and development goals (Forster et al. 2003:87).

Mobilisation of domestic savings does not currently appear as a sufficient solution to this funding problem. In many economies savings are low, nonbank MFIs often face restriction on deposit-taking, and even if a significant amount of deposits is available, they are often short-term and volatile. Thus, at this stage, long-term financing remains a critical issue for many MFIs.

In the long run, MFIs' mobilisation of capital in their domestic markets (savings, bonds and equity) will be the most important factor in achieving sustainable growth without external support. Against this background, we believe that MFIs will have to face structural changes through formalisation, further professionalisation, market exit and merger.[4]

Microfinance investment funds are not a panacea but can be a valuable vehicle, at least until some higher stage of MFI development is reached, and they should contribute to the achievement of that higher stage. Development finance institutions support the expansion and professionalisation of MFIs as a vehicle for new client outreach and poverty alleviation. As public funds are limited, the access of MFIs to other forms of funding may contribute greatly to the sustainability of a development project. According to KfW's evaluation criteria, a financial sector project cannot be deemed sustainable unless it survives the eventual discontinuation of injections of development finance. Thus, preparing MFIs to tap private capital markets is part of KfW's focus, and microfinance investment funds, as presented here, can strengthen this link between MFIs and the international financial industry.

Microfinance Investment Funds – Where Do We Stand?

Microfinance investment funds are defined here as funds that are specifically designed to invest in microfinance institutions and thereby contribute to economic development, while providing adequate financial return to their investors. Some may focus on a higher level of returns, and some may be more socially oriented, emphasising a reputational return with adequate or marginal financial benefits.

---

[4] Chu (1999) predicts that certain MFIs will become industry leaders in the microfinance market. These MFIs will develop into registered institutions and offer not only microcredit but all kinds of other products to their clients. These industry leaders will crowd less dynamic MFIs out of the market. He names the three characteristics of these leaders as superior operations based on operating efficiency, dominant market share and access to domestic and international capital markets.

Vehicles that are created with charitable intent, making donations or providing finance to MFIs at subsidised rates, are not considered as investment vehicles.

Commercially oriented microfinance investment funds have recently shown notable dynamism. But, who is currently active in raising these innovative vehicles? A paper commissioned by Appui au Développement Autonome (ADA) analysed 28 funds worldwide that invest in equity, issue guarantees or make loans to MFIs (Goodman 2003).[5] (Since publication, a few more have appeared.[6]) Twenty-four funds offer guarantees and loans to MFIs, thirteen operate at "market rates,"[7] eleven at "near market rates" and only two funds of the last group – as part of their interpretation of socially oriented activity – are sometimes broadly subsidised. The total size of these funds that provide financing at "commercial terms" is at least € 230 million.[8]

Five of these funds are entirely privately owned and financed, whereas the majority – which could be characterised as PPP projects – include participation by agencies such as NGOs, bilateral institutions or international financial institutions (IFIs).

A remarkable finding by Goodman is that nine funds concentrate exclusively on only one of the three main products (equity, loans, guarantees) offered to MFIs. (Five of the funds make equity investments only.) Another eleven have a concentration of more than 80% of their assets in one product. We believe that this specialisation suggests that these funds orient themselves towards certain types of investors.

Funds can be categorised according to various orientations: risk vs. volume, equity vs. debt, individual investors vs. institutional investors, local vs. international, etc. We identify two basic investment approaches, each with specific advantages and disadvantages. The first we refer to as the "network approach," the second as the "outsider approach."

---

[5] An update of this survey commissioned by CGAP, ADA and KfW was in progress as this article went to print.

[6] These include the Global Microfinance Facility (GMF) and the Africa International Financial Holding (AIFH), in which KfW has stakes. GMF is described later in this article.

[6] See Goodman (2003), pp. 12–13.

[7] "Market rates" and "commercial terms" are in quotes because capital markets often do not exist in countries where MFIs are active, making market rates difficult or impossible to determine. The "market rate" and "commercial terms" are rather based on benchmarks reflecting the payment capacity of the debtor and on rates in similarly high-risk countries having capital markets that can serve as a point of reference.

[8] The exact amount is actually higher: in addition to the amount of € 230 million mentioned above, there are two funds with a combined size of € 265 million that do not invest exclusively in microfinance in developing countries. However, these investments are not broken down in Goodman 2003. Ivatury and Reille (2004) cite USD 270 million as the total of all microfinance social investments funds worldwide. They predict a doubling of size by mid-2004.

The network approach comes from within an existing network of MFIs, such as the ProCredit Bank network of IMI[9] or ACCION Investments in Microfinance (AIM). A central holding company or fund structure is established to mobilise investment, mainly to increase the MFIs' equity base. This bundle of investments is consolidated in a holding company. Usually the holding entity is involved in the management and in strategic decision-making through representation in the MFIs' governing bodies.

The outsider approach is not dedicated to a specific network of MFIs, but to a search for good investment opportunities independent of affiliation to a network of microfinance institutions. The outsider approach is inspired and engineered from the investors' perspective and searches for suitable investments, while the network approach is engineered from the MFIs' perspective in order to fit their objectives and have to look for suitable investors.

The network approach requires an in-depth knowledge of the MFIs in which investments are made. At the core of this strategy, the company which has established or upgraded the MFIs knows their procedures, risks and potentials, and uses this special knowledge to attract investors who will inject growth capital into these MFIs. The funds using the outsider approach do not have this special knowledge, because they concentrate on stand-alone investments and because, in contrast to the network focus, they do not have the same degree of influence on the MFIs. In fact, some may seek no control whatsoever, being passive or "portfolio investors" with relatively small shareholdings or without any shareholding but rather as creditors providing loans, possibly along with a package of other services on a fee basis. Their advantage is that they can "cherry pick," looking for the MFIs best suiting their investment criteria. Thus, they may be able to offer more diversified risk portfolio over countries as well as over types of MFIs. Depending on the funds' objectives, different kinds of MFIs – NGOs, registered nonbanks or microfinance banks – can be targeted for investment. Funds can also work with commercial banks to refinance their microcredit business portfolio, for example. Table 1 contrasts these and other relevant features of both approaches.

Comparing the investments made by each type of fund, the outsider funds appear to have greater latitude, offering a broader variety of products to MFIs. This permits more flexibility in the contract conditions governing the investments. Funds that focus on equity investments also seek long-term refinancing to avoid liquidity problems. So, the equity oriented network funds have to look for patient investors who are content to wait for some before realising capital gains (or losses) by selling their equity in the funds. There may be few such investors, who are of a different kind compared to investors looking for investments with more calculable results. A fund that offers fixed-term loan contracts or guarantees to MFIs may find it possible to obtain fixed-term refinancing for its own operations.

---

[9] IMI is described in detail in the articles by Schmidt and Moisa (2005) and by Alexander (2005) in this volume.

Table 1. Comparison of the two basic investment fund approaches

Fund Development	*Network approach*	*Outsider approach*
Type of relationship with target MFIs	Investment strategy targets MFIs in a particular network	Relation varies based on investment objectives or services provided
Type of target MFIs	"Typical" MFI (usually microfinance banks and registered nonbanks)	All kinds of MFIs, including commercial banks and NGOs
Types of investments	Mainly equity stakes in MFIs	Full range of products
Time horizon of relationships	Medium to long-term	Short, medium, and long-term
Time horizon for the fund	Unlimited period	Defined period or unlimited period
Exit strategy	Sale of shares	Maturity or completion of contract
Legal form of fund	Joint stock company	Joint stock company, other limited liability vehicles, other forms
Management	Managed by a specialised management firm related to the MFI network	Management by a specialised independent management company.
Diversification of the fund's investments	Limited to the MFI network	Regional or worldwide diversification possible
Information advantages and flexibility	In-depth knowledge of network from active role as investor	Can seek the best investment opportunities worldwide
Influence on the MFIs	Involvement in management and strategic issues of the MFI through ownership	Limited to passive portfolio investment, unless significant equity share is obtained
Examples (with KfW participation)	Internationale Micro Investitionen AG (IMI), ACCION Investments in Microfinance (AIM), La Fayette Participations	Global Microfinance Facility (GMF), Africa International Financial Holding (AIFH)

Risk and Return

As previously described, microfinance investment funds are likely to be established as a PPP engaging a variety of parties across a public and private sector continuum, all with different understandings and expectations of (financial) risk and (financial) return. They are often united in their expectation of social return however defined, which most hope to maximise in the most effective way possible.

Earlier, we depicted the risk-mitigating aspects of funds through diversification at the MFI level. We turn now to examine what a fund can offer to investors compared to what a stand-alone MFI can offer. Clearly, a microfinance investment fund can diversify its investment products to suit the risk tolerances of private investors. This can be achieved by using risk tiers ranging from equity equivalent tranches to preferred, senior tranches, each with different risk qualities that offer different potential returns. To illustrate, Box 1 details the structure of the Global Microfinance Facility (GMF) recently set up by a group of development finance institutions and private investors to test the potential for such funds in practise.

Box 1. Structure of the Global Microfinance Facility (GMF)

The GMF is designed as an MFI refinance facility with a global focus. It is as an offshore company with a minimum equity requirement for participating investors. The investors hold:

- *C-Notes (equity equivalent, first-ranking loan, tenor 10 years, up to USD 2.1 million),*

- *B-Notes (equity equivalent, 2nd tier loan, tenor of 10 years, up to USD 8.0 million), and*

- *A-Notes (senior loans up to USD 20.0 million).*

The C-Notes carry the highest risk and are held by the Fund Manager and by IFC (on behalf of the Dutch Government). The B-Notes are held by IFC and KfW, and the A-Notes, carrying the least risk, are held by Crédit Coopératif and BIO. More investors are expected. Corresponding to the risk of the different tranches, the holders are assigned different returns and cancellation clauses.

The Fund is governed by an Assembly of Shareholders and by its Board. Investment decisions are made by an Investment Committee on the basis of proposals by the Fund Manager. The Fund Manager is an independent firm, Cyrano Management, Peru. The Fund targets MFIs in all development and transition countries. About 50 local and foreign currency loans and guarantees are expected to be issued through 2008.

Compared to a stand-alone investor, microfinance investment funds can also mitigate risks through significant information advantages. Through the network approach they already have specific market knowledge about the microfinance industry and about specialised MFIs; through the outsider approach, they acquire it. Specialised fund managers are able to implement, monitor and evaluate benchmark criteria specific to microfinance institutions, which provides valuation tools and guidance for investment or divestment decisions.

This information is of great importance for microfinance investments because ratings – which give investors a basis for ranking the risk of a potential venture – are only partly available for MFIs. The scope of rating services is still limited within the microfinance universe, and none is yet universally accepted. Microrate,[10] the most important MFI rating firm, offers ratings predominantly for Latin America and to a limited extent for African MFIs. Fitch has given local ratings to a number of MFIs, but naturally concentrates on formalised MFIs (banks). However, as the microfinance industry moves towards asset-backed securities and new refinancing arrangements, a respected standard with a worldwide reputation becomes a requisite.

Structure and Governance

Investment funds are commonly managed by a specialised manager. The manager is held accountable through oversight mechanisms that are satisfactory to investors. The manager usually has certain discretionary powers to make investment decisions as determined by investment policies and benchmarks, controlled by the fund's governing bodies and verified by auditors.

In order to document the quality of the information obtained on the MFIs and to increase the confidence of potential investors in the fund manager's competence and loyalty, fund managers usually invest their own money in the fund as well. This confirms the manager's serious interest in identifying good MFI investments. Inadequate due diligence and poor investment choices would not only ruin the fund managers' reputation, as it would a rating agency's, but would also affect the manager directly through participation in the investments' potential losses – unlike a rating agency.

Based on the type of funding received and on his or her capacity as a financial engineer, the fund manager can design a range of financial instruments: equity, convertible loans, credit lines, guarantees, standby facilities, and other local and foreign currency instruments. As an expert in microfinance, a fund manager should be able to design tailor-made instruments suitable for MFIs, thereby creating good investment opportunities.

Linking the observations about the information advantages and specialisation of independent fund managers with their assumed decision-making powers, we found

---

[10] See www.microrate.com

that such funds conform to the structure that Schmidt and Moisa (2004) derive from agency theory and that they recommend as a prerequisite for making good, value-increasing decisions and for protecting the investor: access to good information should be combined with the ability to make decisions.

Why Should Development Financiers Back Microfinance Investment Funds?

The potential for private investors to become involved in microfinance investment funds is clear. Why is there not more private interest? Why and on what basis should public institutions be involved in microfinance investment funds?

We hope the presence of development financiers in microfinance investment funds is a temporary phenomenon. We believe that development financiers – IFIs, bilateral institutions and nongovernmental organisations – are necessary to initiate innovative approaches such as microfinance investment funds. They are needed to step in where the financial market fails to establish self-sustaining, market-driven facilities, which are created and tested largely by development finance organisations.

Why do these presumed market failures occur, and how can development financiers help to overcome them in a lasting way?

The first aspect we see is that development financiers have a different risk perception through a better knowledge of MFIs as well as of difficult markets. Commercial investors outside "the microfinance world" usually lack knowledge about both MFIs and their markets, which might lead them to overestimate risks. As an example, the development finance community is probably more aware than private financial institutions of the notable stress resistance that many MFIs have demonstrated. As Elisabeth Rhyne has pointed out, MFIs survived the crisis in Bolivia much better than many commercial banks, due to the nature of their business (Rhyne 2004). Such experiences lead international and bilateral financial institutions to risk perceptions that make them more willing to take positions which outside investors would assume to be highly risky.

With the growing involvement of private investors in microfinance, their knowledge and trust should also grow. The development financiers' task is to support the spread of information and develop experience in the private financial sector, so that private sector investment in MFIs will increase, which will help MFIs achieve financial sustainability. The involvement of financial institutions in microfinance investment funds is an avenue for the dissemination of information and lessons. These factors will cause the proportion of private funding in microfinance investment funds to increase over time, which will lead the private sector to take over – for an adequate risk premium – the riskier tiers offered by a fund.

In addition, the reputation of experienced development financiers with an extensive knowledge of microfinance will also encourage private investors to join a venture. Development finance institutions' involvement and their "good name" offer a platform for marketing microfinance investments to private individuals at the retail level. From a development perspective, development finance institutions can safeguard target-group orientation as a core principle of successful microfinance.[11] Their temporary presence in investment funds could be necessary to prevent "mission drift" away from the original target group in response to pressure for higher returns from private investors in MFIs.

Mission oriented development financiers are generally prepared to assign a significant amount of their own manpower and other resources for the structuring of a microfinance investment fund and the establishment of a market. This can help overcome market entry barriers that might discourage private investors. The costs of setting up an innovative fund and the risks of its failure can be prohibitively high for private investors. Without start-up subsidies, institutions such as microfinance investment funds that can have a very positive impact in the long run might not see the light of day.

To recap: in the beginning microfinance investment funds are likely to be organised as Private-Public Partnerships (PPPs), and the role of public institutions is that of a market facilitator. It will be a challenge for development financiers to ensure that their own stakes are sold to socially-committed commercial investors in the medium term.

Some argue that the presence of development financiers scares away some investors who feel that their involvement is a signal that instability is likely in the long-run because of a lack of viable concepts. We think that this notion is unproved. The track record of purely private microfinance investment funds so far is very limited. Development financiers therefore have a useful role, launching creative and productive activity that will enhance markets while having a positive social impact.

Conclusion and Open Questions

Microfinance investments funds appear to be a promising type of PPP in the financial sector that should be added to the list of potential activities explored by Schmidt and Moisa (2004) at the close of their article. PPPs can include microfinance investment funds that have specialised owners and that provide capital to MFIs, that offer financially attractive investment opportunities and that attract substantial amounts of capital.

The limited track record of microfinance investment funds and their rapid pace of innovation preclude a final evaluation of their opportunities and limitations. Thus, this response paper presents a work in progress within a general economic framework and based on a growing body of experience.

At the third annual KfW Financial Sector Development Symposium in November 2004, private investors and leaders in development finance will discuss how the fast-growing microfinance industry can access worldwide private capital

---

[11] Schmidt and Moisa (2004) discuss the different incentives of public and private partners in a joint venture.

for refinancing and further enhance its financial technology. The potential partnership between microfinance and private capital to support expansion and professionalisation of MFIs, to strengthen nascent markets in developing and transition countries, and to offer socially and financially rewarding opportunities to private capital markets will be explored in more depth.

With this perspective, this paper attempts to frame a set of key questions for discussion:

- What sorts of risks do different types of investors face? What sorts of returns are realistic?

- What are the best strategies for assessing market timing, market competition, and market crowding?

- How can microfinance funds be structured for optimal accountability? How should a rating scheme be structured? Will it attract new investors?

- What scenarios can be created to optimise involvement of the "big players" in microfinance?

The Symposium will provide many more insights into the opportunities and challenges we face in developing microfinance investment funds. It hopefully will be an important step forward, or from the perspective of actors across the public and private sector continuum, an important step closer to one another.

References

Alexander, Helen: Sustainable Microfinance Banks – IMI as a Public-Private Partnership in Practise, in this volume

Chu, Michael: Tapping Capital Markets: Microfinance as an Emerging Industry. Unpublished, 1999. See http://www.undp.org/ods/areas/area-3/area-mm/title.html.

Forster, Sarah: Seth Greene and Justyna Pytkowska and Set, *The State of Microfinance in CEE and NIS*, World Bank/CGAP, 2003

Goodman, Patrick: *International Investment Funds: Mobilising Investors towards Microfinance*, Appui au Développement Autonome (ADA), Luxembourg, 2003, http://www.microfinance.lu/comas/media/fondsinv_endef1].pdf

Ivatury, Gautam and Reille, Xavier: *Foreign Investment in Microfinance: Debt and Equity from Quasi-commercial Investors*, CGAP FocusNote No. 25, January 2004, www.cgap.org

Matthäus-Maier, Ingrid and von Pischke, J.D. (eds.): *The Development of the Financial Sector in Southeast Europe*, Berlin/Heidelberg/New York: Springer, 2004

Rhyne, Elisabeth: *Surviving the Crisis: Microfinance in Bolivia, 1999–2002*, in: Matthäus-Maier and von Pischke 2004, pp. 89–100

Schmidt, Reinhard H. and Moisa, Nina: *Public-Private Partnerships (PPP) for Financial Development in Southeast Europe*, in this volume

PART VI:

Summary and Conclusions

CHAPTER 29:

An Overview of Banking, Financial Regulation, and Access to Financial Services in Southeast Europe in the Context of EU Enlargement

Ingrid Matthäus-Maier[1] and J.D. von Pischke[2]

[1] Member of the Board of Managing Directors, KfW Bankengruppe
[2] President of Frontier Finance International, Inc., Washington DC, USA

This book explores five themes related to EU accession by Southeast European countries. The first is economic policy and government performance. The second is financial regulation and the implications posed for it by prospects for accession. The third and fourth present bankers and clients' perspectives on the performance of financial markets at the retail level. The final theme is public-private partnerships, including exploration of an example supported by KfW that creates micro and small business finance institutions. These themes are summarised here.

This book continues a storyline developed in a previous publication: *The Development of the Financial Sector in Southeast Europe: Innovative Approaches in Volatile Environments*, published in 2004 by Springer Verlag on behalf of KfW, and which is essentially a measured examination of successful development assistance to financial sectors in Southeast Europe (SEE). The 2004 publication looked backward, distilling the lessons in promoting financial sector development in a post-crisis and transition context. This book looks forward. It tries to identify likely future developments by examining driving forces, identifying key actors and placing them in context.

Stimulating the Economy of Southeast Europe

Paul Hare of the Heriot-Watt University (chapter 1) sets the stage not only for Part I but also for the entire book by looking at the crucial factors and processes promoting stability and progress in Southeast Europe. His theme paper assesses whether the support provided for development has done the job it was designed to do. He emphasises that development objectives can be achieved only if they are well-designed and realistic, and if the environment is receptive.

Hare approaches the subject by focusing on three critical areas of the SEE economy: First, labour markets create the jobs that will lift households out of poverty. Employment generation depends on achieving rapid rates of enterprise formation. Here, micro, small and medium-sized industrial development is essential, complemented by foreign direct investment (FDI). The second critical area is investment in physical infrastructure and in other productive activity. High rates of investment, both foreign and domestic, are required to stimulate growth. Post-conflict aid is declining, underscoring the importance of attracting FDI. Third, trade is essential in the small, open SEE economies. Trade can be facilitated through supportive domestic policies that reduce transaction costs and uncertainty between buyers and sellers.

Hare points out that several constraints retard the pace of reform and act as a brake on investment: ethnic and religious divisions that threaten stability and weaken trust, political fears about the impact of reforms, lack of familiarity with the market economy, and barriers to efficient trade within and also beyond the region.

Three response papers elaborate on core aspects of Hare's theme paper. Marc Franco of the European Commission (chapter 2) deals with EU accession. Bulgaria and Romania are expected to be the first SEE countries to join the EU, and others will follow when they satisfy the Copenhagen Criteria that specify the basic requirements for admission: respect for democratic principles and the rule of law, a functioning and competitive market economy, and capacity to implement and enforce EU legislation. Stabilisation and Association Agreements, flanked by corresponding implementation assistance, provide the framework for accession.

Ewald Nowotny, formerly of the European Investment Bank, (chapter 3) emphasises the interaction between infrastructure investment and financial development. Private investment in infrastructure is important because it applies market criteria, enhancing efficiency. Given that many SEE states are relatively small, regional participation in infrastructure development takes on particular importance. Nowotny also points to the role infrastructure investments can play in opening up and developing local capital markets, for example through local currency bond issues as pioneered in the Czech Republic, Hungary and Poland.

Khalid Sherif of the World Bank (chapter 4) concentrates on the costs of doing business in transition economies and the changes required to bring SEE economies up to the performance levels of the countries that joined the EU in 2004. The challenges he cites include the currently rudimentary financial sectors in these countries, inconsistent tax and regulatory systems that distort incentives, uncertainty and delays in policymaking and implementation, weak judicial structures, and corruption. The legal framework touches on all of these problems and therefore deserves special attention. Recognising that these shortcomings raise the costs of doing business, discourage enterprise and make it difficult to establish a broad tax base, SEE countries are now taking a proactive line.

Financial Regulation for Stability and Protection in Southeast Europe

To what extent can financial regulation improve the investment climate and increase confidence in financial systems in SEE? This question is the central issue treated in Part II by Evan Kraft of the Croatian National Bank (chapter 5). His theme paper discusses two major issues. The first is the role of financial regulation in realising the opportunities opened by the EU accession process, such as improved access to FDI, capital markets, and official loans and subsidies. The second major issue is the challenge facing financial regulators in adapting international supervisory best practice, developed for the regulation of large, advanced markets, to local circumstances that include political interference, limited institutional capacity to administer regulations, and relatively low levels of financial development.

With banks dominating SEE formal financial markets, Kraft views banking supervision as a contribution to sectoral and macroeconomic stability, a means of limiting risks, and a source of discipline and respect for law. These outcomes are most easily achieved when supervisors enjoy political independence, especially when they are part of a central bank.

Kraft believes that the integration of SEE financial sectors into larger regional systems need not be rushed. In general, no major changes are required to comply with EU banking directives. Basel II practices that govern banking in rich, diversified economies should not be adopted until sufficient databases have been compiled to meet rating criteria and until regulators' skills are more fully developed. However, changes will surely be required, especially in the protection of creditors' rights. Awareness and preparation are in order.

Five response papers address regulatory and related issues presented by Kraft. Merab Kakulia of the National Bank of Georgia (chapter 6) offers an example of regulatory standards that are tighter than those of the EU, and a regulatory framework, in place for several years, that has moved systematically to improve standards and performance. However, local laws impose procedural constraints that bank regulators view as unhelpful.

Peter Nicholl of the Central Bank of Bosnia and Herzegovina (BiH) (chapter 7) addresses the impact of foreign banks on local banking practices and standards. He notes that foreign banks operating in BiH span a range of quality. The best ones have the confidence of depositors and have introduced new products and systems, spurring the better domestic banks to innovate and adapt in order to compete. Nicholl points out that foreign banks, especially the older and larger ones, have tremendous reputational capital at risk: their failure in any country would have a significant impact on their standing in the international financial community and among depositors.

Mihai Bogza of the National Bank of Romania (chapter 8) follows Nicholl in exploring the contrasts between foreign banks (owned by foreign capital) and local banks (with a majority of domestic shareholders). According to Bogza, Romanian authorities have found that foreign banks have widely different approaches to doing business, and that these can be roughly categorised by the structure of foreign ownership and by the banking traditions and standards of the home countries in which the foreign parties are based.

Eris Sharxhi of the Bank of Albania (chapter 9) focuses on risk management and its implications, especially in the context of the Basel II package of regulatory improvements. Better risk management has been achieved by SEE banks and by their regulators. However, attempts to manage risks through regulation may have perverse consequences when rules are not aligned with the risks they are intended to manage. Hence, using a range of tools can produce more accurate risk assessments. Sharxhi echoes Kraft in calling for flexibility in content and timing as SEE regulators adapt to Basel II and EU standards.

Christian Fehlker, Arnaud Mehl and Adalbert Winkler of the European Central Bank (chapter 10) analyse the challenges of financial regulation in SEE. Their analysis is based on three factors that determine the effectiveness of financial regulation and supervision: the preconditions for effective supervision, the conduct of supervision and the supervisory framework. The immediate task is bringing SEE practices up to international standards. They conclude that smooth implementation of the currently accepted reform agenda in Southeast Europe is a key challenge. The relatively rapid evolution of best practice makes catching up with international standards a chase after a moving target.

Bankers' Perspectives on Dynamic Banking in a Changing Market

What are the strategies and expectations of bankers in Southeast Europe (SEE), especially in light of the competition among large foreign banks and much smaller domestic institutions? This is the central question of Part III. Sylvia Wisniwski of Bankakademie International notes in her theme paper (chapter 11) that banking is among the most stable of all SEE sectors in scope, depth and commercial dynamism.

Southeast Europe has attracted many foreign banks. This has occurred through proactive financial sector reforms, opportunities to establish trade links with foreign banks' home countries and in response to the chance to develop market potential while there is still little competition. According to Wisniwski, the structure of SEE banking sectors – in which the local banks are typically small – will change as a result of tighter regulation, the introduction of deposit insurance, increased competition and completion of bank privatisation. These factors will fuel a second, more rapid wave of mergers and acquisitions, creating another investment opportunity for foreign banks. As a result, fees and interest rate margins will be squeezed, and foreign banks' market shares will grow.

Wisniwski believes that within this setting, institutions with well targeted products will continue to reap attractive returns. Large foreign banks have an advantage because their systems, liquidity, reputation, market power and staff are well developed and easily expanded to include new markets. However, the greenfield banks devoted to MSE (micro and small enterprise) clients have great market potential, the capacity to consolidate their market positions, and for the time being, relatively little competition from large banks.

The retail market remains attractive: consumer lending is expanding rapidly, attracting new players. Leasing, housing finance and trade finance are other attractive market segments. She cautions that rapid increases in retail lending, especially through consumer finance, could easily erode microfinance banks' niche, and pose the threat of a bubble as aggressive lenders face inexperienced borrowers. Wisniwski concludes that as banks expand, they will need to transform. Two areas of critical importance are risk management and staff training.

Four response papers address Wisniwski's analysis and views. Per Fischer of Commerzbank (chapter 12) discusses the role of foreign banks and of smaller domestic banks. He foresees a declining role for local banks as foreign banks enter and expand their presence in SEE markets, in part through the acquisition of local banks. However, promising opportunities can be seized by independent local banks that build on their market strengths, take advantage of modern banking expertise, employ professional staff, and that move beyond their national boundaries.

Mita Katic of Kulska banka, Novi Sad, (chapter 13) concurs that smaller, dynamic domestic institutions are well positioned to serve the vibrant and strategically important SME sector. The former Yugoslav system, based on large enterprises supported by large banks, is giving way to the current reality in which small and medium-sized firms are the primary providers of jobs and incomes in a liberalised economy. While large foreign banks will continue to serve large enterprises in the region, small local banks can profitably serve micro, small and some medium-sized enterprises.

Focus on smaller clients has been successful for Unionbank, Sofia, as Evgeny Gospodinov describes (chapter 14). Unionbank has carved out a market niche in a financial sector dominated by foreign banks. The strength of this local bank is its access to and understanding of local clients, leveraged by innovative behaviour and client-friendly practices such as flexibility, responsiveness, speedy service and confidentiality. Unionbank cultivated the SME market at an early stage, gained access to external medium-term financing, and expanded its capacity by embracing change and by profiting from its pioneering approach.

Opportunity Bank, Podgorica, (chapter 15) is part of the Opportunity International Network. Keith Flintham states that this bank's purpose is to improve the lives of disadvantaged people by assisting them in their business ventures. Consequently, the micro and SME sector is Opportunity Bank's target group. Flintham notes that this sector offers a number of advantages over corporate lending in Montenegro: larger spreads, client loyalty developed through relationship banking, buoyant demand for loans (especially medium-term loans), limited competition and the opportunity to grow with successful clients, which expands outreach. Engagement in this sector also helps achieve positive economic impacts generally by promoting job creation and business generation.

Clients' Perspectives on Access to Financial Services for SMEs in Southeast Europe

Will the dynamic changes in the structure of the banking sectors in SEE create equally dynamic responses in the rest of the economy? Can the liquidity provided by banks and credit-granting NGOs trickle down and promote economic opportunity at the grass roots level? Sarah Forster of the New Economics Foundation in her Part IV theme paper (chapter 16) takes up these questions by discussing the range of financial services available to the micro and small firms that are a driving force in economic growth in Southeast Europe.

According to statistics presented by Forster, private business in SEE has grown rapidly since the early-1990s. In the decade up to 2001, the private sector's share of GDP rose from around 30% to over 60%, moving closer to the 89% level of the 15 countries constituting the EU prior to May 2004. Drawing on international comparisons, Forster underlines that enterprise growth is essential for overall economic growth, and that funding from sources external to the firm is part of the formula. However, little data are available on the scale and composition of demand for finance in SEE.

Forster concludes that commercial banks in SEE appear to favour lending to larger rather than smaller enterprises, tending to serve first those market segments that are easiest to cultivate, such as large firms and possibly consumer finance. The market gap between the limited supply of finance and the strong demand by MSE is partially met by official donors. Their funds, in the form of grants and credit lines, are channelled to commercial banks, to fewer than a dozen microfinance banks and to about 45 NGOs. As of early 2003, outreach was estimated at 175,000 loans outstanding amounting to USD 420 million.

MSEs searching for credit appear to find commercial bank loans difficult to obtain, reflecting demand- and supply-side barriers. The former include legal and registration problems, low levels of education and familiarity with financial practices, adverse market conditions and small firm size. Among the supply-side barriers are loan decision-making processes, collateral requirements, term structures and currency mismatches.

These barriers are to some extent being overcome by innovation and technical assistance. Banks' innovations on the supply side include expedited decision-making, technical assistance, guarantees, better regulation and governance, and new products and delivery methods. Supply-side innovations by microfinance institutions and other MFIs include decentralised and timely credit appraisal and approval, cash flow lending rather than asset-based lending, client orientation and openness to change. Forster hopes that further innovation could result in greater collaboration between commercial banks and other MFIs.

In the first of five response papers, Albrecht Mulfinger of the European Commission (chapter 17) outlines the responses of the international community to the situation described by Forster, based on the fact that failure to fund MSEs stifles economic growth and job creation. Fortunately, as a result of privatisation, know-how transfer, donor support and foreign direct investment, the numerous obstacles that restrict or prevent MSEs in Southeast Europe from gaining access to financial services are diminishing. The Charter for Small Enterprises is one effort by the EC to tackle the problems facing SMEs seeking finance.

Igor Brkanovic (chapter 18) illustrates this picture by describing the SME loan market in Serbia. The former economic and political system supported neither microenterprise nor SMEs. However, with 99% of enterprises belonging in these categories, the government launched a strategy in 2003 to assist these target groups, given their importance for employment creation, profit generation and ownership in fixed assets. But SMEs have almost no access to commercial bank credit, in part because Serbian bankers consider SMEs to be nontransparent and hence difficult to evaluate. SMEs, on the other hand, are critical of the banks, claiming that they do not keep information confidential, that business plans and other data are misused to their disadvantage, that procedures are cumbersome, and that credit analysis is inconsistent, slow and not suited to MSE operations.

Stefan Kossev of Boliari EAD (chapter 19) provides a view of micro and SME finance in Bulgaria, where financing is hard to obtain in the wake of bad macroeconomic experiences that led entrepreneurs to favour informality. The picture he paints is very similar to the one drawn by Brkanovic. According to Kossev, large projects receive priority at the expense of SME promotion. Even funding provided by donors does not always go to indigenous enterprises. Local firms therefore grow slowly and if they and their local bankers survive at all they may be acquired by large international groups.

Christoph Freytag of ProCredit Bank Serbia, Belgrade (chapter 20) demonstrates that there is more competition among microfinance banks and NGOs in SEE than commonly assumed. Defining competition from a strategic standpoint, based on the similarities of these two types of institutions, reveals that the SEE microloan portfolios of the NGOs and the ProCredit Banks are in the same range, that each have broadly similar rural outreach, and that loans to women as a proportion of total loans to real persons do not diverge as widely as might be assumed. In short, the ProCredit Banks and the NGOs serve virtually the same market, compete for much the same clients and achieve similar results in terms of outreach and target-group orientation.

The widely acclaimed superior performance of microfinance banks in scaling up their operations is based on their ownership, which creates of system of incentives, and on their bank charters. Freytag also says that because their credit technology is appropriate for MSE clients, the microfinance banks' portfolios are of better quality than the MSE portfolios of the commercial banks.

Hayder Al-Bagdadi, Dirk Steinwand and Frank Wältring of GTZ (chapter 20) discuss a new donor strategy for delivering business development services (BDS) – nonfinancial services intended to help entrepreneurs and firms to produce better products and to operate more efficiently. The new approach to providing BDS responds to demand oriented market signals, in conrast to the former supply oriented basis. As a result of this reorientation, BDS providers' relationships with their micro and small enterprise clients is now based on fees for services rendered.

This new strategy addresses more precisely the numerous nonfinancial obstacles that MSE face. The authors believe that this approach will be more successful than the free BDS offered in the past, which required continuing subsidies and undermined the local consulting market or prevented it from functioning.

Looking Ahead – Public-Private Partnerships in the Financial Sector in Southeast Europe

Can public-private partnerships (PPPs), most commonly found in the development and operation of infrastructure projects in the US and UK, be used to promote finance for small and medium-sized enterprise (SME) in transition economies and developing countries? If so, how can the responsibilities of public sector and private sector investors be structured in ways that will achieve superior returns, especially in dynamic situations such as SME finance in Southeast Europe?

Reinhard Schmidt and Nina Moisa of the University of Frankfurt (chapter 22) deal with these questions in their Part V theme paper. They define PPP as an arrangement in which private *capital, management* and *ownership* are used to provide what are typically regarded as public services. PPPs are an institutional form that, when properly designed, enables the public sector to obtain leverage by enlisting private parties in ways that reap the advantages of private economic activity, i.e. initiative, experimentation, innovation and reduced costs.

Schmidt and Moisa state that in order for PPPs to work, the incentives of all parties must be aligned with the project's objectives. Achieving alignment is a complex task and subtle art. Alignment requires that contracts are workable and enforceable, and that they allocate risks and rewards efficiently. Contracts also allocate property rights. Participation in ownership by the private party is a first step towards aligning interests. Ownership is defined primarily in a functional or economic manner as consisting of residual claims, which reside with those who make residual decisions. Residual decisions are those that are not defined in contracts, which means that residual decision-makers bear some risk. As situations change over time and in the course of a project, the likelihood of contract renegotiation increases. Those who have made the most specific investments incur the largest sunk costs and therefore have the most to lose in renegotiation. The economic objective in structuring PPPs is to assign residual decision rights to the party who will use them to make decisions that add the most value to the project. This party must have a long-term perspective.

PPPs are often set up to implement infrastructure projects. A more recent development is to exploit the advantages of PPPs in the finance sector, specifically for micro and small enterprise banks. Schmidt and Moisa describe the highly successful case of the micro and small enterprise banks affiliated with IMI (Internationale Micro Investitionen AG), an investment company that invests in SME banks. The interests of the investors and consultants that establish and manage these banks are aligned in a number of ways: by enhancing the role of reputation, making payment dependent upon performance, ensuring that the consultant has an equity share, and defining as clearly as possible the grounds for intervention by the public party and the possible sanctions that can be used to check the actions of the private party, in this case IPC (the consulting firm that founded IMI and that executes IMI projects). A novel dimension is that the private partners appear to be more concerned about the nonfinancial objective of maintaining the target-group orientation than are the public sector partners.

In the first of five response papers Klaus-Eckhard Hartmann of DEG (chapter 23) describes the fundamental strengths and weaknesses of public sector investment in financial sector development. Public sector investors are often prepared to accept a high level of risk, but their funds are in short supply and therefore should be used strategically as a basis for attracting private funding. The supply of private sector funds is vast, but private investors are almost always risk-sensitive. The trick is to match project risk with the risk tolerance or appetite of the investors. This is accomplished by constructing hierarchical divisions or "risk ladders" that include equity and different types of loan finance tailored for various classes of public and private investors. The ratio between equity and debt is a critical factor for managing risk and distributing it accordingly.

Ira Lieberman of The Open Society Institute (chapter 24) summarises the use and evolution of cooperation involving public and private sector participants as well as the challenges that come with these arrangements. Challenges frequently arise because of the incompleteness of contracts, including means of dealing with *force majeure* in the form of economic crises. Political considerations relating to the pricing of services may make cooperation impossible in sensitive areas such as water and electric power. Corruption is also a problem. Finding off-shore jurisdictions in which the private parties feel comfortable, and which are beyond local conflicts of interest, is critical for productive dispute resolution. In contrast, cooperation in microfinance has worked much more smoothly, beginning with donor engagement of NGOs as implementing agencies and then moving towards support for for-profit institutions with emphasis on sustainability.

Helen Alexander of IMI (chapter 25) notes that IPC's consultancy work grew out of the recognition that the institutions, not the technology, were the barriers to serving the micro and SME target group. This realisation brought about a focus on ownership and governance. This led IPC to create IMI, with the objective of forming new institutions that would be regulated, serve a specific target group and accept local deposits. Official international financial institutions (IFIs) and other investors joined IMI and furthered its agenda.

As of early 2004, IMI's public sector and private sector owners held nearly equal shares, and total equity exceeded €43 million. The total equity of the 18 IMI institutions worldwide was €134 million, much of which was held by the public sector investors in IMI (IFC, KfW, FMO and BIO), joined by EBRD and others that invested in the network but not in IMI. In 2004 and 2005 these investors will swap their shares in the individual banks for shares in IMI, which will become a holding company, a network of banks with essentially one owner and with a common ProCredit Bank logo. In early 2004, network institutions had about

320,000 loans outstanding with a combined portfolio of €700 million. Sixty percent of these loans were for amounts of less than €1,000.

The key to IMI's success is governance and ownership and its close ties to IPC as the manager and driving force behind the IMI banks. IMI has been fortunate in two respects, first, in not being forced by its public sector owners to include local shareholders in its ventures and, second, in having investors with a long-term perspective. A level of trust has been developed that greatly facilitates unity of purpose and economy in governance. The eventual exit of public sector investors creates the challenge of finding a new investor base. IMI plans to take a two-pronged approach by attracting a small number of like-minded, large private investors and also a multitude of small private investors in order to safeguard IPC's leadership role and IMI's target-group orientation.

Syed Aftab Ahmed (chapter 26) provides perspectives on the highly successful IMI public-private partnership in which IFC has played a decisive role as a public investor. He notes that both the private and public investors in this PPP share a common enthusiasm, but in varying degrees, for financial returns as well as for the creation of benefits of another kind, in this case sustainable, expanding financial services for micro and SME clients. In addition to working for these results, both types of investors are "patient" but attach different priorities to exit, that is, to the time horizons of their investments.

Ahmed explains that the effort to counteract market failure that animated investment decisions in the past has been displaced by concern for governance, for creating commercial structures in which incentives are aligned to produce financial results as well as benefits of another kind. In this sort of venture, it appears that investors subject to the discipline of capital markets may have an advantage over other investors who are not so disciplined or who are primarily motivated by eleemosynary ideals.

Subsidies for starting up commercial micro and SME financial institutions are required, and these figure in the effort to align incentives of the public and private parties. Ahmed provides examples of the dynamics of PPPs as they develop and mature. One is that renegotiation, as detailed by Schmidt and Moisa, can lead to conflict. Ahmed concludes that there are really three bottom lines for PPPs with objectives such as those of IMI: financial returns, other forms of desired impact, and governance.

Klaus Glaubitt and Haje Schütte (chapter 27) call for public-private partnerships to promote financial sector development in Southeast Europe, where immature financial sectors will not be modernised by private actors alone. Glaubitt and Schütte argue that as long as public actors respect the principle of subsidiarity and design their interventions in ways that will not lead to market distortions, there is a rightful, catalytic place for public actors in financial sector development. They support their thesis by presenting original data comparing the performance of the microfinance banks of the IMI network – classified by the authors as public-private partnerships – with those of local commercial banks that KfW supports through refinancing lines. The comparison favours the microfinance banks. Glaubitt and Schütte conclude that the incentives of these institutions are better aligned with the project's objectives than are those of the commercial banks assisted by KfW.

Doris Köhn and Michael Jainzik (chapter 28) examine the potential of microfinance investment funds as a vehicle for attracting and mobilising private capital into microfinance. Without the real involvement of private capital, microfinance will be unable to continue to expand its upscaling and outreach efforts, as private capital offers greater financial resources, professionalism, distribution channels, and marketing expertise. The appeal of microfinance investment funds for private investors includes risk diversification, reputational return, and economies of scale. For MFIs, the benefits of such funds include diversification of funding sources, which is an additional element of risk management, as well as cheaper and less constrained funding. Thus properly-designed microfinance investment funds can contribute to economic development through their investment in MFIs, while providing adequate financial return to their investors. According to Jainzik and Köhn, development finance institutions have a critical role to play in the partnership, particularly in helping to support and facilitate the experience gained by the private financial sector, so that their knowledge of microfinance and their investments in MFIs will increase. Investment approaches, various risk tolerances, and issues of structure and governance are all topics visited in the paper, and Jainzik and Köhn conclude by formulating specific questions to be revisited and answered as microfinance investment funds grow and mature.

Outlook and Future Directions

The picture that emerges from the theme papers and the response papers provide a generally positive outlook for the financial sectors of the SEE region. The authors confirm that much progress has been made in developing and reforming the sector so that microenterprises and SMEs are gaining sustainable access to financial services. The progress that is underway is especially remarkable in view of the multidimensional transition processes the region has been going through since 1990: from conflict to peace, from state planning to a market economy, and from authoritarian to democratic political systems.

A very strong component of the large trends that drive this positive outlook is the prospect of eventual EU membership. The Copenhagen Criteria provide a clear statement of the reforms that SEE countries have to undertake in order to join the EU. Substantial assistance in implementing these reforms is being provided by the European Commission and the international community. This assistance will help to reduce persistent high unemployment; to increase investments in infrastructure and in other productive assets, especially from foreign sources; and to open SEE economies to intra- and interregional trade. The prospect of EU accession is also a key facilitator of a broader and deeper financial sector, helping to reduce high country risks and the high premiums private investors and banks require when lending to the region.

While the benefits seem to shine brightly, accession has its costs, as some of the authors warn. There is general agreement amongst the authors that the countries of Southeast Europe should cautiously evaluate the benefits and costs in adopting the *acquis communautaire*. These costs are likely to be high because of the limited (but growing) institutional capacity to deal with the complex package that makes up the *acquis*.

The same caution is called for when adopting Basel II, as the central bankers contributing to this book agree. Basel II will impose high transaction costs on the banks adopting it as well as on the supervisors enforcing it. Staying with Basel I seems to be a good choice for the time being until sufficient experience has been gained by early adopters of Basel II. A mixed picture seems to emerge regarding the implications of Basel II for the issues at the core of this book: lending to microentrepreneurs and SMEs, and financial sector development. The strong risk diversification of micro and SME portfolios should encourage banks to lend because of the relatively modest levels of equity required to support such loans. However, international refinance to the region will be dampened because banks outside the region will have to make stiff equity allocations to support exposures to Southeast Europe that the market perceives as high-risk.

These capital-based factors may explain why the authors seem to disagree regarding the prospects of lending to microentrepreneurs and SME. While bankers agree that these are attractive market segments, especially for small local banks, entrepreneurs voice significant problems in obtaining commercial bank loans. The available data seem to support the entrepreneurs' perception and indicate ample room for SME lending to increase, possibly reaching levels of penetration achieved by the recent EU accession states. Specialised micro and SME banks seem poised to support this trend.

The entry of further foreign investors into the banking sector in Southeast Europe, generally seen as accompanying progress towards EU accession, may also help to close this gap. Further supply-side innovations will lead to an improved provision of financial services. However, the second round of consolidation that may come on the wings of foreign investment may hit just those small local banks that have created market niches in SME lending.

Whatever the prospects for SME lending, long-term refinancing for banks will remain scarce. Strict country limits adopted by or imposed on banks outside the region will place a ceiling on international lending to the region. Local deposits will remain mostly short- to medium-term as citizens' trust in banks slowly grows. A refinancing gap for local institutions is likely to result, especially for those expanding rapidly, such as the ProCredit Banks of the IMI network. Creative and innovative solutions will be required to overcome these barriers.

New and innovative public-private partnerships are likely to emerge as a bridge, with public funds catalysing investment through laddered risk sharing mechanisms. In this regard, the recent establishment of a number of microfinance and SME investment funds is a welcome development in Southeast Europe.

This book and its predecessor convey a largely positive message. This message is important for the countries of the region, especially for its decisionmakers in the public and the private spheres as well as for those in the international community that take an active interest in the region's development. This positive message is also useful for other countries working their way through complex transition processes. The message is: well-designed international assistance can make a positive difference if it is well-designed, if framework conditions are conducive, and if efforts in cooperation fall on fertile ground.

Index of Names

A

Ahmed, S. 198, 247, 248, 279, 297, 348
Alexander, H. 247, 289, 334, 347

B

Bogza, M. 59, 103, 341
Brkanovic, I. 219, 345

F

Fehlker, C. 60, 113, 342
Fischer, P. 128, 163, 343
Flintham, K. 129, 179, 198, 284, 343
Forster, S. 185, 189, 200, 211, 227, 323, 324, 326, 334, 344
Franco, M. 4, 39, 340
Freytag, C. 188, 233, 345

G

Glaubitt, K. VIII, 248, 303, 348
Gospodinov, E. 129, 173, 343

H

Hare, P. 3, 7, 11, 17, 30, 35, 339, 340
Hartmann, K.-E. 246, 277, 347

J

Jainzick, M. 249, 323, 349

K

Kakulia, M. 58, 93, 341
Katic, M. 129, 169, 343

Köhn, D. 249, 323, 349
Kossev, S. 187, 227, 345
Kraft, E. 57, 61, 76, 89, 113, 114, 115, 116, 118, 119, 120, 341, 342

M

Matthäus-Maier, I. IX, 33, 36, 37, 89, 145, 160, 164, 197, 198, 211, 260, 275, 279, 334, 335, 339
Mehl, A. 18, 37, 60, 61, 67, 89, 197, 211, 262, 275, 342
Moisa, N. 244, 246, 248, 251, 323, 324, 328, 332, 333, 335, 346, 348
Mulfinger, A. 187, 213, 344

N

Nicholl, P. 58, 99, 341
Nowotny, E. 4, 43, 340

S

Schmidt, R. H. 244, 246, 248, 261, 269, 275, 312, 323, 324, 328, 332, 333, 335, 346, 348
Schütte, H. VIII, 248, 303, 348
Sharxhi, E. 59, 107, 342
Sherif, K. F. 5, 47, 340
Steinwand, D. 188, 239, 345

T

Thimann, C. 63, 90, 113

V

von Pischke, J.D. V, 33, 36, 37, 89, 145, 160, 164, 197, 198, 211, 260, 275, 279, 285, 334, 335, 339

W

Winkler, A. 18, 37, 60, 61, 89, 197, 211, 262, 275, 342

Wisniwski, S. 127, 131, 138, 145, 160, 342, 343

Index of Countries

A

Albania VIII, 9, 11, 13, 14, 16, 18, 21, 23, 24, 28, 29, 35, 39, 45, 59, 61, 62, 63, 65, 66, 77, 78, 107, 108, 109, 110, 131, 134, 135, 136, 138, 141, 145, 151, 156, 157, 159, 163, 164, 185, 189, 190, 191, 192, 193, 194, 197, 200, 202, 204, 210, 233, 234, 235, 267, 305, 306, 311, 320, 321, 342
Argentina 286
Armenia 306, 313, 317, 318, 319
Austria VII, 58, 69, 70, 77, 133, 134, 136, 149, 159
Azerbaijan 313

B

Belgium 142
Bosnia and Herzegovina (BiH) 8, 9, 13, 14, 16, 18, 21, 23, 24, 26, 30, 35, 40, 58, 61, 63, 65, 68, 73, 74, 77, 78, 99, 100, 101, 102, 131, 135, 137, 138, 140, 142, 143, 145, 149, 150, 152, 153, 155, 156, 159, 160, 161, 164, 189, 190, 192, 193, 197, 200, 201, 202, 204, 207, 210, 211, 213, 233, 234, 235, 267, 268, 300, 305, 306, 311, 314, 317, 318, 319, 341
Bulgaria 4, 8, 9, 11, 13, 14, 15, 16, 18, 23, 24, 27, 28, 29, 35, 39, 45, 48, 61, 62, 63, 65, 66, 73, 77, 78, 129, 131, 134, 138, 145, 148, 150, 152, 153, 159, 160, 164, 173, 174, 175, 176, 187, 189, 190, 191, 192, 193, 197, 203, 204, 210, 213, 214, 216, 227, 228, 229, 230, 231, 233, 234, 267, 285, 287, 306, 317, 318, 319, 320, 321, 340, 345

C

Canada 258
Commonwealth of Independent States (CIS) 8, 21, 26, 163, 190, 191, 192, 283, 284, 285, 326
Czech Republic 4, 15, 16, 18, 36, 63, 66, 133, 148, 163, 191, 192, 193, 204, 340

E

Egypt 132
Estonia 18, 28, 31, 36, 69, 70
European Union (EU) V, VII, VIII, IX, X, 4, 5, 7, 8, 9, 13, 16, 19, 20, 21, 23, 25, 26, 27, 28, 37, 39, 40, 41, 42, 44, 45, 46, 47, 50, 57, 58, 59, 60, 61, 62, 64, 66, 70, 71, 72, 73, 75, 78, 79, 80, 83, 85, 86, 89, 90, 94, 95, 97, 99, 103, 104, 109, 113, 115, 116, 117, 118, 119, 120, 122, 123, 131, 133, 134, 136, 137, 151, 156, 158, 163, 166, 175, 185, 187, 190, 191, 194, 196, 197, 198, 204, 205, 208, 211, 213, 214, 215, 216, 217, 228, 230, 231, 311, 339, 340, 341, 342, 344, 349, 350

F

Federation of Bosnia and Herzegovina (FBiH) 135, 157
Former Yugoslav Republic of Macedonia (FYR Macedonia / FYROM) 8, 9, 13, 14, 15, 16, 18,

21, 23, 24, 26, 28, 35, 39, 190, 192, 193, 197, 204
France 113, 142, 197, 214, 229, 273, 274

G

Georgia 58, 93, 94, 96, 97, 164, 198, 207, 305, 306, 320, 321
Greece 28, 45, 142

H

Hungary 4, 15, 16, 18, 29, 31, 36, 44, 63, 64, 65, 69, 70, 133, 142, 144, 163, 166, 173, 191, 192, 193, 204, 340

I

Italy 58, 71, 77, 99

J

Japan 69, 89, 143, 159

K

Kazakhstan 317, 318, 319
Korea 69, 132
Kosovo 9, 23, 26, 61, 131, 135, 138, 139, 145, 152, 156, 159, 189, 200, 202, 204, 210, 233, 234, 235, 267, 294, 305, 311, 314, 320, 321

L

Latvia 18, 36, 69, 70
Lithuania 17, 18, 36

M

Macedonia 8, 45, 61, 63, 65, 77, 78, 131, 135, 156, 157, 189, 192, 197, 202, 211, 233, 234, 235, 267, 306, 314, 317, 318, 319
Moldova 8, 9, 13, 14, 16, 18, 21, 23, 24, 26, 29, 36, 45, 63, 65, 66, 78, 189, 190, 191, 192, 193, 198, 205, 234, 267, 305, 306, 320, 321
Montenegro 8, 9, 13, 14, 16, 18, 21, 23, 24, 26, 27, 28, 29, 36, 40, 61, 65, 129, 131, 134, 135, 156, 163, 169, 179, 181, 182, 189, 190, 191, 192, 193, 197, 205, 210, 211, 234, 284, 309, 315, 343

N

Netherlands VII, 69, 171, 290

P

Poland 4, 13, 15, 16, 17, 18, 28, 36, 63, 65, 137, 142, 144, 152, 159, 163, 164, 191, 192, 193, 198, 199, 200, 204, 210, 214, 285, 340

R

Republika Srpska 9, 157
Romania 4, 8, 9, 13, 14, 16, 18, 20, 23, 24, 27, 28, 29, 36, 39, 45, 48, 50, 59, 61, 62, 63, 64, 65, 66, 71, 74, 77, 78, 103, 104, 105, 131, 135, 136, 138, 141, 142, 145, 146, 148, 156, 160, 164, 165, 190, 192, 193, 194, 197, 198, 203, 210, 213, 214, 216, 233, 234, 235, 267, 304, 315, 318, 319, 320, 321, 340, 341

S

Serbia 8, 9, 13, 14, 16, 18, 21, 23, 24, 26, 27, 28, 29, 36, 40, 45, 58, 61, 65, 99, 129, 131, 134, 135, 138, 139, 144, 145, 151, 152, 153, 154, 156, 157, 160, 161, 162, 164, 166, 169, 170, 171, 187, 189, 190, 191, 192, 193, 197, 205, 210, 211, 219, 220, 221, 222, 225, 233, 234, 267, 309, 315, 318, 319, 345
Slovakia 13, 18, 63, 64, 65, 66, 142, 148, 163

Slovenia 18, 36, 45, 58, 63, 64, 65, 99, 148, 204
Soviet Union 9, 34, 93

T

Turkey 43, 44, 58, 99, 141, 142, 160, 214, 283, 286

U

UK 27, 69, 173, 196, 202, 203, 208, 209, 244, 251, 258, 273, 346
Ukraine 21, 267, 305, 306, 316, 318, 319, 320, 321
USA V, 74, 339

Y

Yugoslavia 8, 9, 13, 40, 50, 100, 169, 191, 211, 219

Index of Banks and Organisations

A

ACCION International 285, 328, 329
AGROINVEST, Serbia and Montenegro 210
AIG Inc., US 132
Anelik Bank, Armenia 313
Armeconom Bank, Armenia 313
Aval Bank, Ukraine 316, 318, 319

B

Banca Agricola, Italy 164
Banco Turco Romano, Romania 141
Bank Austria Creditanstalt, Austria 149, 159
Bank Daewoo, Korea 132
Bank for International Settlements (BIS), Basel 20, 88, 109, 121
Bank of Baku, Azerbaijan 313
Bank Respublika, Azerbaijan 313
Bannock Consulting, UK 173
Basel Committee on Banking Supervision (BCBS) 68, 72, 78, 81, 86, 87, 88, 114, 120, 121
Bayerische Landesbank (BLB), Germany 74, 100, 140, 151
Belgian Investment Corporation for Developing Countries (BIO) 198, 247, 269, 330, 347
BNP Paribas, France 142
BRD, Romania 164
BRE Bank, Poland 164

C

CARE 285

Central Bank of Bosnia and Herzegovina 58, 69, 99, 102, 135, 136, 159, 341
Citibank, US 132
CKB Bank, Montenegro 315
Commerzbank AG, Germany VI, 128, 155, 163, 164, 171, 213, 307, 343
Consultative Group to Assist the Poor (CGAP) 200, 211, 284, 307, 308, 312, 327, 334
Converse Bank, Armenia 313, 317, 318, 319
Croatian National Bank, Croatia 61, 74, 134, 150, 159, 160, 341

D

Delta Banka, Serbia 154, 155, 160, 162, 164
Deutsche Gesellschaft für Technische Zusammenarbeit (GTZ) – German Technical Cooperation 151, 188, 239, 241, 345
Deutsche Investitions- und Entwicklungsgesellschaft (DEG) 198, 246, 260, 269, 277, 279, 347
Diners Club, US 132
DOEN Foundation, Netherlands 269, 270
DSK Bank, Bulgaria 173

E

Eksim Banka, Serbia 315
Euromarket Banka, Montenegro 309, 315

European Agency for Reconstruction (EAR) 219, 223, 314
European Bank for Reconstruction and Development VI, 8, 64, 139, 141, 155, 173, 191, 192, 197, 210, 213, 247, 260, 269, 285, 291, 307, 347
European Central Bank (ECB) 60, 90, 113, 115, 116, 118, 119, 120, 122, 215, 342
European Commission (EC) 4, 39, 40, 79, 80, 91, 121, 122, 123, 140, 187, 195, 213, 216, 340, 344, 349
European Investment Bank (EIB) 4, 21, 43, 44, 45, 213, 340
Export Credit Bank, Macedonia 314

F

Financial Action Task Force on Money Laundering (FATF) 116, 117, 122
FINCA (The Foundation for International Community Assistance) 284, 285
Forum Bank, Ukraine 316

G

German Federal Ministry for Economic Cooperation and Development (BMZ) 306, 312
Gospodarska Banka, Bosnia 153, 155, 160, 164

H

HypoVereinsbank (HVB), Germany 133, 163

I

Ineco Bank, Armenia 313
ING, Netherlands 171

International Finance Corporation (IFC) VI, VII, 127, 136, 139, 141, 151, 155, 164, 166, 177, 198, 202, 204, 247, 260, 268, 269, 279, 290, 297, 299, 300, 301, 302, 307, 308, 330, 347, 348
International Monetary Fund (IMF) 15, 18, 29, 35, 36, 63, 77, 79, 85, 88, 89, 94, 97, 106, 109, 117, 123, 136, 197
Internationale Micro Investionen AG (IMI), Germany 140, 155, 198, 200, 233, 237, 245, 247, 248, 267, 268, 269, 270, 271, 279, 284, 285, 286, 289, 290, 291, 293, 294, 295, 296, 300, 301, 302, 307, 311, 328, 329, 334, 346, 347, 348, 350
Internationale Projekt Consult (IPC), Germany 173, 233, 245, 247, 268, 269, 270, 271, 279, 285, 289, 290, 295, 296, 299, 301, 307, 310, 347, 348
Intesa BCI S.p.A., Italy 164
Istarska Kreditna Banka, Croatia 164

K

KBC Bank, Belgium 142
Kent Bank, Turkey 141
KfW Entwicklungsbank, Germany V, 306
Komercijalna Bank, Serbia 137, 164, 166, 315, 318, 319
Kreditanstalt für Wiederaufbau (KfW) – German Financial Cooperation V, VI, VII, VIII, IX, X, XI, XII, 7, 43, 139, 155, 166, 171, 177, 198, 200, 202, 207, 213, 247, 248, 249, 269, 290, 303, 306, 307, 308, 311, 312, 313, 316, 323, 326, 327, 329, 330, 333, 339, 347, 348
Kulska banka, Serbia 170, 315, 318, 319

L

LT Gospodarska Banka, Bosnia and Herzegovina 314, 317

M

MEC, Moldova 320, 321
Mercy Corps, USA/Scotland 284
MIRO Bank, Romania 320, 321
Misr Bank, Egypt 132
Moznosti, Macedonia 314

N

Nadra Bank, Ukraine 316
National Bank of Georgia (NBG), Georgia 58, 93, 94, 97, 341
National Bank of Greece, Greece 155
National Commercial Bank, Albania 141
Netherlands Development Finance Company (FMO) VII, 155, 198, 247, 260, 269, 290, 307, 308, 347
New Economics Foundation 189, 203, 211, 344
Nova Banka, Croatia 164
Nova Ljubljanska Banka, Slovenia 135

O

Opportunity Bank, Montenegro 129, 134, 145, 179, 181, 182, 284, 315, 343
Opportunity International (OI) Network 129, 179, 343
Opportunity International, Australia 284, 285, 343
Organisation for Economic Co-operation and Development (OECD) 24, 50, 69, 83, 84, 108, 122, 193
Organization for Security and Co-operation in Europe (OSCE) 9, 26
OSI (Open Society Institute and Soros Foundation Network) 285

P

Para-Bank, Azerbaijan 313
Partner Banka, Croatia 164
Partner Mikrokreditna Organizacija, Bosnia and Herzegovina 210
Privat Bank, Ukraine 316
Privredna Banka, Croatia 164
PRIZMA, Bosnia and Herzegovina 210
ProCredit Bank, Albania 267
ProCredit Bank, BiH 267, 320, 321
ProCredit Bank, Bulgaria 199, 200, 210, 235, 267, 307
ProCredit Bank, Georgia 267, 307
ProCredit Bank, Kosovo 138, 139, 267, 307
ProCredit Bank, Macedonia 235, 267, 307
ProCredit Bank, Serbia 138, 139, 155, 188, 234, 235, 267, 307, 320, 321, 345
ProCredit Bank, Ukraine 267, 307
ProCrédito, Bolivia 290

R

Raiffeisen Bank BH, Bosnia and Herzegovina 133, 154, 155, 160, 162, 314, 317, 318, 319
Raiffeisen Zentralbank Österreich (RZB), Austria 136, 163
Raiffeisenbank, Austria 133
Rijecka Banka, Croatia 74, 140, 151
Robank, Romania 164
Romanian Mortgage Loan Company (Ro-Fin), Romania 145
Rural Finance Fund, Albania 210

S

Small Enterprise Assistance Fund (SEAF) 202, 285
Société Générale, France 164, 197, 229
Southeast Europe Enterprise Development (SEED) 191, 192, 197, 204, 206, 211

T

Turkish Savings and Deposit Insurance Fund (SDIF) 141
Tutunska Banka, Macedonia 314, 317, 318, 319

U

UniBank, Azerbaijan 313
Unicredito Italiano, Italy 141
Unicredito, Romania 141
Unionbank, Bulgaria 129, 173, 175, 176, 177, 343
United Nations High Commissioner for Refugees (UNHCR) 225
United States Agency for International Development (USAID) 146, 199, 202

Universal Bank d.d., Bosnia and Herzegovina 137, 155, 160, 161, 314, 317, 318, 319
UPI Bank d.d., Bosnia and Herzegovina 314

V

Vakifbank, Turkey 141
Varna, Bulgaria 197, 227, 229
Volksbank BH d.d., Bosnia and Herzegovina 314
Volksbank Romania 315

W

World Bank (WB) 5, 14, 15, 23, 37, 46, 47, 53, 85, 86, 87, 88, 89, 90, 94, 106, 109, 123, 136, 144, 191, 194, 199, 210, 211, 283, 284, 334, 340
World Trade Organization (WTO) 21

Z

Zagrebacka Bank BH d.d., Bosnia and Herzegovina 314
Zagrebacka Banka, Croatia 137, 164, 317, 318, 319

Index of Terms

A

accession countries (EU) VII, VIII, IX, X, 4, 9, 39, 41, 44, 48, 57, 61, 62, 70, 73, 78, 79, 86, 89, 90, 99, 109, 113, 131, 134, 136, 137, 151, 158, 163, 187, 208, 228, 231, 339, 340, 341, 349, 350
acquis communautaire 7, 27, 45, 350
automatic teller machine (ATM) 235

B

bad loans 65
banking supervision 57, 62, 64, 67, 68, 69, 70, 71, 72, 78, 81, 86, 87, 88, 93, 94, 99, 113, 114, 116, 117, 120, 121, 123, 304, 341
bankruptcy 20, 29, 32, 52, 66, 115, 117, 286
Basel I X, 57, 59, 60, 61, 62, 80, 81, 82, 83, 84, 85, 86, 90, 94, 95, 107, 108, 109, 110, 111, 113, 115, 117, 119, 120, 128, 134, 151, 158, 217, 341, 342, 350
Basel II 108, 110, 117, 120, 151, 217, 341, 342, 350
build operate and own (BOO) 283
build operate and transfer (BOT) 283, 286
Business Development Services (BDS) 188, 209, 239, 240, 241, 242, 345
Business Environment and Enterprise Performance Surveys (BEEPS) 15

business start-ups 11, 202, 214, 222, 225, 226

C

capacity-building 206, 241, 284, 285
capital adequacy 58, 72, 94, 107, 108, 119, 133, 135, 159, 308, 317, 318, 319, 320, 321
capital markets XI, 4, 44, 57, 62, 67, 69, 70, 73, 84, 144, 146, 165, 185, 202, 235, 248, 263, 277, 279, 280, 284, 287, 299, 304, 305, 323, 324, 325, 326, 327, 334, 340, 341, 348
CARDS Programme (Community Assistance for Reconstruction, Development and Stabilisation) 40, 42
collateral 15, 32, 48, 58, 100, 101, 106, 115, 119, 142, 146, 186, 187, 203, 206, 207, 213, 215, 217, 222, 223, 224, 225, 228, 229, 230, 293, 305, 344
competitive advantage 74, 105, 176, 237
confidentiality 129, 181, 224, 343
consumer credit 105, 142, 143, 159, 160, 195, 198
consumer lending 78, 100, 105, 127, 128, 138, 140, 142, 143, 145, 151, 152, 158, 198, 236, 343
Copenhagen Criteria 4, 27, 39, 40, 340, 349
country risk 187, 228, 311, 325, 349
credit cards 143, 148, 151, 160

credit rating 54, 59, 75, 84, 201, 228
credit scoring 128, 151, 152, 158, 208
creditor protection 48, 66, 67, 304

D

Dayton Peace Accords 9, 26
debit cards 148
debt-equity ratio 278, 308, 319, 321
deposit insurance VII, 58, 79, 95, 97, 119, 127, 342
downscaling (approach) 198, 206, 259, 307, 308, 309, 310, 313, 314, 315, 316
due diligence 58, 74, 325, 331

E

e-banking 151
EU accession VII, VIII, IX, X, 4, 9, 39, 41, 44, 48, 57, 61, 62, 70, 73, 78, 79, 86, 89, 90, 99, 109, 113, 131, 134, 136, 137, 151, 158, 163, 187, 208, 228, 231, 339, 340, 341, 349, 350

F

factoring 186, 188, 194, 195, 196, 204, 205, 211, 215, 230, 272
Federal Deposit Insurance Corporation Improvement Act (FDICIA) 72, 73
fee income 128, 147, 301
Financial Sector Assessment Program (FSAP) 85, 94, 106
financial sector development V, VIII, IX, X, XI, 19, 29, 34, 53, 57, 60, 61, 62, 63, 66, 73, 93, 115, 119, 156, 246, 248, 252, 259, 260, 261, 267, 272, 273, 275, 277, 278, 279, 281, 297, 312, 323, 333, 339, 347, 348, 350
foreclosure procedures 48, 304

foreign direct investment (FDI) 3, 4, 7, 11, 13, 15, 17, 19, 20, 22, 24, 25, 28, 30, 42, 44, 57, 62, 73, 102, 133, 134, 149, 158, 187, 203, 213, 229, 340, 341, 345
foreign exchange (FX) transactions 29, 69, 94, 152, 175, 208
free-trade agreements (FTA) 20, 27, 149

G

governance 30, 48, 52, 53, 93, 107, 115, 165, 186, 207, 245, 247, 248, 271, 285, 289, 295, 299, 301, 311, 331, 344, 347, 348, 349
grant element (GE) 44, 277, 280
greenfield approach 307
greenfield bank 127, 133, 137, 138, 140, 145, 158, 164, 179, 285, 308, 343
grey economy 170, 181, 188, 219, 224, 227, 228
gross domestic product (GDP) 8, 14, 17, 18, 19, 22, 23, 24, 30, 41, 45, 48, 50, 53, 61, 62, 63, 64, 76, 77, 79, 93, 97, 102, 106, 134, 143, 185, 186, 190, 191, 192, 196, 213, 215, 344
gross national income (GNI) 22, 23, 24, 25, 50
guarantees 4, 21, 31, 73, 91, 119, 136, 147, 158, 175, 186, 194, 203, 207, 208, 216, 217, 226, 230, 246, 273, 274, 277, 280, 285, 311, 327, 328, 330, 331, 344

H

household loans 78, 143
housing finance 54, 128, 145, 158, 160, 195, 245, 272, 274, 343

I

information technology (IT) 105, 151, 152, 164, 167, 170, 174, 175
institution-building 40, 209, 259, 278
insurance XI, 4, 19, 21, 44, 47, 67, 69, 71, 78, 79, 86, 88, 89, 91, 93, 97, 117, 118, 136, 142, 186, 195, 204, 205, 215, 304, 324
intermediation 37, 41, 66, 89, 101, 105, 106, 110, 113, 116, 128, 142, 206, 234
internal ratings based (IRB) approaches/models 82, 83, 108, 110
internally displaced person (IDP) 14
International Accounting Standards (IAS) 115
international finance institution (IFI) VI, X, 43, 44, 45, 46, 128, 137, 138, 165, 173, 235, 237, 245, 247, 260, 266, 268, 269, 286, 290, 294, 302, 304, 311, 327, 332, 347

L

leasing 47, 96, 128, 145, 158, 165, 186, 188, 194, 195, 196, 203, 204, 205, 211, 215, 217, 222, 226, 230, 236, 245, 272, 273, 304, 343
leasing services 145, 203, 215, 226, 230
lending boom 62, 75, 76, 77, 78, 86, 88, 89
leverage 3, 216, 244, 269, 277, 278, 279, 280, 281, 346
liquidity gap 153, 154, 161, 162

M

maturity mismatch 128, 146, 152, 155, 158, 278, 280
mezzanine finance 278, 280

micro and small business (MSB) VII, 177, 199, 204, 225, 233, 235, 236, 237, 252, 261, 297, 339
micro and small enterprise (MSE) VI, 127, 138, 144, 177, 183, 185, 186, 187, 188, 189, 190, 191, 194, 195, 196, 197, 198, 199, 200, 201, 202, 203, 204, 205, 206, 207, 208, 209, 213, 214, 215, 216, 217, 220, 224, 227, 228, 229, 230, 231, 236, 237, 245, 252, 259, 260, 261, 262, 263, 265, 266, 267, 268, 269, 270, 271, 273, 274, 285, 289, 298, 299, 302, 305, 343, 344, 345, 346
micro, small and medium-sized enterprise (MSME) 144, 191, 192, 201, 227, 239, 241, 305, 306
microfinance bank (MFB) XI, 129, 138, 139, 145, 164, 165, 186, 188, 196, 198, 199, 200, 201, 206, 207, 208, 210, 229, 233, 234, 248, 268, 279, 289, 290, 291, 293, 294, 295, 296, 301, 307, 326, 328, 329, 334, 343, 344, 345, 348
microfinance institution (MFI) X, 152, 182, 186, 195, 196, 198, 199, 200, 201, 203, 204, 206, 207, 208, 210, 217, 228, 247, 248, 268, 275, 278, 279, 287, 288, 289, 290, 298, 299, 301, 302, 305, 323, 324, 325, 326, 327, 328, 329, 330, 331, 332, 333, 334, 344, 349
most favoured nation (MFN) 21
municipal finance 272, 273

N

non-governmental organisation (NGO) XI, 140, 144, 158, 182, 185, 186, 188, 198, 199, 200, 201, 203, 205, 206, 207, 208, 225, 226, 233, 234, 235, 236, 237, 240, 246, 247, 260, 261, 268, 275, 284, 285, 286, 289, 326, 327, 328, 329, 332, 344, 345, 347 not-for-profit organisation (NPO) 179, 260, 261, 266, 267

O

official development assistance (ODA) 22, 62
off-take agreement 283, 286

P

Partnership and Cooperation Agreements (PCAs) 21, 27
portfolio at risk (PAR) 201, 293, 308, 313, 314, 315, 316, 319, 321
poverty alleviation 3, 13, 326
Private Sector Participation (PSP) 303
prudential problems 78
Public-Private Partnership (PPP) VII, 44, 226, 243, 244, 245, 246, 247, 248, 251, 252, 253, 256, 257, 258, 259, 260, 261, 263, 264, 265, 266, 267, 268, 269, 270, 271, 272, 273, 274, 275, 277, 283, 284, 285, 286, 287, 288, 289, 296, 297, 298, 299, 300, 301, 303, 304, 306, 307, 308, 309, 310, 311, 312, 317, 320, 323, 327, 330, 333, 334, 335, 339, 346, 348, 350

R

rapprochement (EU) 40
residual claimant 244, 253, 254
residual decision rights 245, 254, 255, 256, 263, 266, 267, 346
return on equity (RoE) 102, 146, 200, 201, 208, 247, 270, 308, 309, 313, 314, 315, 316
risk management 228, 309, 325, 342, 343, 349

S

savings VI, 4, 17, 18, 29, 30, 44, 51, 64, 72, 134, 136, 141, 142, 149, 164, 173, 186, 195, 198, 204, 219, 220, 228, 235, 236, 258, 287, 289, 294, 311, 325, 326
small and medium-sized enterprise (SME) VII, VIII, IX, XI, 7, 15, 16, 33, 34, 41, 57, 62, 74, 75, 101, 120, 129, 137, 138, 140, 144, 145, 158, 165, 169, 170, 173, 176, 177, 179, 180, 181, 182, 185, 187, 191, 196, 197, 202, 204, 210, 211, 213, 214, 215, 216, 217, 219, 220, 221, 222, 223, 224, 225, 226, 227, 228, 229, 230, 231, 234, 236, 240, 244, 245, 247, 248, 280, 284, 285, 286, 287, 289, 304, 305, 306, 307, 308, 310, 312, 313, 314, 315, 316, 343, 344, 345, 346, 347, 348, 349, 350
SME lending 74, 129, 144, 173, 176, 177, 179, 180, 181, 197, 222, 229, 307, 310, 350
Stabilisation and Association Agreements (SAA) 4, 21, 39, 75, 340
Stabilisation and Association Process (SAP) 34, 39, 40, 94
Stability Pact 8, 20, 149, 156
subsidiarity 248, 259, 260, 262, 304, 348
supervision 26, 42, 59, 60, 64, 66, 68, 69, 70, 71, 72, 78, 79, 86, 90, 91, 94, 95, 96, 99, 107, 108, 110, 113, 114, 116, 117, 118, 119, 120, 121, 122, 141, 151, 158, 207, 234, 259, 272, 289, 311, 342

T

tariffs 21, 22, 23, 27, 28, 31, 54, 286
technical assistance (TA) 40, 121, 136, 166, 173, 176, 186, 207, 213,

235, 260, 269, 270, 277, 279, 291, 299, 300, 308, 309, 310, 313, 314, 315, 316, 344
trade and protectionism 27
transaction costs 3, 4, 5, 21, 28, 50, 115, 198, 222, 263, 305, 309, 310, 325, 340, 350
transition countries 19, 30, 32, 53, 59, 61, 62, 64, 67, 68, 70, 76, 133, 157, 159, 191, 192, 193, 198, 259, 265, 277, 278, 279, 305, 306, 312, 323, 330, 334

U

unemployment 349

V

venture capital 67, 185, 194, 195, 202, 205, 215, 285

KfW Bankengruppe. Brands for the Future

KfW Bankengruppe (KfW banking group) gives impetus to economic, political and social development worldwide. As bankers we work efficiently every day. As promoters we stand for the sense and sustainability of our actions. The proceeds from our work flow back into our promotional activities and help to secure our promotional potential in the long term. As a creative bank we not only encourage innovations, but we ourselves increasingly develop new financing instruments for our customers and partners. Our competence and experience are combined into five strong brand names.

KfW Förderbank (KfW promotional bank): It is the right address for all measures in the product areas of construction, infrastructure, education, social services and the environment. Through low-interest loans we help many citizens realize the dream of owning their own home and support their interest in environmentally friendly modernization measures. As KfW Förderbank we also provide support for companies investing in environmental and climate protection, for municipal infrastructure measues as well as training and advanced training measures.

KfW Mittelstandsbank (KfW SME bank): The name is the programme. Here we have combined all of our promotional activities for business start-ups and small and medium-sized enterprises. These include, on the one hand, classic long-term loans and, on the other, innovative programmes aiming to strengthen the companies' equity base. Both are offered to our customers through their regular bank. Target-oriented advice is naturally also part of our business.

KfW IPEX-Bank: Our export and project finance has become KfW IPEX Bank, which does business under the umbrella of KfW Bankengruppe. It is customer-oriented and competition-driven and operates at standard market conditions. It is a reliable, long-term partner that supports international companies with taylor-made financings. The financing solutions which KfW IPEX Bank offers to its customers include structured finance, project finance, corporate loans and traditional export finance. The success of KfW IPEX Bank is due above all to many years of experience in the most important markets and industry sectors all over the world.

KfW Entwicklungsbank (KfW development bank): On behalf of the German federal government KfW Entwicklungsbank finances investments and advisory services in developing countries. It typically works together with governmental institutions in the respective countries. Its aim is to build up and expand a social and economic infrastructure and to create efficient financial institutions while protecting resources and ensuring a healthy environment.

DEG: As a partner of the private sector DEG supports companies wanting to invest in developing and reforming countries. It provides financing for profitable, environmentally friendly and developmentally effective projects in all economic sectors. In this way it sets the basis for sustainable economic growth – and better quality of life for the people in these countries.

KfW Bankengruppe has also become a strategic partner of the economy and politics. As an advisor to the federal government we offer our expertise in the privatization of state-owned companies. On behalf of the German government we also handle business for the Federal Agency for Special Tasks associated with Unification (Bundesanstalt für vereinigungsbedingte Sonderaufgaben, BvS) and the Compensatory Fund of Securities Trading Companies (Entschädigungseinrichtung der Wertpapierhandelsunternehmen).

Printing: Strauss GmbH, Mörlenbach
Binding: Schäffer, Grünstadt